CONVERSING WITH

Richard Kostelanetz

Limelight Editions
New York 1988

ML
410
.C24
K68
1988

OCLC # 16579603

Copyright © 1987 by Richard Kostelanetz
Copyright © 1987 by John Cage

All rights reserved under international and Pan-American Copyright Convention. A Limelight Original. Published in the United States by Proscenium Publishers Inc., New York and simultaneously in Canada by Fitzhenry & Whiteside, Limited, Toronto.

Acknowledgments for permission to reprint are noted in an appendix which represents an extension of the copyright page.

Library of Congress Cataloguing-in-Publication Data

Kostelanetz, Richard, 1940–
Conversing with Cage

1. Cage, John Interviews, 2.) Composers—United States—Interviews, Contemporary I.
Title.
ML 410.C24K68 1987 780'.92'4 87-22853
ISBN 0-87910-104—0 (cloth)
0-87910-100—8(pbk)

OTHER WORKS BY RICHARD KOSTELANETZ

Books Authored

The Theatre of Mixed Means (1968)
Master Minds (1969)
Visual Language (1970)
In the Beginning (1971)
The End of Intelligent Writing (1974)
I Articulations/Short Fictions (1974)
Recyclings, Volume One (1974)
Openings & Closings (1975)
Portraits from Memory (1975)
Constructs (1975)
Numbers: Poems & Stories (1975)
Illuminations (1977)
One Night Stood (1977)
Tabula Rasa (1978)
Inexistences (1978)
Wordsand (1978)
Constructs Two (1978)
"The End" Appendix/"The End" Essentials (1979)
Twenties in the Sixties (1979)
And So Forth (1979)
More Short Fictions (1980)
Metamorphosis in the Arts (1980)
The Old Poetries and the New (1981)
Reincarnations (1981)
Autobiographies (1981)
Arenas/Fields/Pitches/Turfs (1982)
Epiphanies (1983)
American Imaginations (1983)
Recyclings (1984)
Autobiographien New York Berlin (1986)
The Old Fictions and the New (1987)
Prose Pieces/Aftertexts (1987)
The Grants-Fix (1987)
Radio Writings (1988)

Books Edited

On Contemporary Literature (1964, 1969)
Twelve from the Sixties (1967)
The Young American Writers (1967)
Beyond Left & Right: Radical Thought for Our Times (1968)
Possibilities of Poetry (1970)
Imaged Words & Worded Images (1970)
Moholy-Nagy (1970)
John Cage (1970)
Social Speculations (1971)
Human Alternatives (1971)
Future's Fictions (1971)
Seeing Through Shuck (1972)
In Youth (1972)
Breakthrough Fictioneers (1973)
The Edge of Adaptation (1973)
Essaying Essays (1975)
Language & Structure (1975)
Younger Critics in North America (1976)
Esthetics Contemporary (1978, 1988)
Assembling Assembling (1978)
Visual Literature Criticism (1979)
Text-Sound Texts (1980)
The Yale Gertrude Stein (1980)
Scenarios (1980)
Aural Literature Criticism (1981)
The Literature of Soho (1981)
American Writing Today (1981)
The Avant-Garde Tradition in Literature (1982)

Books Co-authored & Edited

The New American Arts (1965)

Books Co-compiled & Introduced

Assembling (Twelve Vols, 1970–1981)

Performance Scripts

Epiphanies (1980)
Seductions (1986)

Portfolios of Prints

Numbers One (1974)
Word Prints (1975)

Audiotapes

Experimental Prose (1976)
Openings & Closings (1976)
Foreshortenings & Other Stories (1977)
Praying to the Lord (1977, 1981)
Asdescent/Anacatabasis (1978)
Invocations (1981)
Seductions (1981)
The Gospels/Die Evangelien (1982)
Relationships (1983)
The Eight Nights of Hanukah (1983)
Two German Hörspiele (1983)
New York City (1984)
A Special Time (1985)
Le Bateau Ivre/The Drunken Boat (1986)
Baseball: Americas' Game (1986)
Epiphanies (1987–)

Radio Features

Audio Art (1978)
Text-Sound in North America (1981)
Hörspiel USA: Radio Comedy (1983)
Glenn Gould as a Radio Artist (1983)
Audio Writing (1984)
Radio Comedy Made in America Today (1986)
New York City Radio (1987)

Texts for Composers

He Met Her in the Park/ Motte Henne i Parken (for Charles Dodge, 1981)
Wasting (for Paul Lansky, 1986)

Videotapes

Three Prose Pieces (1975)
Openings & Closings (1975)
Declaration of Independence (1979)
Epiphanies (1980)
Partitions (1986)
Video Writing (1987)
Home Movies Reconsidered (1987)

Films Produced & Directed

Epiphanies (1983; 1981–)

Films Co-produced & Directed

Constructivist Fictions (1978)
Ein Verlorenes Berlin (1983)
Ett Forlorat Berlin (1984)
A Berlin Lost (1985)
Berlin Perdu (1986)
El Berlin Perdida (1987)

Holograms

On Holography (1978)
Antitheses (1985)

Retrospective Exhibitions

Wordsand (1978)

CONVERSING WITH CAGE

Dedicated by RK & JC
To Klaus Schöning
Fanny & Nadia

HOLY SPIRIT LIBRARY
89 0439
CABRINI COLLEGE, RADNOR, PA.

CONTENTS

PREFACE

John Cage gave a marvelous answer, as he so often does.
—Merce Cunningham, *The Dancer and the Dance* (1985).

Few artists of his eminence or his conversational brilliance are as generous with interviews as John Cage, who honors requests from undergraduate newspapers with attention and grace equal to those from slick magazines; and these interviews have appeared all over the world. Since they are individually incomplete, and most have elements lacking in others, it seemed appropriate to select exemplary passages from these interviews, adding details between brackets, and from these selections to compose a sort of extended ur-interview that Cage ideally might have had. I decided to gather his choicest comments under several chapter titles, and then order these comments as though they were parts of a continuous conversation similar to, say, Pierre Cabanne's *Entretiens avec Marcel Duchamp* (1967). While these categories may violate the style and content of Cage's thinking, they nonetheless serve the convenient function of organizing what he would not organize himself, exemplifying perhaps a principal difference between talk and print. Though remarks may not be literature, conversation as provocative and elegant as Cage's, so full of important ideas and original coherence, often attains the quality we call classic. Not only has he been an epitome of an artist as speculative intellectual, but he is one of those rare artists who, fully aware of what he is doing, generally talks about his own works and their implications with more truth than do his commentators.

Since we were making a new book, to take its place beside other books, we decided not to draw from interviews in previous books wholly devoted to Cage's work: his own titles, which now number nearly a dozen; my own documentary monograph, *John Cage* (New York: Praeger, 1970; London: Allen Lane, 1971; Koln: Dumont, 1973; Barcelona: Anagrama, 1974); Daniel Charles's *Pour les oiseaux* (Paris: Belfond, 1976), which at last count has been translated into English (*For the Birds* [Boston & London: Marion Boyars, 1981]) and German (*Fur die Vogel* [Berlin: Merve Verlag, 1984]); Klaus Schöning's *Roaratario* (Königstein/Ts, BRD: Athenäum, 1982), which is bilingual; in addition to *Sounday* (Hilversum: KRO, 1978) and *The John Cage Reader* (New York: C.F. Peters, 1982). To these earlier titles, as well as Cage's work in general, this new book is at once an introduction and a supplement; it may, for some of its readers, over a period of years, perhaps function as both.

I could not have completed this book without the cooperation of John Cage, who, perhaps because he saves so little paper, gave me the right and freedom to put his thoughts together, and then checked the manuscript for errors and infelicities, putting his own addenda between dingbats. This book depends as well upon the cooperation of numerous interviewers and publishers, who kindly sent me their texts and their manuscripts, along with their permissions. Their names are given at the ends of the passages drawn from their texts, with the year identifying the date of original publication (unless the conversation actually occurred long before); all questions are theirs, unless bracketed. As there was no effort to change present tense to past, look to the end of the excerpt to ascertain when Cage was speaking. Further information about the interviews and interviewers is given in the appendices at the back of the book. Chapters of this book previously appeared in *Book Forum, Fiction International, High Performance, Kenyon Review, Perspectives of New Music* and *Temblor,* among other magazines. Otherwise, my fingers did the initial editing on my Kaypro 2; and as J. S. Bach learned from copying his predecessors' scores, so the experience of having Cage's conversation pass through my hands was generally an instructive pleasure.

It would be appropriate, as well as helpful, to conclude this book with a comprehensive discography of tapes and records of Cagean performance; but that would be too long for a volume this size. For the latest data about this, I recommend contacting Mode Record Service, P.O. Box 375, Kew Gardens, NY 11415. To our friend Ernst Brucher of Dumont Buchverlag go our thanks for initially commissioning this; to Melvyn Zerman and his colleagues at Limelight Books for publishing it; to Kathy Antrim, for conscientious copyediting; to Deborah Campana, gratitude for bibliographic additions; and to our assistants, Andrew Culver and Constance Wynne, our thanks for completing our jobs.

Richard Kostelanetz
New York, New York
14 May 1986

EPIGRAPHS

I have never been able to do anything that was accepted straight off.—Marcel Duchamp, in conversation with Pierre Cabanne (1967).

A mind that is interested in changing . . . is interested precisely in the things that are at extremes. I'm certainly like that. Unless we go to extremes, we won't get anywhere.—John Cage, in conversation with Cole Gange and Tracy Caras (1980).

I can distinguish three ways of composing music nowadays. The first is well-known—that of writing music, as I do. It continues. A new way has developed through electronic music and the construction of new sound sources for making music by performing it, rather than writing it. And a third way has developed in recording studios, which is similar to the way artists work in their studios to make paintings. Music can be built up layer by layer on recording tape, not to give a performance or to write music, but to appear on a record.—John Cage, in conversation with Ilhan Mimaroglu (1985).

CABANNE: How did you live in New York?
DUCHAMP: You know, one doesn't know how one does it. I wasn't getting "so much per month" from anyone. It was really *la vie de bohème*, in a sense, slightly gilded—luxurious if you like, but it was still Bohemian life. Often there wasn't enough money, but that didn't matter. I must also say that it was easier back then in America than now. Camaraderie was general, and things didn't cost much, rent was very cheap. You know, I can't even talk about it, because it didn't strike me to the point of saying, "I'm miserable, I'm leading a dog's life." No, not at all.—Marcel Duchamp, in conversation with Pierre Cabanne (1967).

Oddly enough, the interview [with Cage] had a profound influence on my life. I became very immersed in environmental work and the theories of Buckminster Fuller. I am still there, working in my own nonprofit organization seeking innovative (avant-garde?) approaches to social and environmental harmony.—Geneviere Marcus, in a letter (1986).

Andy Warhol asked me if I would interview John Cage for *Interview.* I said, "Sure." I telephoned John Cage and told him that Andy Warhol wanted me to interview him for *Interview.* John said, "Ha, ha, ha; that's the *funniest* thing I ever heard."—Ray Johnson, in a letter (1987).

AUTOBIOGRAPHY

I was born in Los Angeles in 1912. My family's roots are completely American. There was a John Cage who helped Washington in the surveying of Virginia. My grandfather was an itinerant Methodist Episcopal minister. ❧After preaching ineffectively against Mormonism in Utah,☙ he ended up in Denver where he established the first Methodist Episcopal church. He was a man of extraordinary puritanical righteousness and would get very angry with people who didn't agree with him. As a child my father used to run away from home whenever he got the chance. He was regarded as a black sheep.

My mother was married twice before she married my father, but she never told me this until after he died. She couldn't remember her first husband's name.

My father invented a submarine just before the First World War which had the world's record for staying underwater, and he dramatized this by making an experimental trip on Friday the thirteenth, with a crew of thirteen, staying under water for thirteen hours. But it never entered his mind that the value of staying underneath water lay in being invisible to people above. Because his engine ran on gasoline it left bubbles on the surface of the water. So his sub wasn't used in the war, and Dad went bankrupt.—Jeff Goldberg (1976).

My father was an inventor, and he had a very beautiful idea for space travel—going to the moon and such things. He had a theory of how the universe works; it was called "Electrostatic Field Theory." He was able in his laboratory to simulate the universe, and he had little pith-balls of different sizes, in an electrostatic field, that actually went through the revolutions and orbits and so forth that the planets do. The people at the Pasadena institute [Cal Tech] couldn't explain why his thing worked, so they refused to believe it; but they also couldn't explain it away.

He believed that everything in the world has an electrostatic charge. That, in effect, is what gravity is. We don't fall off the earth because of our electrical connection with the earth; but if there were a sphere of an optimum size, we would have to hold it down to keep it here. Otherwise, because of its size, it would assume a charge opposite to that of the earth, and it would automatically move away. He had seen this happen in his laboratory.

Now with Buckminster Fuller's domes and construction devices, it would be perfectly simple to make an enormous sphere. It would then move away from the earth, without force, but, so to speak, in accord with nature. Then my dad's idea was that, since you would be able to do that, you would then be able to do the reverse, which would be to change the nature of the charge and so approach your destination.—Robert Cordier (1973).

My first experience with music was through neighborhood piano teachers, and particularly my Aunt Phoebe. She said of the work of Bach and Beethoven that it couldn't possibly interest me, she herself being devoted to the music of the nineteenth century. She introduced me to Moszkowski and what you might call *Piano Music the Whole World Loves to Play.* In that volume, it seemed to me that the works of Grieg were more interesting than the others.—Roger Reynolds (1961).

I started taking piano lessons when I was in the fourth grade at school but I became more interested in sight-reading than in running up and down the scales. Being a virtuoso didn't interest me at all.—Jeff Goldberg (1976).

When I was twelve years old, I had a radio program. It was for the Boy Scouts of America. I rode on my bicycle from ☙Moss Avenue near❧ Eagle Rock, where we lived, over to KFWB in Hollywood. I told them that I had the idea of having a Boy Scout program and that the performers on the program would be Boy Scouts and that ten minutes of each hour would be used by someone from either a synagogue or a church who would give some kind of an inspiring talk, you know. I was in the tenth grade, and so KFWB told me just to run along.

So I went to the next radio station—KNX. It was nearby, and they liked the idea, and they said, "Do you have permission from the Boy Scouts to do this?" I said, "No, but I can get that." So I went to the Boy Scouts and said that I had the agreement of KNX to have an hour every week for the Boy Scouts and was it all right with them? They said yes, and I said, "Well, will you cooperate with me? For instance, can I have the Boy Scout Band?" And they said, certainly not. They said you can do anything you like, but we won't cooperate; so I went back and told the people at the radio station. They agreed. Every Friday after school—I was still in high school—I would go over to the radio station and conduct the program which I think was at something like four to five in the afternoon or five to six. During the week I would prepare the program by getting as many scouts as I could to play, oh say, violin solos or trombone solos.

If this was in 1924–25, radio was still new to America.

Well, radio was very close to my experience, because my father was an inventor. He was never given the credit for it, but he had invented the first radio to be plugged into the electric light system.

What was your idea for the show?

Well, what I told you: Boy Scouts performing and some ten-minute inspirational talk from a member of the clergy. I no sooner began the program than there was a great deal of correspondence, people writing in; and those letters would be read on the air by me. I was the master of ceremonies. When there was no one else to perform I played piano solos. . . .

Of?

Mostly *Music the Whole World Loves to Play.* There used to be these books with that title. They were on all the neighborhood pianos. It's sad that we no longer have pianos in every house, with several members of the family able to play, instead of listening to radio or watching television.

How long did your juvenile radio career go?

That lasted for two years. Isn't that amazing? And it was so popular that it became a two-hour program, and the Boy Scouts became jealous. They came to the radio station and said that I had no authority and no right to have the program. So, of necessity, the radio station asked me to leave, and they accepted the real Boy Scouts, because I was only second class. I was not even a first-class scout. They accepted the real ones, and the real ones used it in a quite different way. They were very ostentatious and pushy. The result was that after two programs they were asked to leave.

Was there a sponsor?

No, this was before the day of grants.

So, even into the late twenties, your experience of music came mostly from live music.

From piano lessons and so on. It was in church primarily. Aunt Marge had a beautiful contralto voice. I loved to hear her sing, always on Sundays in church and sometimes on weekdays at home. Then in college, at Pomona, I met a Japanese tennis player who had some kind of physical trouble as a result of playing tennis. So he was resting by taking a few classes at Pomona College. He was absolutely devoted to the string quartets of Beethoven, and he had as fine a collection of recordings of those as one could find. His name was Tamio Abe, and he played all those records for me.—Richard Kostelanetz (1984).

Since I was convinced I would be a writer when I was in college, I was also convinced that college was of no use to a writer because teachers required everyone to read the same books. So I persuaded my mother and father that going to Europe would be more useful for someone who was going to write than continuing college and they agreed.—Paul Cummings (1974).

I went to Paris instead of continuing my third year of college, and in Paris I was struck first of all by the Gothic architecture. I spent a number of months studying flamboyant Gothic architecture at the Bibliothèque

Mazarin. A professor I had had in college ◂§José Pijoan§▸ was furious with me for not being involved in modern architecture. He got me working with a modern architect ◂§whose name was Goldfinger. Ironically, he got me to drawing Greek capitals for columns.§▸ And then I heard that architect one day say that to be an architect you'd have to devote your entire life to architecture. And I realized I wasn't willing to do that. I loved a number of others things—poetry was one, and also music.—Rob Tannenbaum (1985).

During the Depression in the early 1930s, I found myself in Santa Monica, California, after having spent about a year and a half in Europe—in Paris, actually—where I rather quickly came in contact with a wide variety of both modern painting and modern music. The effect was to give me the feeling that if other people could do things like that I myself could. And I began, without benefit of a teacher, to write music and to paint pictures, so that when I came back from Europe I was in Santa Monica where I had no way to make a living—I was a dropout from college—and I showed my music to people whose opinion I respected and I showed my paintings to people whose opinion I respected. Among those for painting were Galka Scheyer, who had brought "The Blue Four" [Lyonel Feininger, Alexej Jawlensky, Wassily Kandinsky and Paul Klee] from Europe, and Walter Arensberg, who had the great collection that was formed really by Marcel Duchamp. And I showed my music to Richard Buhlig, who was the first person to play Schoenberg's Opus 11. The sum total of all that was that the people who heard my music had better things to say about it than the people who looked at my paintings had to say about my paintings. And so I decided to devote myself to music. Meanwhile I had gone from house to house in Santa Monica selling lectures on modern music and modern painting. I sold ten lectures for $2.50 and I had an audience of something like 30 or 40 housewives once a week. I assured them that I knew nothing about the subject but that I would find out as much as I could each week and that what I did have was enthusiasm for both modern painting and modern music. In this way I taught myself, so to speak, what was going on in those two fields. And I came to prefer the thought and work of Arnold Schoenberg to that of Stravinsky.—Alan Gillmor (1973).

Schoenberg was approaching sixty when I became one of his students in 1933. At the time what one did was to choose between Stravinsky and Schoenberg. So, after studying for two years with his first American student, Adolph Weiss, I went to see him in Los Angeles. He said, "You probably can't afford my price," and I said, "You don't need to mention it because I don't have any money." So he said, "Will you devote your life to music?" and I said I would. And though people might feel, because I know my work is controversial, that I have not devoted myself to music utterly, that I have spent too much time with chess, or with mushrooms, or writing, I still think I've remained faithful. You can stay with music while you're hunting mushrooms. It's a curious idea perhaps, but a mushroom grows for such a short time and if you happen to come across it when it's fresh it's like coming upon a sound which also lives a short time.—Jeff Goldberg (1976).

How did you, an experimentalist par excellence, come to study with such a formal structuralist twelve-tone composer?

In the '30s we didn't take Bartók seriously. We took Stravinsky and Schoenberg seriously as the two directions that one could legitimately take. I chose Schoenberg, and I think it was right, because toward the end of his life Stravinsky also turned to twelve-tone music.

I worshipped Schoenberg—I saw in him an extraordinary musical mind, one that was greater and more perceptive than the others.—Paul Hertelendy (1982).

Schoenberg was a magnificent teacher, who always gave the impression that he was putting us in touch with musical principles. I studied counterpoint at his home and attended all his classes at USC and later at UCLA when he moved there. I also took his course in harmony, for which I had no gift. Several times I tried to explain to Schoenberg that I had no feeling for harmony. He told me that without a feeling for harmony I would always encounter an obstacle, a wall through which I wouldn't be able to pass. My reply was that in that case I would devote my life to beating my head against that wall—and maybe that is what I've been doing ever since. In all the time I studied with Schoenberg he never once led me to believe that my work was distinguished in any way. He never praised my compositions, and when I commented on other students' work in class he held my comments up to ridicule. And yet I worshipped him like a god.—Calvin Tomkins (1965).

Anyway, Schoenberg lived in a dark, quasi-Spanish house, and he had no grand piano, just an upright. He wasn't tall, and he had very poor taste in clothes. He was almost bald and he looked as though he was haunted. As far as I was concerned, he was not an ordinary human being. I literally worshipped him. I tried to do my work as well as I could for him, and he invariably complained that none of his pupils, including me, did enough good work. If I followed the rules too strictly he would say, "Why don't you take a little more liberty?" and then when I would break the rules, he'd say, "Why do you break the rules?" I was in a large class at USC when he said quite bluntly to all of us, "My purpose in teaching you is to make it impossible for you to write music," and when he said that, I revolted, not against him, but against what he had said. I determined then and there, more than ever before, to write music.—Jeff Goldberg (1976).

He refused to look at my compositions (in class). When I came up with a long fugue subject, he'd simply say, "Put it in your next symphony."—Paul Hertelendy (1982).

Someone asked Schoenberg about his American pupils, whether he'd had any that were interesting, and Schoenberg's first reply was to say there were no interesting pupils, but then he smiled and said, "There was one," and he named me. Then he said, "Of course he's not a composer, but he's an inventor—of genius."—Jeff Goldberg (1976).

You had the good fortune to study with two people who were extremely important for twentieth-century music: Henry Cowell and Arnold Schoenberg. With Schoenberg, there is the famous quote about your "beating your head against the wall" of harmony. You must have talked with Schoenberg a little more than that. Did you feel that it was important to study with him?

At the time that I felt the need to study music, the choice that was open to a student then was to study in the "school"—that is to say, of Schoenberg, or the "school" of Stravinsky. Both of them were in Los Angeles at the time, where I wanted to study. So it was a simple matter to make a choice. I don't think that Stravinsky was teaching, but Schoenberg loved teaching, and I had decided, moveover, that I preferred his music to that of Stravinsky—though I had loved all modern music, not just Schoenberg. I preferred the work of Schoenberg to that of any other modern composer in the sense that if I were going to study, that I would study with him, and studying with him meant believing what he had to say. It didn't mean having an opportunity to argue with him, as so many college students do with their teachers, whom they may not have elected to study with. All they elected to do was to go to a building in which certain people happen to be, but they didn't go to the people; they went to the building. I had already dropped out; I'm a college dropout. So that the only reason I went to study with Schoenberg was because I believed in what he had to say and to teach.

I stayed with him for two years, and when I left him, it was for the reason that your question included. Namely, that though we had gotten along beautifully for two years, it became more and more clear to me and to him that he took harmony fundamentally seriously, and I didn't. I had not yet studied Zen Buddhism, curiously enough. When I did, which was about ten or fifteen years later, I would have had even more reason for not studying harmony. But at that time, it was as though I was wrong, and what I was interested in was noise. The reason I couldn't be interested in harmony was that harmony didn't have anything to say about noise. Nothing.

Wasn't it Cowell who recommended that you go to Schoenberg?

Yes.

I know that Cowell was the founder of the New Music Society and the New Music Edition, and he was responsible, I believe, for directing the attention of so many people toward the music of Varèse, Ruggles, and Ives. I imagine you would have found working with him very congenial then.

I enjoyed him for the reasons that we've mentioned, together with his interest in music of other cultures. What is now called "world music" in the universities. He was, I would say, the instigator of interest in other cultures.

When I studied with Adolph Weiss here in New York, to prepare myself for studies with Schoenberg, I also studied with Henry Cowell at the New School and became his assistant for a while. In that way I didn't have to pay for the classes. I had very little money. To eat and pay my rent and so forth, I was washing walls in a Brooklyn YWCA. I played bridge every evening with Mr. and Mrs. Weiss and Henry Cowell—or sometimes with the Weisses and Wallingford Riegger. About midnight, we would stop playing and I would sleep for four hours, then get up, and between four and eight I would do my exercises for the next day's lesson with Weiss, and then I would get on the subway, at the last possible moment, to go to Brooklyn to wash the walls. The way I knew it was the last possible moment was because I saw the same people every morning, in the same car. Because *they* all went there at the last possible moment; they didn't like their jobs any more than I liked mine. Then, when I got back to Manhattan, I would eat, and then take a lesson with Weiss, and then play bridge again until midnight.—Cole Gagne & Tracy Caras (1975).

My mother had an arts and crafts shop which was nonprofit. Mother was the club editor of the *Los Angeles Times.* She started the crafts shop in order to give craftsmen an opportunity to sell their goods. I had no job. No one could get work. So I either did library research for my father, who was an inventor, or other people—people who were running for governor, who wanted this data or whatever; I would do library research for them. On occasion I also sat in my mother's art and crafts shop and sold the goods and wrote music in the back of the shop. One day into the shop came Xenia, and the moment I saw her I was convinced that we were going to be married. It was love at first sight on my part, not on hers. I went up and asked her if I could help her and she said she needed no help whatsoever. And so I retired to my desk and my music, and she looked around and finally went out. But I was convinced that she would return. Of course, in a few weeks she did. This time I had carefully prepared what I was going to say to her. That evening we had dinner and the same evening I asked her to marry me.

What did she think of this, all of a sudden?

She was put off a little bit, but a year or so later she agreed. I think we were married in '35. So at first we lived in the same apartment house as my mother and father did; and I was, at that moment, studying with Schoenberg.—Paul Cummings (1976).

I ran into Oscar Fischinger, who was a maker of abstract films that he made by following pieces of music; and he used, among other things, the Hungarian dances of Brahms.

It was an idea of a mutual friend that I would write some music that he would use to make an abstract film, and so I worked with him. While we were working together, I was moving bits of colored cardboard hung on wires. I had a long pole with a chicken feather, and I would move it and then have to still it. When I got it perfectly still—he was sitting in an armchair at the camera—he would click it and take one frame. And then I'd move them, following his direction, another inch and so, and then he'd take another frame. In the end it was a beautiful film in which these squares, triangles and circles and other things moved and changed color. In the course of that tedious work, he made a remark which was very important to me. He said that everything in the world has a spirit which is released by its sound, and that set me on fire, so to speak.—Joel Eric Suben (1984).

When I was studying with Schoenberg in the thirties, Stravinsky came to live in Los Angeles, and an impresario who was our local Hurok advertised a concert of his music as "Music of the World's Greatest Living Composer." I was indignant and marched straight into the impresario's office and told him that he should think twice before he made such advertisements in a city where Schoenberg was living. I was *extremely* partisan. I was like a tiger in defense of Schoenberg, and I was less and less interested in Stravinsky's music as time went on. Then, circumstances were such that while Stravinsky was alive there was a celebration of his work at Lincoln Center and a performance with Lukas Foss conducting *L'Histoire du soldat.* Rather than present the whole thing with dancers and whatnot, they had decided to have three composers read the three different parts. Aaron Copland was the narrator, Elliot Carter was the soldier, and I was the devil. Everyone thought I was well cast. Anyway, Stravinsky was in the audience, and he was delighted with my performance, so I asked him whether I might come and see him. I visited him in a hotel on Fifth Avenue. We had a very pleasant conversation, and I found him an extremely interesting man, so I said something to this effect: "You know, the reason I never made an effort to see you before was because I was so partisan and so devoted to the work of Schoenberg." He made this rather remarkable statement: "You know, the reason I've never liked Schoenberg's music is because it isn't modern." This reminded me of things which I'd heard Schoenberg say when he was teaching us. He would take a particular group of four notes and he would say, "Bach did this with these four notes, Beethoven did this, Brahms did this, Schoenberg did this!" In other words, it was as Stravinsky was saying. Schoenberg didn't think of himself in any sense as constituting a break with the past.—Jeff Goldberg (1974).

Xenia played in my percussion orchestra, but she was primarily an artist and learned how to draw very beautifully and painstakingly. She became interested in making mobiles using balsa wood and paper, which moved and cast very beautiful shadows. She now does curatorial work for a museum.—Jeff Goldberg (1976).

Xenia was interested in crafts and in bookbinding, and she did later those valises for Marcel [Duchamp]. We went to live in a large house in Santa Monica run by Hazel Dreis, a very fine bookbinder. I mean a real bookbinder—not a casemaker, but a real binding. And we both bound books. Xenia did most of it. I enjoyed designing the covers and so forth. I also wrote music there. Then, in the evening all the bookbinders became musicians and played in my orchestra. So because it was percussion music, I think, it brought the interest of modern dancers. I wrote a few pieces for this dance group at UCLA, which was nearby, and also for the athletic department that had underwater swimmers who swam underwater ballet. That was how I discovered dipping a gong in a tub of water and making a sound that way. Because I found that the swimmers couldn't hear the music when it was above water, but could if it was both in and out. So this connection with the dancers led me to the possibility of getting employment working with dancers. I went one day to San Francisco and got actually four jobs in one day and of the four I chose to work with Bonnie Bird, who had been in the Martha Graham group and was teaching at the Cornish School in Seattle. The Cornish School was extraordinary because of Nelly Cornish's insistence that each person not specialize but study all of the things that were offered. I worked with Bonnie Bird and wrote music for her, and I organized the percussion orchestra and made tours around the Northwest and to Mills College every summer. And that's where I met Moholy-Nagy and all those people from the School of Design in Chicago, and was invited to go to Chicago and join the faculty there.—Paul Cummings (1974).

The recording medium at that time was wire. Did you ever think of working creatively with wire?

I did some library research work in connection with my father's inventions. Because of that, when I became interested in recorded sound for musical purposes or even for radio plays, I then did library research for myself about the new technical possibilities; and they included, as you say, wire and film. Tape wasn't yet, in the early forties, recognized as a suitable musical means; but wire and film were.

Did you work with them yourself?

No, I just wanted to. I wrote letters, I think it was in '41 or '42, to corporations and universities all over the country trying to establish a Center for Experimental Music, and I didn't get anywhere. Well, actually, I got a little where. The University of Iowa's psychology department was interested through the presence there of, wasn't his name, Carl Seashore, who made many ways of finding out about intelligence and so on. He was interested in my project. Dr. Aurelia Henry Reinhardt, isn't that right, who was president of Mills, was interested. She was a very tall, big, imposing, and brilliant woman. She had a great collection of Gertrude Stein books. So was Moholy-Nagy at the School of Design in Chicago. But none of these people had any money. They said, if I could raise the money to establish it, they would be willing to have it as part of their activities. For two years I kept trying to do that, and that's when I, so to speak, didn't get anywhere.

What did you imagine this center having?

Well, I was working with percussion instruments. One characteristic of percussion is that it's open to anything else than what it already has. The strings in the orchestra are not that way—they want to become more and more what they are; but the percussion wants to become other than what it is. And that's the part of the orchestra that's open, so to speak, to electronics or to . . . And so I thought of recording means as instrumental to percussion music.—Richard Kostelanetz (1984).

[Did you serve in World War II?]

Fortunately, I never had to go to war. My father was an inventor, and I did research work for him. I didn't have to go to World War II, which otherwise I might have gotten involved with. He was doing work in seeing through fog for airplanes, and I did library research work in connection with that; and, of course, it was indirectly related to the war. It was pleasant for me not to have to get involved. Had I been drafted, I would have accepted and gone into it; I would not have refused. There are so many examples of people who were able to continue their work in the Army. The first I think of is the philosopher Ludwig Wittgenstein, who wrote his *Tractatus* in the trenches in Italy. Christian Wolff, more recently, wrote more music in the Army than he did out of the Army, etc. In other words, I believe in the principle of Daniel in the Lion's Den, so I would not want to keep myself out of it, if I were obliged to go into it. On the other hand, I am glad not to have gone into it, as I have never in my life shot a gun. As a child I was very much impressed by the notion of turning the other cheek. You know, if someone struck me on one cheek, I actually *did* turn the other cheek. I took that seriously.—Alcides Lanza (1971).

Xenia had inherited a small amount of money, and at the end of that year we decided that since the fan mail for the Patchen play had been very good [in Chicago], we would come to New York and make our fortune. I would write music for radio and films and so forth, using sound effects, because I was still working principally with percussion. Well, it turned out that when I got here, all the fan mail that was received by CBS here was negative. So there was no possible employment. We were penniless, absolutely penniless.—Paul Cummings (1974).

[What persuaded you to stay in New York?]

It was a marvelous place to land because it was not only New York which I think, when one first comes to it, is extremely stimulating, but it was the whole gamut of the world of painting. Through circumstances in Europe, many painters were living here in New York—Mondrian was here, for instance, and Breton was here; and so in one fell swoop or series of evenings at Peggy Guggenheim's you met an entire world of both American and European artists. She was already involved with Jackson Pollock, and Joseph Cornell was a frequent visitor. Marcel Duchamp was there all the time, and I even met Gypsy Rose Lee. It was absolutely astonishing to be in that situation.

How did you first meet Duchamp?

I'd come from Chicago and was staying in the apartment of Peggy Guggenheim and Max Ernst. Peggy had agreed to pay for the transport of my percussion instruments from Chicago to New York, and I was to give a concert to open her gallery, "The Art of This Century." Meanwhile, being young and ambitious, I had also arranged to give a concert at the Museum of Modern Art. When Peggy discovered that, she cancelled not only the concert but also her willingness to pay for the transport of the instruments. When she gave me this information, I burst into tears. In the room next to mine at the back of the house Marcel Duchamp was sitting in a rocking chair smoking a cigar. He asked why I was crying and I told him. He said virtually nothing, but his presence was such that I felt calmer. Later on, when I was talking about Duchamp to people in Europe, I heard similar stories. He had calmness in the face of disaster.—Jeff Goldberg (1976).

To continue with Duchamp a bit: Was he a good chess teacher?

I was using chess as a pretext to be with him. I didn't learn, unfortunately, while he was alive to play well. I play better now, although I still don't play very well. But I play well enough now that he would be pleased, if he knew that I was playing better. So that when he would instruct me in chess, rather than thinking about it in terms of chess, I thought about it in terms of Oriental thought. Also he said, for instance, don't just play your side of the game, play both sides. That's a brilliant remark and something people spend their lives trying to learn—not just in chess, but everything.—Paul Cummings (1974).

So when did you hook up with Jean Erdman?

Well, Merce Cunningham and Jean Erdman were working with Martha Graham at Bennington College and before they left, they asked me to write some music for a dance which they would make that summer. And so I wrote it [*Credo in Us*] and in return for writing the music Jean and Joe Campbell gave us their apartment which they still live in on Waverly Place. So we had a place to live, but no money for food, I mean literally. There was one of those days I felt relieved because I found that I had not even a cent—nothing. I think before I had nothing I had written some letters to people telling them of the situation and in that way I received something like fifty dollars through the mail. And at that time that was a good deal. And in the course of it, John Steinbeck, who was an old friend, came along and invited us to the 21 Club for lunch. I was so horrified because lunch cost over, well over, a hundred dollars. I never particularly like to have lunch anyway because it breaks into the day, and you can't get anything done!—Gwen Deely (1976).

When I first came to New York, something had been written to me by Martha Graham that led me to believe she would give me a job as an accompanist for the dance classes in her school, and that she would consider my writing music for her. So when I first came to New York, I went to see her. I remember it was a late afternoon, it was quite dark, it must have been in the colder part of the year. She didn't turn any lights on. She seemed very mysterious and very powerful, and I was already put off. Then it turned out that she hadn't meant anything, that she didn't want me to work for her at all, even as a dance accompanist. Then I felt somewhat liberated, I remember, when I left, from her kind of power.—David Shapiro (1985).

Can we talk about your [1943] concert at the Museum of Modern Art? Wasn't that a very important event for you at that time?

I thought it was. It was not as important as I thought. It was highly publicized and highly reviewed, even in *Life* magazine, so I thought that my fortune would be made. I was very naive and quite ambitious, but I discovered very quickly that no matter how well known you are, it doesn't mean anything in terms of employment or willingness to further your work or do anything.—Paul Cummings (1974).

I had heard one lecture given by Nancy Wilson Ross at the Cornish School late in the thirties on Zen and Dada, which had impressed me very much, but which had not impressed me sufficiently to get me to reading Zen texts. It was only in the middle forties when, through personal circumstances that ended in my divorce from Xenia, that I required help as an individual who needed help, and that was going to come as usual from psychoanalysis, but it didn't—and I recount the story in my book [*Silence*, 1961]. But instead I got involved with Oriental philosophy and that performed for me the function that psychoanalysis might have performed. But, in performing it, Zen is almost characterized by an insistence on an utterly realistic approach and one that ends in humor.

Then all of these things that have been talked about you and Dada really aren't Dada at all, because their roots would be in Zen.

Well, except you have to go back to the beginnings of these remarks. I had been brought up on the twenties. I was very impressed by geometrical abstract art, and I was aware of Duchamp and so forth. I liked Dada very much. That interest in Dada became enforced by my interest in Satie, who himself was a Dadaist. I preferred Dada to its successor.

Surrealism.

I think so.—Irving Sandler (1966).

When I was growing up, Church and Sunday School became devoid of anything one needed. The public schools avoided such "needs," and what I was forced to do in school was what I no longer wished to do—including Shakespeare. I was almost forty years old before I discovered what I needed—in Oriental thought. It occupied all of my free time (aside from musical work) in the form of reading and attending classes of Suzuki for several years. I was starved—I was thirsty. These things had all been in the Protestant Church, but they had been there in a form in which I couldn't use them. Jesus saying, "Leave thy Father and Mother," meant "Leave whatever is *closest* to you." In Zen, one speaks of "no-mindedness." The idea of Nirvana is not a negative statement, but the "blowing out" of what is seen as an impediment to enlightenment. The ego is seen as the one barrier to experience. Our experience, whether it comes from the outside or from the inside, must be able to "flow through." Irrationality, or "no-mindedness," is seen as a *positive* goal, which is "in accord with" the environment.—C. H. Waddington (1972).

I remember meeting with de Kooning. It was at the time that I was first involved with chance operations, and I wrote those six or seven Haiku; and I made calligraphic copies of them on Oriental papers. I don't know if you've seen them, but there's one line of music at the bottom of the page and the rest of the page empty; and I dedicated these to people who had helped me or who were trying to help me with the problem of livelihood, which was serious then. Bill de Kooning must have been one of these because I dedicated one of the Haiku to him, and I went to his studio to give it to him. He had what has never appealed to me, and he explained to me that he had it, which was the desire to be a great artist. I remember that he didn't turn the light on, and it was getting dark outside, and he said, "You and I are very different. I want to be a great artist."—Gwen Deely (1976).

In the late forties, when we [Merce Cunningham and I] were making a tour, we wrote, as to other colleges, we wrote to Black Mountain asking for an engagement. And they wrote back and said that they would like to have us come but that they had no money to pay us, and we accepted that arrangement anyway. They agreed to put us up and to feed us. And so between two engagements—I think one was in Virginia and the next was in, oh, Chicago perhaps—we went to Black Mountain. I forget how long we stayed, but several days. And it was a great pleasure. There were many parties. And when we got in the car to drive away . . . We had parked it in front of that building where the studies were, and hadn't used it while we were there. So that when we drove it back, we discovered this large pile of presents that all the students and faculty had put under the car in lieu of any payment. It included, for instance, oh, paintings and food and drawings, and so on.—Mary Emma Harris (1974).

I only took other employment if it was absolutely necessary, to eat; but I could go a long time without working, I mean without getting a job. It was when I began the *Music of Changes* in the early fifties that I decided to limit my work to my composition, not to look for another kind of work.—David Shapiro (1985).

From all I've read, it appears that those early meetings on Monroe Street with Feldman and Wolff and Tudor were very significant meetings. The image that comes out is one of daily activity and daily changes of attitude.

Yes.

How long did that last?

It lasted a year, maybe two years. Then I went to Colorado and met Earle Brown and Carolyn Brown, and they became so interested in the work that they decided to leave Colorado and come to New York and live here. I, meanwhile, had started a tape music project with Louis and Bebe Barron and David Tudor. And Earle went into this. Well, the appearance of Earle Brown on the scene infuriated Morton Feldman, so that the closeness that I had had with Morty and David and Christian was disrupted by the advent of Earle Brown. Later, that whole problem was resolved by our raising the money to present a concert of the music of Brown and Feldman at Town Hall. Then both Earle and Morty became friends, and had a truce.

Did the intensity of that group of people extend outside of the group?

Oh yes. There were other people who wanted to enter the group and enjoy the exchange of ideas and so forth, but Morty refused to let that happen. He insisted upon its being a closed group. It was through my acceptance of Earle Brown that Morty then left. The group then dissolved. Morty was literally furious that anyone else was allowed into the group. Another one who might have been in it, but wasn't, was Philip Corner. And I don't know, but I imagine Malcolm Goldstein and James Tenney. However, the fact that they weren't brought into it made it come about that they formed their own group, which was called Tone Roads. And they did beautiful work.—William Duckworth (1985).

What attracted you to mycology?

Well, the building that I lived in in Manhattan [in the late forties and early fifties] had a marvelous situation. It was at Grand Street and Monroe, and I had half of a top floor of the tenement. I could look up to 59th Street and I could look down to the Statue of Liberty, and I was spoiled by this involvement with the sky and air and water and so forth. When they tore this building down, I went to the people in charge and I said, could I have an apartment that would have the same view when you put up the new building? And they said, we can't take such things into consideration. And so at that moment, it was a coincidence, as it generally is, some friends of mine, who had come together through one association or another with Black Mountain College, had the notion of starting a cooperative community in Stony Point, New York, up the Hudson, and asked me to join in and I did. And it was August. I had lived in the privacy of New York, and I was suddenly introduced to a farmhouse in Stony Point before the buildings that we now live in were built, and I found myself living in small quarters with four other people, and I was not used to such lack of privacy, so I took to walking in the woods. And since it was August, the fungi are the flora of the forest at that time. The brightest colors (we are all children), they took my eye. I remember that during the Depression I had sustained myself for a week on nothing but mushrooms and I decided to spend enough time to learn something about them. Furthermore, I was involved with chance operations in music, and I thought it would just be a very good thing if I get involved in something where I could not take chances. However, I've learned to experiment, and the way you do that is, if you don't know whether a mushroom is edible or not, you cook it all up, and you take a little bit and then you leave it until the next day and watch to see if there are any bad effects. If there aren't any, you eat a little more, and presently you know something.—Yale School of Architecture (1965).

[*How did your involvement proceed?*]

I decided to learn [about mushrooms] and other wild edible plants. First I got books and found the books confusing. And then I met Guy Nearing, and I finally began to learn a good deal about mushrooms. Then four years later [in Italy], I was on a TV quiz show, which I won by answering questions about mushrooms; and that was the first consequential amount of money I'd ever earned. (It was two years later, in 1960, that I began to make some money with my music.) So I began giving classes at the New School of Social Research in mushroom identification, and then that class developed into the New York Mycological Society, of which I'm a founding member. Now I have one of those honorary things from the People to People Committee on Fungi, which is centered in Ohio, for having done a great deal for amateur mycology. And I'm a member also of a Czechoslovakian mushroom society. But I've now given away all my mushroom books—there were over three hundred of them I'd collected—since I figure I have enough in my head. And I've published with Lois Long a portfolio of twenty lithographs—ten are by her which illustrate fungi, and ten are by me which write about fungi in relation to all my other interests.

I think that when I focus my attention on something, it goes dead; but when I place it in a space that includes things that are not it, then it comes alive.—Robert Cordier (1973).

There's pleasure in eating, don't you agree?

But you couldn't live on mushrooms?

No, they're not nourishing.

Do you have favorites?

I like the ones I have. If you like the ones you don't have, then you're not happy.—Lisa Low (1985).

Did you notice the mushrooms at Black Mountain?

No. I had always lived in the cities, and when I went to Black Mountain, I had, even then, the feeling that the insects and whatnot in the country were far more irritating than the cockroaches in the cities. And it was only in Stony Point that I discovered that I was starved for nature and took to walking in the woods. And my whole attitude toward insects changed.

You prefer insects to cockroaches now?

I prefer being bitten by mosquitoes to cockroaches. Yes.—Mary Emma Harris (1974).

At what point in your composing did you become interested in Zen and in Buddhism?

It happened between '46 and '47, and the involvement didn't take place immediately. It began with Oriental philosophy and then Suzuki came from Japan and was teaching at Columbia, and I attended his classes for some three years. So that, that takes us up to about '51 or something like that. Now the effect it had was first to change what it was that I was trying to say in my work. And, second, to change how it was I was making my work. And what it was that I was saying was very much influenced by such Oriental notions as creation, preservation, destruction, and quiescence; and I was most involved in this understanding of the seasons. And then the Indian notion of the emotions that are necessary to make a work of art, the four white ones and the four black ones and the central one, without color, of tranquility, this being the one that must be expressed no matter what others are expressed. All that I tried to express in certain works. Then I began composing in that way, first with charts, in which I made moves on the charts, regardless of my intentions. In other words, a spirit of acceptance, rather than a spirit of control. And then testing my life by my art, etc.—Yale School of Architecture (1965).

Most people who believe that I'm interested in chance don't realize that I use chance as a discipline. They think I use it—I don't know—as a way of giving up making choices. But my choices consist in choosing what questions to ask.

And also choosing how to follow the answers you get.

Well, my use of the *I Ching* in my work is just a mechanism of the chance operation. But I think if you use the *I Ching* as a book of wisdom, there, too, it's difficult to know how to ask the questions.

Very often you can ask a question and then find out that it gives you an answer that makes you aware of another dimension you haven't thought of.

If I ask the *I Ching* a question as though it were a book of wisdom, which it is, I generally say, "What do you have to say about this?" and then I just listen to what it says and see if some bells ring or not.

So do you use it for . . .

On occasion when I'm troubled. But I haven't been troubled for quite some time—that is to say, I haven't been so troubled that I felt the need to ask it.—Robin White (1978).

The number 64 which is the number that the *I Ching* works with—I found a way of relating it to numbers which are larger or smaller than 64 so that any question regarding a collection of possibilities can be answered by means of the *I Ching* which I now have computerized, so that I can very quickly do something using the *I Ching* actually as a computer. I found when I made *HPSCHD* with Lejaren Hiller that if you have a question for which you want a great number of answers, then it is economical to use the computer. But if you have a question which you only want one answer to, then it's better to do it yourself. And when I do it myself I use the printout of the *I Ching* which is now computerized. Mostly I want only one answer to a question, and therefore I can work at home without going to a computer laboratory. And this box over here that has ropes around it is full of *I Ching* printouts. So I have a great supply of answers to questions which I have not yet asked.—Hans G. Helms (1972).

Why do you have such a strong interest in chess, which is a rigid, closed system?

In order to let it act as a balance to my interest in chance. I think the same thing is true of Marcel Duchamp. Because when he gave me his book on chess, I asked him to write something in it, and he wrote ☙in French❧: "Dear John, Look out, still one more poisonous mushroom." Because both mushrooms and chess, you see, are the opposite of chance operations.—Art Lange (1977).

[Chess] is pretty directed then?

Yes. On the other hand, I like games anyway. I even like poker. I don't play it very often. Sometimes if you get in residence at a university you have to play games with the teachers. Poker is very popular at universities.—Mark Bloch (1987).

I work a great deal and enjoy working, but life is so complicated—circumstances arise and we're not always able to do the work we think is the proper work for us to do. It is precisely being able to accept those interruptions, to be able, temporarily, to let the work go and do the thing that comes and asks to be done.

I spend most of the day working. Sometimes I interrupt my work to go mushroom hunting or to play chess, which I don't have a gift for. Marcel Duchamp once watched me playing and became indignant when I didn't win. He accused me of not wanting to win. You must have an extraordinary aggressiveness to play well.

I was twenty-three when I married, but the marriage only lasted ten years. Now I share my apartment with Merce Cunningham.

I met Merce Cunningham in the thirties, before he joined the Martha Graham Dance Company. I began to write music for him, and we toured the country together. Then I became musical director for his own company. I still tour with them and give lectures, which is one reason why I don't teach. I move around too much. Continuity is extremely important in a teaching situation.—Jeff Goldberg (1976).

The first time I left Stony Point must have been '60 or '61, when I was made a fellow at Wesleyan University and then in '67, when I was made a composer-in-residence at the University of Cincinnati. And then the two following years, '67 through '69, I was at the University of Illinois, and then at the University of California, Davis. And I needed the large income that all of these fellowships and residencies gave me, because I became in their late life the sole support of my mother and father. So that I was obliged to make a great deal of money, whereas up until 1958, I never knew where the next dollar was coming from. And it was in '58 that I won the TV quiz in Italy. That was the first sizeable income that I had, and I spent most of it to buy a Volkswagen bus for the dance company so we could tour.—Mary Emma Harris (1974).

If I notice that I'm disturbed if the phone rings and not giving my full attention to whomever it is, then I think I am not doing my work properly. I should be able to be interrupted. I mean, it's being done well if being interrupted is not upsetting it. I've noticed many people who protect themselves from those interruptions make that separation between work and their lives. I enjoy being at the telephone when I am there and I enjoy my work when I am *there.*

Some people consider me a poor musician whereas they think some of my ideas are interesting. So they say, he's not a musician, but he's a philosopher, whereas most philosophers say he's not a very good philosopher but he's a good musician. And they ask me sometimes which I think are more important—my compositions or music or my texts, and the answers are the ones we've been giving all through this conversation—when we're writing music, that's what's important, and when we're writing ideas, that's what's interesting. And I would like to extend it to as many other things in my life as I can—to cooking, to answering the telephone. And life actually is excellent at interrupting us.—Rose Slivka (1978).

Well, I began to make money not from actually writing music but from lecturing, concerts, and all such things, what you might call the paraphernalia of music, when I was fifty. Now I could get along without giving any concerts if I chose to live in a poor corner of the world. My income from past work is sufficient to live on in a very modest situation. I used to suggest to Merce Cunningham that it was time to retire, and he said, "Where would you go?" And I said, "To Bolivia." He said, "Why" So I said, "Because surely no one there is interested in modern music." I'd like to be somewhere where the phone doesn't ring. You see I refuse to have an answering service. I consider it a form of twentieth-century immorality.

In what way?

Well, it means that you disconnect yourself from the society. And at will. It's a form of selfishness.

Do you have your name in the telephone book?

No, I don't, but that's not my wish. That's Merce's wish because he's involved with a large company of dancers and a school, so if his name were in the telephone book, it would be awful. Anyway, people find out what your number is whether it's in the book or not.—Stephen Montague (1982).

I think that one of our most accessible disciplines now is paying attention to more than one thing at a time. If we can do that with equanimity, then I propose paying attention to three things at the same time. You can practice it as a discipline; I think it is more effective than sitting cross-legged.

In meditation?

I think the meaning of meditation is to open the doors of the ego from a concentration on itself to a flow with all of creation. Wouldn't you say? If we can do this through the sense perceptions, through multiplying the things to which we're able at one and the same time to pay attention, I think we can accomplish much the same thing. That's my faith.—Terry Gross (1982).

When you taught at the New School, around 1956, you worked with performance material as well as with music. What kind of assignments did you give?

The course "in the Composition of Experimental Music" generally began with my trying to bring the students to the point of knowing who I was, that is, what my concerns and activities were, and I wanted them to find out who they were and what they were doing. I wasn't concerned with a teaching situation that involved a body of material to be transmitted by me to them. I would, when it was necessary, give them a survey of earlier works, by me and by others, in terms of composition, but mostly I emphasized what I was doing at that time and would show them what I was doing and why I was interested in it. Then I warned them that if they didn't want to change their ways of doing things, they ought to leave the class, that it would be my function, if I had any, to stimulate them to change.

Did many leave?

Well, there never were many, and they mostly stayed. Eight or ten at the most. Some people did quite conventional musical work; they knew that I would try to get them to budge a bit. And some of them did. After this basic introduction, the classes consisted simply in their showing what they had done. And if I had anything to say I would say it. I also got them to say things about their work, . . . but this is a common progressive education practice, isn't it? We had very little to work with: a closet full of percussion instruments, a broken-down piano, and things that people brought with them. The room was very small, so we simply did what we could do in that room.

I reminded them that because we had so little they had to do things that would nevertheless work. I didn't want them making things that couldn't be done. Practicality has always seemed to me to be of the essence. I hate the image of an artist who makes things that can't be done.

Wasn't it surprising to have painters in a music class like that?

It wasn't surprising to me because I had, before that, in the late '40s and the early 50s, been part and parcel of the Artists Club. I had early seen that musicians were the people who didn't like me. But the painters did. The people who came to the concerts which I organized were very rarely musicians—either performing or composing. The audience was made up of people interested in painting and sculpture.—Michael Kirby & Richard Schechner (1965).

Your music wasn't published until Peters gave you an exclusive contract late in the 1950s. How did your signing with them come about?

I was living in the country then, and I had quite a problem supplying copies of my music to people who wanted to have it. I first took all of my music to Schirmers, and Mr. Heinsheimer said my music would only be a headache for them. The only piece he liked was the *Suite for Toy Piano,* but he said, "Of course we'll have to change the title." So I said, "There's no need for you to do that; I'll just take my music away." And I took it back to the country.

People kept writing to me asking for copies, and I kept on writing music. Finally, one day—it was while I was writing the incidental music for Jackson Mac Low's play called *The Marrying Maiden*—I put my pen down, and I determined not to write another note until I found a publisher. So I picked up the Yellow Pages and I ran down the list of music publishers, and I stopped at Peters. The reason I stopped there was because someone—I think someone in some string quartet—had said that Mr. Hinrichsen was interested in American music. So I simply called and asked to speak with him. He said, very cheerfully over the phone, "I'm so glad that you called. My wife has always wanted me to publish your music." That day we had lunch and signed the contract.

One of his great virtues was that he made no effort to censor, or to like or dislike the music. He felt that his function was not that, but was to publish it. If he decided to publish something, he didn't question it. I think it's for that reason I have an exclusive contract with them. He accepted everything I had done, and gave me *carte blanche.* I can do anything I want. That was not my privilege until I was nearly fifty years old, and that's true in both writing music and in writing texts. Now it's true that anything I do do is used in this society. Formerly it wasn't true. Walter Hinrichsen was the first to open that door.—Cole Gagne & Tracy Caras (1980).

In the fifties, when I gave a concert, I would advertise it, and at the most 125 people would come. When I gave *HPSCHD* in Illinois last year, somewhere between 7,000 and 9,000 people came, and they came from all over the country—and even from Europe! I gave a music circus in Illinois the year before and 5,000 people came, and the concert was free. I gave one in Minneapolis this year; another 3,000 people came, and it was free. Things are changing.

There are people saying that you as an "avant-garde artist" are the jester of the bourgeois society. What do you answer to this reproach?

The situation is different and has been different for many years in the U.S. from what it is in Europe. The people in Europe who concern themselves with art are for the most part not students, who are busy studying in Europe, but are rather the people who have the leisure to pay attention to art. Therefore, Europe considers itself more cultivated than the U.S., which is considered by Europe to be a little far away from tradition and from culture, and to be a little bit barbarian.

Well, what is happening in the U.S. is this: When you get a job in society and enter in the economic-political structure of capitalism, you no longer have any time for art. You're not interested in art any longer; only a few people are. The people who are interested in the arts are the students. Therefore, if I make a tour in the U.S., I go from university to university. If I make a tour in Europe, where do I go? I go from festival to festival, or from radio station to radio station, and from one concert hall to another. The public is changing now, but formerly it was entirely a grown-up group without children. That means that the idea of being a court jester is a European idea.—Max Nyfeller (1970).

After many years of doing what you do, how do you handle criticism? Do you think people are more aware, and more kindly disposed?

They certainly are. We performed in a museum in Columbus, Ohio. It was winter—I think it was '49, when food had to be flown in to Indians in Arizona, because the snow simply covered the United States—and we were on a tour. We left Chicago and the next place we were to get to was Portland. The only way we could get there was down through Arizona; we had to park the car in Sacramento and take a train. And then we flew from there to Denver and then back to Sacramento to get the car, and then across to Columbus. When we got to Columbus, there was no time to rest before the performance because of the problems with travel. At that time Merce did a series of solos and I played the prepared piano. The stage was very poor—every time Merce jumped, his head disappeared from view. Afterward, there was a party for us, and all the people did at the party was tell us that our work was terrible and that we shouldn't do what we were doing—that we had no notion of what music was or dance or anything. We thought that that performance in Columbus was a complete failure and that it ought never have taken place. Well, ten years later, I received a letter from a young man who said he had been in the audience and that it had changed his life.—Middlebury College (1981).

Do you feel it doesn't matter what people say about you?

Of course it doesn't matter. Because it is *their* action at that point. I learned very early to pay no attention to criticism. A review of a concert I gave in Seattle was to the effect that the whole thing was ridiculous. I knew perfectly well it wasn't. Therefore, the criticism was of no interest. In fact, it taught me that if people like what I am doing, I should look out. It's important that I live as I did before society became involved in what I am doing.

Do you resent society?

I think society is one of the greatest impediments an artist can possibly have. I rather think that Duchamp concurred with this view. When I was young and needed help, society wouldn't give it, because it had no confidence in what I was doing. But when, through my perseverance, society took an interest, then it wanted me not to do the next thing, but to repeat what I had done before. At every point society acts to keep you from doing what you have to do.

When you say society, you don't mean an audience?

I'm objecting to society as an audience, but I like society as what you might call an ecological fact.—Moira & William Roth (1973).

An audience is a group of people listening. The more devotedly this is done, that is the more attentive one is to each sound and the more curiosity one has about those to come, the more an audience *is* an audience.—Bill Womack (1979).

So you are concerned with people and unconcerned with the audience. You want the audience to turn into people.

I'm out to blur the distinctions between art and life, as I think Duchamp was. And between teacher and student. And between performer and audience, etcetera.—Moira & William Roth (1973).

Bob [Rauschenberg] knocked on the door to my studio one day, and brought in a painting he had just finished. It was a new one in the black series. I think he felt my reaction to it was not sufficiently enthusiastic. I had been very enthusiastic about his work, and he may have felt I was disappointed. In any case, I suddenly realized that he was terribly upset, close to tears. He asked me if there were something wrong with the painting. Well, I gave him a good talking-to about that. I told him he simply could not be dependent on anyone's opinion, that he could never, never look to another person for that sort of support.—Calvin Tomkins (1980).

I think our questions are stupid and corny.

Well, my answers are too, so it makes no difference. We're just a group of stupid people talking nonsense. I feel very stupid now. I feel myself, in the present moment, of just not knowing what to do at all; and I hate to do what I have done. And yet I don't know what to do now.

In the last few years, I've done a great deal of traveling, and lecturing, and performing; and I am not a good performer. David Tudor is a much better performer. It would be better if I would stay home and work, or even just pick mushrooms, in order that I might find what to do. But as I travel around like this, I'm like a traveling salesmen, or a minister traveling from one town to another preaching the gospel. Formerly, when I had the occasion to give a lecture, I would write a new lecture; but now I have so many engagements. I have no time to write a new one. So I simply read one of the old ones. And none of this is conducive to life, but rather to death, because it is the same kind of repetition that you get with printing, like the Renaissance. Nevertheless, the fact that I move around is related to McLuhan's description of the world as just one village. He says we live in "a global village."

Now the fact that I work by moving from one town to another is something that I'm not used to. I'm still used to the idea that I need time and some space in order to function as a composer. I think, for instance, that I need to be at home for, oh, at least three weeks with an empty head before any idea will come into it. This is an old romantic Renaissance idea, but I still have not found a way to travel around the world and to have ideas come into my head.

And you like to travel very much.

No, I would prefer, I think, to stay at home. On the other hand, I begin to realize that my home is all around the world. So we have changed from one culture to another with respect to traveling; but in this sense, as in many others, we tend to have one foot in a previous culture and the other in a new one. And we have not learned the way to act with ease in this new situation. This is one of our problems nowadays.—Lars Gunnar Bodin & Bengt Emil Johnson (1965).

If, for instance, you go to Paris and spend your time as a tourist going to the famous places, I've always had a feeling you would learn nothing about Paris. The best way to learn about Paris would be to have no intention of learning anything and simply to live there as though you were a Frenchman. And no Frenchman would dream of going, say, to Notre Dame.

So you managed to do that with Duchamp, live in Paris and not sightsee?

That was my intention: to be with him as often as circumstances permitted and to let things happen rather than to make them happen. This is also an Oriental notion. Meister Eckhardt says we are made perfect not by what we do, but by what happens to us. So we get to know Marcel not by asking him questions, but by being with him.

What happened when you played chess?

I rarely did, because he played so well and I played poorly. So I played with Teeny (Mrs. Duchamp), who also played much better than I. Marcel would glance at our game every now and then, and in between take a nap. He would say how stupid we both were. Every now and then he would get very impatient with me. He complained that I didn't seem to want to win. Actually, I was so delighted to be with him that the notion of winning was beside the point. When we played, he would give me a knight in advance. He was extremely intelligent and he almost always won. None of the people around us was as good a player as he, though there was one man who, once in a blue moon, would win.—Moira & William Roth (1973).

When did you start working with words?

Well, back in the thirties people found my music unusual and had questions about it, so my writings actually began as responses to people's questions in an attempt to let people know what it was that I was doing. More and more I began doing in writing what I was doing in music, so that I wouldn't answer questions literally but would give instances of how I was working. The "mesostics" on the name of Joyce are something else. They are a form of poetry which I devised that enables me to read all the way through a book that otherwise I would not read through. I find that if I involve myself in some kind of discovery, then I can get through a situation in which I otherwise have difficulty. If I had set out to try to understand *Finnegans Wake,* I wouldn't have been so attracted to read it. But if through reading it I made something, which is a discovery, then I'm excited.—Robin White (1978).

Is there a human being who has influenced you more than anyone else?

As time goes on I feel more influenced by more people.

Is there any area in which you prize your achievements more than any other area?

No.

What would you say is your most important legacy to future generations?

Having shown the practicality of making works of art nonintentionally.

What is your favorite piece of wisdom?

The Huang Po Doctrine of Universal Mind. This is a text, not a phrase.

Why?

I have no idea.—Jay Murphy (1985).

And what are your favorite objects?

I'm very careless about objects. That's why I give everything away. That's why I've given my mushroom books away to this university «§UC-Santa Cruz; materials re music to Northwestern and re the humanities to Wesleyan§». I keep boxes and put things in them, and give them away almost immediately or send them to places, because I am searching, you see, for this emptiness all the time. I'm a magnet in this society for material. Things are sent to me continually. I have no way to survive unless I get rid of them. It seems ruthless, but it is necessary.—David Cope (1980).

The photographer Mark Haven has commented that in your loft there is more a suggestion of contemporary graphics, with the Jasper Johns prints and so forth, than music. There does seem to be very little suggestion of your work as one walks around.

Well maybe, except there was an Italian article recently with photos about this loft that said it was musical. Everything here is as visible as sound is audible. The pictures unevenly placed are like notes on a staff. But the thing about this place that is musical is the street noise from Sixth Avenue.

Do you like all the noise?

I love it!—Stephen Montague (1982).

I love living on Sixth Avenue. It has more sounds, and totally unpredictable sounds, than any place I've ever lived.—Michael Zwerin (1982).

I wouldn't dream of getting double glass because I love all the sounds. The traffic never stops, night and day. Every now and then a horn, siren, screeching brakes—extremely interesting and always unpredictable. At first I thought I couldn't sleep through it. Then I found a way of transposing the sounds into images so that they entered into my dreams without waking me up.—Stephen Montague (1982).

Now I don't need a piano. I have Sixth Avenue, the sounds. I translate the sounds into images, and so my dreams aren't disturbed. It just fuses. There was a burglar alarm one night and I was amazed because the pitch went on for two hours, was quite loud. It seemed to me to be going slightly up and slightly down. So what it became in my dreams was a Brancusi-like shape, you know, a subtle curve. And I wasn't annoyed at all.—David Sears (1981).

I was thinking about things to ask you and they all seemed kind of stupid or insignificant. But then in doing this piece [recording the noisy plumbing in your house] I had some sort of reference point. Was that a piece that I did or a piece that you did?

It's just the recording of some things that happened. Right? The water was turned off today, so some air got into the pipes. I'm afraid I exercised the pipes too much before you came. If I hadn't, you would have gotten more of the spitting sound. Or that explosive, forceful sound. But I think sounds are interesting whether they're forceful or not. It's something that wouldn't have been made if you hadn't made it, so in that sense you made it. But you have no control over what's happening, so you haven't made it in the sense of giving it its shape. It's what you might call "a music of contingency," which means that you're necessary but not in control.

I guess you were necessary, also, because they happen to be your pipes.

I don't know. I was less necessary. I was playing chess.

Was that sound of me running the water bothering you at all?

No, no. I like sounds. Sometimes there are marvelous percussive sounds from those pipes up in the skylight—really very forceful. They can wake you up if you're sleeping.

Why do some of us like the shocking sounds more than the nonshocking sounds?

I guess they oblige us to listen—no alternative.—Mark Bloch (1987).

A new development in my life that interests me very much is gardening. I've never thought of myself as a gardener, but as a hunter. And now in New York, I have a loft situation with a twenty-by-twenty-foot skylight. It's the old B. Altman department store. There are seven large windows, so the place has plenty of light. I have between eighty and ninety plants now.

What appeals to me is the fact that everything, even though you're growing certain species, varieties for certain characteristics, each one is an individual. You get to recognize the individuality of each tree.

I have two mangoes and one is doing very well and the other is not. The other, when it gets new leaves, they just dwindle and fall. Whereas the strong one gets bigger and bigger. Grete Sultan says one has good genes and the other doesn't.—Andrew Timar et al. (1981).

[Has this new interest in growing changed your diet?]

We are also eating, the ones who have money and so forth, wrong food. The vegetables are not good for us through the agribusiness. The meat is not only not good as animal fat but the chickens have all been ruined with those hormones. So that the diseases we have, and the *amounts* of disease we have are astonishing. These are the problems that should be addressed rather than the protection of one country against another. We should approach *immediately,* as soon as possible, the question of air, the question of water, the question of food, the question of shelter, etc. All those things.

A quick change in food intake will affect the health of the whole society. Drastically. My arthritis, all the pain from my arthritis, disappeared in one week from changed diet. It stands to reason that if you keep putting things into you and it keeps going out that it's like flushing—a system that changes quickly. Same is true of the rivers, and the same is true of the air. If we change the way we treat it, it will change.

If you go now to Iceland you go into a land situation where the air is good, and the water is good. I mean really good. There's no industry. Englishmen going there for a vacation are frequently so astonished at the pleasures of having good air and good water that they don't go back; they stay there. I was amazed. You just can't believe what a pleasure it is to breathe good air and drink good water.

I now distill water with a machine, and then having taken everything out of it, I then put essence of seawater back into it—not to taste it, but in order to have proper minerals in the water.—Sean Bronzell & Ann Suchomski (1983).

The foods are all poisoned, systematically poisoned. It all accumulates. And now, I won't even buy vegetables in the regular stores. But whether I succeed in getting vegetables that are free of pollution, I doubt, because I think that pollution is global. I don't think there is any escape from it.—Monique Fong & Françoise Marie (1982).

How did you become interested in macrobiotics?

Some years ago I had a case of blood poisoning in my foot which ended with numbness in the toes of the left foot and then seemed to be going to the right foot. The doctors did what they called sophisticated tests, and there was no indication of what was wrong. The blood circulation seemed to be all right, everything was all right. Everything was *fine,* but my toes wouldn't move! That continued for several years, and also since 1960 I had had arthritis. It was in my wrist, and my fingers were enlarged. That lasted for all those years—over fifteen years. I was taking twelve aspirin a day, which was the only thing they advised me to do. I could see that things were getting worse, and I happened to be in Paris for a number of months and thought that acupuncture might help. A Chinese man came and he said, "Acupuncture will only help you palliatively." He said, "What you need is ◂§to have your blood tested and then to make§▸ a change of diet. Someone will have to do that for you." I asked him how much I owed him for this advice. He said, "I haven't done anything for you," and he wouldn't accept anything. He wouldn't give me any acupuncture either.

Well then, finally, not on that trip to Paris but during a later one, a little over two years ago, a book of mine was being published, and I had many interviews. It was very strenuous. One was for TV, and it was in a basement without any heat. That night I couldn't sleep because there was a pain behind my left eye—just unendurable. I knew that the ◂§orthodox§▸ doctors wouldn't help me, so I began complaining to my friends. ◂§I had been told by my astrologer, Julie Winter, that my health would be improved by a change of diet prescribed by an unorthodox doctor.❧ I complained to Yoko Ono and John Lennon, among others. They've followed the macrobiotic diet for eight years. Yoko said to me, "What you need to do is go to Shizuko Yamamoto, in New York, and she will change your diet." Well, immediately bells rang. I didn't hesitate; I went immediately. ☙Shizuko Yamamoto means, in Japanese, Tranquillity at the Base of the Mountain.❧

The first thing Shizuko said was extremely impressive to me, because I also had the good fortune in the late forties to attend the classes of Daisetz Suzuki in Zen Buddhism for two years, and that had a determining influence upon my music and my thinking. When she said, "Eat when you're hungry and drink when you're thirsty," it sounded exactly like Zen Buddhism. I was delighted. She went on to explain the importance of whole grains as the staple. I found it extremely convincing. At that time, however, I had been cooking following the books of Julia Childs—plenty of butter and cream and so forth. The idea of cooking without butter and cream was extremely difficult for me. I didn't know what to do. Finally, John Lennon, through one of his assistants, sent me a whole stack of macrobiotic cookbooks. Then I felt encouraged so I began to explore the whole thing and immediately saw that it would be a pleasant experience.

When did you meet Shizuko?

Just about two years ago. I began following the diet immediately. Since then I haven't taken any medication, and I have no pain anywhere. Within a week after the changed diet, the pain behind the left eye went away. My wrists are still not as flexible as they should be, but there's a great deal of improvement. Also I lost a good deal ☙thirty pounds❧ of excess weight.

Before I changed my diet I had always had problems with constipation, but now there's nothing like that. The other thing I find remarkable—you can see this so easily in relation to other people—is the way that your energy asserts itself the moment you wake up at the beginning of the day, and it remains constant. It doesn't go up and down, it stays level, and I can work much more extensively. I always had a great deal of energy, but now it is extraordinary.

I remember recently in California I was invited to make etchings, and at one point we were working until three o'clock in the morning. Every two hours or so, the other people I was working with would say, "Oh, let's stop and rest." Resting didn't seem necessary to me. I just continued working. They were not only resting but they were taking coffee too to keep themselves going, then they would get that much more exhausted afterward. They were constantly going up and down whereas I was not doing that.

Since this change I think I've been more active than I've been since 1952, over twenty-five years ago. I'll be sixty-seven this year. Let's see, I was around forty, and I was very, very active; my mind went in many directions. But three books are being published this year, five editions of etchings, and many, many new pieces of music. I think it is largely due to this change. At the same time, I'm much more equable in feeling; I'm less easily agitated.

Do you find that macrobiotics restricts you?

When people invite me to dinner, I say, "You know I follow this diet, and I prefer to bring my food with me." They either let me bring my food or they actually change their menu. I find it happening more and more that people are willing to change their food entirely.

This evening I'm going for dinner to the house of a friend who was actually opposed to the macrobiotic diet, and this evening she will cook a macrobiotic meal—and she'll enjoy it herself too!

I find it easy to eat macrobiotically when traveling. I take along a Panasonic rice steamer and an electric wok. They turn a motel room into a kitchen.—Maureen Furman (1979).

Would you like to share one of your favorite recipes with us?

I have one I like very much now; I call it Lentil Pâté. You slow-boil two cups of lentils in eight cups of water in a heavy, uncovered pot for fifteen minutes, after which you add a cup of bulghur—which you must stir frequently because it absorbs the liquid. Let that cook for fifteen minutes, then turn it off. You then sauté a large, chopped onion in sesame oil, and add it to the mixture with a teaspoon or so of salt. I have a pepper-grinder and I count to fifty while grinding it, then add two heaping tablespoons of Dijon mustard or that delicious mustard made of green peppercorns. You can eat this hot or cold, or you can spread it on bread—taking the place of butter.—Paul Hersh (1982).

I used to smoke at least three packs a day. Everything that happened was a signal to light a cigarette. Finally I divided myself into two people: one who knew he'd stopped, the other who didn't. Every time the one who didn't know picked up a cigarette to light it, the other one laughed until he put it down.

Do you always drink Guinness stout, or Irish whiskey?

Well, now I don't drink alcohol because of my macrobiotic diet. It's a funny thing. I don't have any desire for it either. But when I was drinking, it was a very fine single malt whiskey. Let's see, what do I like to drink now? I guess I like water. It quenches the thirst.

Do you ever go to the cinema?

No.—Stephen Montague (1982).

Do you read the papers?

No. I read them over people's shoulders, or across the aisles. I figure that if something is happening that I ought to know, someone'll tell me about it.—Paul Hersh (1982).

What do you do for leisure?

I don't have any leisure. It's not that I have my nose to the grindstone. I enjoy my work. Nothing entertains me more than to do it. That's why I do it. So I have no need for entertainment. And my work is not really fatiguing, so that I don't need to relax. Merce's work is physically tiring, so he likes to look at television. But I don't so much enjoy that. Or put me down in a situation where I have plenty of energy and I'm not permitted to do my work, then I'll look at television.—Stephen Montague (1982).

I come home after a tour with a lot of mail to pay attention to. I'm here now for two days before I go off on another tour. I'm perhaps going too much, but I'm committed to do it, and I think that that's the excuse that everyone gives, that through circumstances they're overcommitted, whereas they didn't think when they became committed, that they would be ☙in the end❧ overcommitted.

I take my work with me wherever I go, so that if I, for instance, have a doctor's appointment I take it with me and use the time in the doctor's office. I also work at home, of course, so I'm prepared to work at the drop of a hat. I learned to do that because of my long association with dancers, who in the course of rehearsals frequently leave gaps of time that can be filled up with one's own work. I've made that a habit through the years; otherwise, I wouldn't have gotten all the things done that I have done. Even people who are not very familiar with my work generally comment on the volume of it.—Tom Darter (1982).

So you don't have any real secrets about how you manage all this?

Well, you begin by watering the plants, and you end the day by playing chess. And I have to do my exercises. And I shop, generally, though I didn't do that today.

So by having a game of chess at the end of the day . . .

I'm making a balance with my use of chance operations. Because if I make a wrong move with my knight, I lose. Games are very serious success and failure situations, whereas the use of chance operations is very free of concern. It's like being enlightened.—Kathleen Burch et al. (1986).

My most recent interest is in stones.

Stones?

Yes, I collect them for my garden from all over the world. Some of them are quite big. I ride along the road and I stop and I look at stones. I have a very large stone waiting for me now in a van in North Carolina.

There are so many faces to this particular rock that it's like an exhibition of several works of art.—Lisa Low (1985).

What do you think about the fact that you're now an establishment figure?

I'm not sure that's the case, although it is partly the case. But it's very curious that the critics go on saying how bad my work is.—Geneviere Marcus (1970).

My name has become well known, but the experience of my music is as unknown, I would say, as ever. That's partly due to the fact that I've written a great deal of music and it's not all the same, and I'm always making new music, so no one knows what they're going to hear when they hear some of it. Through my being, you might say, notorious, certain things are expected by some people and certain things by other people. They get preconceptions about what the experience is going to be like, and very often they're disappointed. And if the program has an intermission, there's a decidedly smaller audience after the intermission than at the beginning of the concert. Sometimes there's such a large crowd waiting to hear it that the hall fills up again with new people when some of the first group walk out.—Tom Darter (1982).

Do you believe your self-creation came about as a result of your relation to your work? If so, how did you avoid the separation between life and work? Would you agree that the artist is a person who believes in work for the sake of work, in art for making the artist, to make life into works and works into life?

It reminds me of what Thoreau said, and I feel so too. "It's not important what form the sculptor gives the stone. It's important what sculpting does to the sculptor." I don't think being an artist is essential. People can be plumbers or street cleaners or be like artists if they do their work as their lives; what and how they do makes how they live, and gives them the love and pleasure of living. The situation of being constantly on the brink of change, exterior and interior, is what makes the question that has been asked difficult to answer. One never reaches a point of shapedness or finishedness. The situation is in constant unpredictable change. It makes me think again of Thoreau and *Walden* because *Walden* sets out from the question: Is life worth living? The whole book is a detailed and affirmative reply. He found that out by simply keeping his ears and eyes open and in his daily work being present at each moment.

In the last two years I've been doing a great deal of work reading and writing out of James Joyce. Then I thought to simplify my life by leaving the Merce Cunningham Dance Company for one year. I had to do it for one year because of the symphony commitments during the bicentennial.

During my leave, I felt such a gap, such a loss of something that was a large part of my life. So I'm back with it and I find I can write more music as I tour around the country with the dance company than I can staying home, simply because people don't know where I am. I'm like that Chinese animal who climbs into the tree during a snowstorm and no one can see where it is because the snow has covered its tracks.—Rose Slivka (1978).

My attitude toward old age is one of gratitude for each day. Poor Henry David Thoreau died at age forty-four. You know he had the habit of walking through the streets of Concord in the dead of winter without any clothes on, which must have certainly disturbed the local citizens no end. Later there was a lady who each year would put flowers on Emerson's grave and mutter as she would pass Thoreau's: "And none for you, you dirty little atheist!" Anyway, as I get older and begin to be almost twice as old as Thoreau, I am naturally grateful for all this time. It strikes me that since there's obviously a shorter length of time left than I've already had, I'd better hurry up and be interested in whatever I can. There's no fooling around possible. No silliness. So where I used to spend so much of my time hunting mushrooms, I've recently become interested in indoor gardening. I now tend to spread myself thinner and thinner. I'm always looking for new ways of using my energy but meanwhile continuing other activities.—Stephen Montague (1982).

I was interviewed recently and asked how it felt to be so old, to have grown so old, and one of the things I found myself talking about is the constant opening up or opening out to other possibilities. I remember that it seemed to be essential when I was in my twenties to focus my attention on one thing and I made a choice between music and painting. I chose music, but now it seems perfectly natural to open out to every single thing I possibly can do because I'm not going to be here much longer. The best thing is to enjoy to do as much as possible while I am here.—Rose Slivka (1978).

About five or six years ago, I was invited to make etchings at the Crown Point Press in California. I accepted immediately, even though I didn't know how to make them, because about twenty years before, I was invited to trek in the Himalayas, and didn't. I later discovered that the walk was going to be on elephants with servants, and I've always regretted that missed opportunity. I thought I was too busy. I am now multiplying my interests because it is my last chance. I don't know what will turn up next. The doctor told me at my age anything can happen. He was right. I got rid of arthritis by following a macrobiotic diet; work is now taking on the aspect of play; and the older I get the more things I find myself interested in doing. If you don't have enough time to accomplish something, consider the work finished once it's begun. It then resembles the Venus de Milo, which manages quite well without her arms.—Stephen Montague (1982).

Are you concerned that the things you've done will exist after you don't exist anymore?

I'm afraid they will. I've now done so much work in so many different directions that it would be very hard to . . . I mean writings, graphic work, and the music. All of that would be hard to get rid of now. Even for me, say I decided I wanted to get rid of it, that would be impossible—there's too much, and now too many copies of it. I'm afraid it's here for a long time. It could go into a decline as a person does who gets ill, but then it might recover.

The I Ching *was in decline for several hundred years and it came back.*

Generally, if something does go into a decline a kind of sympathetic action takes place in some part of the population, and they take care of it and bring it back.

Does that please you?

I don't think it is a concern that I have. My own concern now is to live as long as I can, to do as much more work as I can, and to let my work that is already finished live, so to speak, its own life.—Robin White (1978).

I don't think of success any more than I think of good or bad. I do think sometimes my work is superficial, but then when I notice that it's superficial I try to make it more radical. That's what happened in the *Apartment House.* My first attempts to change harmony were superficial. But my later attempts, I think, were quite radical.—Art Lange (1977).

Well, one of the things I'm thinking of getting now is a word processor. That will help me with my writing and that will also be a computer so that it can help me with some of my *I Ching* calculations. It's conceivable that if I could get into that computer all the necessary information about multiphonics so that I wouldn't have to think about it, that I might be able to deal with it.—Morton Feldman (1983).

With the breakthroughs in computer technology we can program, or "superimpose," the collected works of any composer. Would you enjoy hearing your music organized this way?

Yes.

Who else's?

Anyone, or any number of them together. I really would. I've learned to amuse myself when signing things for people by asking them if they want a "single" or a "double," and a double is the signature over a signature, which turns it into a drawing.—Paul Hersh (1982).

Have you ever thought that you were going crazy?

The feeling is not familiar to me. I used to have a feeling, which was that I had, so to speak, a guardian angel. I have the feeling now that I might die in an accident or something, whereas formerly I thought that I wouldn't, because I had work that needed to be done. Now I have the feeling which may be presumptuous—I hope it is—that I've done more or less what I was obliged to do. Therefore I could just as well die. Nothing much would be lost if I did.—Jeff Goldberg (1976).

Have you ever had any big disappointment? What has been your biggest disappointment?

I don't think it's an interesting question, forgive me.

I've learned so much in the book *Conversations with Marcel Duchamp,* and on the very first page he is asked that question; and he says I have nothing to complain about. I've enjoyed it all, the whole thing. And the same remark comes from Thoreau, when on his deathbed a relative asks him if he'd made his peace with God and he said I wasn't aware that we'd ever quarreled.—Rose Slivka (1978).

As I get older, every birthday that ends in a 5 or a 0 is cause for a celebration of some sort. And when you have celebration going on all over the world, it usually takes a year before and a year after those birthdays to get them all in. That leaves me with a year or two every five years to do my work.—Harry Sumrall (1986).

This is your seventieth year—the beginning of a new decade for you. Your life-style and the macrobiotic diet seem to agree with you. You're in good health and seem very fit.

I'm gradually learning how to take care of myself. It has taken a long time. It seems to me that when I die, I'll be in perfect condition.—Stephen Montague (1982).

PRECURSORS

If you could speak to anyone of the past, whom would you like to talk with? Thoreau would, of course, be one . . .

James Joyce, Gertrude Stein, Erik Satie. If we went back further, I wouldn't mind meeting Mozart.

Why Mozart?

I think he was a great musician. It's his tendency toward complexity and away from unity. Now I would let Bach stay on his side of the street. And I also wouldn't bother with Beethoven or Haydn.

Why not Haydn?

The cadences are impossible ☙if you have, as I do, less and less interest in punctuation❧.

How about some composers you'd like to meet in the nineteenth century? Wagner for example.

I would have enjoyed meeting Grieg. He had an independent mind. He was able to write all those fifths when they were forbidden in what was considered good writing.—Stephen Montague (1982).

I remember loving Bach. At the time that I did I knew a very great musician, Richard Buhlig, who made an arrangement of *The Art of the Fugue* of Bach for two pianos. And I had the very great pleasure of hearing many performances of that *Art of the Fugue* in Southern California when Buhlig was alive. I had the feeling that I needed no other music really than that to hear. I was so deeply involved in it. And I remember being surprised one day when Buhlig said that he hoped he lived long enough to play Mozart. And I said what do you mean? . . . He went on to say that Bach was all good and well, but the great musician was Mozart. And that he wanted to end his days playing Mozart, but that he thought it would be too difficult.

And later, fortunately, I had two experiences: one of listening to Mozart and another time a kind of study of Mozart that led me to a view of music that was different than the view that the music of Bach gave. The difference is the difference between everything fitting together, as it does in Bach, and coming out to reassure us about the existence of order. Mozart does another thing. He provides us with a music which is characterized by multiplicity. And you have the feeling that if there were something, if he had been able to give us some other thing than he did in *Don Giovanni*, that he would have willingly given it. That he left the doors open to the unknown and the excitement and the affirmation of life, rather than the affirmation of order, is what I love in Mozart.—Anne Gibson (1984).

If you examine any page of Mozart, you're apt to discover not one idea but many. I think in the case of Mozart there is an implicit tendency toward multiplicity. That tendency interests me more than the tendency toward unity. It seems to me to be more characteristic of nature. If I look at a tree, a single tree, and start looking at the leaves, all, admittedly, have the same general structure. If I look at it carefully, I notice that no two leaves are identical. Then I begin with that attention to differences to enjoy every glance at the tree, because everything I see is something I haven't memorized.—Bill Shoemaker (1984).

What do you feel is the importance of the music of the past?

What do you mean?

I mean the works of Beethoven, Haydn, and others.

The past is not a fact. The past is simply a big field that had a great deal of activity in it. I asked a historian once, "How do you write history?" and he said, "Oh, you have to invent it." Well, the way we invent history is by doing what we do; and the more we do, the more we look into the past to see if there is anything that is like what we are doing. If there is, we get interested; and if there isn't, we don't. Almost all of us now don't repeat themes the ways those people you just mentioned did. I must say that I find it very annoying that they do that. It seems to me that if we hear a melody once, that's enough. The other thing that bothers me, besides the melody and the regular rhythm, is the harmony.

Then you tend to subscribe to the Oriental notion of continual variation.

That's also implied in Schoenberg. The whole notion of twelve-tone music is that of continual variation. That marvelous notion of Schoenberg's that as the development continues, the variations can become more far reaching. That's a good idea; it is analogous to that desire on the part of Ives, to have a music that makes us stretch our ears.—Anthony Brown (1975).

What was so thrilling about the notion of twelve-tone music was that those twelve tones were all equally important, that one of them was not more important than another. It gave a principle that one could relate over into one's life and accept, whereas the notion of neoclassicism one could not accept and put over into one's life.—Alan Gillmor (1973).

How about people in other fields like literature, painting, poetry?

Well, I think anybody in his right mind would have enjoyed meeting Leonardo. Joyce loved the work of Ibsen, did you know that? Dostoevski, but then I would have had to learn Russian. I'm very glad to be alive in the twentieth century with respect to painting. I don't find previous periods of painting as interesting as it is now, but Giotto might have been interesting. I would like to have known Meister Eckhart, a contemporary of Dante. And I would have dearly loved to have seen Milarepa floating in the form of a thistle over the landscape of Tibet. Milarepa was the great Tibetan saint, if saint is the right word, or yogi, whatever.—Stephen Montague (1982).

I'd like to ask you when you first discovered the music of Ives?

Not until much later and not through my own curiosity but through that of Lou Harrison. Two of the inspiring books—inspiring because they gave me the permission to enter the field of music—were *New Musical Resources* by Henry Cowell and *Toward a New Music* by Carlos Chavez, the Mexican composer.

And in this respect Henry Cowell was a rather important influence.

That was very important to me, to hear through him music from all the various cultures; and they sounded different. Sound became important to me—and noise is so rich in terms of sound. Surprisingly, you can even read statements in the early fifties from young composers in Europe, who are otherwise revolutionary and adventurous, to the effect that sound has no importance in music. Do you realize that? They tended to think that the thoughts, the constructions, the ideas that form the relationships of sounds were important, but that the sounds themselves were of no importance.—Alan Gillmor (1976).

What sort of man was Charles Ives?

Well, I never actually went to see him because it was known, since 1920, that he was suffering from a nervous disease. Any loud sound like the ringing of a doorbell or a telephone disturbed him greatly. He was also very shaky, not only in his hand but in his ear as well. His sensation of tone would wobble.

He was an important insurance man. He could have been many times a millionaire but he was very moral. So he never took more from his company than he needed to live in a simple way.—Jeff Goldberg (1976).

I appealed to him for money once on behalf of another composer who needed help and he gave it promptly. I didn't appeal to him over the telephone or by going to the door. I simply then tossed a note through the mail.—Joel Eric Suben (1984).

Ives was similar to Mao Tse-tung. He wanted to make an amendment to the Constitution so that rather than voting for people we would vote for things which should be done. Mao says, "We must firmly believe that the great masses of humanity are good," and Ives said, "We must believe that the majority is right."—Jeff Goldberg (1976).

What relation do [Charles] Ives's ideas and experiments have to some of your own works?

Well, now of course I find Ives quite relevant. But I didn't come across Ives's work until the late 1940s, and as I said, through Lou Harrison. He had an enthusiasm for Ives. What had put me off Ives was all the Americana business. I didn't like that. You see, in modern painting I was devoted to Mondrian; just as I had chosen Schoenberg in music, so I chose Mondrian in painting. And it was not through my own inclinations but through the excitement and work of Robert Rauschenberg that I came to be involved in representational work. If, then, I could accept representation in painting I could, of course, accept the Americana aspect of Ives. But even still, deep down, when I listen to a piece of Ives, what I like about it is not the quotation of hymns and popular tunes—nor do I particularly like that in Satie, by the way. What I like is the rest of it, the way it works, the process of it, the freedom of it, and "do this or do that, do whatever you choose"—that I love.—Alan Gillmor (1976).

What distinguishes Ives's music for me is that it has both inherent in it this social aspect of music, through the reference to, the nature of, familiar tunes, and then it has something mysterious in it that we don't know and come to only through the experience of Ives, and that is what, in a text in one of my books, I call mud, musical mud, so that out of this fertile mud for me is this other thing which is suggestive of the presence of people, not just one person, but society; and we're allowed in his work, because of the mud, I think, which makes it mysterious at the same time it makes something you can clearly experience, though what you experience you're not sure of; but in order to come out of the listening experience with any shape of your own, you have to finish the experience in your own way.

Marcel Duchamp said it was the function of the observer, or the listener, to complete the work of art; so that he brought this social aspect of music over into the art of painting. Painting in and of itself and before him, was not so social; but that was one of the things he did in changing twentieth-century art—to give it the character of music.—Joel Eric Suben (1984).

Schoenberg convinced me that music required structure to differentiate parts of a whole. At first, when I worked with [the abstract filmmaker Oscar] Fischinger, I used the serial technique in connection with musical cells which I did not vary at all. Then I began to work with rhythm. Each piece was based on a number of measures having a square root so that the large lengths have the same relation within the whole that the small lengths have within a unit of it. One could then emphasize the structure at the beginning and move into far-reaching variations.

Fischinger told me that everything in the world has a spirit that can be released through its sound. I was not inclined towards spiritualism, but I began to tap everything I saw. I explored everything through its sound. This led to my first percussion orchestra.—Joan Peyser (1976).

When, in the middle forties, I was searching to find out why one would make a work of art in this society, I was thinking not in terms of theater, but specifically in terms of music. My search for a reason for making art came about because of this.

I had been taught in the schools that art was a question of communication. I observed that all of the composers were writing differently. If art was communication, we were using different languages. We were, therefore, in a Tower of Babel situation where no one understood anyone else. So I determined either to find another reason or give up the whole business.

Lou Harrison and other composers joined with me in this quest. At the same moment, a musician [Gita Sarabhai] came from India alarmed over the influence that Western music was having on Indian traditions. She studied in a concentrated fashion with a number of teachers of Western music over a nine-month period. I was with her nearly every day.

Before she returned to India, I learned from her the traditional reason for making a piece of music in India: "to quiet the mind thus making it susceptible to divine influences."

Lou Harrison, meanwhile, was reading in an old English text, I think as old as the sixteenth century, and he found this reason given for writing a piece of music: "to quiet the mind thus making it susceptible to divine influences."

Now the question arises: What is a quiet mind? Then the second question arises: What are divine influences? One of the things that is happening to society now is that the East and the West no longer are separated. We are, as Fuller and McLuhan point out continually, living in a global village.

Formerly, we thought that the Orient had nothing to do with us; that we had no access to it. We know better now. We learned from Oriental thought that those divine influences are, in fact, the environment in which we are. A sober and quiet mind is one in which the ego does not obstruct the fluency of the things that come into our senses and up through our dreams. Our business in living is to become fluent with the life we are living, and art can help this.—Stanley Kauffmann (1966).

The function of art traditionally (according to Ananda K. Coomaraswamy) was to imitate nature in her manner of operation, and I think the function of enlightenment, the goal of Buddhist action, is to come to terms with the mind in relation to all of its aspects, which include nature; so that the person flows with his experience, whether it comes to him from without or from within, rather than going against it.

Art can be practiced in one way or another, so that it reinforces the ego in its likes and dislikes, or so that it opens that mind to the world outside, and outside inside.

In the Lankavatara Sutra to the question "Does enlightenment come gradually or suddenly?" the Buddha said it comes gradually and then he gave examples from nature like the germination of a seed. And then without any transition or explanation he said it comes suddenly and he gave the example of the flash of lightning.

Is one of your intentions with your music to change the way people think about music?

Since the forties and through study with D. T. Suzuki of the philosophy of Zen Buddhism, I've thought of music as a means of changing the mind. Of course, my proper concern first of all has been with changing my own mind. I wanted to change it because I was, in the forties, in certain ways very confused both in my personal life and in my understanding of what the function of art in the society should be. It was through the study of Buddhism that I became, it seems to me, less confused. I saw art not as something that consisted of a communication from the artist to an audience but rather as an activity of sounds in which the artist found a way to let the sounds be themselves. And in their being themselves to open the minds of the people who made them or listened to them to other possibilities than they had previously considered. To widen their experience, particularly to undermine the making of value judgments.

Given that definition, does this demystify the whole concept of musician? Doesn't this make everyone a musician?

It doesn't make the virtuoso not a musician. He remains a musician as he has been, but the other untrained people can become musicians also. I think it comes about through placing the center everywhere, in all the people whether they're composing or listening, and furthermore placing the center too in the sounds themselves. So there is then an interpenetration of unlimited centers. This is a fundamental of Buddhism.

The value judgment when it is made doesn't exist outside the mind but exists within the mind that makes it. When it says this is good and that is not good, it's a decision to eliminate from experience certain things. Suzuki said Zen wants us to diminish that kind of activity of the ego and to increase the activity that accepts the rest of creation. And rather than taking the path that is prescribed in the formal practice of Zen Buddhism itself, namely, sitting cross-legged and breathing and such things, I decided that my proper discipline was the one to which I was already committed, namely, the making of music. And that I would do it with a means that was as strict as sitting cross-legged, namely, the use of chance operations, and the shifting of my responsibility from the making of choices to that of asking questions.—Bill Womack (1979).

John, the late 1940s was a period of fresh discovery for you. I'm thinking of your study of Eastern philosophies, in particular Zen, and your contact with Gita Sarabhai, who revealed to you that the reason for making a piece of music in India was "to sober and quiet the mind, thus rendering it susceptible to divine influences." Is that a view you still hold?

Certainly. I might alter it slightly now and not state it so "churchily." I would say that the function of music is to change the mind so that it does become open to experience, which inevitably is interesting.

Is it not possible that a movement, a slow movement, say, or a Mozart symphony or string quartet could serve the purpose of sobering and quieting the mind?

On occasion Mozart can do that. On other occasions he's quite incapable of it, and it's due to the performances. I had the occasion to hear a performance of *Don Giovanni* in New York in the 40s that was magnificent. I later heard the same piece in southern France at Aix-en-Provence and it was a farce. And I heard so much Mozart in two weeks—they had a Mozart festival in Aix-en-Provence—that I wished at the end of those two weeks never to hear another note of Mozart in my whole life. It seemed all frivolous, all decorated, all ornate. Impossible! Of course I love Mozart; but there are ways to hate Mozart.

Well, I was going to say that you do have some special affection for Mozart's music. In fact, it plays a rather significant role in your 1969 work HPSCHD, *for example. How do you explain your particular preference for this classical composer when you have rejected so many others, in fact, almost all of the others?*

I like Mozart because he moves toward multiplicity, whereas in contrast Bach moves toward unity. When you have six or seven voices or four voices or whatever you have in a Bach composition, they all add up rhythmically to a motor rhythm, which goes ta-ta-ta-ta-ta-ta-ta consistently, and there aren't any pauses of any kind. Also pitch-wise the Bach business is all organized so that nothing is extraordinary, everything moves in the same way, whereas in a Mozart work everything works in a different way and in two or three measures of Mozart you can have many ways rather than one way of doing things.

What about the question of form? This seems to me a significant fact. . . .

. . . form is a very different word. . . .

Mozart is a closed form and Bach is an open form.

I find it just the reverse.

How do you explain then the regularity?

. . . Don Giovanni bursts into flames; how could it be more open than it is?

I'm thinking, of course, more of symphonic music, the sonata-allegro principle as opposed to the open-endedness of fugal procedures.

When I think of Mozart I really think of *Don Giovanni.*—Alan Gillmor (1976).

Why is Henry David Thoreau important today?

Because we are finally paying attention to him.

Why is this nineteenth-century anarchist relevant now?

Because the fact of separate governments endangers continued life on this planet. Our proper concerns are not political but global.—Jay Murphy (1985).

I'm amazed that in reading Thoreau I discover just about every idea I've ever had worth its salt. I find Thoreau very lively, and continually invigorating. Take, for instance, something that I came across this last year: "If, when I am in the woods, the woods are not in me, what right have I to be in the woods?" It's what I have been saying in my books all along. More recently, I am enlivened by Thoreau's drawings; I think I may be the first person to declare them beautiful. Thoreau said that no page in his journal is as suggestive as one that includes a rough sketch. I think they become more suggestive the more they are removed from any possible interpretation.—Anthony Brown (1975).

Thoreau and the Indians and I have said all along that the sounds all around us are equivalent to music. In India they say that music is continuous; it only stops when we turn away and stop paying attention. Thoreau said that silence is like a sphere. Each sound is a bubble on its surface. I want to keep from interrupting the silence that's already here.—Michael Zwerin (1982).

What brought you to Thoreau?

It was a circumstance when I was at the University of Cincinnati, and the Cunningham Dance Company that I've worked with so long was performing just south of Cincinnati in Kentucky; and there was a meeting of students with questions and answers as there often is when we tour. A very tall man stood up and asked such interesting questions and made such interesting remarks that I made a point of meeting him later, and he was the poet Wendell Berry. He taught at the University [of Kentucky] and he lived in a valley nearby where his father and his grandfather and his great-grandfather had lived, and there was a sense of his connection with the land that is so rare with people. So I later went to visit him when I was making a trip in the direction beyond that valley, and we went mushroom-hunting together with his wife and children. In the evening he brought out the journal of Thoreau and just opened it at random; and the moment I heard him reading it, I knew that that was a book I needed to become familiar with. And I've worked with it all the time since then. That was 1967.—Gwen Deely (1976).

Once someone asked you a very dull question, trying to show that you had been inconsistent in a line of reasoning, and I remember that with that marvelous laugh of yours you said, "Well, you won't find me consistent."

Emerson felt this way about consistency, you know; but our education leads us to think that it's wrong to be inconsistent. All consistency is, really, is getting one idea and not deviating from it, even if the circumstances change so radically that one ought to deviate.

So that gives us flexibility as human beings.

I think there is a grand difference between German philosophy, which has tended to insist upon consistency and unity and such things, and the philosophies of India, which have separate goals.—Ellsworth Snyder (1975).

Are you familiar with Keats's line, "The poetry of earth is ceasing never"?

No, but that's lovely.

Do you know that your ideas about chance operations have been compared with Keats's idea of negative capability?

I don't know that term.

"Negative capability" is Keats's idea that the artistic personality dissolves and becomes a part of whatever is around him. A stone, a sparrow. And he opposes that to what he calls the "egotistical sublime," the artistic personality that overwhelms what it sees, making whatever it is become him.

I don't like that idea. I like the first idea. What did you call it?

Negative capability.

Yes, I like that very much. Thoreau got up each morning and walked to the woods as though he had never been where he was going to, so that whatever was there came to him like liquid into an empty glass. Many people taking such a walk would have their heads so full of other ideas that it would be a long time before they were capable of hearing or seeing. Most people are blinded by themselves.—Lisa Low (1985).

When I was young, the poets who were of interest, particularly, were Cummings, Pound, Eliot, Joyce, and Stein. That was our world. And Cummings was fascinating because of the typography, and the many kinds of experimentation. Nowadays I think we might link him with Apollinaire. But I loved *The Enormous Room* and *Eimi* and other things, and I collected his books. Of those five, the first to drop from my interest was T. S. Eliot.

And the second was Cummings. And Stein, I think, goes next. The two who remain absolutely fascinating and as lively now as they were then are Pound and Joyce.—Art Lange (1977).

I used to go [to an Anton Webern concert, in the late forties] with my hair on end and sit on the edge of my seat. It was so completely different from anything I'd ever heard. Of course he cannot compare to Schoenberg. Schoenberg is so clearly magnificent. Boulez is responsible for the shift to Webern, and I think I understand why. Schoenberg's music is traditional. It continues the past magnificently. Whereas Webern *seems* to break with the past. He gives one the feeling he *could* break with the past. For he shook the foundation of sound as discourse in favor of sound as sound itself. But in Schoenberg the supremacy of pitch relations remains. And so he was really tied to an earlier time. In Satie [by contrast], the structures have to do with time, not pitch. Virgil Thomson introduced me to Satie just at the time I first heard Webern. I connected the two composers in my mind.—Joan Peyser (1976).

In the late forties and the early fifties, you were an outspoken admirer of Webern's music, but by the late sixties you remarked in an interview that you'd rather walk out of the concert hall than listen to it. The question is really in two parts: (1) Could you explain this loss of interest, and (2) have you had a similar reaction over the years to Erik Satie's music?

No, I was always devoted to Erik Satie's music, and I still am. You don't really have to be interested in it in order to enjoy it. Whereas in the case of Webern, I think you're obliged to be somewhat interested.

You mean interested in the construction of it?

And all of the ideas and everything. Otherwise, I don't think it's that seductive. Certainly some pieces are not at all. Whereas Satie is. The fact that he's interesting even though he is charming makes him for me still very lively. I think he's one of the liveliest musical figures, certainly of this century.

Long ago I wrote that text comparing him with Webern. Maybe if I paid more attention to Webern now I would like him again, but I don't feel any need for it. But the remark against him is simply against any use of music that you already know, and an insistence on the music that you haven't yet heard—or the music you haven't yet written. Many people collect music that they like and surround themselves with it. I do the reverse: I don't keep music around me; I keep noise.—Cole Gagne & Tracy Caras (1980).

Satie certainly is a composer who has not been given his due; and even when he is performed, oftentimes the performances seem not satisfactory; and that may be partially because of the way we now think about performing music.

I think people try to make it something rather than letting it happen. Don't you think that's true also of Ives?

I do.

Ives seems to me to be best played, and Satie too, by people who don't play very well, who aren't, as Satie would say, paralyzed. I mean to say, they know so much, how to behave, that they can't behave in any other way that the way in which they are paralyzed to play.—Ellsworth Snyder (1985).

If we talk about the principle of simplicity or rhythm and of repetitiveness of rhythm in Satie's writing, I think that the extreme of it might be the *Vexations,* in which you have a thirteen-measure cantus firmus, followed by its repetition with two voices above it; then the cantus firmus is repeated and then the two voices are heard with the top one now in the middle rather than the other way. This goes on for eighteen hours and forty minutes. Now what happens when something so simple is repeated for such a long time? What actually happens is the subtle falling away from the norm, a constant flux with regard to such things as speed and accent, all the things in fact which we could connect with rhythm. The most subtle things become evident that would not be evident in a more complex rhythmic situation. We have, I believe, many examples in contemporary visual art of things brought to an extraordinary simplicity. I recall, for instance, the white paintings of Robert Rauschenberg, which don't have any images. It's in that highly simplified situation that we are able to see such things as dust or shadows carefully painted, as in Rembrandt, any other shadow entering the situation would be a disturbance and would not be noticeable, or if noticeable, a disturbance.

I think that a proper performance of Satie's music will bring about subtle oscillations simply because it would be intolerable to have that music, with its more or less regular beats, kept extremely regular. In other words, the very fact of their simplicity and regularity calls for the kinds of subtle differences that go with, say, breathing. And I think, finally, the rhythm of Satie becomes not interesting at the point of the beat, but it becomes definitely interesting at the point of the phrase. And there you will find that the phrases are not repeated, but are in fact varied in the most interesting way. I would say that they're far more interesting, say, than Beethoven, from a rhythmic point of view.

And than Stravinsky? That's so totally different that I think the question is unfair.

The trouble is I haven't studied Stravinsky very much. You see, I'm partisan, and I was devoted to the music of Schoenberg. But I would say offhand, with some assurance, that the rhythm of Satie is more interesting than the rhythm of Schoenberg.

You made avant-garde history by presenting, with a team of ten pianists working in shifts, the world premiere of Satie's Vexations, *which, as you're suggesting already, is a rather innocuous series of thirty-six diminished and augmented chords which the composer directs to be repeated 840 times. The performance lasted eighteen hours and forty minutes and was covered, I believe, by a team of eight critics from the* New York Times.

Now Darius Milhaud, who was, as you know, intimately acquainted with Satie in the 1920s, has taken exception to this performance. He suggested that Satie would not have approved of such a caper, that his essential pudeur, *or modesty, would not have allowed it. How would you react to Milhaud's criticism?*

I think that the piece was a perfectly serious piece which the French, including Milhaud, had not taken seriously. I first found it in a drawer at Henri Sauguet's; he brought it out as a joke on Satie's part which he claimed that Satie himself had not taken seriously. But if you just look at the manuscript of *Vexations* you see how beautifully it was written. It was written no less beautifully than anything else he wrote. Curiously enough, the textual remarks in connection with the *Vexations* are not humorous; they are in the spirit of Zen Buddhism. It says at the beginning of the piece not to play it until you have put yourself in a state of interior immobility, and it very clearly says that it is to be done 840 times. Satie had a concern for inactivity and for repetition far beyond, say, even Andy Warhol, not only in terms of time but in terms of the extent of activity. There was not the true connection between Milhaud (and Les Six) and Satie that we have automatically taken for granted.

I think they were all quite different from Satie, and I don't think they really understood much Satie. I have another example of how they didn't understand Satie, and this is from Milhaud himself. In 1949, I think it was, I was in Paris for an extended period of time, and I went to those collections at the Conservatoire. I did everything I could to find pieces of Satie that I was unfamiliar with, and I came across at the Conservatoire notebooks in which there were just numbers written by Satie; and I myself write such lists of numbers—or did at the time—in relation to my own musical compositions. So I immediately saw these as rhythmic structures for pieces that he had either written or was about to write. I was very excited about them because they gave me confirmation to a rhythmic analysis of Satie's works that I had been making which I've written about in *Silence*—you may have seen that article—and they have to do with symmetry, either, as I expressed it, horizontally conceived or vertically conceived. When I saw Milhaud the next time, after having all this experience, I told him what I thought I had discovered, and he pooh-poohed my ideas. He said: "Oh, those were shopping lists." He denied the fact that Satie was interested in rhythmic structures—Alan Gillmor & Roger Shattuck (1973).

If I said, well, here's one thing that I think is very important, very few other people may think it important. Discover for sure how many pieces of Furniture Music Satie wrote. I mean: end the matter. Just find out. Now that may not be important to anyone. •§Furniture Music was Satie's most far-reaching discovery, the concept of a music to which one did not have to listen.§• I came here [to the University of Illinois] bearing gifts to this university. I brought three pieces of Satie's Furniture Music that I had with difficulty found. And I went straight to John Garvey who has in general been interested in music. Chapters are written in any book on Satie about his Furniture Music. None of it is published and I had it right there. I gave it to him. It was of no interest to him. He returned it to me. There was no interest here. It simply hasn't been performed here. So seeing that, I performed it at Mills in California when the occasion arose, and I'll do it at Davis again, but I would like to know if Satie wrote any more. Then, of course, I want to find out how he wrote those beautiful pieces. And could that give people ideas about what to do next and so on? And this is how many projects will be that anyone will have. My project here sounds rather esoteric. If you went through the town here, where there are a hundred thousand people, you might find four people who thought it was a good thing to do. [Darius] Milhaud doesn't know how many pieces of Furniture Music Satie wrote.

I asked him, and I asked Henri Sauguet, and I asked all the people who'd written books on Satie. It is a very difficult problem to solve. Not one of those people devoted to Satie took the matter seriously.—Don Finegan et al. (1969).

They liked us [at Black Mountain College], our being there, and invited us back then for the summer, and asked me to arrange a series of concerts. And I chose the music of Satie, because there were few musicians in the Black Mountain community. Most of them were painters. And I knew that I could play much of the music of Satie and that I could probably find in the community others so that we could be able to go through the whole body of his work. Whereas, if I'd chosen just modern music in general, we would just get a smattering of this, that, and the other. And many things that would be important, such as the work of Schoenberg, wouldn't be able to be well represented, because there weren't proper musicians there, nor could I play it. So the the first thing that developed was that since the community was largely German, if not really German . . .

The music community definitely was.

Well, also the art community was from the Bauhaus, for instance. The whole feeling was German, and many of the people were German. So that Albers' first question to me was, "Won't you also give a series of lectures, because we see no reason for listening to French music. And you will have to explain to us why we should listen to something so trivial," and so un-Germanic, you see, as the music of Satie.—Mary Emma Harris (1974).

So I gave twenty-four short lectures, and I gave one long lecture, in which I denounced Beethoven, the peak of German music. And that was necessary to do, from Satie's point of view, because Satie himself spoke against Beethoven. So I pointed out to the Germans that Beethoven's music was a mistake fundamentally, and that Satie's music was correct. The reason is that Beethoven's music is based on a marriage of form and content, involving beginnings, ends and middles, and all kinds of ideas and expressions of individual feeling that have nothing whatsoever to do with sounds, whereas Satie's music is essentially based upon an empty space of time, in which one thing or another could happen. There is no other way to explain some of the pieces he wrote around 1912, which simply don't do any of the things that German music told everyone that music should do. From Satie's point of view, all that he was doing was getting rid of sauerkraut.—Robert Cordier (1973).

No Germans take French music seriously. When Debussy went to visit Brahms in Vienna, the servant answered the door, and Debussy had not warned Brahms that he was visiting. But he happened to be in Vienna, and went to his house, knocked at the door, and the servant came to the door and said, "Who are you?" And he said, "I'm Claude Debussy." And Brahms sent back word, "Who is that?" And Debussy sent back word, "French musician." And Brahms said, "There is no such thing." He refused to see him. It has been that strong, that feeling. And even with Schoenberg. He said in one of his letters that his discovery of a way of composing music by means of the twelve tones ensured the supremacy of German music for the next hundred years. And that attitude was not separated from Black Mountain thinking; it was essentially through Albers a Germanic situation.—Mary Emma Harris (1974).

[Do you think of your music as counterculture?]

I think the idea of a counterculture, and also naturally of an avant-garde, was an idea formerly more useful than now. It suggests that there is a principal culture, or as people used to say, a mainstream. I don't think that that mainstream any longer exists, or rather that anything that was a counterculture is now as well established, as alive and as flowering, so to speak, as the mainstream. I met in Paris a very interesting musicologist. He gives this image, which I think very useful, of a river in delta. The river has divided, and we don't any longer know which stream is the principal stream. We are in fact living in a society in which a multiplicity of directions are being taken, and no one who is in one of them would say that the others are more interesting than the one he is in. In other words, if a person is alive to what he's doing, it can be quite different from what someone else is doing, and be equally a part of what's going on. I don't see it as worthwhile to say that one is more important than the others.

I remember being offended by an evening arranged with Louise Varèse by Pierre Boulez at the New York Philharmonic. It was a program of music by [her late husband] Edgard Varèse, and Boulez explained that, in his opinion, Varèse was an eccentric, which was to say someone not in the mainstream. But from the point of view of some of these streams in the delta, Varèse is absolutely essential. It was he who fathered forth noise into the twentieth century. But there are many others going on now, so you wouldn't know which to call the avant-garde now, because all these many directions are taking place, and each one is equally interesting.

Why do you place Varèse in the mainstream?

For someone interested in noise, like myself, if you start from the beginning of my work, after I studied with Schoenberg, I began by hitting things in the environment. I wanted to find a way of making music that was free of the theory of harmony, of tonality; and so I had to find a way of composing with noise. And I came to the conclusion that the important aspect, or as we would say in the twelve-tone language, the important parameter of sound, is not frequency but rather duration, because duration is open to noise, as well as to what has been called musical. When you take such a pont of view, you can shift your allegiance, as it were, to Varèse; or you could move it over, as many did, from Schoenberg to Webern, who seemed to have an awareness of the importance of duration, which Schoenberg didn't seem to have as much.

Since I studied with Schoenberg, I was aware of the importance that he gave to the notion of structure, of that division of the whole into parts. Since I had no feeling for harmony or tonality, I was in no position to define those parts by means of cadences. So, these empty spaces of time would be as hospitable to noise as musical sound, and they could be clarified by a variety of means, including silence. If, for instance, you want to separate one section of a composition from another, you can have sound through one of them and then begin the next one with silence, or make it entirely silent.

Silence is just the negative part of music.

No, it is the aspect of sound that can be either expressed by sound or by its absence, either positively or negatively, whereas pitch can be expressed only by sound. It can't be expressed by the absence of sound. Nor can the parameters. So I deduced that the parameter of duration was, shall we say, more hospitable, a more reasonable structural means for music, than pitch had been.—Frans Boenders (1980).

[What do you think of "Time and Space Concepts in Music and Visual Art"?]

The subject gave me the idea of reexamining the ideas that I continue to hold and that I have held in the past. I tend to have ideas and then keep them if they continue to be useful, or drop them if they seem not to be useful. I have no trouble with time, nor trouble with space. But I do have trouble with the word "concept." I think one way or another we would want to get rid of it. And I think there are precisely two ways to get rid of it. This comes to me from a lecture by Daisetz Suzuki. At the beginning of the lecture I am thinking of, he went to the blackboard and drew an egglike shape on the board and put two parallel lines halfway up the left side. Pointing to those two parallel lines, he said this is the ego, and pointing to the egglike shape, he said this is the structure of the mind. And he said that the ego had the capacity to close itself off from its experience, which went up and out through the senses to the world around us—what we might call the relative world—and then it continued down, to what Meister Eckhart called the "ground" and came back to the ego through dreams. So that the ego could cut itself off either by saying it liked things on the outside or didn't like them, making judgments and so forth. And memorizing what it didn't like and so on, and then having dreams about that, which sometimes get things turned upside down. So that one way or another you could be alone or you could be flowing full circle so that you would come out, in the end, in that case, like Rilke looking at a tree and wondering whether you were yourself or were the tree. Suzuki said that's what Zen would like us to do, rather than use the ego to separate oneself from one's experience.

This lecture, and other experiences, convinced me that I would take the outward path, rather than the inward path of meditation, since if it was a circle it went all the way around. So my notion then was how to go out through the senses and yet not have any concepts.

You see, you could go in through the dreams or through sitting square-legged or through deep breathing—all those Yoga exercises—and you could come to the same conclusion: no concepts. Certainly all those koans of Zen Buddhism are aimed to reduce any concept that one may have to such a state of pulverization that it doesn't exist.

That's why I have used chance operations. I use them in a way involving a multiplicity of questions which I ask rather than choices that I make. So that if I have the opportunity to continue working, I think the work will resemble more and more, not the work of a person, but something that might have happened, even if the person weren't there. Something like that.

It seems to me that, in an art like the dance, the discipline is not what mine is, of sitting still and putting ink on paper, but is a daily discipline connected with the body. It closely resembles the disciplines of going in (and sitting, breathing, etc.). And though Merce Cunningham also uses, not always and not as I do, but in his own way, chance operations, it seems to me that the dance frees the body from the closing-in-on-itself aspect of the ego: what happens is that a concept disappears and simply a movement is made.

There was another lecture that Suzuki gave that I keep thinking of all the time. We have in the West this business of trying to find out, among a plurality of events in time and space, which one is the best. And then thinking of ourselves as separate from that and as desirably moving toward it. But in the Kegan philosophy which Suzuki taught, each being, whether sentient as we are, or nonsentient as sounds and rocks are, is the Buddha: and that doesn't mean anything spooky. It simply means that it is at the center of the universe. So that what you have in Kegan philosophy is an endless plurality of centers, each one world-honored.—Richard Kostelanetz et al. (1977).

We understand things by means of what we do. That is to say, without doing *something* we tend to be blind to everything, but the moment we do do something that action opens our vision to the things in the past and the things in the future. By doing, I mean making something or creating something, or devoting ourselves to something. That act enables us to see other things. When we say that such and such a thing is a generalization or a conclusion, it is because what we are doing enables us to see it as such; but if we did something else, we might see some of the things that we thought were of no importance as being extremely interesting. I spent many, many years finding the music of Charles Ives of no use; and then, because of changes in my own music, Ives became of paramount importance to me.—C. H. Waddington (1972).

When I began to study Oriental philosophy, there was still the idea with us that the Orient was not for us—that we had no right to it and that if we took it, it wouldn't fit us. So I kept coming back to Western thinking to find the same idea in it, and more recently, in reading the *Journal* of Thoreau, of course, I find all of those ideas from the Orient there, because he actually got them, as I did, from the Orient. And Christian thinking, very early, this thing that I just said about the plurality of Buddhas, you have the same idea in Gnostic Christianity: split the stick and there is Jesus.

Here's another idea that comes from the Orient which still means very much to me and is very useful. It's that we don't live by means of one principle, but by a series of principles which can change according to the situation in which we find ourselves. From a Western point of view this sort of flexibility and changeability of mind might seem, what would you call it?—hypocritical. But in Indian philosophy, there is a division of thinking into four parts: *artha,* which means goal seeking, such goals as exist in cooking, hunting wild mushrooms, or winning a game, or subduing an enemy, etc; *kama* concerns beauty and the giving of pleasure and the enjoyment of sex; and *dharma* is, as I understand it, the true and the false, or the good and evil; and *moksha* is liberation from all these concerns.

From the European point of view, if one heard of liberation in opposition to those others, one might be led to choose it, and to let the others go, but then you would shortly die if you were looking for wild mushrooms.

This idea has been very helpful to me because when I was younger, I would express an idea such as my devotion to chance operations, and not know quite what to say when people said, very logically, that if I looked for mushrooms that way I would kill myself and so why did I write music that way? But writing music is one thing and looking for mushrooms is another.

Categories describe work, not people.

Right. Another idea that I continue to be interested in, and which doesn't so much come from the Orient, is just our present circumstance; we moved from giving attention to an object to what we can call environment or process. The art that dealt with beginnings and endings has to do with object, whereas the kind of art that doesn't deal with such things can go on any length of time, or exist in any space, and we see this kind of art being made now, whether in visual arts or in music or in theater. We can have them both in view of what I just said about Indian philosophy. Sometimes one, sometimes the other, sometimes mixtures.—Richard Kostelanetz et al. (1977).

When I was teaching at Black Mountain College in the earlier '50s one summer, I had come through my study of Zen Buddhism with Suzuki to an appreciation of a particular text: I liked it more than the others connected with Zen Buddhism—it's called *The Huang Po Doctrine of Universal Mind.* So one evening at Black Mountain, with Elaine de Kooning (or was it Francine du Plessix, who is now Francine Gray, I forget), we read the entire *Huang Po Doctrine* with all the notes and everything. And the reason there were two of us was because part of it is a dialogue, question and answer. And after that experience, which took several hours, three or four hours, people told me their lives had changed.—Alan Gillmor & Roger Shattuck (1973).

I understand Duchamp's not doing things, and it seems to me that I am somewhat in Duchamp's situation now, except that instead of not doing things I will keep on doing whatever there is to do. ☙Duchamp had "gone underground." We now know that he was as busy as ever, making, among other works, his *Etants donnés.*❧ What I like very much to think about in this connection is the final image from the Ox-Herding Pictures, the Zen text that teaches by means of illustrations instead of words. There are two versions of the Ox-Herding Pictures, you know. One version ends with an empty circle—nothingness—the example of Duchamp. In the other version the final picture is of a big fat man, with a smile on his face, returning to the village bearing gifts. He returns without ulterior motive, but he returns. The idea being that after the attainment of nothingness one returns again into activity.—Calvin Tomkins (1965).

What do you think of Marshall McLuhan and his theories?

I am very devoted to him. He has examined many aspects of twentieth-century life and come to views that corroborate the views of poets, painters, and musicians in society, things that we did dimly, that we actually acted upon but often did not realize in terms of words. But he made all these things very clear. His mind moves in an extraordinary way. I think sometimes he happens upon points that are not immediately perceived as useful. Other times, they coincide with the perceptions of artists.—Nikša Gligo (1972).

Do you think there has been a concerted effort to minimize or suppress McLuhan's work? Do you think his ideas are threatening to the academic/political intelligentsia?

I think that the ideas remain. So that if there was a concerted effort, it was ineffective. I think of McLuhan's work often.—Paul Hersh (1982).

I just thought—I haven't given my attention to this before and so it interests me now—of the correspondence between Thoreau and Satie, and I think it is evident over and over again. For instance, in those pieces of Satie that I mentioned before, say, between 1912 and 1914, where one phrase following another seems to be followed by discontinuity rather than continuity—it's almost the opposite of the *Gymnopédies*—where suddenly there'll be a little waltz, say, and then there'll just be a glissando or—I forget what—some chords or something, something that seems to be unrelated. In Thoreau's *Journal,* from paragraph to paragraph, or even from sentence to sentence, there is this state of discontinuity, just as there is in McLuhan, which is so irritating to so many people in McLuhan, that rather than developing his ideas, he simply gives you a series of ideas.—Alan Gillmor & Roger Shattuck (1973).

In the time that I've known Bucky Fuller, since the late forties, he has had a vision of how it [his synergetics] could influence music; and he has several times explained it to me. And I have as many times not understood. And the reason I don't understand is because I'm so busy doing the work that I am doing. So that when I hear about another way of working, I'm not as open to it as I would be if I didn't have this way to work that I do. Which in itself is changing. But the thing that puts me off is the presence of mathematics, which has to do with specific relationships.

On the other hand, I've been so devoted to Fuller's work that I was alarmed at the time [my book] *A Year from Monday* was being published. I was alarmed whether or not he thought of my work as antithetic to his own work. In other words, the use of chance operations—did he think they were opposed to his views? He didn't. He found them perfectly compatible. And it may be that it should be the work of someone else, rather than my own work, to bring the vision and ideas of Fuller into music.—Walter Zimmerman (1975).

HIS OWN MUSIC (to 1970)

What was your first music like?

It was mathematical. I tried to find a new way of putting sounds together. Unfortunately, I don't have either the sketches or any clearer idea about the music than that. The results were so unmusical, from my then point of view, that I threw them away. Later, when I got to California, I began an entirely different way of composing, which was through improvisation, and improvisation in relation to texts: Greek, experimental writing from *transition* magazine, Gertrude Stein, and Aeschylus. Then, becoming through Richard Buhlig and others aware of my disconnection with musical technique or theory, I began studying the books of Ebenezer Prout. I went through them as though I had a teacher, and did all the exercises—in harmony, primarily. I don't think I did counterpoint. It was later, with Schoenberg, that I studied that.—William Duckworth (1985).

Have you ever worked with serial composition methods?

Yes, in my very earliest works. That was why I studied with Schoenberg. It was because I had devised a twenty-five-tone row that Henry Cowell said I should study with Schoenberg. Twelve was more economical than twenty-five.

There was a tendency, very strong even apart from twelve tones, to find a way not to repeat pitches, and this resulted in the chromaticism of Carl Ruggles in the United States; it affected many people. When I was very young, it made me think of this way of writing with two octaves, twenty-five tones—to play each one of those notes before I repeated any one of them. And to keep, when I had two voices with one octave in common—to keep the tones of that octave as far apart as possible. And I was able to keep them, say, eleven tones apart; but I didn't use the series. But after I studied with Schoenberg, I agreed with Henry Cowell that twelve tones is simpler than twenty-five. And so I began to write a twelve-tone music.—Lars Gunnar Bodin & Bengt Emil Johnson (1965).

I showed Adolph Weiss my first compositions, which were of a curious, original kind of twelve-tone music in which I divided the row into fragments or motives, but instead of varying them as most composers would, I kept them static but had ways of making mosaics out of them that used all the transpositions, and the inversions and the retrogrades, and so forth, and almost never expressed the row itself. Well, in that situation, I equated the absence of any of those motives with their presence. So that I could express a fragment of a row by its duration, and that would mean by silence. So when I would send such a composition to Weiss, he would say, "Why, when you've just started your piece, why do you stop? You're not supposed to stop until you get to the end. Why do you stop in the middle?" Well, I thought about this a good deal, but I had a strong inclination toward this stopping; it was because I wasn't *going*. The music was not going, therefore it could perfectly well stop, since stopping was as much a part of it as sounding; not sounding was the same as sounding.—Cole Gagne & Tracy Caras (1975).

Schoenberg later characterized you as an inventor of genius and you rose to prominence with some intriguing works for bones, bottles, specially designed percussion instruments, and the prepared piano.

Well, I have become convinced that everything has a spirit and that everything sounds. I became so curious about the world in which I lived, from the sonic point of view, that I began hitting and rubbing everything I came near—whether I was in the kitchen or outdoors, and I gradually assembled a large collection of unconventional instruments.—Tim Page (1986).

In 1938 Syvilla Fort, a magnificent black dancer/choreographer in Bonnie Bird's company at the Cornish School in Seattle, was giving a dance program on Friday, and I was the only composer around. She asked me to make the music for her *Bacchanale.* The space was small, and there was no room for percussion, only room enough for a grand piano. So I had to do something suitable for her on that piano. And that's what happened. She asked me on a Tuesday. I got to work quickly and finished it by Thursday.

Were you trying to re-create African or Oriental music?

At that time, because I had recently been studying with Arnold Schoenberg, I wrote either twelve-tone music or percussion music. I first tried to find a twelve-tone row that sounded African, and I failed. So I then remembered how the piano sounded when Henry Cowell strummed the strings or plucked them, ran darning needles over them, and so forth. I went to the kitchen and got a pie plate and put it and a book on the strings and saw that I was going in the right direction. The only trouble with the pie plate was that it bounced. So then I got a nail, put it in, and the trouble was it slipped. So it dawned on me to put a wood screw between the strings, and that was just right. Then weather stripping and so on. Little nuts around the screws, all sorts of things.—Stephen Montague (1982).

The objects work as mutes, and the sound becomes softer than an ordinary piano, and quite a bit different. I find it as fascinating to prepare a piano as it is to walk along a beach and pick up shells.—Tim Page (1986).

I invited Mark Tobey and Morris Graves over to listen to it, and they were delighted. And so was Syvilla, and so was I, and so was my wife,

Xenia. We were all so happy, happy as could be. When Lou Harrison heard it, he said: "Oh damnit! I wish I'd thought of that!"—Stephen Montague (1982).

When I finished [studying with Schoenberg], I was suddenly an active member of the musical world. As such, it was my responsibility to say something, because at that time—it was in the thirties—people said an artist "must have something to say." So I tried, as composers do, or poets, or whatnot, to see what I had to say, and to say it. For instance, when the Second World War came along, I talked to myself, what do I think of the Second World War? Well, I think it's lousy. So I wrote a piece, *Imaginary Landscape No. 3,* which is perfectly hideous. What I meant by that is that the Second World War is perfectly hideous, and I meant incidentally that *Time, Life* and Coca-Cola were also hideous, that anything that is big in this world is hideous.

Logically I thought that anything that is small and intimate, and has some love in it, is beautiful. Therefore, I wrote a piece for prepared piano, which is very quiet. It is called *Amores,* and it is about my conviction that love is something that we can consider beautiful. But then shortly I discovered that I was being divorced and going through all the troubles associated with disrupted love life; so that even love has its aspects which are not beautiful. So what is beautiful? So what's art? So why do we write music? All these questions began to be of great importance to me, to such a great importance that I decided not to continue unless I could find suitable answers. So I tell about going to a psychoanalyst in *Silence* and so won't repeat that story now; but the result was that I did not accept psychoanalysis or undergo it as a process, but I did accept Oriental philosophy, and did undergo that, not as a disciplined process, but as a study in terms of reading books and going to lectures, at a time that I was in such serious necessity that I was on the edge of being unable to function. I was ill, or could have become ill, had this not happened, though I do not want to blame Zen Buddhism with what I have done. I would not have done what I have done, except for it; and so I am very grateful for it. On the other hand, Zen Buddhism is not the only way to come to the kind of actions to which I came.—Lars Gunnar Bodin & Bengt Emil Johnson (1965).

I might even say, or someone else might say of me, that my whole dedication to music has been an attempt to free music from the clutches of the A-B-A. When I was just beginning to write music I made a list of all the permutations of numbers such as would produce forms or relationships of parts in a musical composition. And I made them for all the numbers from 2 through 11. By the time you get to the number 11 the possibilities are extraordinarily numerous. Now, when you look at all those possibilities of formal or structural relationships, you see that European music has used only a tiny number of them, whereas if you simply listen to environmental sound you're over and over struck by the brilliance of nonorganization.—Hans G. Helms (1972).

I thought, if I'm not going to have tonality in my music, I'll need something to make an alternative structure; and that was rhythm. I examined the nature of sound, which has pitch, duration, overtone and amplitude. Then I examined silence; and of those four things, silence had only duration. Therefore, in discovering the need for a rhythmic structure I was finding a correct structure for music—whereas the European structure, based on tonality, would not admit noises or pitches outside the major and minor scale, and was incorrect.—Michael John White (1982).

I have, so to speak, no ear for music, and never did have. I loved music but had no ear for it. I haven't any of that thing that some people speak of having—knowing what a pitch is. The whole pitch aspect of music eludes me. Whether a sound is high or low is a matter of little consequence to me.

So this in fact was the great attraction that percussion music had for you; it could liberate you from . . .

. . . noises delight me; each one of them interests me; and time interests me. And when I saw that time was the proper basis of music, since it included both sounds and silence, I saw that pitch and harmony and counterpoint and all those things that had been the basis of European Music were improperly so and had made it into the boring thing that for the most part it symphonically became. I agree with the African prince who went to a concert in London and afterward was asked what he thought. He had heard a program of music that began before Bach and went on up to modern times, and he said, "Why did they play the same piece over and over again?"—Alan Gillmore (1973).

I remain a percussion composer whether I write for percussion instruments or not. That is, my work is never based, structurally or as an instance of process, on frequency but rather on duration considerations. Within time I write for friends who are virtuosi, strangers who play in orchestras, myself growing old, indeterminately or determinately, always nonintentionally. Since 1968 I have found two ways of turning intention toward nonintention: musicircus (simultaneity of unrelated intentions); and music of contingency (improvisation using instruments in which there is a discontinuity between cause and effect).

Did your early involvement with percussion music in some way influence you in *composing with "chance" methods and* to *compose with "chance" methods?*

Variation in gongs, tomtoms, etc. and particularly variation in the effects on pianos of the use of preparations, prepared me for the renunciation of intention and the use of chance operations.

What are the special responsibilities, as you see it, that we percussionists have in the world today?

I still believe what I wrote in 1939, "Percussion music is revolution." New music: new society. I don't think, as some seem to be thinking, that the percussion should become like the other sections of the orchestra, more expressive in their terms (overtone structure, frequency). I believe that the rest of the orchestra should become as noisy, poverty-stricken, and unemployed as the percussion section (or at least grant its acceptability in musical society). I do not mean anything hierarchical. I just mean accepting the fact that noises are sounds and that music is made with sounds, not just musical sounds. Hopefully, new society based on unemployment. Why have labor-saving inventions otherwise?—Stuart Smith (1983).

Lou Harrison and I wrote *Double Music* [1941] together. It is a "voiced" percussion piece. One of us wrote the soprano and tenor parts. The other wrote the bass and alto. After agreeing on a rhythmic structure, the phrases and the sections, we worked independently. When we brought the parts together in rehearsal, no notes had to be changed. We were delighted.—David Shapiro (1985).

We'd like to begin with your works from the 1930s and 1940s. Do they seem remote to you now? Did you have to unlearn from them in order to compose your indeterminate works of the last thirty years?

I suppose the answer to both those questions is yes. I'm always more interested in what I haven't yet written than in what I've written in the past—particularly that long ago. Although now so many people are beginning to play the old music, and they invite me to the concerts, so I hear it a good deal. Some of the pieces are good and some of them are not. There are two that are quite popular that I think are good pieces: *Credo in Us* and the *Third Construction.* I think the *Second Construction* is a poor piece ◂§though it is sometimes played very well§▸. I wasn't quite aware that it was poor when I wrote it; I thought it was interesting. But it has carry-overs from education and theory; it's really a fugue, but of a novel order. In this day, I think fugues are not interesting (because of the repetition of the subject).—Cole Gagne & Tracy Caras (1980).

I admit I've been inclined as others have been inclined to get rid of bad pieces, you know, and there are some that are definitely very poor. There's an amusing point here. You have heard about that business of the *Imaginary Landscape* and the *Marches,* and there is one *Imaginary Landscape* that I decided was so bad that it should simply be forgotten, and that's brought about a curious numbering.

Was it an early one?

Yes, it was Number Two, which I thought was really pointless.

And that's published.

I don't think it is now—I think it's gone.

What would make [that work] bad?

I think what makes things bad generally is that in the circumstances in which we are working we are working on many other things too, so that we are not able to give full attention to any one of the things we are doing when we are doing too many things. So that a piece of music was a rhythmic structure for me living, so to speak, in that rhythmic structure; and when the life in it isn't lively but also not simply repetitive as, say, in *Vexations* of Satie, but is somewhere in between it, a very dull lusterless point, it seems to me it's not good.—Gwen Deely, with Jim Theobald (1976).

The percussion part of the program is interesting to me because of this wonderful piece Credo in Us *which involves the use of prerecorded materials. Did you start this piece with the idea of involving radio or recordings?*

Both. It was done for a dance which was choreographed by Merce Cunningham, and he made it with Jean Erdman. It's a kind of satire on America.

So the "Us" is the U.S.?

And it's also you and me.

And what is the "Credo"?

That we believe in all that.

What was the imagery in the dance?

I was always busy playing the music, so I have no way of knowing; but there are many holes in the music, and in the holes there were words of a text that Merce Cunningham had written.

And he spoke them as they danced.

That may be, or they may have stopped and talked to one another.

So the irony is also romantic, classical music bursting out of the speakers, and that was America's idea of culture.

And the cowboy solo, and the jazz solo, and so forth.

So how are you doing it here [tonight]?

The phonograph is playing Tchaikovsky, and the radio, of course, is playing whatever you put on the air.—Charles Amirkhanian (1983).

There [in *Sonatas and Interludes*] I had a written structure so that I knew the length of the phrases of the piece from the beginning to the end. I placed objects on the strings, deciding their position according to the sounds that resulted. So, it was as though I was walking along the beach finding shells that I liked, rather than looking at the ones that didn't interest me. Having those preparations of the piano and playing with them on the keyboard in an improvisatory way, I found melodies and combinations of sounds that worked with the given structure.—Bill Shoemaker (1985).

[The piece deals with the] "nine permanent emotions" of the Indian tradition. Coomaraswamy insisted that certain ideas were true and that these ideas were to be found in both the Occident and the Orient. My first reaction was to express this idea as far as I could in discourse. So I wrote *Sonatas and Interludes.* In it there are some pieces with bell-like sounds that suggest Europe, and others with a drumlike resonance that suggest the East. The last piece is clearly European. It was the signature of a composer from the West.—Joan Peyser (1976).

You see, I don't hear music when I write it. I write in order to hear something I haven't yet heard. My writing is almost characterized by having something unusual in the notation. The notation is about something that is not familiar.—Joel Eric Suben (1984).

In 1949 you went to Europe for a few months, and shortly after your return you began to use the I Ching *in your composition. Had you encountered things in Europe that led you in this direction?*

No, it was rather my study of Zen Buddhism. At first, my inclination was to make music about the ideas that I had encountered in the Orient. The *String Quartet* [1950] is about the Indian view of the seasons, which is creation, preservation, destruction, and quiescence; also the Indian idea of the nine permanent emotions, with tranquillity at the center. But then I thought, instead of talking about it, to do it; instead of discussing it, to do it. And that would be done by making the music nonintentional, and starting from an empty mind. At first I did this by means of the Magic Square.

The third movement of the *String Quartet* uses a canon for a single line ☙half way through it repeats itself, going backward to the beginning altered somewhat by the exigencies of the rhythmic structure❧, and it's a kind of music which doesn't depend on one's likes and dislikes; it's the following willy-nilly of a ball which is rolling in front of you. But there are at least two pieces that are in transition: the *Sixteen Dances* and the *Concerto for Prepared Piano and Chamber Orchestra.* Both of those use a chart like the Magic Square. They established moves on it which distinguished, as I recall, one phrase from another. It can be used compositionally to make differences by changing the move that's made on the chart. Instead of having numbers, as the Magic Square would, the chart of course had single sounds, intervals, and aggregates. The aggregates and intervals are made on either one instrument or several.—Cole Gagne & Tracy Caras (1980).

[Pierre] Boulez had been working with a similar diagram at the time, but he put numbers into the squares whereas I put in aggregates of sounds. They had no relation to harmony. They had no necessary direction. Each was a musical fact, without any implication at all. If one moves in this way one produces a continuity of sound that has nothing to do with harmony and is freed, at the same time, from the imposition of one's own taste.—Joan Peyser (1976).

It was while I was doing such work that Christian Wolff brought me a copy of the *I Ching* that his father had just published. I saw immediately that that chart was better than the Magic Square. So I began writing the *Music of Changes* and later the *Imaginary Landscape No. 4* for twelve radios. The reason I wrote *that* was because Henry Cowell had said that I had not freed myself from my tastes in the *Music of Changes.* It was my intention to do that, so I wrote the music for radios feeling sure that no one would be able to discern my taste in that. However, they criticized that too because it was so soft. So I just kept on going in spite of hell and high water.—Cole Gagne & Tracy Caras (1980).

Normally a musician writes in measures, and then assigns to the unit of those measures a metronomic figure. So we have andante and largo and all those things. In a piece called the *Music of Changes,* which I composed using the *Book of Changes* [*I Ching*], all the things I could discern in a piece of music were subjected to chance operations. Among the things I noticed and subjected to chance operation was tempo. If you look at the *Music of Changes* you see that every few measures, at every structural point, things were speeding up or slowing down or remaining constant. How much these things varied was chance-determined. David Tudor learned a form of mathematics which he didn't know before in order to translate those tempo indications into actual time. It was a very difficult process and very confusing for him.—Michael Kirby & Richard Schechner (1965).

What I did was to develop rhythmic structure from a fixed tempo to changes of tempo. I had not yet moved to a renunciation of absolutely all structure.—Joan Peyser (1976).

After that I altered my way of composing: I didn't write in tempos but always in time. By the time I was teaching at the New School this was one of the facts of my work, and they «the students» caught on readily because it gives one enormous facility in the field of time to know by means of a clock when something's got to start.—Michael Kirby & Richard Schechner (1965).

How did you come to write the Suite for Toy Piano?

My works just before that had been for prepared piano. I had written the *Three Dances* and the *Book of Music* for two prepared pianos, and I had also written the *Sonatas and Interludes,* so that I was familiar both with percussion music and with the complex nature of the prepared piano, and I wanted to find a way of writing for unprepared or normal instruments. And I thought the place to begin would be with the simplest aspect of the piano, namely, the white keys, and so I wrote the *Suite for Toy Piano.* So many of the black keys on toy pianos are merely painted on and don't refer to different pitches, and the instrument itself is generally a white key instrument with a small range. I tried to write in such a way that these pitches, which were the most conventional, would become new to my ears.

I was still working within a rhythmic structure. Schoenberg had impressed on me the importance of tonality and harmony as a structural means to divide a whole into parts, and when I decided to make a music that would include noises, I couldn't have recourse to tonality, because the noises aren't part of it; so I needed a different kind of structure. And I made a rhythmic structure —generally a structure having a total number of measures that had a square root; this enabled me to give the same proportions to the large parts within a whole that I gave to the phrases within a unit of the whole— which was as open to noises as it was to the pitched tones. With the *Suite for Toy Piano* I wanted to approach each sound as though it were as fresh as a prepared piano sound. I wanted to discover again, as though they were completely unfamiliar, the most familiar sounds. Actually, the *Suite for Toy Piano* can be played on any keyboard instrument. I like the sound of a toy piano very much. It sounds like a gamelan of some kind.—Tom Darter (1982).

I think perhaps my own best piece, at least the one I like the most, is the silent piece [*4′33″*, 1952]. It has three movements and in all of the movements there are no sounds. I wanted my work to be free of my own likes and dislikes, because I think music should be free of the feelings and ideas of the composer. I have felt and hoped to have led other people to feel that the sounds of their environment constitute a music which is more interesting than the music which they would hear if they went into a concert hall.—Jeff Goldberg (1974).

They missed the point. There's no such thing as silence. What they thought was silence [in my *4′33″*], because they didn't know how to listen, was full of accidental sounds. You could hear the wind stirring outside during the first movement [in the premiere]. During the second, raindrops began patterning the roof, and during the third the people themselves made all kinds of interesting sounds as they talked or walked out.—John Kobler (1968).

People began whispering to one another, and some people began to walk out. They didn't laugh—they were irritated when they realized nothing was going to happen, and they haven't forgotten it 30 years later: they're still angry.—Michael John White (1982).

I had friends whose friendship I valued and whose friendship I lost because of that. They thought that calling something you hadn't done, so to speak, music was a form of pulling the wool over their eyes, I guess.—Ellsworth Snyder (1985).

Most composers like some of their own pieces better than others, or feel some are more important than others. Which piece or pieces of yours would you consider the most important?

Well, the most important piece is my silent piece.

That's very interesting. A lot of people would agree with that.

Uh-huh.

But you feel that way as well.

Oh yes. I always think of it before I write the next piece.

Really? Tell me how you came to do that piece?

I had thought of it already in 1948 and gave a lecture which is not published, and which won't be, called "A Composer's Confessions." It was given at Vassar College in the course of a festival involving artists and thinkers in all fields. Among those was Paul Weiss, who taught philosophy at Yale University. I was just then in the flush of my early contact with Oriental philosophy. It was out of that that my interest in silence naturally developed: I mean it's almost transparent. If you have, as you do in India, nine permanent emotions and the center one is the one without color—the others are white or black—and tranquility is in the center and freedom from likes and dislikes. It stands to reason, the absence of activity which is also characteristically Buddhist . . . well, if you want the wheel to stop, and the wheel is the Four Noble Truths. The first is Life is Activity, sometimes translated as Life is Pain. If the wheel is to be brought to a stop, the activity must stop.

The marvelous thing about it is when activity comes to a stop, what is immediately seen is that the rest of the world has not stopped. There is no place without activity. Oh, there are so many ways to say it. Say I die as a person. I continue to live as a landscape for smaller animals. I just never stop. Just put me in the ground and I become part and parcel of another life, another activity. So the only difference between activity and inactivity is the mind. And the mind that becomes free of desire. Joyce would agree here, free of desire and loathing—that's why he said he was so involved with comedy, because tragedy is not so free from these two. So when the mind has become in that way free, even though there continues to be some kind of activity, it can be said to be inactivity. And that's what I have been doing, and that's why critics are so annoyed with my work. Because they see that I am denying the things to which they are devoted.—Stephen Montague (1982).

You see I was afraid that my making a piece that had no sounds in it would appear as if I were making a joke. In fact, I probably worked longer on my "silent" piece than I worked on any other. I worked four years . . .

. . . just to get up the guts.

Actually what pushed me into it was not guts but the example of Robert Rauschenberg. His white paintings that I referred to earlier: When I saw those, I said, "Oh yes, I must; otherwise I'm lagging, otherwise music is lagging."—Alan Gillmor & Roger Shattuck (1973).

What other works of yours do you feel have also been very important?

All the others.

But the silent piece stands above all the rest.

It's more radical. I think the pieces since the silent piece in a sense are more radical than the ones that precede it, though I had an inclination toward silence that you can discern in very early pieces written in the 1930s. One of my early teachers always complained that I had no sooner started than I stopped. You can see that in the *Duet for Two Flutes,* or those early piano pieces that were written in the thirties. Then I'm always introducing silence right near the beginning when any composer in his right mind would be making things thicker and thicker, I was getting thinner and thinner.—Stephen Montague (1982).

In *34'46.776" for 2 Pianists,* instead of specifying the piano preparation, I not only specified it only roughly with regard to categories of materials like plastic, rubber, metal, and so forth, leaving the decisions free to the performer; but another element entered into the musical composition which was X, in other words, something not thought of at all. So that it gave a freedom to the individual performer.

This giving of freedom to the individual performer began to interest me more and more. And given to a musician like David Tudor, of course, it provided results that were extraordinarily beautiful. When this freedom is given to people who are not disciplined and who do not start—as I've said in so many of my writings—from zero (by zero I mean the absence of likes and dislikes) who are not, in other words, changed individuals, but who remain people with particular likes and dislikes, then, of course, the giving of freedom is of no interest whatsoever.

But when it is given to disciplined people, then you see—as we have seen, I believe, in our performances with David Behrman, with Gordon Mumma, with David Tudor, with Alvin Lucier, with Lowell Cross, sometimes all of us together, or in a piece that included many of those whom I've just named, together with Marcel and Teeny Duchamp and myself in Toronto, a piece called *Reunion*—in that case you give an instance of a society which has changed, not an individual who has changed but a group of individuals, and you show, as I've wanted to do, the practicality of anarchy.—Hans G. Helms (1972).

In a lecture in 1937 [reprinted in Silence*], you said, "The principle of form will be our only constant connection with the past." You went on to identify this connection as "the principle of organization, or man's common ability to think." Later you associate form with the "morphology of a continuity" and "expressive content." Would you trace your developing view of form?*

I'm now more involved in *dis*organization and a state of mind which in Zen is called *no-mindedness.*

Those statements, given in 1937, are given as a sort of landmark to let the reader know from where I set out. There are certain things in that lecture that I would agree with and some that I would not. I imagine that when I used the word *form* then, that I meant what I later called *structure* (the divisibility of the whole into parts). Later I used *form* in the same sense that people generally use the word *content* (that aspect of composition which is best able to be free, spontaneous, heartfelt, and so on).

That attitude towards form is sort of in the middle between my present thought and my early thought. Now I don't bother to use the word *form,* since I am involved in making processes, the nature of which I don't foresee. How can I speak of *form?*—Roger Reynolds (1961).

Last night you told a student that he should not have any ego involvement in the performance of your compositions, but rather should perform it in the spirit of the piece. But I feel that, in your music especially, there is a necessity for ego involvement because you leave so much for the performer to decide.

No. The performer can use similar methods to make the determinations that I have left free, and will if he's in the spirit of the thing. When I have a number of musicians, some of them decide that because I've given them this freedom they will do whatever they please, and generally, in order to make my work appear foolish, they turn themselves into clowns. Actually, they've succeeded in showing how foolish they are. I've given them freedom and I would hope they would use that freedom to change themselves rather than to continue being foolish.

Have you heard that Town Hall recording of my *Concert for Piano and Orchestra?*

Yes . . .

At one point, one of the woodwind instruments quotes from Stravinsky . . . I think it's *Le Sacre.* You could look at the part I had given him and you'd never find anything like that in it. He was just going wild—not playing what was in front of him, but rather whatever came into his head. I have tried in my work to free myself from my own head. I would hope that people would take that opportunity to do likewise.

Yes, but it's like society. You want to give people freedom, to have an anarchic situation, and now you're saying that they do tend to misuse it sometimes, and this is what people are afraid of for society too, that they will misuse freedom in an anarchic situation.

Well, the reason we are afraid is because we have this overlap situation of the Old dying and the New coming into being. When the New coming into being is used by someone who is in the Old point of view and dying, then that's when that foolishness occurs. For *Atlas Eclipticalis* I gathered all that equipment, electronic equipment, to electrify the whole orchestra and to produce a situation that had never been heard before. Eighty-six instruments amplified and transformed and filtered to the public. An absolutely amazing situation. What did the musicians do? Tear their microphones off the things and stamp on them in fury!

Oh! What orchestra was that?

The New York Philharmonic, Bernstein conducting. And then do you know what they said. Quite pleased with themselves, passing by me in the hall, they said, "Come back in ten years. Maybe we'll take you seriously(!)"—Geneviere Marcus (1970).

I finished *Atlas Eclipticalis* in 1961, and it took me nine months to write. I've always thought that composition was for me either something that took a long time or something that took a short time—the difference between oil painting and water color; and I've tried to have ways of working slowly and ways of working quickly. Now when I travel all the time, I can only use the ways of working quickly, because I don't have much time. At least that's how I feel. So I have tried to write in these last two years only quickly written music. One was *0:00.* and then *Variations III* and *Variations IV.* These three pieces have in common no measurement of time, no use of the stopwatch, which my music for the previous ten years had—the structure of time, or the process of time; but in these pieces I'm trying to find a way to make music that does not depend on time.

In an earlier interview, when I'm asked what aspect of sound interests me the most, I say *time;* but this view that I'm trying to express now is one in which time is abandoned. This is very difficult, because a greater part of my experience as a composer has to do with measurement. And it is precisely this capacity for measurement that I want to be free of.

Just briefly, *0:00,* which is about two years old now, is nothing but the continuation of one's daily work, whatever it is, providing it's not selfish, but is the fulfillment of an obligation to other people, done with contact microphones, without any notion of concert or theater or the public, but simply continuing one's daily work, now coming out through loudspeakers. What the piece tries to say is that everything we do is music, or can become music through the use of microphones; so that everything I'm doing, apart from what I'm saying, produces sound. When the sounds are very quiet, they become loud through the use of microphones. And I may not do again in performance what I did once before.

So there's no notation for this piece.

It's verbal.

Variations III, you know, has circles that are all the same, but each one is on a different sheet of transparent plastic. When they are tossed onto a surface, they overlap. The ones that do not overlap the principal group are removed; so what you have in the end is a complex of overlapping circles. Some overlap more circles than others. For instance, the lowest will be one overlapping one other, whereas the highest will be seven, eight or nine circles overlapping.

What I mean by that is that our activities . . . We are constantly active; we are never inactive. There is no space in our lives. But there is a greater or lesser number of things going on at the same moment; so that if I'm not doing anything other than listening, the fact that I'm listening is that I'm doing something by listening. That's what *Variations III* is.

When you have these overlappings, how do you transform them into activities?

They can be any activities, providing again they are amplified. The only reason for amplification is that it's in the field of music. By means of electronics, it has been made apparent that everything is musical. Also, we know through modern physics that this table [here] is in vibration, and all we need is some way to protect this table from its environment and within that protection to put a microphone; and we will shortly hear the table.

Ultimately then, a music could be made that would be quite ritualistic in which all you would do for musical pleasure would be make audible the sounds that are already in existence. And I think that's very beautiful. If here, for musical pleasure, I could make audible to you what this book sounds like, and then what the table sounds like, and then what that wall sounds like, I think we would all be quite delighted; and we would have had as much musical pleasure as we need have.—Lars Gunnar Bodin & Bengt Emil Johnson.

In 1952 we had a duration structure with compartments which had been arrived at by chance operations. But in my more recent work [early sixties] I'm concerned rather with what I call process—setting a process going which has no necessary beginning, no middle, no end, and no sections. Beginnings and endings can be given things, but I try to obscure that fact, rather than do anything like what I used to do, which was to measure it. The notion of measurement and the notion of structure are not notions with which I am presently concerned. I try to discover what one needs to do in art by observations from my daily life. I think daily life is excellent and that art introduces us to it and to its excellences the more it begins to be like it.

Is there a difference between a group of people deciding to go to the beach and watching what happens on the beach, and a group of people deciding to go to an Event or an Activity and watching or participating in it?

If a person assumes that the beach is theater and experiences it in those terms I don't see that there's much difference. It is possible for him to take that attitude. This is very useful because you often find yourself, in your daily life, in irritating circumstances. They won't be irritating if you see them in terms of theater.

In other words, if you remove yourself from them.

Can we say remove, or use your faculties in such a way that you are truly at the center? We've been speaking of the central factor being each person in the audience.

Let's take a hypothetical but possible event. I'm involved in an auto wreck in which I'm not hurt but in which my best friend is killed. Well, I imagine that's a few steps above irritating—but if I look at it as theater, as happening to another but not to me, I can learn from the experience, respond to it but not be in it; then perhaps I can remove the irritants.

I didn't mean by putting the person at the center that he wasn't in it, I meant rather to show him that he was at the very center of it.

I don't see how this can remove the irritation then.

Do you know the Zen story of the mother who has just lost her only son? She is sitting by the road weeping and the monk comes along and asks her why she's weeping, and she says she's lost her only son, and he hits her on the head and says, "There, that'll give you something to cry about." Isn't there something of that same insistence in Artaud, in the business of the plague and of cruelty? Doesn't he want people to see themselves not in a pleasant world but in something that is the clue to all things that we normally try to protect ourselves from?

Sure. My only quarrel is whether one really enjoys it or not. When the mother gets hit over the head she has two things to cry about.

Another thing about structure. Isn't the difference between the beach and the theater that the beach is not rehearsed and the theater is? The thing that bothered me about the Happenings I've seen is that they are obviously rehearsed but badly done. Either they shouldn't have been rehearsed, or they shouldn't have gone halfway. In one Happening there was a man choking another and it became very theatrical for me in a bad way, because I knew that they weren't really choking each other . . .

And you know what the word "theatrical" should mean . . .

Convincingly. Either they should have done it well or not at all.

I couldn't be in greater agreement. If there are intentions, then there should be every effort made to realize those intentions. Otherwise carelessness takes over. However, if one is able to act in a way that doesn't have intention in it, then there is no need for rehearsal. This is what I'm working on now: to do something without benefit of measurement, without benefit of the sense that now that this is finished we can go on to the next thing.

Let me give you one example. In those two boxes over there are some ninety loops of tape. They vary from small loops that are just long enough for a tape machine, to ones which are, say, forty feet long. We gave a performance [of *Rozart Mix*] last week, at Brandeis, with six performers—the number that turned up at the time that the setup was made—and thirteen tape machines. The performance simply consisted of putting the loops on the various machines and taking them off. Doing this, a complex stage situation developed because we had to set up stands around which the tapes would go, and these things were overlapping. The number of loops made it fairly certain that no intention was involved in putting on one rather than another loop. The number of people and the number of machines also created a situation that was somewhat free of intentions. Another way is by making use of electronic circuits to involve the performers in manipulating the amplifiers. Somebody might be working at a microphone or a cartridge point when another person is at the amplifier altering it. Both people are prevented from successfully putting through any intentions.

But those cases depend upon the use of a machine that will short-circuit human intention.

If you have a number of people, then a nonknowledge on the part of each of what the other is going to do would be useful. Even if one of them was full of intentions, if none of them knew what the others' intentions were . . .

. . . tend in a nonintentional, unstructured direction, and would resemble what I referred to as daily life. If you go down the street in the city you can see that people are moving about with intention but you don't know what those intentions are. Many, many things happen which can be viewed in purposeless ways.—Michael Kirby & Richard Schechner (1965).

Even though each individual thing may be very structured, the combination would . . .

I'm often asked what I think of the new computer, and I don't particularly like it. Yet it is said that the computer would be perfectly natural for me to want to use. It may be a natural instrument for me to use, and I may be old-fashioned in not understanding that. But in one of McLuhan's books, he quotes a modern physicist who quotes an ancient Chinese story, and I'm also always quoting ancient Oriental stories. It's about a farmer who is irrigating the land with great difficulty, and someone comes and explains to him that by changing his technique he would be able to get a great deal of work done in a short time, and the Chinaman replies that he would be ashamed to change his technique in order to save time.

It is precisely time which we have to use. It does not annoy me to spend nine months tossing coins. It interests me to do that. I doubt whether the computer will do what I did, even though I know that there is a button there for aleatoric arrangement of information.—Lars Gunnar Bodin & Bengt Emil Johnson (1965).

My recent work has all been such that it has this indeterminate quality with respect to, certainly, its length. I tend, given the practicality of it in social terms, to make it long. I like, for instance, to start a piece without the audience's knowing that it has started. That can be done in several ways. And to conclude it without their knowing that it has stopped. That appeals to me very much.—David Sylvester & Roger Smalley (1967).

I don't believe you ever incorporated any photographs of plywood in your . . .

Oh, I did. I wrote a piece for carillon. Yes. I went to a girls' school with Merce in southwestern Virginia [in the mid 1960s], and they had a carillon in the school; and the carilloneur said, "Have you music for carillon?" And I said, "Yes I do, but I didn't bring it with me." He said, "Well that's a pity because I would have played it." So I said, "Well, wait a minute," and thinking of Marcel [Duchamp] I went around the theater. There was lots of time—during a dance rehearsal they don't need me—and I looked for a carillon piece, like a found object, you see. And I saw pieces of plywood, they were plywood blocks just the size of organ music, and the carillon is a form of organ music. So I took one. First I asked him how many bells his carillon had. He told me. So then I let him look at that block and I said, "Would you be able to play this?" He smiled and said yes. So within the hour I had written ten pieces on ten pieces of plywood. I had five pieces of plywood, and I wrote a staff on each side. And I gave it to him. I said, "Please play as long as you like this piece, and then remain silent as long as you think it took you to play it. And then play the next one and so on. Play all ten with silences between each." So that afternoon—this all happened in one day—that afternoon he played the ten pieces for carillon [Music for Carillon No. 5], and we stood outdoors and listened; and it was perfectly beautiful.—David Shapiro (1985).

Would you tell us about Variations VII *and its performance?*

It was done in New York, sponsored by EAT (Experiments in Art and Technology). That was several years ago, in '67, I think. The air, you see, is filled with sounds that are inaudible, but that become audible if we have receiving sets. So the idea of *Variations VII* is simply to go fishing, so to speak, in a situation you are in, and pick up as many things as you can, that are already in the air.

Is this similar to LaMonte Young's butterfly piece? He said that butterflies made a sound, though it is inaudible to human ears, but it really is music too.

No, mine was more like fishing for things that were already there.

What were the fishes you caught?

Well, there were ordinary radios, there were Geiger counters to collect cosmic things, there were radios to pick up what the police were saying, there were telephone lines open to different parts of the city. There were as many different ways of receiving vibrations and making them audible as we could grasp with the techniques at hand.—Max Nyffeler (1970).

Composition is like writing a letter to a stranger. I don't hear things in my head, nor do I have inspiration. Nor is it right, as some people have said, that because I use chance operations my music is written not by me, but by God. I doubt whether God, say he existed, would take the trouble to write my music.—Michael John White (1982).

Could you explain the difference between chance operation and indeterminacy?

Chance operations can be used to make something that is fixed. That is how I made the *Music of Changes.* I used the *I Ching* in order to write down something that enforced a performer to go through a particular series of actions. Then later, when I began my series of *Variations,* I was intent on making a kind of composition that was indeterminate of its own performance, a composition that didn't itself prescribe what would be done. In other words, I was intent on making something that didn't tell people what to do. At this point I attack, if I may say so, what seems to me to be a questionable aspect of music. Music is, after all, not like painting; music is a social art, social in the sense that it has consisted, formerly, of people telling other people what to do, and those people doing something that other people listen to. What I would like to arrive at, though I may never, what I think would be ideal, would be a situation in which no one told anyone what to do and it all turned out perfectly well anyway.

If absolute or total indeterminacy is not possible, is it then futile to attempt merely to approach it?

It's not futile to do what we do. We wake up with energy and we do something. And we make, of course, failures and we make mistakes, but we sometimes get glimpses of what we might do next.—Alan Gillmor (1976).

How did you come to make a piece like HPSCHD?

When I was at the University of Cincinnati a year ago, [Lejaren] Hiller called me from Urbana and said he could arrange for me to do a piece using computer facilities and would like to know if I was interested in doing it and what it would be if I did something with computer. The original notion was that another person, Gary Grossman, would do the programming, since I don't know how to program and didn't intend to learn how. It turned out when I arrived at the University of Illinois, Grossman was too busy to do the programming. So, Jerry Hiller did the programming for me, and, since he's had so much experience in the field (and is himself a composer), the piece has become a collaboration between us. The original idea, I thought, was more or less tailor-made for a computer: that is to say, an enormous project—enormous in the sense of having so many details in it that, were one to sit down with pen, ink, and paper, it would be a project exceeding the time one could spend at a desk—one that would be suitable for a computer. The original idea came from a notion I had about Mozart's music and how it differed from Bach's music. In the case of Bach, if one looked at a few measures and at the different voices, they would all be observing more or less the same scalar movement, that is, each voice would be using the same scale. Whereas, in the case of Mozart, if one looked at just a small amount of music, one would see the chromatic scale, the diatonic scale, and a use of chords melodically, like a scale, but made up of larger steps. I thought to extend this "moving-away-from-unity" and "moving-toward-multiplicity" and, taking advantage of the computer facility, to multiply the details of the tones and durations of a piece of music. So this piece divides the five octaves into all divisions: from five tones per octave to fifty-six tones per octave. Then, having observed large chordal/melodic steps, the diatonic and chromatic, even smaller steps were made, which would be microtonal with respect to each one of the tones in any one of these octaves. This arose from the *I Ching* which uses the number "sixty-four" and from the binary function which is so implicit in the computer—zero or one. Multiplying sixty-four by two, you would get, for each one of these tones, one hundred and twenty-nine possible pitches. We have very small steps—microtonal, small steps—chromatic, larger steps—diatonic, then, the very large steps consisting of leaps in all the divisions from five to fifty-six. This still doesn't explain why it's called *Harpsichord.* That happened as a result of a commission from Antoinette Vischer in Switzerland. She had for years wanted me to write a piece for harpsichord. I had been asked years before to write one for Sylvia Marlowe. I must admit I've never particularly liked the instrument. It sounded to me like a sewing machine. The fact that it had so little change in dynamics, and the quality of sound seemed to obscure the—I don't know—life of the sound, the pitch of the sound, or what you wish.

We have tried—Jerry Hiller and I—to give a quality of fine division not only to the pitches but to the durations and also to the timbre, which will be, in general, imitative of harpsichord sound: an attack followed by a decay that has an inflection point. The decay is not a straight line but a line with a bend in it. It starts down and then continues at a different descending angle. Now, that inflection point can be moved and the angle changed and so give "microtimbral" variations, and *that* we've related to the chart of the *I Ching.* The first "subroutine" we made for the computer was to substitute the manual tossing of coins—to obtain the numbers one to sixty-four. This subroutine was used in order to find at which point this inflection—this change of decay, this place in the sound—changes from note to note. It ought to be, in the end, not only microtonal and microdurational, but microtimbral. Each tape is a single, monophonic tape. The performance will introduce elements of indeterminacy, whereas the computer, in order to function, requires complete determination.

How are you introducing indeterminacy into the performance?

In the end there will be the tapes, each one of a different division of the octave. There will be fifty-one tapes, and there will be the seven solos for live harpsichord. They'll probably all be amplified to be equal volume with the tapes. In effect, there will be a maximum of fifty-eight channels. The piece could be expressed by a performance of one to seven live harpsichords and one to fifty-one tapes, according to how large a performance one wishes to give. The solos are obviously all for the twelve-tone scale, one of them being the computer output for the twelve-tone scale made into notation for live performance. Another will be the *Dice Game* that has been attributed to Mozart, of which twenty passes of sixty-four measures each have been programmed by the computer. Two other solos start with the *Dice Game* but then substitute other pieces of Mozart, which are in other tempi but which have been translated into the notation of the dotted-half equals 64 mm. But in one of those—a second pass of sixty-four measures, still using the *Dice Game*—you move instead to another piece of Mozart, still according to chance operations and on to a third, fourth, fifth, sixth, seventh, and eighth. In each pass, I think twenty measures of new material comes in. It gets more and more complex, naturally, departs further from the original *Dice Game,* and both hands go together. Then, in a third version the hands go separately through this process: from the *Dice Game* of Mozart to other pieces of Mozart in other tempi.

Then, we divided history from Mozart to the present time—that is, to

Hiller's work and my own work—into roughly twenty-five-year periods, making an historical shift from the *Dice Game* through Beethoven, Chopin, Schuman, Gottschalk, Ives, Schoenberg, and ending with a binary choice between a piano sonata by Jerry Hiller and my *Winter Music.* In all of this movement through history we've had, in some cases, to slightly change the music to fit into the five-octave gamut which we limited ourselves to, so that Chopin runs start up, but as they reach the limit of our gamut, we have them running back down the same way. That accounts for four: going through history "right-and-left-hands-together," going through history "right-and-left-hands-separate"—that's four—the computer's output is five, the pure *Dice Game* is six, and the seventh is simply one page of directions permitting the harpsichordist to play any Mozart of her choice in either of two manners: as though she were at home without an audience, practicing and playing for her own pleasure; or as though she were in public, performing, or any combination of those. All of that material can be superimposed in any way. So it would produce a variety of performances. Parts can be omitted. The performance can consist of, say, a dozen people with a battery of tapes, shifting the tapes from machine to machine, and so on.

How long are the tapes?

The tapes are twenty minutes long. And so are the solos. The solos going through history, with those different tempi all translated into one tempo of dotted-half equals 64 mm, produce complex relationships of thirteen to twenty-seven to twenty-four, and so on. The notation, which is proportional in space, results in one hundred and twenty pages of manuscript for each of those solos. The *Dice Game* will be a sixty-page manuscript; or perhaps, it's forty pages. Altogether, there will be five hundred and eighty-one pages of manuscript for live performance and those fifty-one tapes.

One more thing that has interested me in this, and I hope it will interest more and more people who work with computers, is the large amount of time and painstaking work that goes into making a subroutine operable. For instance, teaching the computer to toss coins as I had been doing manually, following the mechanism of the *I Ching*—to produce that subroutine took six weeks. To produce this whole piece, which is not yet operating, has taken ten months, which is one month longer than I spent on the *Music of Changes,* or on *Williams Mix,* or any other piece that took me a long period of time. This work that goes into subroutines gives it the character that, I think, chords had for composers in the past. The notion that the chord belongs to one person and not to another tends to disappear, so that a routine, once constructed, is like an accomplishment on the part of society, rather than on the part of a single individual. And it can be slightly varied, just as chords can be altered, to produce quite other results than were originally intended. The logic of a routine, once understood, generates other ideas than the one which is embodied in it. This will lead, more and more, to multiplication of music for everybody's use rather than for the private use of one person.

We often hear of the effect of technology on our lives, reducing work. For instance, people speak of the problem of leisure in the future. I find this in great contrast to the simple fact that we have worked for ten months on this piece without finishing it and, Lord knows, how many more months, or indeed, whether our work will be accomplished, or whether, when accomplished, we will not immediately think of some other way to make it. Leisure, just from this point of view, is not a problem. The question is, rather, "How is our energy? Do we have as much as we had? And how are we going to get more?"

I'm interested in your comment that your work here might introduce a possibility for music for everyone, that is, music for someone, or music for everyone, or whatever.

I'm just saying that more and more people will be using computers, and that more and more routines will exist, and that the possibility of making programs which utilize a routine made here, for instance, with one made there, with one made in some other place and adding others to it, will produce a music which has not yet been heard; and this can be enjoyed, surely by some, maybe by many. Oh, we've got another idea about this piece. A program is being made. . . . One of the first projects that has to be fulfilled is the project of recording the piece which has been contracted for Nonesuch Records—*HPSCHD* on one side, and the microtonal quartet of Ben Johnston on the other side. We are now making a program called "KNOBS" for the listener that will produce twenty computer outputs, suggesting to the listener when and what dials of the stereo to turn. There will be twenty different ways of listening to the record, which ought to suggest that one would listen also in other ways. We will have the solo, which is the twelve-tone computer output, equally on both channels; on one channel, but not on the other channel at all, will be the *Mozart Dice Game;* on the other channel, then, will be the passage through history with the right and left hands separate; and each channel will have twenty-five of the computer tape outputs, probably even numbers on one channel and odd numbers on the other. Then, if you shift the volume and tone controls . . .—Larry Austin (1968).

I read a criticism of my work recently in which the writer said my music was extremely interesting as sound, but it was unfortunate that it didn't have any substance. I wondered what he would have meant by substance, then I realized he meant the *relationships* of the sounds. I have carefully weeded out relationships through the use of chance operations, and what the writer was lamenting was the fact that I had succeeded.—Paul Hersh (1982).

You based one of your works, Cheap Imitation *[for piano, 1969] on Satie's* Socrate. *Could you tell us the genesis of the piece?*

In the late 1940s, through my interest in Satie and so forth, and the fact that I also worked with Merce Cunningham, he made a dance, a choreography, for the first movement of *Socrate;* and since we went around the country and for the most part the music was piano solo, I made a two-piano arrangement of the first movement of the *Socrate.* And when we would arrive in a town I would get some other pianist to play with me, and that way we provided the accompaniment. I told Merce at the time that if he would go on with the other two movements that I would go on with the arrangement. And in 1968, I think it was, he said, well, that's what I'm doing: I'm going on with my company to complete the choreography for the *Socrate.* So I said, well, I'll continue the arrangement, and I was very busy as the time with a piece called *HPSCHD* that was very time consuming. So I got a fellow named Arthur Maddox at the University of Illinois to study the arrangement of the first movement and to make sketches for the second and third, and so on. Then I went over them, and finally at Davis, California, I finished the work, which was a collaboration between myself and Maddox of the arrangement of the *Socrate.* Then, belatedly, I thought of applying to Eschig, who controls the copyright, for permission to make a two-piano arrangement of the *Socrate,* and they refused permission. I've never known the details of why they refused, because they didn't even wish to see the music, and it's a faithful, if I do say so, and serious piece of work. I have heard it in private at a concert at Davis where people paid no admission, so that we weren't infringing copyright by playing it. Everyone was delighted with the arrangement. And when the copyright runs out I will be able to publish it and other people will enjoy it. And I think it would be a useful arrangement to have, since it would make a work that's otherwise hard to come by more generally available. Anyway, the performance of Merce's choreography was just a month off when I got final news that I couldn't have the rights to arrange it. So I told Merce not to worry, that I would imitate the *Socrate* in a piano solo, which I did. I wrote it in a month by means of *I Ching* chance operations, and by this time you could say I understood the *Socrate* less or I understood it more than I had before being so close to it—I don't know which is appropriate. At any rate, I was struck by the fact that the modes—the piece is modal, you know, but the successive phrases often have chromatic relationships, did you know that?

So it's not a typically modal piece; in fact, it's a chromatic modal piece, which is unusual. Successive phrases will often, in terms of mode, have the relationship of the minor second, which is unusual; it's unheard of in modal music. Therefore, my questions to the *I Ching,* by means of which I write my music since the last twenty-five years, were: Which of the seven modes, if we take as modes the seven scales beginning on white notes and remaining on white notes, which of those am I using? Second question: Which of the twelve possible chromatic transpositions am I using? Third question: Now for this phrase for which this transposition of this mode will apply, which note am I using of the seven to imitate the note that Satie wrote? And where he repeated a note I also repeated the chance-given note—but then for each note I asked again which note I am to use and I maintained the rhythm and that was all. For the second and third movements I maintained the intervallic relationships for half a measure. Otherwise, I asked these questions all the time. And I was able in that way to write a piece which was not the *Socrate* but which would fit a choreography based on the *Socrate.* So I called it *Cheap Imitation.* My title was also an imitation of Satie's titles.

Have you not also called it Second Hand?

That's the title of the dance, and it followed my choice of title, which was *Cheap Imitation.* So Merce thought *Second Hand* would go well with *Cheap Imitation,* you see. It's the same as my present project which is based on the *musique d'ameublement*—to call it *musique démeublement* ☙§Apartment House Music§❧. It's an interesting title that corresponds, I think, in some way—it's perhaps not as brilliant—but it has something of the quality of Satie's interesting titles. So then I grew so fascinated by my *Cheap Imitation* that I decided to orchestrate it, and that took me three years. When I finished the orchestration, a performance was announced in several different countries, and on each occasion, except once here in New York, they failed to be able to play the music, because they refused to rehearse. They'd only looked at the music the day of the performance and then found that it was too difficult to play. Having glanced at it a week before, say, they thought, oh, we won't have to look at that. And it turns out to be a very difficult piece to play, and needs devoted attention, which I would say is true of Satie's music. A simple piece like the *Gymnopédies*—it appears that someone who only knows piano for two years could play it. But I think the best performance will come from someone who devotes himself to it as seriously as he would to the most difficult piece.—Alan Gillmor & Roger Shattuck (1973).

HIS OWN MUSIC (after 1970)

You have said that the function of composers is to hide *beauty.*

That has to do with opening our minds, because the notion of beauty is just what we accept. If we hide beauty by means of our music, we have enlarged the field of the mind.

I don't quite understand that.

It seems clear to me! If I just made everything "beautiful," then I wouldn't help either myself or anyone else. No change would take place.

So you do *think about people when you write.*

Not particularly, no. I don't know what my music sounds like until I hear it. I don't know how I would compose if I were thinking about what someone else would be hearing. I try to do my work as well as I can. That's the best I can do. If I thought about the listeners, I wouldn't know which ones to think about.—Arnold Jay Smith (1977).

Every now and then, in my writing of music which gives freedom to the performers, I encounter a performer who says, "I don't want to be free. I want to be told what to do." I have a piece for people I don't know which gives both the possibility of freedom and the possibility of being told what to do. The piece is called *Etcetera* (1973), and it has conductors. The musicians can either go to the conductors or stay by themselves. . . . I try in that piece to give an instance of this society that would have both freedom and no freedom. And then, in other pieces, I give instances of how it is to be free, and in still others I give instances of how it is not to be free. I think it's true that some people need to be told what to do. They can't use freedom. But there are other people, like myself, who hate to be told what to do, who need freedom. We're going to have, I hope, in the future all those varieties of people.—Monique Fong & Françoise Marie (1982).

Could you tell us about this Thoreau piece that you've just done?

It's called *Lecture on the Weather.* My understanding was that they [the Canadian Broadcasting Corporation—CBC] wanted a piece in the neighborhood of thirty minutes long, the way broadcasts go. Since the bicentennial is an occasional piece in referring to the past, I thought besides referring to the past of the United States, I would refer to my own past too, which is basically my silent piece *4′33″* [pronounced four-minutes, thirty-three seconds] ☙or four feet, thirty-three inches❧, which I wrote in '52. All of my music since then I try to think of as something which doesn't fundamentally interrupt that piece. So I multiplied 4′33″ by different numbers, and you come to the conclusion of course that any length of time is a multiple of 4′33″, that it's only our mathematical system that would let us settle on five times 4′33″, and six times, and seven times. There are other ways of having multiples, and there isn't anything that isn't a multiple of it. It's a sliding field situation. So it becomes a question of proportions.—Cole Gagne & Tracy Caras (1975).

The *Journal,* as you know, is illustrated by Thoreau, and I removed his drawings and then in chance-determined spaces put musical notations having the duration of one breath, and surrounded by speech; so that the performer has a book which is illustrated with musical notations, and he speaks, he reads, he vocalizes those single breaths. The piece as a whole is a multiplication of the proportions of my silent piece of years ago, and it begins, as the first performance of that did, at Woodstock, with the sound of breeze. In the second movement rain begins, as it did when David Tudor played it in Maverick Hall in the woods near Woodstock. In the third movement originally, the people began speaking when they saw that no sounds were going to be produced by the pianist. But since they're speaking all the way through this work, the *Lecture on the Weather,* the progression is not breeze to rain to speech, it's breeze to rain to thunder. In the live performance in the hall, which will be broadcast, the lights will also go down, and the drawings of Thoreau will appear as lightning in the last part.—Ellsworth Snyder (1975).

I've done a number of works involving environmental sound, ambient sound, and one of them was *Score with Parts* (1974), which I did for the St. Paul Chamber Orchestra. I used the environmental sound of dawn at Stony Point, New York, where I had written the music, and David Behrman made that recording, and he made another recording for me for the piece called *Etcetera.* Again it was ambient sound not at dawn, just anytime during the day. It was composed for a dance that Merce did in Paris called *Un Jour ou deux (One Day or Two).* And when I was invited by the CBC to make a bicentennial piece called *Lecture on the Weather,* I thought also of asking David Behrman to make a recording of wind, rain, and thunder for the whole thing. Somehow he didn't receive the letter that I sent him. He was at York University in Toronto, and it went to the wrong part of the university. It just wasn't received. Finally I telephoned him, but he was then committed and couldn't do it and thought I should engage Maryanne Amacher, for, he said, she did the best recordings of ambient environmental sounds. I knew that her work was very beautiful. I had heard it, and I agreed with him immediately. So I engaged her to do that and her friend Luis Frangella, an Argentinean, to make a film of lightning with the drawings of Thoreau as the flashes of light. So that Thoreau himself became the thunder. And the speakers preferably would be people who had given up their American citizenship and were becoming Canadians, so it was a *dark* bicentennial piece. Like Thoreau, it criticized the government and its history. And the twelve speakers are speaking quotations from the essay on the duty of "Civil Disobedience," the *Journal,* and *Walden,* according to chance operations.

Which are coherent quotations, not fragments, as in Mureau *or* Empty Words*?*

They're coherent, but they're so superimposed that you can't understand anything. It's the same experience you could have if you had twelve radios going at once. Or if you had tuned between stations and could hear several going at once.

That's not the same experience at all, because with Thoreau you're dealing with a fixed and highly charged body of material.

That's true; you're right.—Richard Kostelanetz (1979).

My piece is called *Renga* with *Apartment House 1776,* and right in the title you see rather than one thing being done, two things are being done. The *Renga* has 78 different parts, whereas most pieces for orchestra, I would say, have four parts, because of the theory of harmony; but this isn't using harmony, the *Renga* part. It's a graphic notation, and the graphism comes from the drawings of Thoreau. They have been taken apart so that they read from left to right, as music conventionally does, for an orchestra of 78. In addition to those 78 different parts, there is the *Apartment House,* which in the title is simply the second part. It has four quartets, four instrumental soloists, and four vocal soloists representing four of the people who lived here two hundred years ago—the American Indian, the Sephardic Jew, the Negro slave, and the Protestants. So that with the singers, the soloists, and the quartets, you have twelve more things happening at once. So you have a situation that can't be considered an object but rather resembles an environment.—New England Conservatory (1976).

I'm working now on a piece for orchestra. It's the other bicentennial commission for the Boston Symphony. There were six orchestras, and they commissioned six composers, each orchestra commissioning a single composer; and then the six orchestras have access to these works, though they're not obliged to play them. The only one that's obliged to play is the one that commissioned it. It was the Boston Orchestra, with Seiji Ozawa as conductor, who asked me to write, and I agreed. I don't know the precise nature of what I'm doing yet, but I know that it includes a *renga,* which is Japanese linked poem. *Waka* is a single poem of five-seven-five (which is haiku), plus seven-seven. But *renga* goes on and on, any number of *wakas.* So that this will make a longer piece than the one I wrote a year ago for the St. Paul Chamber Orchestra, which was *Twelve Haikus,* followed by a recording of the dawn at Stony Point [NY]. The notation is not in conventional notation, but is in graphic notation, in that the drawings are the drawings of Thoreau, from his *Journal.* So they can be played by Western instruments or Oriental instruments, and I don't specify or distinguish between string and wind instruments, even. So that for the Boston Orchestra I will write 102 parts, and the conductor will have the score, which gives the drawings, and tells how many instruments are playing in a drawing, and how loud it is. The parts that the players are given will be literally parts of the drawings, so that when all of them play together, the drawings are all expressed. But the expression of the drawing in sound is not the same as the expression of the drawing on paper. Though one would logically look for a connection between the two, poetically one wouldn't. Now whether or not there will be other things in this piece for the orchestra than the *Renga,* I don't yet know. But if I follow my present inclinations, there will be a circus of music that one might have heard in 1776. By "circus" I mean many pieces going on at once, rather than one alone. Because seen from a particular point of view, music is simply the art of focusing attention on one thing at a time. In my recent works, since about '68, I have tried not to focus the attention on one thing at a time, and have used this principle that I call "musicircus"—of having many things going on at once. Which is what takes place in the *Musicircus* [1967] itself, which is not written down but has been performed, and it takes place in *HPSCHD* [1969], and in the *Song Books* [1970].—Cole Gagne & Tracy Caras (1975).

You could make a work in which you only thought of one thing. I have a piece called *Variations IV,* which says nothing about the sounds in it. It says only where they are to be produced. Rather it gives means of finding where these points in space are. You could also make a composition in which you said nothing about the sounds. Your only concern would be when.—Richard Kostelanetz et al. (1977).

How did you come to write Renga *with* Apartment House, 1776*? Can you say anything about the composition itself?*

Yes. There are two pieces which are played together, for the purposes of the Bicentennial Celebration. One is called *Renga,* which is a form of Japanese poetry. The shortest form of *renga* is 36 groups of 5–7–5–7–7 syllables, and that's what my piece is. But instead of having ordinary musical notation, it has drawings of Henry David Thoreau which came from his *Journal,* placed by means of chance operations in spaces comparable to this poetic structure; then taken apart in 78 parts so that they read from left to right. I did that in order that the parts could be played either by contemporary instruments or by instruments of the 18th century, or other instruments including Oriental instruments. Not much advantage has been taken of that by the various orchestras, but nevertheless that possibility exists. Together with that I made a piece called *Apartment House 1776.* I wanted the "1776" to sound like an address. Through chance operations I found 64 pieces, either anthems, hymns, tunes, ballads, two-steps or quick-steps for the military, marches, and imitations of Moravian music. Through that I had to face what I hadn't faced previously in my work: the question of harmony, and I found a way finally of writing harmony that interested me, which was, actually, to subtract from the original pieces, so that the music consisted of silence-sound-silence. So that each sound that occurs in those harmonies is preceeded and followed by a silence. Then the sound comes from its own center, rather than from a theory.—Art Lange (1977).

Satie has avoided problems of being understood through seeming to people to be too simple to bother to analyze, I think—so that people leave his work alive without analyzing it. But I didn't do that. I analyzed it and I still find it beautiful. I think it was because he had, as I've had, a rhythmic (empty time) structure rather than a structure connected with the surface result (the notes). I'm arguing on the other side of the fence from critics who say that my work is trivial since it can't really be analyzed in the conventional sense. What can be analyzed in my work, or criticized, are the questions that I ask. But most of the critics don't trouble to find out what those questions were. And that would make the difference between one composition made with chance operations and another. That is, the principle underlying the results of those chance operations is the questions. The things which should be criticized, if one wants to criticize, are the questions that are asked.

I had the experience, in writing *Apartment House 1776,* of wanting to do something with early American music that would let it keep its flavor at the same time that it would lose what was so obnoxious to me: its harmonic tonality. My first questions were superficial and so resulted in superficial variations on the originals. Not having, as most musicians do, an ear for music, I don't hear music when I write it; I hear it only when it's played. If I heard it when I was writing it, I would write what I've already heard; whereas since I can't hear it while I'm writing it, I'm able to write something that I've never heard before. The result was that I was working so fast, and against a deadline in the case of *Apartment House 1776,* that my first questions were simply questions about subtraction from the original [William] Billings. Namely, seeing that a situation had four notes, I would ask, "Are they all four present, or only three, or two, or one?" And unfortunately, the first time I did it, I did it with respect to a piece that was interesting in itself, so that when I subtracted from it, it remained interesting. When I played it, it was new and beautiful. And so, not being able to hear them, I then did that with respect to the forty-three other pieces, and it took me a long time. When I got to a piano and tried them out, they were miserable. No good at all. Not worth the paper they were written on. It was because the question was superficial. I hadn't found what was at the basis of my trouble with tonal music. I hadn't rid the music of the theory. The cadences all remained recognizable.

Then I thought I should include silence. I did that (asking, "Are four present, or three, or two, or one, or none?") and again wrote a beautiful piece. I again wrote all forty-four pieces and again they were not good. So I came back to the problem and saw that I had to go deeper into it. Finally I took—my question was for each line—which tones of fourteen tones in one of the voices were active, and I would get through chance operations an answer like this: number one, seven, eleven, and fourteen. The first sound I would write from [William] Billings, put it down, and extend it all the way up to the seventh tone; and at the seventh tone, a silence would begin that would last to the eleventh tone. I would then write the eleventh tone, and it would last to the fourteenth, and at the fourteenth, a silence. Therefore, the cadences and everything disappeared; but the flavor remained. You can recognize it as eighteenth-century music; but it's suddenly brilliant in a new way. It is because each sound vibrates from itself, not from a theory. The theory is no longer in power. The cadences which were the function of the theory, to make syntax and all, all of this is gone; so that you get the most marvelous overlappings.

The reactions to that piece have been extraordinary, particularly in Los Angeles about two years ago.

That's because of the superimposition of so-called spiritual musics, which offended some of the Jewish people in the audience.

It was not intended in any way to do this?

No, I was concerned. I knew that something might happen because people who sing such music don't have the habit of singing while another person is singing something else. And I had to explain to each singer carefully what was going to happen to get them to accept that before they did it. It was particularly hard with Helen Schneyer, who said that she didn't think that she'd be able to sing while other people were singing, that her work meant too much to her. She said, "I won't like it," and so I used a simple device. I said, "Life is full of things that we don't necessarily like." But now she loves it. They all love it because it is a kind of ecumenical feeling to have everything, all the churches, so to speak, together. The Indian chief was marvelous; he mostly wouldn't let me talk at all when I first met him.

He talked you over?

Yes, because for years he had given powwows in a tourist trap between Montreal and New York and so he didn't know how to stop talking. Finally I said, "Swifty, I must tell you what it's going to be like for you to sing in this piece." He put his hand on my knee and said, "Don't bother, I understand. There are going to be many things happening all at the same time."—David Cope (1980).

Were the Etudes Australes *the result of a commission?*

No. Grete Sultan was working on my *Music of Changes,* which I had written for David Tudor, that involved hitting the piano with beaters and also with the hands, and it didn't seem to me that an aging lady should hit the piano, and so I told Grete that I would write some pieces for her, and these are the result.

Did you cast around a while before finding the ideas?

Took me months before I got it.

When you came up with the idea of using the star maps?

No, I had that idea at the beginning, but the idea of writing études for the two hands, each hand separate from the other, was original to this piece. I don't think anyone has thought of doing that before. The lower pair of clefs in each system is for the left hand, and the upper pair is for the right, and they both go through full ranges. The right goes from the low A in the bass clef to the top of the piano, and the left goes from the bottom of the piano to the C above the treble, so that the hands are continually crossing. That's what characterizes these études.—Tom Darter (1982).

It uses, as I always do, the chance operations of the *I Ching* whenever a question needs to be asked; otherwise, it uses star maps of *Atlas Australis*—that's why the pieces are called *Etudes Australes.* They move, as not all of my music but a great deal of it does, from one situation to another, so that the first étude has the fewest aggregates, the fewest chords, and the last one theoretically has the largest number of aggregates or chords—two notes at a time, three, four, and five at a time. I had made a catalogue of what triads, quatrads, and quintads could be played by a single hand unassisted by the other, and I found that there were around 550 four-note chords and five-note chords for each hand. This permitted the writing of a music which was not based on harmony, but it permitted harmonies to enter into such a nonharmonic music. How could you express that in political terms? It would permit that attitude expressed socially. It would permit institutions or organizations, groups of people, to join together in a world which was not nationally divided.—Ellsworth Snyder (1975).

How were star maps used in composing the piece? It's obvious that you didn't simply place the maps on some music paper.

I put a transparent strip of about three-quarter-inch width over the maps. It was the width that diminished the number of stars. The trouble with star maps is that there are too many stars to make a piece of music. And within this width I was able to distinguish the twelve tones of a single octave, so this became like putting a strip one octave wide over the map. Then through chance operations I broadcast these tones to the available octaves for the right and the left hands, so that these—the notes on the page—are not the positions of the stars vertically, though they are horizontally; but not all of the stars, because the maps I used were in a variety of colors, and according to chance operations I traced just the blue and green or the red and orange or the yellow and violet stars, or combinations.

What relationship did that have to those aggregates you mentioned before?

After I had the notes, one of the questions I asked was, which of these notes are aggregates, and which are single notes? In the first *Etude* that question is answered by only one number [out of sixty-four possible, through the *I Ching*], whereas in the thirty-second *Etude* it is answered with thirty-two. It ends with a situation which is half aggregates and half tones, or potentially that.

Do you have any interest in synthesizers?

I've worked with David Tudor in what we call live electronic music. Synthesizers lead toward a taped version of something that is fixed, and I've tried to keep things changing. I myself don't keep a collection of records. The few records I have I don't use as records because I don't have a machine to play them on.

The things you've done with David Tudor have used electronic circuits that were created specifically for the purpose of that performance.

Cartridge Music is an example. The situation gets quite confused, with people turning different knobs, the effects of which they have no way of knowing.

And more recently, in pieces called *Child of Tree* and *Branches,* I amplify plant materials with contact microphones and simple sound systems. There I give directions for improvisation because the improvisation can't be based on taste and memory since one doesn't know the instruments.

How exactly does that work?

If I have a piece of cactus, either by means of an alligator clip attachment or by means of a cartridge with a needle in it, I can connect the cactus and the spines with the sound system, and then by plucking one of the spines or touching it with paper or cloth or something, I can get a very beautiful pitched sound, and the pitch relations between the spines of a single piece of cactus often will be very interesting—microtonal.—Tom Darter (1982).

Could you tell us something about the structure of Branches?

It's improvisation within a structure determined by chance operations, so that what each musician has is eight minutes divided by chance operations into smaller groups, not of seconds, but of minutes. So it would be, for example, four minutes, two minutes, one minute, one minute. Or it might be four minutes, four minutes; or it might be three minutes, two minutes, two minutes, one minute. Then there are ten instruments, and what is an instrument can be determined by each performer. For instance, one spine could be one instrument, another spine another. Or the whole cactus could be an instrument, and there are ten of those, and the tenth one is the pod rattle and must go in the last section of the eight minutes. Then between one eight-minute performance and another there is to be silence, also determined by chance.

I had thought of it, if it were to be played by a number of people, as it was the other evening, as being determined by each person independently of the other. But what the Nexus group did was to determine it for the whole group, and to play it in what you might call vertical harmony, rather than, as I had imagined it, contrapuntally, with each person independent of the other. I explained to them that their understanding of the piece was different from mine, but my directions are actually always ambiguous, and I do that in order to leave the door open for a musician to make an original use of the material.

Did you work with Nexus on Branches *prior to the performance?*

No. No, I just let them do what they do. If you would ask me—because they probably would if we had a chance to talk—of what I thought of the performance and so forth, I would lead them away from continual activity to a sense of silence as activity. So that within one of the structures, say, four minutes, it's not necessary to be continually making sound. You can fill that four minutes by simply putting one sound halfway through the third minute. Instead of being a lawmaker I would like to have my work take on the character of stimulus or suggestion. I don't mean that in terms of license, but in terms of poetry.—Laura Fletcher & Thomas Moore (1983).

Most people knowledgeable with your life know that you are an expert in mycology. How has your study and work with mushrooms paralleled your work with sound, or has it?

I certainly think that is true in my case with mushrooms. I've had for a long time the desire to hear the mushroom itself, and that would be done with very fine technology, because they are dropping spores and those spores are hitting surfaces. There certainly is sound taking place. I mentioned this in the last article in *Silence,* in that humorous article. I would still like to do that. It leads, of course, to the thought about hearing anything in the world since we know that everything is in a state of vibration, so that not only mushrooms, but also chairs and tables, for instance, could be heard. One could go to an exhibition of sounds in which you would see something and hear it as well. I would like to do that.

Are you familiar with some of the work that was done about eight years ago with wiring plants with electrodes and tying these through synthesizers?

Yes, I've done that.

What were the results?

It was most interesting, and I have a project (unfortunately it hasn't taken place yet) to amplify a city park for children. It was to be done at Ivrea near Turino where the Olivetti company is. There is a marvelous hill in the center of the city that is high and has a beautiful view of the Alps, and is isolated enough from the traffic sounds so that you could hear the sounds of the plants. The project fell through, but I was invited to do the same kind of project in Rome and also in Zagreb; but I haven't accepted it until I accept the place. I was spoiled by that marvelous situation in Ivrea where the silence—when you weren't playing the plants—was very audible and beautiful; you could hear it as if you were in a concert hall. In other words, I wanted the silence of the mountain to be heard by the children after they had heard the sounds that they themselves had made by playing the plants. We were going to have a programmed arrangement so that every now and then the plants were going to become unplayable, and the children would be obliged to hear the silence. Otherwise the children would have been making noises continually.

Did you hear the music with cactus [*Child of Tree*]? That was what that came out of. For a dance of Merce Cunningham's I used cacti. I made the sounds on cacti and a few other plant materials. That led to the idea of amplifying a park, and that's led to the idea that I've found quite fascinating: a piece of music performed by animals, and butterflies, which sounds fantastic now but is almost within reach, I think, with our technology.—David Cope (1980).

Have you done some things with water before?

I have a piece called *Inlets* [1977] where there's water in conch shells and you can fill them to any level you wish. And as you tip the shells they gurgle. If that's amplified, it can be heard.

Then I did a piece called *Water Walk* [1959]. I think that was a piece for television. I had a bathtub, a piano, I forgot what else. And then another called *Water Music* [1952]. Handel had done that before, except mine had real water in it.—Mark Bloch (1987)

Do you consider works such as Branches *and* Inlets *to be an extension of something that you were doing in* Cartridge Music, *or does the inclusion of natural objects have a significance that makes the works totally different?*

No, they're a move in the direction of improvisation.

You've frequently spoken out against improvisation, because it relies so heavily upon habit and personal taste.

I'm finding ways to free the act of improvisation from taste and memory and likes and dislikes. If I can do that, then I will be very pleased.

In the case of the plant materials, you don't know them; you're discovering them. So the instrument is unfamiliar. If you become very familiar with a piece of cactus, it very shortly disintegrates, and you have to replace it with another one that you don't know. So the whole thing remains fascinating, and free of your memory as a matter of course.

In the case of *Inlets,* you have no control whatsoever over the conch shell when it's filled with water. You tip it and you get a gurgle, sometimes; not always. So the rhythm belongs to the instruments, and not to you.

Cartridge Music has several people performing programs that they have determined by means of the materials. But one person's actions unintentionally alter another person's actions, because the actions involve changing the tone controls and the amplitude controls. So you may find yourself playing something and getting no sound whatsoever.—Cole Gagne & Tracy Caras (1980).

I received a letter from the very fine violinist Paul Zukofsky, and after I finish the work I'm working on now, I will work on a piece for him. He said that since my return, through the piano études that I wrote for Grete Sultan, the *Etudes Australes,* a return, as he put it, to stricter notation of music, that he would hope that I would write something for violin. When I went to see him the other day, I asked him what he thought was lacking in strictness about the piece I wrote in the fifties for a string player that is graphic, and for some reason he thought that that was suggestive of spontaneity. Whereas nothing could be more strict than graphic notation, since you could take a ruler, as I took to write it, and find out exactly what was to be played. In fact, that notation is so strict, that I felt that I was putting the performer in a strait jacket. It was that tendency, which is exhibited also in the *Music of Changes,* that was one of the things that led me toward greater indeterminacy, leaving freedom to the performer.

There are two works for a string player that can still come out sounding very different from performance to performance, in terms of the arrangement of the graphs themselves. Was it the problem that the graphs were so specific that bothered you?

No. They could sound different because I don't specify what can be done on a single string. I had found through talk to the New Music String Quartet—Broadus Erle, Claus Adam, [Matthew] Raimondi, and [Walter] Trampler—that no one is in agreement as to what can be done on a stringed instrument. Ask two people how many notes can be played on the G string, and you'll get two different answers. Zukofsky now is writing and studying very carefully the possibilities of the violin, and I have somewhere here in these papers now tables that he gave me—and he's going to make further tables—of what can actually be done, and what the physical action is in playing the violin.—Cole Gagne & Tracy Caras (1975).

He really likes—I suppose most violinists do—things to be in conventional notation. He's willing to play what we loosely call quarter tones and so forth, but he wants to be told how much of a quarter tone it is. He told me that he was like a surgeon and that if he knew what it was that he had to do, he could do it. And he is a marvelous musician. Anyway, I don't play the violin, but I've gotten involved through this collaboration with him in the writing again of a very difficult music that has to do with the making of something that requires a great deal of rehearsal. But, that rehearsal is not on the part of an orchestra; it's on the part of a dedicated soloist.—Jack Behrens (1981).

Now I'm making some songs with the same title [*Ryoanji*] and I thought that I should make a difference. First I wrote some songs that were just like the oboe pieces. It was as though I was continuing writing for the oboe, and instead was writing for the voice. And I thought, "No, that's wrong, the voice is different, and I must write it differently." I began to write something different, and again I felt myself to be "ungifted," in the dark, not knowing how to do it.

I was watering the plants, and I had rather clearly in my mind the impression of how I would go about writing for the voice. And so I picked up the phone and called the singer and I made an appointment, actually for yesterday at two. This was two days ago. So then when yesterday came, and it was getting closer and closer to the time of seeing the singer, I was almost on the point of saying, "No, it isn't right," and calling her up and saying that there was no need for it. But then I decided to go on with it, and I showed her what the new idea was and then what the oboe idea was, and it was the oboe idea that was right. You could tell when she sang it, not only from how it sounded but from the way she seemed to be when she was looking at the music; so then actually the new idea was getting closer to the drone, and the old idea wasn't anywhere near the drone. So I think what's happening is that when I start to work now I'm trying to go in response to those drones, and that I haven't found my way yet.—Morton Feldman (Bunita Marcus and Francesco Pellizzi) (1983).

I'm now calling these pieces ☙*Branches, Inlets* & *Child of Tree*❧ *Improvisation 1* and *2*, then there will be *3* and *4* ☙and, more recently, for *BL Lacerta, A* and *B*❧. Number *3* is the piece we do for Merce's dance called *Duets* and number *4* is the one we do for *Fielding Sixes.* And there we use cassette machines, playing cassettes in a special way. Number *3* is simply playing them all pianissimo, and there must be four players. Then each one in the period of the whole time is allowed one crescendo. It makes a very nice situation. Each person has the same material. In that case we have six cassettes. And in the case of *Fielding Sixes,* John Fullemann made an arrangement so that you can slide the speed of the machine. Then we have twelve recordings and they're constantly sliding. Four people playing the same ones and different ones going on at the same time—sometimes the same, but never at the same moment. ☙This piece was being revised in 1986 to be more like *Improvisation 3,* its mirror version. That is, rather than one crescendo, there will be "descents" into silence from a general mezzo-amplitude; and there will be no sliding.❧—Andrew Timar et al. (1981).

At what stage are the Freeman Etudes *now?*

The first sixteen were finished, and then [Paul] Zukofsky discovered that I had learned a little bit too much about what was violinistic. When I had a B above the treble clef, it could be played on any one of the four strings. But if it seemed to me to be more appropriate to the first or the second string, I would then not involve the third or the fourth string in the chance operations. When he discovered that, he suggested—and I agreed—to go back over the string indications to find out again what string should be used when it was at all physically possible. Then I go over it with him again, and where it's literally too difficult, just impossible, then he refuses the chance operation. He accepts some and refuses others, so it never gets to be a pure chance situation. But it goes more toward that than it did.

So they're being revised. The first six are finished, and two more have been revised but not yet copied. Then we'll go on through to the sixteenth. I've begun work on the last sixteen. ☙They will be recorded not by Zukofsky, who recorded I-VIII, but by Janos Negyesy, who now plays I-XVI.❧

It's given Zukofsky notions of things that could be done that he didn't know about. I'm keeping a record of all of his answers to my questions, and he proposes to go over them and publish them.—Cole Gagne & Tracy Caras (1980).

Some of these works are very difficult.

They are, yes, they're very difficult.

Did you have a virtuostic element in mind?

Yes, and these are intentionally as difficult as I can make them, because

I think we're now surrounded by very serious problems in the society, and we tend to think that the situation is hopeless and that it's just impossible to do something that will make everything turn out properly. So I think that this music, which is almost impossible, gives an instance of the practicality of the impossible.—Laura Fletcher & Thomas Moore (1983).

Are you distressed that the interest in [your early] works might be at the expense of your more recent works?

No, I don't think that that's the case because some people play the newer music too. In particular, the recent études for piano and violin interest many people. So I don't think that there's any problem.

My basic attitude toward all this is that I have my life, and my music has its. The two are independent of each other. I'm of course interested in the life of my music, but after a while I'll die and it'll have to take care of itself, so I'm trying to let it take care of itself to begin with.

In your recent music, do you feel a carryover from one piece to the next?

No, another thing happens with me. I work in many ways in a given time period. And not only do I make music, but I write texts, and now I make etchings. I do all of these things in different ways. Some ideas that I have I drop, and others I pick up from the past, and so on. So it's not a linear situation. It's more like overlapping layers. For instance, at one extreme you have the *Freeman Etudes* for violin, which are very determinate; they are written down in as exact a notation as I can make. (That was a request of Paul Zukofsky, with whom I've been writing them.) But at the same time I'm developing an interest in improvisation, which is probably freer than anything I've done before (including the indeterminate music).—Cole Gagne & Tracy Caras (1980).

How do you use the chance operations?

In the particular case of these violin études I start with star maps and I place transparent sheets on them. I place the star map at a point which is convenient for the paper. The maps I use have blue, green, orange, yellow, red, and violet colors. I combine the blue and green, the red and orange, the yellow and violet, then make these colors singly or in pairs, or all three; and that gives seven different densities. My first question to the *I Ching* is, "Which of those seven possibilities (blue/green, red/orange, yellow/violet, red/orange, blue/green with red/orange with yellow/violet) am I dealing with?" Meanwhile I have made a table relating the number 7 to the number 64. The number of hexagrams in the *I Ching* is 64. If I divide 7 into 64 I get 9 with a remainder of 1. That means one group is a group of 10. The six groups, 1 from 7, are groups of 9. I arrange the tables so that three groups of 9 are the beginning of the 64 and then the group of 10 is in the middle, then the other three groups of 9 are at the end. Then

I can toss three coins six times or I can use as I do a computer printout. A young man at Illinois [Ed Kobrin] made a computer program for me. It makes my work quicker than it would be if I used coins or the yarrow sticks.

The result is I quickly know which stars I am to trace. Then my next question is how many stars am I to trace? I take simply a number, 1 to 64, and then after I've done it, I ask, "What next am I to do?" Then when I finish enough tracings to make two pages of music—which was my decision at the beginning, to have each étude have two pages (so the violinist wouldn't have to turn pages)—I now have a band of tracings of the stars, and it's been designed so that it's wide enough for me to distinguish the twelve tones. These twelve tones can appear in different octaves in the violin. My next question is which octave it is in. I put that down, then I take the papers, and I can then transcribe the stars to paper.

Each one of the stars is not a single tone, it might be an aggregate, it might be two tones or it might be three or it might be legato or not and so forth. My next process was to find which passages are legato and which passages are détaché. Instead of making it even—that is to say, 1 to 32 being détaché, and 33 to 64 being legato—what I do is I ask the *I Ching* where the dividing point is between legato and détaché, and it might say it's number 7, so then 1–6 would be détaché and 7–64 would be legato. And then I ask the *I Ching,* "For how long does that last?" and it might say for fifty-three events. After fifty-two events, I ask again. Then all the other questions that can make a tone in detached style special and different from another one are posed. I list all the possibilities and then find out which ones are operative.

When I start building up intervals or triads or quatrads on the strings, I then through chance operations find out which finger is touching which note on which string. Then I call up Paul Zukofsky to ask what he can reach with which other finger which chance determines; then I catalogue his answers. I index them in a book. He thinks we will eventually publish his responses because we're getting to know what is possible in the way of 2-, 3-, and 4-note chords in the way that he himself is surprised at. He is surprised at what we are learning in this work we are doing together. Rather than working from choices I work from asking questions, so that the composition is determined by the questions that are asked and you can quickly tell if your questions are radical. By radical I mean penetrating. If they are not radical, the answers aren't.

If they are basic, then what happens is something that you haven't heard before.—Maureen Furman (1979).

Are you rigorous in your subscription to chance?

Yes, and I suppose there's a contradiction there.

How does your composition differ from a mechanical dice roller inscribing notes in paper? Is the intellectual input all in the initial concept of the composition's structure?

Yes. In my new piece for Cabrillo [music festival], *Dance/Four Orchestras,* I divide the orchestra into four parts, with four conductors, going at four speeds. My idea was to subject the choice of strong beats to chance.

The material is conventional, but its use is unconventional. It's a circus situation because four things are going on at once—a four-ring circus!

How did you choose the title?

I divided the orchestra into four parts because that way the manuscript would fit my publisher's 11-by-17-inch reproducing machine.—Paul Hertelendy (1982).

When you work with percussion, you work with instruments that you actually have in hand. If you leave those instruments where they are and go to another city and look for the same instruments there, you won't find them. You may find similar instruments, but if you listen to the sounds they produce, you'll hear that they produce different sounds than you heard in the previous city from the first collection of instruments. The nature of percussion music, then, is quite open and often quite unpredictable. If you listen to the sounds around you, no matter where you are, you will enjoy the sounds if you hear them in that open fashion, so that you become attentive to what happens rather than insistent about what should happen.

I just finished a piece for orchestra called *Ryoanji,* which is the name of a garden in Kyoto [with fifteen stones in raked sand], but the piece preceding it, which is like it, is for solo percussionist. In making the piece for orchestra, I didn't really change it radically from what it was as a percussion piece. There will be twenty instruments in the orchestra piece, but no instrument is specified. It could be any twenty instruments, and any one of the twenty parts could go to any of the twenty instruments. All of the instruments will play the same rhythm, and all of the instruments can produce any sound, or any combination of sounds, the instruments can produce. Once a musician decides what sound he is making, he must, throughout that rehearsal or performance, make the same sound, as though he becomes the player of a single percussion instrument. There are notations in the score for playing a little ahead of the beat, or a little behind the beat, or on the beat. There are also notations for playing a short sound and playing a sound for its full length. Those are the only variations. It means that piece, each time it is played, will have a different sound that can't be predicted by the composer, the performers, or the listeners. And yet, each time they heard it, they would know what was happening.—Bill Shoemaker (1984).

I think what I'd like is to talk to you about the most recent experiences I've been having with sound, which were surprising to me. They concern drones that are so much with us when we're inside houses or even concert halls; I spent my life thinking we should try to get rid of them. We of course never do get rid of them, because if the drone of the refrigerator, for instance, stopped, we'd call someone and get him to start it going again. We'd be more concerned with keeping the food in good condition than with the acoustic experience. But what has happened is that I'm beginning to enjoy those sounds, I mean that I now actually listen to them with the kind of enjoyment with which I listen to the traffic. Now, the traffic is easy to recognize as beautiful, but those drones are more difficult and I didn't really set out to find them beautiful. It's just that in, say, the last three months they are, so to speak, coming to me.

Well, we try to ignore them or we walk away from them like a person who has a refrigerator in his house that acts up occasionally.

The ones that behave erratically—I don't know about your refrigerator, but the expression "acts up" suggests that it's not a plain drone, it's something else; and that would be obviously beautiful. But it's just the ordinary drone that's becoming interesting to me. And, as I said, I have a feeling that it's as though the sound was finally reaching me rather than I was reaching it.

Well, actually—by just concentrating, by accepting it—you're probably just getting into its focus like any other tone; you're accepting it as a very focused tone.

What's beginning to happen that goes along with that is a heightened awareness and interest in *where* sounds are. For instance, this one that we're hearing now that comes from the humidifier, in back of me, and you can see that it is as interesting as a rock or something. It defines a point in space.

Do you think of inventing your own drones?

I'm writing a number of different pieces with the same title, *Ryoanji*, after the garden in Kyoto. I made a piece for percussion that looks less to me like any music I've ever written; but today when I was looking at it, and I knew you were coming, suddenly it looked to me like hearing these . . .

You asked whether I would invent a drone; well, this comes close to that except it's not really a drone, because it's metrical music for percussion. I don't say what instruments, but I do say that there should be at least two instruments in unison, and I told Michael Pugliese who's playing it, for whom I wrote it—that if he could use five or six and get a constant unison, I would like that very much.—Morton Feldman (Bunita Marcus and Francesco Pellizzi) (1983).

I have spent most of my time in recent years working with what are now called acoustic instruments, rather than electronic instruments, the reason being that many young people now work with electronics very beautifully—and my longtime associate, David Tudor, and David Behrman do also—so that I have the feeling that work is being done. What I've tried to do in recent years is find freshness and newness in the situations that are the most conventional—acoustic piano without preparations, and the violin, and recently, the flute, the voice, and the double bass. My recent work is not electronic. I have been exploring in this set of pieces called *Ryoanji*—not the ones for percussion or for orchestra, but for soloists: oboe, flute, voice, double bass—glissandi within that limited range. The ranges change from one piece to another. Some are very narrow, and some are wider; but none are wider than an octave. What I was searching for in each case with each instrument was that part of the range that yielded a very smooth glissando.—Bill Shoemaker (1984).

One difference between [Harry] Partch and myself—also a difference between myself and Lou Harrison—is that they became interested in intonation and control of microtones, whereas I went from the twelve tones into the whole territory of sound. I took noise as the basis of it. I don't try to make the situation between what is musical and not musical more refined as both Partch and Harrison do; but I start from the other direction, from noise, and don't use sounds that don't do honor to noise.

And I suggest that the same thing might bring about an improvement in society; that instead of basing our laws on the rich as we have, that we would do well to base them on the poor. If we can have laws that make poverty comfortable, then those laws will do well for the rich; but the other way around is oppressive.—David Cope (1980).

I'm listening now to the sounds in the street; and I'm writing a new piece that will have as part of it, of its material, a recording of this traffic.

Especially this sound of cars driving over manhole covers?

Yes, which recurs.

So it doesn't have any regular rhythm?

Well, the rhythm it has is going to be so slow, the beat of this music is going to be so slow, that I don't think you would be able to understand it as rhythm.—Birger Ollrogge (1985).

I always want to start from zero and make, if I can, a discovery. Some works, of course, fall together in a group as, for instance, the *Sonatas and Interludes* or, recently, the Quartets for Concert Band and Amplified Voices, and for orchestras and *Hymns and Variations* for 12 amplified voices form a group. So that a new piece in such a group is one more in a field of possibilities, the field itself already having been discovered. Sometimes this discovery is of material (plant materials as in *Child of Tree* and *Branches,* water-filled conches as in *Inlets,* or, earlier, radios as in *Imaginary Landscape No. 4*) and sometimes it is of compositional means as in the *Music of Changes* or, currently, the *Freeman Etudes* for unaccompanied violin and *Roaratorio* for folk musicians, speech and tape. I do not know what role this desire to start from zero plays in my music except that my father was an inventor and in my work I have tried to follow in his footsteps though he was an electrical engineer and not a musician.—*The Composer* (1980).

Do you have any unfulfilled ambitions?

I have unfulfilled projects. In particular, the thing I would like to do is make what I call the "Thunder Piece," which is to record an actual thunder storm and then use the thunderclaps of *Finnegans Wake* sung by a chorus and electronically transformed ☙to fill up the sound envelopes❧. And then the orchestra would be the rain. This is a project suggested years ago by Marshall McLuhan.—Jeff Goldberg (1976).

You've mentioned a work about rain.

That is "Atlas Borealis and the Ten Thunderclaps." I haven't begun it yet.

Then you don't mind talking about your ideas before you've begun to realize them. Aren't you fearful that someone will steal them?

We don't own ideas anymore, so no one can steal them. If someone gets the notion of doing "Atlas Borealis and the Ten Thunderclaps," then I won't have to do it, and so I publicize it as much as possible.—Geneviere Marcus (1970).

Would it be accurate to say that there is a polemical feature to your work as a composer? Are you more interested in changing the way music is perceived by audiences, performers, and composers than you are in changing the shape or history of music itself?

I think there is a didactic element in my work. I think that music has to do with self-alteration; it begins with the alteration of the composer and conceivably extends to the alteration of the listeners. It by no means secures that, but it does secure the alteration in the mind of the composer, changing the mind so that it is changed not just in the presence of music, but in other situations too.—Cole Gagne & Tracy Caras (1980).

Do you perhaps think of your music as serving the hoped-for deinstitutionalized future, or the future of deinstitutionalized society?

I hope that it is, but I am not certain that it is usefully so.

Why not?

Well, because I know in my own case that I can change myself through what I do in music, that I can become a different individual. My mind can change. My thoughts about sounds and my experience of sounds has changed through my making of music. And the change that has taken place is that, rather than depending upon music for the expression of ideas or the experience of emotions, I find my greatest acoustic, esthetic pleasure in simply the sounds of the environment. So that I no longer have any need not only for other people's music but I have no need really for my own music. I am happier without any music. And the only reason I go on making it is because people insist upon it.

Now, since I have seen this revolution take place in my mind with respect to music, and since I agree with Marshall McLuhan that the whole society is now an extension of the central nervous system, I could hope that the world mind of which we all are a part could change; but I am not certain that it would change as a result of music.

What would you do if people did not ask you to make music?

Perhaps we have to go back to my silent piece. Implicit in this piece which is called *4′33″* and which has three movements, implicit in it is that the movements can be of any length. I think what we need in the field of music is a very long performance of that work. It is the fulfillment of my obligations in some way to other people, and I wanted to show that doing something that is not music is music.—Nikša Gligo (1972).

Then why do you bother writing music?

The answer is simple. I promised Schoenberg—my teacher—to devote my life to music. The fact that I enjoy all these sounds doesn't mean that I should stop writing music which may lead other people in this direction, don't you think?

Besides, how would I spend my life? Of course, I have lots of things to do, and as I get older there are more and more things that interest me, including macrobiotics. But I'd go on writing music even though personally I have no need for it.—Maureen Furman (1979).

HIS PERFORMANCES

As far as I know, all my music has been performed. One of the things that impressed me when I worked with Adolph Weiss was that he had written a large amount of music and almost none of it was played. He was somewhat embittered because of this, and I determined then and there that if I did get to the point of writing music I would consider my responsibility only half-finished if I didn't get it performed. I don't think of music as finished when it's simply written down.—Jeff Goldberg (1976).

My rule is that I won't write something unless it is going to be performed, and I will make every effort to get it performed. So, when I travel, whether I was young, or now, it is generally in relation to that. Roughly I would say 1952, or perhaps 1954, is the turning point. Before that time, I had to make the effort to get it performed. Now other people make the effort and I have to respond by traveling.—Alcides Lanza (1971).

What's your definition of theater?

I try to make definitions that won't exclude. I would simply say that theater is something that engages both the eye and the ear. The two public senses are seeing and hearing; the senses of taste, touch, and odor are more proper to intimate, nonpublic situations. The reason I want to make my definition of theater that simple is so one could view everyday life as theater.

Is a concert a theatrical activity?

Yes, even a conventional piece played by a conventional symphony orchestra: the horn player, for example, from time to time empties the spit out of his horn. And this —when I was as a child, taken to an orchestra concert— frequently engaged my attention more than the melodies, harmonies, etc.

How about listening to recorded music?

I find that most interesting when one finds something in the environment to look at. If you're in a room and a record is playing and the window is open and there's some breeze and a curtain is blowing, that's sufficient, it seems to me, to produce a theatrical experience. When you're lying down and listening, you're having an intimate, interiorly realized theater which I would—if I were going to exclude anything—exclude from my definition of theater as a public occasion. In other words you're doing something by yourself that's extremely difficult to describe or relate to anyone accurately. I think of theater as an occasion involving any number of people, but not just one.—Michael Kirby & Richard Schechner (1965).

In the earlier indeterminant works, such as Variations II, *which can be for any complement of performers, I'm curious about your feelings toward the results. Does it make a difference to you how it comes out? Are you concerned as to how one performance of* Variations II *will sound as opposed to another?*

When it's clear that the person who is realizing the work is doing his work not only in the spirit of the composition, but in such a way as to free him from his choices, then I think it makes no difference what the results are, because we're not really interested in results. Results are like deaths. What we're interested in is things going on, and changing, not in their being fixed. But when someone uses a piece like that, that they think is free, in order to do anything they want to do, when I say, for instance, "Make a disciplined action," I'm not saying, "Do whatever you like," and yet that's precisely what some people now think I'm saying. That's why recently in Buffalo there was a seminar in which I was obliged after what I thought was a very poor performance of the *Song Books* to speak as I am speaking now, and point out not uncertainly that the freedoms I've given have not been given to permit just anything that one wants to do, but have been invitations for people to free themselves from their likes and dislikes, and to discipline themselves.—Cole Gagne & Tracy Caras (1975).

Performers: need they dress formally?

They're just relating to the previous costume, aren't they? It's also a little bit of comic costume. That is a possibility. It could be comic, revolutionary. It could be an attempt to give stature to what the public might consider debatable as music. I did it originally. Well, the first concerts I gave, I gave in unconventional costume. The girls had blouses and skirts, the men had shirts and slacks. That was all. Then when I gave my first percussion concert in '43 at the Museum of Modern Art, we all dressed up formally and I think it was an attempt to say that, too, was music. Then I dropped all that.

. . . or could they be heard and not seen?

Fortunately, I had an experience very early about this. I had organized four people to rehearse to play professionally, and we did all kinds of odd things to make sounds. I invited my mother to come hear it, and she said she thought the sounds were very interesting, but all the things we were doing to produce them were very distracting, and that she would like to hear it without seeing those distractions. So we pulled a curtain across. Then when people heard the music, they said, it's very nice but we wonder how in heaven's name you make the sounds.—Don Finegan et al. (1969).

Even a bad performance may help to educate musicians and listeners to the possibilities of this new work, and stretch their capabilities to be interested in their experiences.—Calvin Tomkins (1965).

But if somebody performs your music in a way that is completely different from your initial concept, from your compositional idea, what would you then think of him?

Oh, I would think that was excellent. In Zen Buddhism, which has interested me for a long time, if the student asks the teacher a question and the teacher gives the answer and then the teacher asks the student the same question and he gives the same answer, he gets hit over the head.—Nikša Gligo (1972).

You said once, "I try to get it so that people realize that they themselves are doing their experience and that it's not being done *to them." Isn't all art done to you?*

It has been, but I think we're changing that. When you have the proscenium stage and the audience arranged in such a way that they all look in the same direction—even though those on the extreme right and left are said to be in "bad seats" and those in the center are in "good seats"—the assumption is that people will see *it* if they all look in one direction. But our experience nowadays is not so focused at one point. We live in, and are more and more aware of living in, the space *around* us. Current developments in theater are changing architecture from the Renaissance notion to something else which relates to our lives. That was the case with the theater in the round. But that never seemed to me to be any real change from the proscenium, because it again focused people's attention and the only thing that changed was that some people were seeing one side of the thing and the other people the other side.

It could, of course, produce more interesting conversation afterward or during intermission, because people didn't see the same side. It was like the story of the blind men with the elephant. More pertinent to our daily experience is a theater in which we ourselves are in the round, in which activity takes place around us. The seating arrangement [in the first "Happening'] I had at Black Mountain in 1952 was a square composed of four triangles merging toward the center, but not meeting. The center was a larger space that would take movement, and the aisles between those four triangles also admitted of movement. The audience could see itself, which is, of course, the advantage of any theater in the round. The larger part of the action took place *outside* of that square. In each one of the seats was a cup, and it wasn't explained to the audience what to do with this cup—some used it as an ashtray—but the performance was concluded by a kind of ritual, pouring coffee into each cup.—Michael Kirby & Richard Schechner (1966).

I think that the Happening business came about through circumstances of being at Black Mountain where there were a number of people present—Merce was there, David Tudor was there, there was an audience.

. . . The Happening resulted from the fact that there were many people and many possibilities and we could do it quickly. In fact, I thought of it in the morning, and it was performed that afternoon—I was able to sketch it all out.—Deborah Campana (1985).

What were you trying to do?

Well, M. C. [Richards] had translated *The Theater and Its Double* of [Antonin] Artaud, and we got the idea from Artaud that theater could take place free of a text, that if a text were in it, that it needn't determine the other actions, that sounds, that activities, and so forth, could all be free rather than tied together; so that rather than the dance expressing the music or the music expressing the dance, that the two could go together independently, neither one controlling the other. And this was extended on this occasion not only to music and dance, but to poetry and painting, and so forth, and to the audience. So that the audience was not focused in one particular direction.

So, actually, there was planning behind this event, and intent?

Of course. It was very quickly arranged, but the ideas were all there. And a score was made.

I made a score, which I don't think I have any longer, that gave what I called "time brackets." So that [Charles] Olson, instead of reading his poetry when he wished, had a particular "time bracket" within which he could do that. And the lecture that I gave included long silences.—Mary Emma Harris (1974).

Would you describe the whole performance?

At one end of a rectangular hall, the long end, was a movie and at the other end were slides. I was up on a ladder delivering a lecture which included silences and there was another ladder which M. C. Richards and Charles Olson went up at different times. During periods that I called time brackets, the performers were free within limitations—I think you would call them compartments—compartments they didn't have to fill, like a green light in traffic. Until this compartment began, they were not free to act, but once it had begun they could act as long as they wanted to during it. Robert Rauschenberg was playing an old-fashioned phonograph that had a horn and a dog on the side listening, and David Tudor was playing a piano, and Merce Cunningham and other dancers were moving through the audience and around the audience. Rauschenberg's pictures were suspended about the audience. . . .

Those were the "white paintings."

Right. He was also painting black ones at the time, but I think we used only the white ones. They were suspended at various angles, a canopy of painting above the audience. I don't recall anything else except the ritual with the coffee cup. I remember a lady coming in at the beginning, Mrs. Jalowetz, who was the widow of the man who had formerly headed the music department. She had made a point of coming very early in order to get the best seat. And she asked me where the best seat was and I said they were all equally good.—Michael Kirby & Richard Schechner (1965).

[What drama have you truly liked?]

I think I can count on one hand the plays I have seen that have truly interested me or involved me.

However, this bleak state of affairs has produced not just a state of inactivity in the theater, but it has produced two things I would like to point out.

First of all in this country, the movement of the modern dance, which, I think, essentially, as it diverges from the classic ballet, is a new form of theater. We have many varieties of it.

Then, after the development of the modern dance here, say in the thirties, in the forties many of us become aware of the thinking and action of Antonin Artaud. This indicated a theater . . . that would not use all of its means toward a literary end so that a form of theater other than the one he has spoken of would develop, and it has. We call it the Happening.

Now, I really believe and practice that a mediocre Happening will be more meaningful, more useful to us as a theatrical occasion, than even attendance at a literary theatrical masterpiece.—Stanley Kauffmann (1966).

Would you regard yourself as antitheatrical the way Jasper Johns is sometimes called antitheatrical?

No. I love the theater. In fact, I used to think when we were so close together—Earle Brown, Morton Feldman, Christian Wolff, David Tudor, myself [in the early and mid-1950s]—I used to think that the thing that distinguished my work from theirs was that mine was theatrical. I didn't think of Morty's work as being theatrical. It seemed to me to be more, oh, you might say, lyrical. ☙Morty is a great poet, and he is often inspired.❧ And Christian's work seemed to me more musical, more really purely musical. That's not true of his later music, which is politically idealistic. ☙I've changed my mind. Wolff's music remains musical because he keeps the principles of repetition and variations.❧ Earle's seemed to me, oh, more conventional, more European. He was still involved, you might say, in musical discourse ☙or soliloquy❧, whereas I seemed to be involved in theater. What could be more theatrical than the silent pieces—somebody comes on the stage and does absolutely nothing—David Shapiro (1985).

So you advocate a return of the condition of art that perhaps it was in the Renaissance, when it existed, but people weren't so aware of it. They banqueted in halls and they were surrounded by great paintings and they listened to music, but they talked while the music was on. Do you see this as a future position of art, perhaps?

I see it as the present one, actually. It began for me, I mean this experience began for me in Washington. David Tudor and I were performing my *Variations VI.* First those left who found the whole thing insupportable, then those who were interested stayed and began moving around the room and conversing and those who were most interested came close to see what we were doing, and shortly they began talking with us while we were performing, sometimes relevantly and sometimes irrelevantly. Now in *Variations IV,* in the case of the performance in Hollywood about two years ago, some people came up to me while I was performing (it was in an art gallery) and I was unwilling to talk to them because I thought I was performing, and when they talked to me, I didn't reply, or if I did, I think I did to one person who was quite insistent, I simply said, "Don't you see that I'm busy?" Whereas in the case of *Variations VI,* this whole need to be busy had dropped away. The work was being done, which reminds me of that haiku poem *Taking a Nap.* What is it? "Taking a nap, I pound the rice." That is to say, by doing nothing, everything gets done.

That is true and false.

I think we have to say yes to what you just said. Yes, it is true and false, but it's very true.

Do you see music at all related to ritual, as a ritualistic act?

Well, I imagine now a music in the future which would be quite ritualistic. It would be simply by means of technology a revelation of sound even where we don't expect that it exists. For instance, in an area with an audience, the arrangement of such things so that this table, for instance, around which we're sitting, is made experiential as sound, without striking it. It is, we know, in a state of vibration. It is therefore making a sound, but we don't yet know what that sound is.—David Sylvester & Roger Smalley (1967).

You see, the old idea was that the composer was the genius, the conductor ordered everyone around, and the performers were slaves. In our music, no one is boss. We all work together.—Arlynn Nellhaus (1968)

What we are trying to do basically is to get three people to work together who [otherwise] make each other miserable. I've gotten more interested in the social aspect of making music. If people can work together well, it is an optimistic notion of society.—Robert Commanday (1968).

Old music was competitive. It divided people, just like the social system. New music brings people together to work and use technology for the common good. It's changing society.—Arlynn Nellhaus (1968).

How did you move into the theater thing?

Experience with the dance led me there. The reflection that a human being isn't just ears but also has eyes, I think it was this. Around 1945, '46, '47, I became concerned about music, and I determined not to continue with this activity unless it was useful, and unless I found answers that struck me as being sufficient reason to devote one's life to it. I found through Oriental philosophy, my work with Suzuki, that what we are doing is living, and that we are not moving toward a goal but are, so to speak, at the goal constantly and changing with it, and that art, if it is going to do anything useful, should open our eyes to this fact. Before the *Theater Piece* [1960] I did two pieces for television. One was called *Water Walk* and one was called *Sounds of Venice* [1959]. I called it *Water Walk* [1959] because of the *Music Walk* [1958]; and the *Music Walk*, I think you would agree, is a theatrical work. Before the *Music Walk* was the *Water Music* [1952]. Those titles wish to show that all those works are connected. The *Water Music* comes from 1952, I believe—the same year as the Black Mountain show—and was my immediate reaction to that event.

Could you describe it briefly?

The *Water Music* wishes to be a piece of music, but to introduce visual elements in such a way that it can be experienced as theater. That is, it moves toward theater from music. The first thing that could be theatrical is what the pianist is looking at—the score. Normally nobody sees it but him, and since we're involved with seeing now, we make it large enough so that the audience can see it. I was working at the time on chance operations and a chart that enabled me to determine what sound pops up at what time and how loud, etc. So I simply put into the chart things that would produce not only sounds but that would produce actions that were interesting to see. I had somewhere gotten the notion that the world is made up of water, earth, fire, etc., and I thought that water was a useful thing to concentrate on. So the possibilities that I put into the chart involved, not exclusively, but largely, water.

What were some of these?

Well, pouring water from one cup into another, using a whistle that requires water to produce sound, making that whistle descend into the water and come out of it.

Do you remember any of the nonwater images?

There was a glissando on the keyboard, also a dominant seventh chord. I was already interested at that time in avoiding the exclusion of banal elements. In the development of twelve-tone music there was an emphasis on consonance, to the exclusion or very careful treatment of consonances. Octaves as well as fifths and particularly dominant sevenths and cadences became things that one shouldn't do. I've always been on the side of things one shouldn't do and searching for ways of bringing the refused elements back into play. So I included sounds that were, just from a musical point of view, forbidden at that time. You could talk to any modern composer at the time and no matter how enlightened he was he would refuse to include banal musical sounds.

When you came to the Theater Piece *in 1960 . . .*

Before that came a time-length piece, which is thirty-four minutes for a pianist approximately. I had been commissioned to write a piece for two prepared pianos, but I introduced an "X" concept of auxiliary noises. Thus I had other groups of noises: one was produced inside the piano, one was produced outside the piano but on it, and then there were noises separated from the piano—whistles. The parts are not in a scored relation, they are independent of one another. Then I wrote a lecture to go with them, involving combing the hair and kiss sounds and gestures that made the lecture theatrical. So I think you could find the theatrical continuing in my work.

In Milan, when I was invited to perform on a quiz show, the first performance was of *Amores,* an early piece for prepared piano, and the next two especially for television. I used the *Fontana Mix.* They are overlaying transparencies involving points and curved lines which don't cross over themselves. A given line doesn't cross over itself but it goes in curving, meandering ways from one side of the page to another. These curving lines are six in number and are differentiated by thickness (three are dotted) and you simply place them over the sheet with points—one sheet with points and one sheet with curved lines—and then a graph with one that is inside, and one measures the intersection of the curved lines with this straight line with reference to the graph vertically, to determine the kind of thing that would happen. The horizontal measurement gives the time. I used the *Fontana Mix* to make a tape piece ◂§and an *Aria*§▸, and I used it to make television pieces. I don't think I used all six of the lines. I used as many as I thought were necessary. And then I made lists of actions that I was willing to involve myself in. Then through the intersection of those curved lines and the straight line I could see within what amount of time I had, for instance, to put a rose in a bathtub, if that came up. If at the same time playing a particular note—or not a particular note—on the piano came up, those two things had to get done within the time allotted. I ended up with six parts which I then rehearsed very carefully, over and over and over again with people watching me and correcting me, because I had to do it within three minutes. It had many actions in it and it demanded what you might call virtuosity. I was unwilling to perform it until I was certain that I could do it well.

You say there were many things you had to do within the three-minute time; could you mention a few of them?

They're all listed in the score. What is more interesting, I think, is that my chart included far more activity than what came up through the measurements, so that a lot of my preparatory planning and thinking was, from a normal point of view, wasted.

Have the charts been published?

You can buy them, you can buy the *Fontana Mix,* and you can also buy the *Theater Piece.* The *Theater Piece* carries this kind of activity up to an abstract point, because none of the things to be done are verbalized. But what an actor will do in a given time space is up to him. He follows my directions—and I think many people perform that piece without following my directions—and puts verbs and nouns on cards. He conceals the order from himself by shuffling the cards. Then he lays them out so he can tell which is one and which is two, up to twenty. Reading the numbers, which are the only things which are in my score, he will be able to make a program of action just as I made one for the *Water Walk.* And if he did it as I did it he would, I know, arrive at a complex situation. But what people tend to do is to get ideas of what they will think will be interesting and these, of course, are a limited number of things, because their imaginations are lazy, and they do fewer things rather than more and they are satisfied to do one thing over an inordinately long duration.

When I was writing the *Theater Piece* I started out in terms of process, just overlaying these things and taking measurements, and I went far enough with that concept to put it on paper, but not to specify verbally. I left that up to the performer. I stopped the process before it was realized, leaving the realization up to the individual.

This is why . . . I had a conversation earlier that year with Karlheinz Stockhausen, and he asked, "If you were writing a song would you write for the singer, or would you write music?" I said I would write for the singer. He said, "That's the difference between us. I would write music." He was at the time thinking about writing a song for Cathy Berberian, and he wanted to make use of as many ways of vocal production as he could think of. He was interested in African clicking, and she was able to do that, so he put it in. He was also interested in whistling. It didn't occur to him that she couldn't whistle. She's absolutely incapable of whistling. So he gave her things to do that she was unable to do. That was why I left the *Theater Piece* unspecified. I didn't want anyone to do something he couldn't do.

The words could be taken by chance from a dictionary.

Right.

Yet they're supposed to be the basis of the action.

Right. I wanted to leave the performer free. I didn't want him to get involved in a situation that he wasn't willing to carry through.—Michael Kirby & Richard Schechner (1965).

How would you react if somebody, during the performance of your music, falls asleep or shouts or protests. Would you be hurt, offended, discouraged?

No, each person is doing his own life. And even when someone is listening, he is listening in an original way. So there is no point in being offended because we are, so to speak, a multiplicity of centers.

Your first remark about that man at the concert who goes to sleep reminds me of this haiku poem: "By going to sleep, I pound the rice." Which means that someone is sleeping and someone is pounding the rice.

You mean, everybody has his own rights and nothing more?

Yes, and we are, so to speak, working together so that there is no need for the person who is pounding the rice to sleep and there is no reason for the sleeper to be singing, you see.—Nikša Gligo (1972).

What happened after the Theater Piece*?*

At about that time my music was published, and it took a long time to make up a catalogue for it. In 1958 I began some pieces called *Variations.* The first one was involved with the parameters of sound, the transparencies overlaid, and each performer making measurements that would locate sounds in space. Then, while I was at Wesleyan [University], in this first piece I had had five lines on a single transparent sheet, though I had had no intention of putting them the way I did, I just drew them quickly. At Wesleyan while talking to some students it suddenly occurred to me that there would be much more freedom if I put only a single line or a single notation on a single sheet. So I did that ☙with *Variations II*❧, but it still involved measurement. Then *Variations III* came along. I had been working very early with structure, with this process that could be seen as structure; it always involved space, which struck me as distinguishing what we now call neo-Dada from earlier Dada. I admired modern architecture with all its open space. I admired those Japanese gardens with just a few stones. I had been committed to the notion of activity and nonactivity, just as earlier I had been committed to sound and silence.

Just as I came to see that there was no such thing as silence, and so wrote the silent piece, I was now coming to the realization that there was no such thing as nonactivity. In other words the sand in which the stones in a Japanese garden lie is also something. Why this had not been evident to me before, I don't know. There isn't any nonactivity. Or, as Jasper Johns says, looking at the world, "It appears to be very busy." And so I made *Variations III,* which leaves no space between one thing and the next and posits that we are constantly active, that these actions can be of any kind, and all I ask the performer to do is to be aware as much as he can of how many actions he is performing. I ask him, in other words, to count. That's all I ask him to do. I ask him even to count passive actions, such as noticing that there is a noise in the environment. We move through our activity without any space between one action and the next, and with many overlapping actions. The thing I don't like about *Variations III* is that it requires counting, and I'm now trying to get rid of that. But I thought that performance was simply getting up and then doing it.—Michael Kirby & Richard Schechner (1965).

The two kinds of music now that interest me are on the one hand a music that is performed by everyone. . . . So I like that; music by many, many people. And therefore, more and more in my performances, I try to bring about a situation in which there is no difference between the audience and the performers. And I'm not speaking of audience participation in something designed by the composer, but rather I am speaking of the music that arises through the activity of both performers and the so-called audience. This is a difficult thing to bring about, and I've made only a few attempts so far and with mixed results, you might say. I think the most enjoyable from my point of view was last fall at the University of Wisconsin in Milwaukee when I was asked to give a demonstration of sounds of the environment. And about three hundred people came into a concert hall, and I spoke to them much as I am speaking to you now about the enjoyment of sounds of the environment. And then, through *I Ching* chance operations we subjected a map of the university campus to those operations and made an itinerary for the entire audience which would take about forty-five minutes to an hour. And then all of us, as quietly as possible, and listening as attentively as possible, moved through the university community. It was a social experience.

Rather than a musical one?

It was also musical and was discussed as such and as society when we returned to the hall.

The other kind of music that interests me is one that has been traditionally interesting and enjoyable down through the ages, and that's music that one makes oneself without constraining others. If you can do it by yourself, you're not in a situation of telling someone else what to do.

But I find the conventional musical situation of a composer telling others what to do—I find that something which I now don't myself instigate. If someone plays my earlier music in which that situation takes place, then I don't make any objections; but I myself would not have organized that concert.—Hans G. Helms (1972).

Do you like to speak with performers before they perform one of your pieces?

I like to make suggestions and then see what happens, rather than setting down laws and forcing people to follow them. Since I don't hear music in my head to begin with, I don't lose anything at all by leaving a little more freedom. The use of chance operations leads to certain freedom, and the providing of suggestions, rather than law, adds to it.—Terry Gross (1982).

In Allan Kaprow's Happening with the mountain [*Courtyard*], he says that there is this symbol business about the girl and the Earth Mother. That strikes me as drawing relationships between things, in accord with an intention. If we do that, I think then we have to do it better than people in history did it. Happenings don't do it better because they have this thing we've spoken of as carelessness in them. Carelessness comes about through—to use your words—"nonmatrixed activity." The only way you're going to get a good performance of an intentional piece, that furthermore involves symbols and other relationships which the artist has drawn in his mind, is to have lots of rehearsals, and you're going to have to do it as well as you can; rather than using one symbol, you might find another, more effective symbol. You've involved in a whole thing that we have been familiar with since the Renaissance and before.—Michael Kirby & Richard Schechner (1965).

If you read [Ferruccio] Busoni's curious essay written a long time ago—it's called "Sketch of an Esthetic of New Music" [ca. 1911], and it really should be read—he says, for instance, in speaking of the new music in which notation is too rigid, that music must be freer than that, the thing that has made it rigid is the tendency toward architecture, and that this tendency toward architecture, the division of the whole into parts, has been very pleasing to the academic, because it is very easy to teach; but it has nothing to do with the proper spirit of music. It has only to do with the spirit of the academy. That it is, in fact, opposed to the spirit of music, because music is free of all such constraints, since it exists in the air. It's a marvelous essay.

If someone makes a Happening, very often it is an individual expressing an idea or a feeling, and he makes a kind of scenario or plan for the Happening, which will express this idea which he has. He does not engage the people in any discipline, but leaves them completely free. What he is doing actually is something like a Renaissance work—namely, the expression of an idea or a feeling that an individual has, and he is doing it in what amounts to a careless way, because it is undisciplined. If one is going to let anything Happen, which is the basis of how the Happenings developed—namely, that anything can Happen—it must be because one does not have an idea nor a feeling to express, but is willing to give all that up and to move into a situation in which anything may happen, because one is interested not in expressing ideas or feelings but in increasing one's awareness and curiosity. Now if one has the feelings of open awareness and of utter curiosity, and if he wants to make a Happening, then he will make a situation that is extremely complex, in order that something may happen—not that what happens will be something that he had in his mind, but that it will precisely be something that he did *not* have in mind. Most of the Happenings that we have had in New York have been things that people had in mind and then produced. And that is what the Renaissance did, and we're not interested in that; and if we are, we know the discipline we must follow to produce a Renaissance work of art. But the Happening comes about in a situation where we have renounced the Renaissance; and where we wish to have happen something that we have not had in our minds, and that will increase our awareness and goad our curiosity. A Happening should be like a net to catch fish the nature of which one does not know.

And at this point the word "discipline" means what it originally meant—namely, giving up oneself in order, one could even say, to know oneself.—Lars Gunnar Bodin & Bengt Emil Johnson (1965).

I think what we're doing is something else and not that. So when I go to a Happening that seems to me to have intention in it I go away, saying that I'm not interested. I also did not like to be told, in [Allan Kaprow's] *Eighteen Happenings in Six Parts,* to move from one room to another. Though I don't actively engage in politics, I do as an artist have some awareness of art's political content, and it doesn't include policemen.

I think we all realize that anarchy is not practical; the movement of philosophical anarchism in the United States that did quite a lot in the nineteenth century finally busted up because in the large population centers its ideas were not practical. We look at our lives, at the anarchist moments, or spaces, or times, or whatever you want to call them, and there these things that I'm so interested in—awareness, curiosity, etc.—have play. It is not during organized or policed moments that these things happen. I admit that in a policed circumstance I can take an aesthetic attitude and enjoy it on my terms.

But why do you think that so many Happenings have become intentional?

I think that those people for one reason or another are interested in themselves. I came to be interested in anything but myself. This is the difference. When I say that anything can happen I don't mean anything that *I want* to have happen.

But don't you in some way structure your work?

You're aiming now at a purity we are never going to achieve. When we say "purposelessness" we add "purposeful purposelessness." You'll find this more and more being recognized not as double talk, but as truth. That's why I don't like definition; when you succeed in defining and cutting things off from something, you thereby take the life out of them. It isn't any longer as true as it was when it was incapable of being defined.

But some people can't do things unless you define them for them.

That kind of sight is not going to enable them to see. The whole desire for definitions has to do with the Renaissance in which we demanded clarity and got it. Now we are not in such a period and such definitions are no longer of use to us.—Michael Kirby & Richard Schechner (1965).

I'm glad to report that I haven't had the feeling that anyone in the [Boston] orchestra was angry with me, whereas formerly they were.

Just fifteen or sixteen years ago in New York—and now I wish to correct a misstatement of fact on the part of a rather sensationalist critic in this town who reported that I asked the Philharmonic to smash their instruments, and that they complied. That is simply not the case. What happened was that, at great expense, I managed to amplify by means of contact microphones the entire New York Philharmonic and to send it out by means of twelve channels, in *Atlas Eclipticalis,* when Leonard Bernstein gave a kind of avant-garde festival.

What happened at the first performance was that many in the orchestra were furious at the music and tore the microphones off their instruments and stamped on them and smashed them. And the next day, which was Friday, I repaired or brought new microphones for all the ones that had been broken, and they again smashed them. And on Saturday they again smashed the new ones. On Sunday, Mr. Bernstein gave them a sermon, and they played rather nicely, but then they were not ashamed of their behavior. And one of them came offstage smiling, and he shook my hand, "Come back in twenty years and we'll treat you better"—New England Conservatory (1976).

In the sixties, people were very irritated by your works, and today . . .

Oh, you mean today you don't think they're so irritated.

People are not accustomed to it.

I just performed *Muoyce* which is a whispered version of my *Writing for the Fifth Time Through Finnegans Wake,* and it was done in Frankfurt. It lasts for two and a half hours. Klaus Schöning of Hörspiel WDR told the audience which was large, about four or five hundred Joyce scholars, that the doors were open; that once the performance began, they could leave as they wish, and that they could also come back if they wanted. After twenty minutes, they began to leave, and he told me later that only about half of the audience was there at the end. So I think that the work is still irritating. People think, perhaps, that they are no longer irritated, but they still have great difficulty paying attention to something they don't understand. I think that the division is between understanding and experiencing, and many people think that art has to do with understanding, but it doesn't. It has to do with experience; and if you understand something, then you walk out once you get the point because you don't want the experience. You don't want to be irritated. So they leave, and they say the avant-garde doesn't exist. But the avant-garde continues, and it is experience.—Thomas Wulffen (1985).

Obviously there seem to be some differences between the European and the American audiences concerning the reception of your work.

I suppose there are differences. I think the European audiences are mostly mature people. The audiences in the United States are more generally in the universities and are people who are not yet economically members of the society.

But hasn't that changed within the last ten years? Or in the United States, are there still mostly young people as audience for your music?

My impression is that the universities are the places where American society as a whole enjoys art. When they graduate from the universities, only some of them enjoy it.—Birger Ollrogge (1985).

Does the computer alter the concept of "audience"?

I think that not the computer itself, but the ideas that I and others have, in the field of music, have done this already, so that we think of the concert more and more not as something that begins and ends but as a process that continues and sometimes [is] very long so that people could come and go—again, flexibility. And one of the things that's so annoying about concerts to people who are themselves, let us say, not music lovers, is this business of sitting in rows in a theater situation, and our tendency now is to remove that by having a space in which people can move or sit, go out, come in . . . in the course of the performance of music.

Will there be any future need for concert halls and museums?

No, but this notion of ☙only❧ having what we need—it seems to me can be laid at the door of the Germans; I think it's a false idea that they've buffaloed us into—I think we can perfectly well do things that are not necessary, and that it will seem pleasurable to us to get together and have an unnecessary concert. . . .

On whether concerts are more pleasurable experienced by groups of people:

Well, I think there is a great difference between an original painting and a reproduction, and between a live performance of music and a recording, and the general experience as numbers increase will be of recordings as things develop in technology, and people may even learn to prefer them to the original, but others will want to see the original and will realize that there is a difference.—Don Finegan et al. (1969).

I believe in practicality, that's why I'm so devoted to the piano, because it's available everywhere; but I'm not so devoted, for instance, to the bassoon, because the bassoon is becoming rapidly an instrument of the past. It can't compete with the brass instruments, and in Hollywood, for instance, they no longer employ bassoonists . . .

. . . in their orchestras . . .

. . . because they don't make enough noise, so that fewer and fewer people are learning to play the bassoon, which I think is a good thing, because the bassoon vibrates in such a way as to turn the man who plays it insane. Almost everyone who learns to play it loses his mind. And now we don't have so many bassoonists, so it's all very good.

[But the piano and other things?]

But the piano is very useful, because there is one everywhere. If I wrote only for the bassoon, I also would be disappearing as a useful individual. More and more it's practical to write for electronics, because wherever you go there are electrical circuits—amplifiers, loudspeakers, and microphones. We carry with us our contact microphones now, but I think ultimately they'll be available too.

What I want to do now, and what David Tudor wants to do also, is to have a period of laboratory research in which we work with amplifiers, microphones, and loudspeakers to discover other possibilities than the ones with which we are familiar. And I think the fact that we're not working in laboratories is one of the things that makes the problem of composition difficult. In other words, at the present moment, my ideas tend to be removed from physicality, and what is needed, so that we will have our feet on the ground, is physical contact with sound, with new possibilities, in a laboratory. At this time, and here [in Sweden] too, electronic laboratories for music are developing everywhere; but they are all related to fixing music on tape. And this is related to the Renaissance, and not to electronic technology.

So it's a question of distribution. You do not believe in tapes and records.

This is an enormous problem now. The electronic distribution of our activities is becoming more and more magical with Telstar, for instance. McLuhan says that anything that happens at any point happens everywhere because of the electronic media. It's in the nature of our understanding of electronic technology, and so we speak of the global village.

The notion of the physical distribution of ten thousand books is another problem, not so much electronic, as it is mechnical. The machine [of the book] belongs to the Renaissance. The things of intangible distribution belong to electronic technology. When Bengt Emil Johnson speaks of the poetry that will not so much be consigned to books as to recording, the moment they become recordings they will be able to be distributed with great ease, with no difficulty whatsoever, throughout the world. But once they've been experienced, the tendency of technology will be not to keep them but to ask you for another one, something new—this is the spirit, I think, of the new culture: not to keep but to constantly give.

So this question of distribution is related to museums, and to monuments, and so on. Of course, we will have that problem, but it will be a disease rather than something simple.

Do you have some ideas to solve this?

We can't be satisified with distribution now because it won't be very good. For instance, my book [*Silence*], published in the United States, is very difficult to get outside the United States, and that won't be solved, because all of the publishing problems of books, and objects, and things in quantity are still those of the previous culture. Yet with the number of people who work now—the number of composers, the number of authors, and so on—has vastly increased over the nineteenth century; but the number of [music] publishers has *not* increased. The result is that you have traffic problems, so you have the kind of problems that all large cities encounter with automobile traffic. And I hear, where I go now, that in the future we may expect that private traffic in large cities will be forbidden. It may then equally be forbidden to produce a book that would require people to distribute it, but it will not be forbidden, certainly, to send information by electronic media throughout the world.—Lars Gunnar Bodin & Bengt Emil Johnson (1965).

[What about live theater?]

The difficulty with the theater, as I see it, is that it has—because of the complexity involved and probably because of the economics—tended to close the circle around it rather than to open it out. This is true also of the symphony orchestra. Whether or not people inside the circle are going to enter into the dialogue is very much an open question. Occasions will arise when dialogues will occur, but in the case of theater it's extremely difficult. I was up at Wesleyan University for discussions about the performing arts. There was a man who had performed Hamlet at the Tyrone Guthrie . . .

George Grizzard?

Yes, and the director associated with him.

Alan Schneider?

Alan Schneider. I certainly wouldn't have gone had I known what was going to take place. It was a warm evening and they began by taking their coats off, and trying to give the feeling of informality; they even went so far as not to use the chairs but to sit on the table that had been placed in front of them. They proceeded to say that they had nothing to tell the audience, that what they wanted were ideas from the audience, in other words they wanted to have a discussion. Of course there were no questions. So they had to chat and supplement one another's loss of knowledge of what to do next. The whole thing was absolutely disgusting: the kind of ideas and the kinds of objectives, the vulgarity of it, was almost incomprehensible. The chairman of the meeting was also disgusted and at one point he interrupted Schneider and Grizzard and knowing that I was in the audience, asked me to speak my piece. I asked them what they thought of Happenings and learned that they had no knowledge of them whatsoever. They don't go. They weren't interested. They were concerned with the *Hamlet* situation.

This is the difficulty. When a painter comes to a Happening, he brings a painting tradition; when a musician comes he brings with him a music tradition. But no one in the theater brings anything . . .

Except a quality of mind, namely, a tremendous ego. You could see that in Grizzard. He kept being humble in order to show that he wasn't so stuck up. But it was clear that he was as stuck on himself as he could be, and that he wanted the best thing to happen to him that would happen. He thought it was nice and ethical of him to have preferred to do *Hamlet* instead of something on Broadway. That kind of shoddy ethic is just intolerable.

I said this sort of thing. I was quite heated. I normally don't like to talk against things, but I had been asked to. When we couldn't discuss Happenings because they had no knowledge nor interest, and didn't think it was as serious as *Hamlet* and thought they were being virtuous, then I said, "Well, what do you think about TV?" They weren't interested in TV. And yet they're living in an electronic world where TV is of far more relevance than the legitimate theater.

Why don't we think of those theater people as what they are? They're a form of museum. And we are going to have museums and we should just be grateful to them for doing what they're doing and not bother them.—Michael Kirby & Richard Schechner (1965).

Your music has always been elusive when people try to record it. Do you agree?

I like live music. I don't stop my music from being recorded because other people like it. But I've always been opposed to records.

You often work with electronic equipment. It seems to me that the spontaneity and good humor of your approach helps to humanize such devices.

The piece we're setting up now [*Cartridge Music*] uses electronics, but it also uses junk things that are part and parcel of everyday life. We have a complex situation with three performers, and objects with cartridges and contact microphones. We enter a situation that resembles people trying to get through the tunnel into New Jersey.

In terms of sound?

No, in terms of what we have to do to produce the sounds. One person may be turning down the amplitude while someone else is playing something. Causes and effects get disconnected. The personal element seems to make the machinery not quite work properly.

Is a concert hall a good place for such an experience?

Yes. If we have a concert such as this, people can then listen when they go outside, and the noises won't seem as disagreeable as they'd thought.

Would it be good if all the sounds of life eventually replaced the concert hall altogether?

Not altogether. In the future, it seems to me, we should want all the things we've had in the past, plus a lot of things we haven't had yet.

It seems to take a lot of work and trouble to achieve the randomness and spontaneity you seek. Is this a contradiction?

It's an attempt to open our minds to possibilities other than the ones we remember, and the ones we already know we like. Something has to be done to get us free of our memories and choices.—David Sterritt (1982).

I think the only real difference between theater and music is that more and more things happen that aren't, superficially, making sounds. The moment that you have singers, such as you have in *Renga* and *Apartment House,* you've already left the situation of music, at least in the view of the musicians' union. Singers, you know, belong to AGMA, which is the theater union. That became extremely clear both in the performance of [Mr.] Swift Eagle and in the reaction of the audience. The audience acted as though it were not at a musical concert; it didn't occur to them to stop making noise themselves, but they moved into a theatrical reaction.

For us, as spectators who didn't participate in this disruption, Swift Eagle's performance seemed to belong to "theater," as such, rather than music. That is, the people sitting beside me might protest against the music, but, when he would start doing his things, then some of them became so fascinated, in spite of themselves, that they would simply pay attention again. However, he was a very appropriate performer for one of your pieces. I think, because, while he could relate to the audience and deal with that, still he was intent on doing what he was also doing. He was able to exist on many levels of his reality, and this was very good.

I disagree first of all with the idea of a performance as separate from a rehearsal. So that rather than a performance being a special occasion, it simply becomes the general nature of the performer. At that point, I think, one could decide whether or not he was interested in the performance.—Dick Higgins (1976).

A few years ago, several orchestras across the country played your Renga *with* Apartment House 1776. *It usually provided a rather vicious reaction from at least a good portion of the audience. Did you anticipate such a response?*

No. I thought it would be a cheerful piece, and that it would be celebrative of the bicentennial—which I think it is. I'm always surprised that more people didn't recognize it as having that character. But many people faced with sad music laugh, and faced with witty music start crying, and so forth. It seems to me that music doesn't really communicate to people. Or if it does, it does it in very, very different ways from one person to the next.

Many people become annoyed, I think, simply because I superimposed the spiritual songs of four different peoples. Yet if you engaged them in a discussion on ecumenical thought, you'd probably find that they agree with the idea that there are different ways of approaching God.

It was not bad in Cleveland or in Boston. It was bad in New York, Chicago and Los Angeles. That's largely because of the orchestras, which are not good orchestras. There are good people in each of the orchestras, but there are in them a large number of people who aren't good, who don't play faithfully what they are given to play. Faced with a music such as I had given them, they simply sabotaged it.

It sounds like the same things that happened with the New York Philharmonic and Atlas Eclipticalis.

Yes, of course it is. The New York Philharmonic is a bad orchestra. They're like a group of gangsters. They have no shame—when I came off the stage after one of those performances, one of them who had played badly shook my hand, smiled, and said, "Come back in ten years; we'll treat you better." They turn things away from music, and from any professional attitude toward music, to some kind of a social situation that is not very beautiful.

In the case of *Atlas,* they destroyed my property. They acted criminally. They tore the microphones off the instruments and stamped on them, and the next day I had to buy new ones to replace them for the next performance. It was very costly. And they weren't ashamed.

In light of your musical differences with Pierre Boulez, do you feel he performed properly?

Well, Boulez and I have had a difficult friendship, one might say, but a long one. I met him over thirty years ago. He gave me the manuscript of the *Second Piano Sonata.* So although we don't see eye to eye, we nevertheless have a window or a door open on the other one, with a kind of sympathy.

So he did well with your work, but the orchestra was just intractable?

He did as well as he could. He couldn't do very well, and the orchestra certainly could do badly. He worked with the *Apartment House* aspect of the piece and did that very beautifully. I've since followed all his directions for the instrumentation of the quartets. The assistant conductor prepared the orchestra, and he had done it very well. But when Pierre heard the sliding tones—he hates sliding tones—he insisted that they be removed from the piece. He said that without consulting me. The sliding tones are essential to the orchestra part because they make it sound like nature. (Seiji Ozawa had done that so beautifully.) But Boulez insisted that instead of sliding, they make it like an arpeggio. It was perfectly awful. I couldn't countermand what he had said at the last minute; there would have been complete chaos in the orchestra.—Cole Gagne & Tracy Caras (1980).

You see music, from the point of view of its being written and performed and then heard, becomes, in contrast to painting, a social situation. A social situation, when it involves a group of people, is very different from a social situation which has reference to individuals, because, when a group of individuals becomes a group, they in a certain sense are no longer individuals. So that most of the music I've written has been for individuals who have developed a virtuosity, who've devoted themselves to this work in a way that involved them in discovery and such things as stamina. The perfect example, of course, is David Tudor. But when you come to a group of musicians who are not individuals, but have become a group exceeding four . . .

[So it has to do essentially with how many people?]

This question of numbers is exceedingly interesting to me. I have a friend in India who owns a textile factory in Ahmedabad. His name is Gautham Sarabhai. He has calico mills you may have heard about. That beautiful exhibition at the Museum of Modern Art of Indian textiles was all provided by the Sarabhais. Just as Paris has suffered from the glacierlike effect of technology, so this textile factory in India realized the need to give up the ancient procedure of a man making a piece of cloth from beginning to end by himself. It had to adopt certain factory conventions that are of an assembly line, really, so that one person would do something to a piece of cloth, and another person would do something else. And in the end no one [person] had produced it. It has been produced by a group that was not a group of individuals even. And the effect in India was striking, because all the people became extremely unhappy. Before that, they had been happy. He's a good man—Gautham Sarabhai. He wanted to solve this problem of accomplishing more work, which is the desire of the twentieth century, in order to make more money and so forth, and yet not to make his workmen miserable. At first they introduced some Japanese specialists, who had been studying this problem of factory work, but they got nowhere. Finally, someone came from the United States, someone who made systematic experiments; and he discovered that two people have difficulty working together, because they tend to divide into one against one. This accounts for all the divorces. Three people divide into two against one, so that two people become happy and make the third one miserable. Four people divide into two against two, and they can't work well together. Five people can work well together, they discovered. The same is true of six, seven, eight, nine, ten, eleven, and even twelve. They can develop an esprit de corps, a spirit of the group, which does not deny the individuality. Thirteen is impossible, in their experience. This thirteen may be the trouble with the Christian religion, because besides Jesus there were the twelve disciples.

Right. For it to work, they had to get rid of one of them.

It's very amusing, for offhand from the musical point of view, we would say that the number *four* works very well. For we have so many examples of string quartets. But then the Indian experience may prove that wind quintets are superior to string quartets. I noticed in the forties we had in the United States an excellent string quartet called the New Music String Quartet. And very shortly they split up.—Robert Cordier (1973).

In the course of writing *Renga* and *Apartment House,* a long work to write (it took me thirteen months and well over a thousand pages, contacting all those singers, organizing everything), anyway, I was taking my laundry one day to the laundromat, and crossing Eighth Avenue I suddenly got an idea for another piece for orchestra, because the problem is how to deal with those one hundred people. And I was already aware that, after all the work and trouble and everything, I was perhaps making something that would not function, could not be performed, could not be quickly done in this union money-making situation. Anyway, I suddenly got an idea that I thought might work. And then when I ran into this musician on Fifty-first Street and he said, "What did you think of the rehearsal?" I said, "I think it was awful." And then I described to him the new piece that I had thought of. I've already composed it; it is now being copied; it's eight Quartets, in three different versions, for twenty-four, forty-one, and ninety-three people. But only four play at a time, so you see you suddenly have a quartet of the fifteenth first violinist, the third second violinist, the fifth horn, and the fifth 'cellist.

And these people will be obliged to be real people.

I said, "What do you think will happen?" He thought for a moment and then said, "I don't think they'll fool around." They'll realize that if they fool around, they'll be fooling around themselves. And the orchestra, as it stands now, gives them no room for feeling that they've done anything, so they can be bad children because it won't make any difference.—Dick Higgins (1976).

Do you always use transparencies for scoring?

Yes, when I use scores, this can go directly to the publisher. In the piece I'm currently making for flute, clarinet, piano, percussion, violin, and cello, there won't be a score that connects all of the parts. There won't be a fixed relation between those instruments, but rather a flexible relation between them. It resembles, perhaps, that aspect of architecture in, say, San Francisco where, because of the fault in the earth, the architecture has to be flexible and be able to move, so when there is an earthquake, the building will simply shake instead of falling down.

I'm thinking now, and have been for several years, of kinds of music which will survive, so to speak, any relationship of the parts. In a piece called *Thirty Pieces for Five Orchestras,* and in another one, *Thirty Pieces for String Quartet,* I literally made thirty pieces for each group of instruments in the orchestra and each instrument in the string quartet. Those pieces could begin anywhere at any point of time between zero and forty-five seconds, and end at any point of time between thirty seconds and one minute, fifteen seconds. The whole composition, which is a series of thirty of these, would last approximately thirty minutes. Any one segment of a piece, or any one of the pieces of those thirty, could be played in one tempo or another, because of this latitude or flexibility in the beginning and ending. What's happening in the present piece ⟨*Music for . . .* , with the title completed by the number of players⟩ that didn't happen in the earlier pieces is that the lengths of time and the positions of those flexible beginnings and endings are changing, so that rather than all of the instruments having the same degree of flexibility, they have different degrees of flexibility. Another thing I'm going to do is change the range in which the instrument plays at any given time, so that it may move from a very narrow range, as in the piece I've just showed you, to a wider range, according to chance operations. You'll have a togetherness of differences—not only differences in ranges, but differences in structure.—Bill Shoemaker (1984).

After the experience that I had in Kalamazoo with the rehearsal and performance of *Mureau,* I went to Montreal and did the same work with the entire audience without a rehearsal, as I suggested in the foreword to *M.* Afterward, when I left Montreal, I took a plane to New York. It happened that I arrived at Kennedy at the same time that Margaret Mead the anthropologist arrived. She was coming from another place, but we were both in the same baggage pickup area. We drove to town together, and I told her what I had done in Montreal. She is involved more and more now with the notion of ritual, which is a way of involving all of the people present in an activity. She asserted again, as I had heard it before, the importance of food and eating where there is a large number of people together. What is desired, as Ivan Illich would say, is a feeling of conviviality.

The work that I have been doing during the past year is a four-part text called *Empty Words,* a continuation of *Mureau. Empty Words* gradually does without parts of speech. The first part is without sentences; the second part is without phrases; the third part is without words; and the last part is without syllables. I thought of it as something that could be read through the whole night, with intermissions of, say, half an hour between the two-and-one-half-hour sections, with the presence of food, following the suggestion of Margaret Mead, and timing the last part, which is nothing but silences and letters, so that it would end at dawn along with the opening of the windows and doors of the world outside. You might say that my concern is social, but what has impressed me about Oriental and Buddhist practice and thought is not just thinking of individuals or society, but thinking also of the environment. It's only necessary to recall that in Buddhism all beings are Buddhas whether they are sentient as we are, or whether they are not sentient as stones and cigarette butts are not. I remember the meaningfulness in the Buddhist service in Kyoto, early one morning when I was there, of the opening of the doors. All those things get mixed up, so that why I have the recording of the dawn as the second part of my present piece for orchestra is that I have become through *Empty Words* aware of the dawn, and even awake at that time in order to hear it, you know, morning after morning.

I had an astonishing experience recently with the *Empty Words.* It was in Boulder, Colorado. I had been invited to do whatever I wished for the Naropa Institute, a Buddhist Institute headed by Rinpoche, or most precious jewel. The school is very well organized; it had not just studies of Buddhism, but also the arts, music, poetry, and dance. There were also teachers of science and so on, brought together through their common interest in Buddhism. I had just finished the fourth part of *Empty Words*, and had in some performances read the first part with electronics, changing the timbre of my voice, and changing its position in space; in other words, varying a number of, as we say, parameters of sound; and also using in the two-and-a-half-hour period a chance-determined program of slide projections of Thoreau drawings. There would be a hundred and fifty in two and one half hours, which means a slide changing somewhere between one second and four minutes. At any rate, when I finished the fourth part, with its long silences up to eleven and twelve minutes, and just a few letters otherwise, I felt there was no need to change the timbre of the voice, and also no need to speed it up and slow it down as I had in the first and second parts, but to establish a tempo for a line whether it had letters in it, or whether it was part of a silence, so that there would be a movement toward a center, or a coming to quietness, or you might even say, a coming from the loss of the aspects of language, to a having of the simplest elements of music. I thought that this would be appreciated in a Buddhist situation. I also thought that instead of one hundred and fifty slides, that there would be just five slides in the two and one half hours, and those not always shown, so that they would suggest a meditative experience. Then I recalled that the Bodhidharma (when he came from India to bring Buddhism into China) sat facing a wall in China for ten years. At one point, one of the people cut off his right ear, but he didn't budge. So thinking along these lines, I sat in Boulder with my back to the audience. It was a large audience, about fifteen hundred people. There had been a program printed, saying that this was simply a mix of letters and silences from the *Journal* of Thoreau. Well, after twenty minutes, an uproar began in the audience, and it was so intense, and violent, that the thought entered my mind that the whole activity was not only useless, but that it was destructive. I was destroying something for them, and they were destroying something for me. The social situation was really miserable; however, it divided the audience, and at one point a group of people came to protect me. Things were thrown, people came up on stage to perform, and it was generally an upsetting situation. Afterwards, instead of just leaving, there was a discussion between those who remained and myself. I said that I thought that we were due for a period of self-re-examination. Later, I was with friends, Allen Ginsberg, Anne Waldman, Diane di Prima, George Quasha, and other poets, and they said that I had succeeded in bringing the monsters in among the Buddhas. This, of course, had not been my intention.—Anthony Brown (1975).

Did you enjoy the noises?

I was doing something I had never done before. And the reason that

I decided to do it here was that it occurred to me that it would be very beautiful and very appropriate for this circumstance. But then due to my becoming so foolishly famous, many people come to such a performance who have no reason for coming except foolish curiosity. And when they discover that I'm not nearly as interesting to them as they thought I might be, I don't understand why they don't go away.

Isn't that the chance response you deal with?

I know it, I know what limb I'm out on. I've known it all my life, you don't have to tell me that.

It's just like those slides you showed, the response was just a different thing.

Nonsense. Those slides are by Thoreau and in my opinion they are extremely beautiful. The catcalls and imitations were stupid criticisms. The thing that is beautiful about the Thoreau drawings is that they're completely lacking in self-expression. And the thing that made a large part of the public's interruption this evening so ugly was that it was full of self-expression.

Did you end the piece the way you wanted to end it, or did you end it because people were making noise.

I didn't end it the way I wanted to end it. I ended it the way it was to end.

Why is it that when I go to hear someone and I don't like what is going on, instead of interrupting it, I say to myself, why don't you like it? Can't you find something about it that you enjoy? People insist upon self-expression. I really am opposed to it. I don't think people should express themselves in that kind of way.

But isn't that what you're doing right now?

I don't think so. I'm discussing this situation, which, although you say you enjoyed it, I think could have been a lot more successful.

Haven't you said that you want to incorporate outside noises into your work?

I haven't said that. I've said that contemporary music should be open to the sounds outside it. I just said that the sounds of the traffic entered very beautifully, but the self-expressive sounds of people making foolishness and stupidity and catcalls were not beautiful, and they aren't beautiful in other circumstances either.

What were your expectations of your performance tonight?

I don't have expectations.

If you're disappointed, then you have expectations.

That goes back to what I said at the beginning, that I felt that it would be beautiful to do this piece in this situation.

Aren't you glad you got an honest response?

If we are talking about the interruptions, that's not to be classified under honest, that's to be classified under the complete absence of self-control and openness to boredom—and boredom comes not from without but from within. —Anne Waldman et al. (1974).

I had a wild time there [in Milan] because I read the third part of *Empty Words,* and I'd no sooner begun than the audience began an uproar. They didn't leave the hall—there was a large audience of three thousand people—they didn't leave the hall, but they joined me, so to speak, in performing. Some of them were opposed to what I was doing and some of them were in favor of what I was doing, and many of them wanted to do whatever they wanted to do. And so this continued for two hours and a half. Nobody left. Some people were rather wild and destructive, and they tried to destroy the slide-projecting machine, and to remove the drawings of Thoreau, which I thought was very sad because they're so beautiful. On the other hand, the fellow who was controlling the slide projector was very energetic, and he fought and kept it going. And one person came up and took my glasses off to keep me from reading, and also the light that I was reading by was smashed; but another person put in a new bulb immediately, and I looked at the fellow who took my glasses off, and something about the expression on my face made him put them right back on. So I continued for two hours and a half. At the end I went to the front of the stage and showed no anger, but I made a kind of embracing gesture with the arms out, and up. And then there was a kind of wild applause, and I was told later that it had all been very successful. I didn't see how it could be termed successful in terms of my work, since it was impossible for anyone to hear what I was doing; but it was a kind of social occasion.—Geoffrey Barnard (1980).

[What do you think of performances past?]

Our situation as artists is that we have all this work that was done before we came along. We have the opportunity to do work now. I would not present things from the past, but I would approach them as materials available to something else which we were going to do now. They could enter, in terms of collage, into any play. One extremely interesting theatrical thing that hasn't been done is a collage made from various plays.

Let me explain to you why I think of past literature as material rather than as art. There are oodles of people who are going to think of the past as a museum and be faithful to it, but that's not my attitude. Now as material it can be put together with other things. They could be things that don't connect with art as we conventionally understand it. Ordinary occurrences in a city, or ordinary occurrences in the country, or technological occurrences—things that are now practical simply because techniques have changed. This is altering the nature of music and I'm sure it's altering your theater, say, through employment of color television, or multiple movie projectors, photoelectronic devices that will set off relays when an actor moves through a certain area. I would have to analyze theater to see what are the things that make it up in order, when we later make a synthesis, to let those things come in. Now in terms of music I thought of something manually produced, and then of something vocally produced, wind, etc. This includes all the literature. And then I thought of sounds we cannot hear because they're too small, but through new techniques we can enlarge them, sounds like ants walking in the grass. Other sounds are city sounds, country sounds, and synthetic sounds. I haven't analyzed all the things that go into theater, but I think I could.

What are some of them?

It's extremely complex because it involves, as I said earlier, seeing and hearing, We know, or think we know, what the aspects of sound are, what we can hear and how to produce sounds. But when you're involved with sight the situation becomes more complex. It involves color, light, shapes that are not moving, shapes that are moving; it involves what in Buddhism is called "nonsentient" being and then goes again in relation to what is called "sentient being"—animals, etc. I would refer back to Artaud's thinking about theater. He made lists that could give ideas about what goes into theater. And one should search constantly to see if something that could take place in theater has escaped one's notice.—Michael Kirby & Richard Schechner (1965).

How did you come to do what you did last night?

I didn't really know what I was going to do. I was in this house doing my work, hearing those [filing] cards I was using ☙while writing through *The Cantos* of Ezra Pound❧—I thought how beautiful. My first thought was I'll continue doing my work onstage, shuffling the cards, turning pages, and so on—and that I'll do it without amplification. Then when I saw the hall, I thought, well, we'll have to have it. I generally make sound in the *Dialogue* in relation to circumstances of the place. ☙Merce Cunningham is onstage doing his work at the same time.❧

You've written that music should not do anything to the audience; that the audience should do something to the music—to make its own performance, as it were. How did this happen last night?

Well, music is not just composition, but it is performance, and it is listening. The amplification of those cards, though it was high, almost at the level of feedback—which we heard now and then—produced sounds that were still so quiet that one could hear the audience as performers too. And I'm sure that they noticed that themselves. You noticed, for instance, the man in the back who was having trouble with his digestion. And I would hear many different kinds of coughing and I'm sure that people heard those themselves as sounds, rather than as interruptions. I hope, and I've hoped this now for thirty years, when I make music that it won't interrupt the silence which already exists. And that silence includes coughs. I thought the audience behaved/performed beautifully, because they didn't intend to cough—they were obliged to cough; the cough had its own sound—and they didn't make any opposing sound. All the sounds, I thought, interpenetrated—nothing obstructed anything else.

It's called a "Dialogue," which implies some intention in interaction between you [and Cunningham]. What kind of form does that take? When you design a piece, how do you think of the dialogue?

I think it is probably a misnomer. The only way you can rationalize the title, it seems to me, is in terms of each member of the audience; he's the one who has to make the dialogue.

It's the dialogue with the audience, then?

Not with the audience, but the audience creating the dialogue, or looking at two things at once.—Middlebury College (1981).

Some of your critics have mentioned to me that one major factor in being alienated from your thoughts and music is that of a sense of avoiding skills, or avoiding a practiced or virtuoso approach. Their notion of "skill" and "virtuoso" is based on deciding something is good and working to intensify that narrowly as a goal until it is spectacular. Do you agree with the criticism (or even believe it to be a criticism), or are such critics simply missing the point of your ideas?

That's a mistake on their part. Most of my music is written for virtuosos. The orchestra music is not written for virtuosos because orchestral musicians are not virtuosos. But the *Music of Changes* was written for David Tudor, and he is a virtuoso pianist. The *Etudes Australes* were written for Grete Sultan, and are probably the most difficult piano pieces ever written, demanding skills that include even how to sit at the piano. I receive over and over again letters from virtuoso pianists who find these pieces fascinating, most recently from Roger Woodward. He says he's fascinated by them. I've heard different pianists play them, and I'm delighted to see that the pieces will have a long life; again, in opposition to the general critical thought that my music will evaporate into thin air the day I die—which I don't think is true. If it did, I think there is enough of it around that it would germinate again, that it would come back. But I'm not concerned, really.

The pieces that I'm writing now for Paul Zukofsky he says are the most difficult violin pieces that have ever been written. He objects to that difficulty, and he can't work at them for more than about five minutes at a time. He has to stop and rest. Too difficult. On the other hand, he has explained to me, since I don't play the violin, that the history of violin literature has been one of increased difficulty as time goes on, so that it's only reasonable that these pieces should be more difficult than previous pieces for the violin.—David Cope (1980).

Do you have any ideas yet about the orchestral piece for Japan?

It will be called *Etcetera No. 2. Etcetera No. 1* was written for the ballet of Merce Cunningham, which he made for the Paris Opera and which is being revived in January. The music begins with the musicians unconducted, acting freely as individuals; and when they choose, they move to one of four conductors in front of them. Pardon me, I think it is three conductors. And the conductor cannot conduct until he has a full complement of the musicians for whom there are empty chairs in front of him. And four is the maximum actually—four, three, I think of two even—I don't know. I forget. Anyway, that is the character of *Etcetera 1,* and *Etcetera 2* is going to begin with the musicians all conducted, and there are going to be four conductors. And each pair of musicians will have one stand with the music on it. It is very curious. That took me a long time to figure out. It's important that there be two, because when one of them leaves the conducted situation to go to an unconducted melodic situation, he needs to know, when he returns, where everybody is. And the one who is sitting there can tell him.

What I thought was fascinating was that they said to you that you could choose what other works would be on the program with your new work.

Not only that I could, but would I build the programs by choosing a piece that had seemed very important to me in connection with my own work, and then to choose music among our contemporaries (which I took to be younger people), music which was not yet well known, but that I thought was important. So I've chosen for ⊰Hiroyuki Iwaki for the Suntory International Music Program in Tokyo in 1986⊱ to play either the *Socrate* of Erik Satie or the *Symphony,* Opus 21 of Anton Webern, or both, because the Webern is only ten minutes. In addition, Christian Wolff is writing *Exercises 24* and *25,* two short pieces. Satie's *Socrate* will be welcome because it's thirty to thirty-five minutes. It's very rarely played beautifully.

Have you ever heard it played with an orchestra beautifully?

Never.

Have you ever heard it played with an orchestra?

Yes.

And what do you think was wrong with it?

Well, what I thought was wrong was that the transparency and the subtlety didn't seem to appear.

Didn't seem to come through?

Well, I heard that recently in Bonn, Germany, at the Satie festival where I was asked to talk, and I looked forward so much to hearing it with a good orchestra and sopranos.

That by the way seems to be another one of the problems.

It certainly is.

The singers there had vibratos which were so wide that you couldn't tell what the pitches were. And in my reply to Takemitsu, I said, "If you choose to include the sopranos in the program, make sure to have singers who don't vibrate but who sing as folksingers do and use microphones, and the microphones shouldn't be amplified too much either. We want to hear the melodies in relation to the orchestra." I thought hearing it with the vibrating voice business was terrible. When I was asked to write the opera, I said, "Can I get the singers not to vibrate?" And the conductor said, "No, that's what they do."—Ellsworth Snyder (1985).

[Given your taste for theater, why haven't you worked in opera?]

I was asked to write an opera, and I have never written one. It means a lot of work. It means a theater piece with all those singers. And you see, I've come to the desire to free each person in the performance from anyone like a conductor. Instead, what I want the opera to be is a collage of sorts, of a pulverized sort, of European opera; and my title, I think, is excellent. It's *Europera,* which is the words "Europe" and "opera" put together. Originally I thought to have the music be the music in the repertoire of operas of that particular opera house. So that both the sets and the costumes would already exist. They would simply be collaged in a different way than conventionally. So instead of having one opera, you'd have them all in one evening. And it's a very nice idea and relatively practical, but it turns out that operas—I was told, as I never go to the opera, of course. I was told that the opera had become quite modern, the sets were not what I imagined, and the costumes too were often not what I would think they had been in the past. Furthermore, the conductor who had asked me to accept the commission is going to be a new conductor, and he didn't want my work to reflect on the previous conductor, which it would, if you took the costumes and sets you see that they had. So he wants it to refer to opera in general, rather than his predecessor. In that way, my first idea had changed a great deal, and I find as I travel about, for instance, yesterday evening, I got another idea from going to a dance concert, about what I would like to do with the lighting. Rather than have the lighting focused on the activity, I would like to have the lighting done by means of chance operations. I'll probably find out what is the minimum lights, so that the singers won't fall down or something. And what would be the maximum lighting. Then to play between those, with what must be very good technology now. And that won't be too difficult. I'm disconnecting not only the lighting from the singers but the costumes from the roles and the background from the activity, and I'm going to introduce a number of what I think of as stage effects, things happening, so that the whole performance will be like not a choreography involving a dance, but still a kind of movement in this space without benefit of a plot.

I was on my way to Frankfurt to tell them I wouldn't do it, and I went to sleep on the plane. When I woke up, it was just dawn, and seeing the dawn was so marvelous, and that struck me as being the right backdrop for the opera. So that instead of being a single day, or act or one performance, I thought there will be two performances, two *Europeras,* 1 and 2. There will be a series of days, days of different lengths, that is they go from dark to lightest to dark. And there will be through chance operations a determination of different effects of weather. Then I'm going to have many of the dancers dressed in black, helping the singers around—suggesting that, even though the subject is European, the conventions are Oriental.—Ellsworth Snyder (1985).

I had a very good performance of an orchestral work, *30 Pieces for Five Orchestras,* done on the 1981 Metz Festival in France. And it was because I had written into the contract that there were to be ten rehearsals devoted entirely to this work. That is to say, thirty hours of rehearsal. About three quarters of the way through rehearsals, the musicians obviously became interested in what they were doing, so interested that they wanted to hear it. Every time they had a chance they would leave the group to go out and listen, then go back. The performance was excellent! Do not write for orchestra unless you have in the contract some way that will hurt them—plenty of rehearsals.

Your music suffers from the problem that it looks easy . . .

And we don't have to practice it.—Stephen Montague, (1982).

I now not only don't object to my music being recorded but I even help people record it. However, I never listen to the records.

Not even if you would play them all at once?

That would be to have a specially arranged happening, which may happen actually in California. When I'm 75 years old, they're planning a week of my music, and it will begin with the *Musicircus* of the different kinds of music that are already in Los Angeles. And it will end with a kind of *Musicircus* of my own work. And in that way we might very well play as many records at once that we could find. I think I'll do that.—Birger Ollrogge (1985).

HIS WRITINGS

I left college actually before the thirties; I dropped out of college. And I had the intention of becoming a writer, first of all, and I went to Europe. What had impressed me in art was the art of the twenties; and in literature, *transition* magazine, Joyce and Stein, Pound and Eliot, and Cummings. The socially conscious poetry that came up during the thirties didn't interest me. I quickly discovered that I couldn't see eye to eye with the Communists of the period, who were very lively, because they weren't really interested in experimentation; and I am the son of an inventor, and the only way I would make myself useful was to discover new things.—Irving Sandler (1966).

Why are you in the habit of presenting your lectures in some unusual manner?

If a lecture is informative, then people can think that something is being done to them, and that they don't need to do anything about it except receive it. Whereas, if I give a lecture in such a way that it is not clear what is being given, then people have to do something about it.—Roger Reynolds (1961).

[What about your much-reprinted art catalogue essays on Robert Rauschenberg, Marcel Duchamp and Jasper Johns?]

How did I write the texts?

The Rauschenberg text was written rather quickly and followed a musical score of mine. It has been my habit for some years to write texts in a way analogous to the way I write music. Say I have four subjects that I am willing to discuss. Then I take a sheet of paper with four shapes on it. Over that I place a circle which in the case of music refers to time and in the case of a text, such as these, refers to lines on a page. I have the lines, I have another sheet with points on it (these sheets are transparent); and as the points fall over the one that has shapes, some of the points are within the shape, some are outside. Now the circle with the numbers and other circles—another page not with points, but with O's (circles) also is laid over this complex, then a dotted line that is wiggly (meandering) is laid over this so that it intersects at least one of the points which is within one of the shapes and intersects also the first circle. It will possibly, very more likely than not, intersect with other points that are either within or outside of this shape, and the circles. In the case of the Johns's text, if it intersects with the circles, then I am obliged to present an idea. If these points and circles are within the shapes, the stories and ideas are relevant to his work; if outside, relevant to his life. And all of that within the number of lines that is given by the intersection of the dotted lines with the first circle.

The Duchamp text was written in a simple way. You know the *I Ching* business of tossing three coins six times to get a number from one to sixty-four, and I got the number twenty-six which meant that I had only to write twenty-six statements. Then I tossed coins for each one of the statements to see how many words were to be used in each one. That is why there are sometimes single words, because I got the number one.

Now I searched and searched for a way to write about Johns which would not only fulfill my musical obligation but would somehow suggest his work, or something that I felt about it. And one of the things I feel about it, that I don't feel about, say, Rauschenberg, or some other painters, is that the whole surface of the painting has been worked on. There is no emptiness in it. There is no place that something hasn't been done. There are a few exceptions to that, but few. So I made a text, fulfilling this obligation that I mentioned that produces jobs like this. And then I filled in the gaps, so that I too would have filled up the time, whereas in the Rauschenberg one I tried to give some reflection of that by the spaces that I left in time—there were spaces between these various obligations that I had to write. To write the Johns text, the actual writing took me, I think, about three weeks; but the coming to how to write it, this way of writing, took me five months of constant application to this problem of writing about it.—*Artforum* (1965).

Originally my idea for Jasper Johns was to write a text in which I myself didn't write anything. This came perhaps from thinking about his involvement with things that are not himself—letters, numbers, flags. There's also obviously the element of great complexity—things over things, many layers—in his work.

So I had the notion of making a text having superimposed letters and words, of different sizes. Perhaps I was thinking of music in general (which is many things going simultaneously), or my piece for twelve radios in particular. Or even "Where Are We Going? and What Are We Doing?" which is four lectures at once. Here I decided to do eight things at once, and so I made on graph paper eight things at once, each made up of a series of letters and/or numbers of different sizes. I used *I Ching* chance operations. If I have eight lines, there is the possibility of a letter being in every place, in each line—a thick block of print. But through chance operations, a letter can be twice as large and take the place of two. And if it is two, it could be in any position; but another might come that would take up all eight. Meanwhile, the text is running along underneath.

The question then arises: do these texts connect from this letter? What

I wanted was a text that would come out of little letters into a larger one and then continue. That's very difficult; it becomes like a puzzle. I worked eight months on this, and finally abandoned it. That's not exactly faithful to Johns. He would not have given up.

How I was going to complete them was again determined by chance operations—a text of 453 characters, letters, would have been written by someone whose name began with S, on a subject having nothing to do with Johns, whereas another one having 23 characters, whose author's name began with B would have been written with Johns in mind. This was going to be a collage in which I had written no words, but for which I had determined the whole process. The result would have been a composition of mine. That might be able to be done where one wasn't so . . . in love, because I was wishing to convey a love of the work of Jasper Johns.

In other words, I was confined in my use of words to the notion of communication, which in the case of sound I have been willing to abandon. Towards what I have to say, I haven't been willing to change my notion of communication from what is conventional and accepted. My own use of language tends toward saying what I have to say, rather than what the words themselves have to say. I did tend in this direction, but I abandoned it.—Lars Gunnar Bodin et al. (1965).

Words and information have a terrible way of getting in and sticking and preventing anything else from getting in. They merely clutter up your head.—Susan Reimer (1973).

I've been asked to make a text for *Art in America* dealing with Marcel Duchamp whom I knew quite closely in recent years, particularly in Cadaqués [his Costa Brava home]; before he died we were sometimes two weeks together. So I agreed, naturally, to do something but said I would like to do what I've been wanting to do: to make a text that had no syntax. And so I subjected the dictionary to chance operations—the *I Ching.* All the words, so that I could divide all the pages of this dictionary—1,428, including the boys' and girls' names at the end—I could divide that by 64, producing groups of pages of 22 or 23. That comes out to 64. Then I subject 22 and 23 to 64, to get groups of 2 or 3, so that when I get a second hexagram I know precisely which page I'm on. Then I count the words on the page and relate *that* to 64 and know immediately what word I'm dealing with. Then I ask how many forms does the word have—if it's a noun, if it's a verb; is it singular or is it plural. If there's an illustration, is it the word or the illustration, etc. So that I finally pinpoint what it is I have to do in the text. Then *where* on the page does it go?—The page is likewise submitted to the *I Ching.* And I did it very finely so as to avoid a module. Again, by means of abundance; quantity not quality.

You see from Corbusier's point of view, which is quality, a module becomes of great importance. From a quantitative point of view, which I'm trying to work with, a module becomes, if *necessary,* then something to obscure. Anyway, the place, the direction of the word, and then submitting each letter to the chance operation—is it present? Is it in the process of disappearing, as Duchamp himself had disappeared, you see? Is it disappearing structurally? If it's an E, it has four parts, the three horizontals and the vertical; which one of them is missing, if one is missing? Or is it being eaten by some disease—as the poor man, too, was. Then you have in the end when you superimpose many realizations of this process with that instant lettering business, you know, when you have 261 typefaces, you then work into a very rich situation. And some of the typefaces are—from a value point of view, qualitative point of view—clearly poor typefaces, but from an abundant point of view, they are *Yatha butham*—just as they are. And when they are just as they are in this rich configuration of things, they are beautiful. And the Lord must have had a similar idea in mind.

Have you seen the book on notations that was just published [*Notations,* 1969]? This is the collection that I made for the Foundation for Contemporary Performance Arts. Painters had given the Foundation paintings and they had been sold and so we got money for music, theater and dance, and so on. Then I thought of this project of collecting musical manuscripts, hoping that musicians could help themselves by ultimately selling it to a university or to a library, and then using the money to support the works of the musicians, dancers, and performing artists. And the book has this character that I've been speaking about of no value judgment placed—so that in one and the same collection, there are good things and what people would say are poor things. And there are things of all kinds, and they're not organized into any categories. So that it's like those aquariums where all of the fish are in one big tank. As a result I think it's very beautiful. And then the text is mainly different intensities of typefaces, like music notation which has light and dark in it.—Don Finegan et al. (1969).

Let me show you my recent text. It is called *Mushroom Book.* I had for many years wanted to write a mushroom book, and I found that when I concentrated on mushrooms it was not interesting. So what I did was to list all the things that interested me. So: mushroom stories, excerpts from mushroom books, remarks about mushroom hunting, excerpts from Thoreau's *Journal* about mushrooms, excerpts from Thoreau's *Journal*—anything, remarks about life and art, or art and life, life and life, or art and art. By that I mean life becoming art, and I think of Fuller.—Nikša Gligo (1972).

I had the notion when I was asked to write for the Walker Art Center in the series on "The Meanings of Modernism," to write a text against the "march of understanding," and to make clear the virtues of remaining ignorant in the face of art. [Professor Louis] Mink says that it is no longer possible to take this naïve attitude, that enough is known about *Finnegans Wake* to make it imperative to know more and, ultimately, to destroy it. I work at . . . keeping it mysterious. Instead of understanding it, I would like, if I can, to help keep the work of Joyce mysterious.—David Cope (1980).

I have become interested in language without syntax. One of the things that separate the people of the world is not only the various cultures, but the different languages; and we see already the development of language which is graphic—anybody can understand it, regardless of where they come from. This has become necessary through travel by air. I noticed in the plane I took to San Francisco recently that it didn't say No Smoking. Instead, it has a picture of a cigarette with an X across it and the same for putting the belts around yourself. Also, when people love one another, they don't speak so much; or if they speak, they don't make sense. They tend to make nonsense, when they love one another; so I think we need to have more *nonsense* in the field of language, and that's what I am now busy in doing.

In other words, your words will have no *meaning?*

I have noticed that people looking at these things I am doing, instead of following a line, begin jumping over the page, inventing words that I don't even know are there; and that is what I wanted to do with music—to let people hear it in their *own* way. And now I am hoping to find a language in which people can read in their own way, no matter where they come from.—Alcides Lanza (1971).

Having agreed to write a text about electronic music, and having noticed that HDT—that's Thoreau—listened to sound as electronic composers listen to it, not just to musical sounds but to noises and ambient sound generally, it occurred to me that making a chance-determined mix of his remarks in the *Journal* about sound, silence and music would make a text relevant to electronic music. Therefore, I gave it the title *Mureau*—*Mu* (music) *reau* (Thoreau).

What was your method?

I went through the index of the Dover edition of the *Journal*, and I noticed every occurrence in the index of anything that could be remotely thought to be connected with music, and then I listed all of those appearances; then I subjected it all to chance operations in terms of sentences, phrases, words, syllables, and letters. I made a permutation of those five possibilities, so that it would be each of the five alone, or in any groups of two, or any groups of three, or any groups of four, or finally all five.

In gathering the original material for Mureau, *you took phrases out of Thoreau and sentences out of Thoreau and words out of Thoreau.*

First I listed all the things having to do with sound.

Listed in what form? Sentences? Words? Page references?

Page references, just as they appear in the index. Then I asked, what it was of all those permuted possibilities I was looking for, whether I was looking for all five together or a group of four of them, or a group of three or a group of one or two. And when I knew what I was doing, my next question was for how many events was I doing it? And the answer could be anywhere from one to sixty-four. Let's say I got twenty-three. Then if I knew that I was looking for twenty-three events which were any of these five, then I ask of this five which one is the first one. Which is the second? Which is the third? So I knew finally what I was doing. And then when I knew what I was doing, I did it.

By what kind of process did you identify a syllable?

I used the syllables as they appear in the dictionary—the breakings of the words.

You took the words as they existed in Thoreau and simply broke them apart and thereby made them part of your syllable collection.

If I was looking for syllables.

So you have a syllable collection, along with a word collection, along with a letter collection.

My letters become quite interesting. Letters are either vowels or consonants. But it was the diphthong that taught me to think of letters as possibly being in combination. AE, for instance, is a diphthong. Therefore, I thought if vowels can join together to make diphthongs, why can't they join in larger groups and why can't consonants join one another? And I decided that they would. Then, if I landed, by chance, on the letter T in the word "letters," the T is connected with another T. My next question would be: Do I take just the T that I landed on, or do I take the one adjacent to it also? And if it were B and J in the word "subject," and if I landed on the B, I would accept the J if chance said I should.

By what process did you land on the B?

Well, by counting the letters in the line, and then relating that number to the number sixty-four and the *I Ching,* giving me the number that would give me the B.

I think you've skipped a step of your process. Let's say there are one hundred and twenty-eight letters on the line; you consult the I Ching *and get, say, the number four. That would mean you'd use the numbers eight and nine? I'm making a very simple example—one hundred and twenty-eight letters. Let's make it really simple—sixty-four.*

And we get the number fifty-three, so it would be the fifty-third letter. The letter, say, is a B and it's adjacent to a J and preceded by a vowel. So we ignore the vowel, since we're dealing with consonants. . . .

And the word in this case is "subject."

And I ask whether I use just the B or the B and the J.

You make it then an either/or question.

If I throw one to thirty-two, it would be the B alone, with the J being thirty-three to sixty-four. But say there were five consonants. Here are four: N, G, C, H—the NG from the word *I Ching* and the CH from "chance." Then my question is, since I've landed on the G, do I take the N in front of it and the C and H after it? Or what do I do? My first possibility would be to take the G alone. My second would be to take the NG, because it's in the same word. The next would be to take NGC, and the fourth would be to take NGCH. Is that right?

There are more possibilities.

What are they?

Well, if you landed on the G, why not take just the G and the C that follows it?

Because the N came before and belongs in the same word. That's how I worked anyway. I did leave out the GC; you're quite right. Or the GH too. I took the G as being primary. . . .

If you took the G as being primary, therefore the G is necessarily connected to the N because both come from the word "Ching," but is not necessarily connected to the letters of the second word.

Well, you're quite right. Now I think that that's a very good question. What you suggested could bring about a change in the way I work, because I realize I've omitted certain possibilities. I didn't mean to. What would you do? You would have the C, the NG, the CG, the NCG, and the NGCH; would you accept that as the limit? That's five. Then one to twelve will be the first, thirteen to twenty-five the second, twenty-six to thirty-seven the third, and thirty-eight to fifty-one the fourth, and fifty-two to sixty-four the fifth.

And that's how you divide the sixty-four options of the I Ching *when there are five alternatives.*

That's how that works.

One reason why your poetry is so distinctive is that no one else writes poetry in this way—no one. Then how did you decide to begin work, in the case of Mureau*?*

I wanted to make a text that would have four parts, and it was written for a magazine in Minneapolis called *Synthesis.* And they were written to be columns.

Written to be columns?

I was a columnist for the magazine. I don't think of these texts as lectures. They were conceived as columns, initially, and if you'll notice, the columns have different widths. I did that on purpose.—Richard Kostelanetz (1979).

But I'm really interested in the piece you're writing now about the weather.

It responds to a commission by the Canadian Broadcasting Corporation in relationship to the Bicentennial of the United States. Since it came from Canada, I accepted immediately. The man who wrote me in the first place suggested that I work with the writings of Benjamin Franklin; but after reading a little bit of Franklin's work, I felt that I couldn't do that, that I was still, as I have been for many years, devoted to Thoreau. I tried to take myself for this occasion away from Thoreau; and I bought several books that are anthologies of American writing. But I found that I can't take myself away from Thoreau. I'm still too fascinated.—Walter Zimmerman (1975).

Are you going to do music for dance soon again?

Well, I've written this text which I'm beginning, and I'll go on with it, called *Empty Words;* and I think it will be very suitable for dance accompaniment. It doesn't make any ordinary sense, but I think we know now from our own experience (and we may as well cite Artaud again) that there isn't such a thing as a thing that doesn't make sense. So language that we thought had to make sense in a particular way can make sense in other ways. I can read you a little passage of this, which I think makes a great deal of sense, but what sense it makes we're not sure. You're not sure what it's saying, but you can get some kind of an idea.—Robert Cordier (1973).

In Empty Words *you went back . . .*

I was continuing *Mureau,* but extending it beyond Thoreau's remarks about sound and music to the whole of the *Journal.* To begin with, I omitted sentences, and I thought of *Empty Words* as a transition from literature to music.

You would agree, then, that Mureau *is a literary work basically. It's meant to be printed in a magazine or book.*

Yes. In the first notebooks of *Empty Words,* each part is called a lecture.

So Empty Words *was initially conceived as a performance piece.*

It was something to be read aloud, and therefore I made it a length that some people would consider excessive; I made a length of two hours and half for each lecture.

How did you determine that?

Most people consider this excessive, and they don't want me to give it as a lecture. I think that's because the average lecture, say, in a college, should be forty minutes.

Why did you make your own lectures nearly four times as long?

I don't know whether I can answer that question. I had been very impressed by an experience I had in Japan, in 1964, of going to a Buddhist service in a town called Nagoya, the one where all the temples are. It's in the same valley as Kyoto. Anyway, we went to an evening service there that went on for hours and hours, and we had been warned that it was going to be tiresome. I was with Merce Cunningham and the Dance Company. It was very cold, and we were not protected by any warmth. They had told us it would be uncomfortable and long, but we were told also that we didn't have the right to leave once we had decided that we wanted to stay. So we all suffered through it, and it went on and on and . . .

How long? Three hours?

No, more than that. It was like six, something like that. And then a few days later, or maybe it was on another trip to Japan, I was in a Zen temple in Kyoto. When I was invited to go to an early morning Buddhist service, I did. I noticed that after a lengthy service they opened the doors of the temple, and you heard the sounds coming in from the outside. So, putting these two things together, the long night business and then the dawn of the opening of the doors, I thought of the opening of the doors occurring at dawn, and making four lectures and the fourth would begin at dawn with the opening of the doors to the outer world so that the sounds would come in—because, you see, it was a transition from literature to music, and my notion of music has always been ambient sound anyway, silence.

Let me go back to the origins of the work. Why does it have the title Empty Words*?*

It comes from a description of the Chinese language that was given to me by William McNaughton, who has made marvelous translations of both Japanese and Chinese texts. The Chinese language, he said, has "full words" and "empty words." Full words are words that are nouns *or* verbs *or* adjectives *or* adverbs. We don't know in Chinese which of these a full word is. The word is so full that it could be any of them. For instance, the word "red" is an adjective. It could be—I'm hypothesizing now—it could be the same as ruby or cherry, if those were names for red.

It is a full word because it has several semantic possibilities?

It can mean any one of those things.

An empty word, by contrast, is . . .

A connective or a pronoun—a word that refers to something else.

Or it has no meaning by itself. For example, if I say to you "it," that would be an empty word.

Yes. I'm not being at all scholarly about my use of the term "empty words." I'm suggesting something more in line with what I've already told you, namely, the transition from language or music, and I would like with my title to suggest the emptiness of meaning that is characteristic of musical sounds.

That is to say, they exist by themselves.

Yes. That when words are seen from a musical point of view, they are all empty.

They're empty semantically?

How do you mean?

"Semantic" refers to meaning. They are also empty syntactically.

I would rather say that they're empty of intention, And now we come back to the emptiness of full words. Because we don't know if the full word intends to be an adjective or a verb or a noun, it's the reader who brings the intention to it.

Which is to say, when you say the word "red" in Chinese, you can . . .

You can go in any one of four or five different directions. And the person who lets it go there is the receiver.

No, but when you say the word "red," you may mean nothing more than the word "red"; but when I hear the word "red," I think of red apples, red cherries, red beans, and so forth.

I think this is going even further than I meant to go. I would like to go back to the difference between red and blush and cherry—because that's very basic—that's more basic than a red apple or a red cherry. It's whether it's a noun or a verb or an adjective. In other words, we don't know at all what it is.

It doesn't know what it is. We *give it a syntactical context.*

And it could be any one of these things. It is without intention. And I think haiku poetry is somewhat without intention. I think it may be that the author, if not without intention in writing a haiku poem, has a plurality of intentions, more than one.

How so?

In writing a haiku poem, which as you know is just five, seven, five syllables, there are so few ideas present. An example is: *Matsutake ya/ Shiranu ko no ha no/ Hebaritsiku,* which is "Mushroom/ ignorance, leaf of tree/ adhesiveness." That's all there is in the poem. And it's by Bashō. And what does it mean? R. H. Blythe translates it: "The leaf of some unknown tree sticking on the mushroom."

He inserts a lot of syntactical connection that is not present in the original.

He has to; he is obliged to. Now we don't know what Bashō meant. It could be, "Mushroom does not know that leaf is sticking to it."

There are all kinds of connectives the translator or reader can put between Bashō's words.

Many.

Those words are full words.

Yes, but you see, what I'm saying now is that, full as they are, they are somehow in Bashō, too, devoid of intention. But then if he was intending something, why wasn't he more explicit?

So you had this notion of Empty Words *in your mind at the beginning. You also had the notion of developing a piece that would be away from something that was just read on the page to something that would be performed, as it approaches music.*

The approach to music is made by steadily eliminating each of the aspects of language, so that as we start Lecture One of *Empty Words,* we have no sentences. Though they did exist in *Mureau,* now they've gone. In the second one, the phrases are gone, and in the third part the words are gone, except those that have only one syllable. And in the last one, everything is gone but letters and silences.

So you've had a further reduction within the piece. But let me go back a step. Were the same compositional methods used in manipulating the material from Thoreau in Mureau *as were used in* Empty Words*?*

Yes.

Then why is Mureau *generally written continuously, like prose?*

Because it was a column to be printed in a magazine.

And as we can see, Empty Words *was written with lots of white space between the various parts.*

Empty Words is a lecture. In fact, the whole thing is, through chance operations, put in the form of stanzas.

Poetic stanzas or musical stanzas?

Well, just stanzas. That is to say that one part of it is separated from another part.

Okay, parts; let's say parts.

And the parts were determined by the appearance of a period following whatever word, syllable, or letters that were chance-obtained.

When you found a period in Thoreau, that punctuation mark ended your stanza and forced you to go on, vertically to another part.

That made a situation that brought about too many parts. Let's see if I can give you an example . . .

You're now showing me notebooks that have Roman numerals.

The Roman numerals are volumes of Thoreau's *Journal.*

Page numbers, and then occasionally English words.

Right. Now I'm trying to find an example of too many periods close together. Well, here's one. There's a period. "Hauling off" period. And before it is "teenth" period.

As part of, say, "nineteenth," you had just a syllable there.

And "hauling off."

Which you took as a phrase.

And each was followed by a period. And I did not want there to be so many parts that every time a period came that would be a stanza. So when they are adjacent like that, I asked the question, Which one of them disappears?

By a decision of taste, you decided that one of them should disappear?

Yes.

Then you used the I Ching *to decide which one should disappear.*

Now when they were that close I had another device to see whether one of them disappeared and in this case they didn't necessarily disappear. It was just more difficult for them to disappear. So that sometimes two words can make a complete stanza, as in this case: "comes hawk."

These two words are vertically aligned. Where do they come from?

One comes from the eleventh volume, and the other from the sixth volume. But they were both . . . let's see what . . . they were both words.

Now I'm lost. Go back again.

Here I have the notation "W 32."

That means you had to choose a word. And "32" means . . .

There are thirty-two words to be found. One, two, three, four, five, six, seven, eight, nine, ten, eleven, twelve . . .

Thirty-two words in that section.

And now we have phrases, words, and syllables, and there are fifty-four of them.

So then you found fifty-four, and once you found fifty-four . . .

Then I found word, syllable, word, syllable, syllable, word, phrase, phrase, phrase, phrase, word, phrase, word, phrase. . . . It's an interesting way to work, and it follows the title—it's empty-headed.

I understand that. But it's still dealing with a very pregnant, resonant, and, to you, very relevant, text in Thoreau's Journal. *So there was an exercise of choice in selecting it, rather than another book, and that choice would influence an awful lot.*

I know, as you know too, that, were the same kind of thing done with *Finnegans Wake,* the result would be entirely different.

Or if it were an urban writer, it would be different. If it were done with a . . .

Or with a different language. Or with a combination of languages. It was certainly suggested by *Finnegans Wake* that one should do that.

Since Finnegans Wake *is a combination of languages—that is its principal linguistic characteristic—any work derived from it would reflect that fact.*

Let me go back to the question of the four major sections, or "Lectures" as you call them. When did one of them end?

When there were 4,000 events at least.

In other words, there had to be 4,000 separate extractions from Thoreau.

In the case of the First Lecture, there are 4,061, and the reason for that excessive number is this: when I got to the 3,997th event . . .

You threw a sixty-four.

Right, I threw a sixty-four, and it took me up to 4,061.

What are those half-moon marks in your notebook—half-moon marks that we use to connect letters to each other over space, as when we make a superfluous space in typing. You have these all over the text; what are they about?

It was the last thing I did before I finished the text. I went through and found out which things were to be read as connected to each other, so that this "R" from "hear" instead of being separate from the "TH" of "the" in the following word goes together with it, so it's "RTH," instead of "R,TH."

The letters are printed together in the text, and pronounced together when you speak them. So these were derived from an either/or situation with the I Ching. *So, half the bits—should we call them "bits," or is "events" your word?—are concerned, and half of them aren't. How did you decide, in typing out this work, to go on to another line? How did you decide that the space should not be a space between words, so to speak, but a space between lines?*

I set up a certain number of characters for each line, a maximum, and I did not permit the breaking of a word, and I used commas as ends of lines.

So, whenever there was a comma in the original text, that indicates the end of a line.

Or any other kind of punctuation.

Including a period—a period that you ruled would end a stanza. So, it's simply a matter of when the words or bits fill up the available line, then you go on to the next line.

I hope I can show you that.

We're looking now at Empty Words, *Part One, as it appears in your book.*

. . . "notAt evening comma," so that was the end of the line.

A comma in the original ended the line in your text, but that comma is not reproduced here in the book.

That's right.

"Right can see," and there's a hyphen. And those three words are separated.

"Suited to the morning hour."

And those five words are separated from the following stanza. Now, in the opening line, the first two words "not" and "at" are run together, into "notAt," because by the I Ching *process that was thrown they had to run together. You kept the capitalization of "A" in "at," which was in the original Thoreau.*

Yes. Then the indentation here is obtained by subtracting the number of characters in the line from the maximum number, which is probably something like forty-two or forty-three.

If you have forty-three characters in a line, what do you subtract?

Subtract the number of characters in the first line from the maximum. And then subject that number to chance operations to discover where the indentation was.

I'm lost; I'm sorry.

There are one, two, three, four, five, six, seven, eight, nine, ten, eleven, twelve, thirteen characters in "notAt evening." I subtract that from forty-three, and I get thirty. And now I relate thirty to the number sixty-four to find out how many spaces in from the edge I should indent the line. Say I got the number two. I'm working with thirty characters here. The *I Ching* works with the number sixty-four. So looking at the table that relates thirty to sixty-four, taking my next *I Ching* number, I found out, if I get the number one, for instance, I got something very small. I have to begin the line one space in from the left. But the next time, instead of being right underneath the first line, is indented toward the middle.

In the second line again, by the same procedure, you counted the number of characters, subtracted that from forty-three, put that number through the I Ching *with its sixty-four options, and thereby determined where your second line begins.*

Now, when there was no comma, because it looks like there wasn't one here, then I went as far as I could in the line, up to the maximum, without breaking the line and without breaking the word. If there were only one or two, then I left just an either/or about the indentation, and it looks like it . . .

Started flush left, until you go to one of those punctuation marks that would prompt you to go on to another line.

That's right.

And continued to do the same thing.

Right.

And in Empty Words, Three, you removed the possibility of words, so you had just syllables and letters, and then in Four, just letters.

I had one further idea, and that was to sit in profile for the first one, then face the audience for the second one, to sit in profile again but on the other side for the third, and then with my back to the audience for the fourth. And it was actually at Naropa that I sat with my back to the audience, and they became infuriated.

Each of the four works comes with a preface—actually each section has a preface that incorporates the prefaces of its predecessor, until there is a four-part preface for the last one. What are they meant to do?

All the information, all the answers to all the questions, such as those you now are asking me, are given as conscientiously as I can in these introductions. I tried to imagine what it is anyone would want to know, and then I give them that information in the introduction, but not in any logical sequence.

How were these prefaces written?

The first thing I did was find out how many words I had at my disposal for the first remark or for the first answer: one, two plus three plus two plus two plus two, eleven. I had eleven words. Now I thought, well, what shall I say. And it occurred to me to say at the beginning how it was that I came to be in connection with Thoreau. That seems to be a reasonable beginning.—Richard Kostelanetz (1979).

But isn't it important for a poet to make sense?

Just the opposite. A poet should make nonsense.

Why?

Well, for example, if you open *Finnegans Wake,* which is I think without doubt the most important book of the twentieth century, you will see that it is just nonsense. Why is it nonsense? So that it can make a multiplicity of sense, and you can choose your path, rather than being forced down Joyce's. Joyce had an anarchic attitude toward the reader so that the reader could do his own work.

Do you write with intent?

People read thinking I'm doing something to them with my books. I'm not. They're doing something to themselves. . . . What intention could I have possibly had in writing *Empty Words?*

Well, you may have wished to speak of Thoreau.

No, he was just the source. I picked Thoreau only because his journal had two million words. I don't want my reader to experience *Empty Words* except in his own way.

And if I find Empty Words *obscure?*

That's your problem. You're interested in other things.—Lisa Low (1985).

[Did you perform the text as well?]

Ever since I stopped smoking about six years ago a kind of cloud has come over my voice, and more and more my interests move toward the voice and toward the use of the voice in connection with music in performance. I had in mind, for instance, to read all of *Empty Words,* which could take a whole night long. I wanted to read the first three parts, which would take seven and a half hours or, with two intermissions of a half hour each, would take eight and a half hours. I would have that eight and a half hours precede the dawn, so that the fourth part would begin by opening the door, wherever it is, to the sounds outside. By now I don't know whether my voice would put up with it. Not knowing whether I can do something leads to a decision to learn how to be able to do it. What it has to do with is breathing—a whole area to be investigated.

That is now a new frontier for you.

Breathing and speaking and the use of them for the voice. I know enough about it to know it has an effect upon the mind.—Rose Slivka (1978).

I still think our time sense is changed, or that we have changed it. With all these pieces that I've written in recent years, they can be quite long, hours long. All of them can also be just a few seconds long, did you know that?

No.

They don't have to be played for any particular length, that is part of the principle of indeterminacy.

But would you prefer them to be longer than shorter?

No, no. It doesn't make any difference to me. I wish to be, as it were, useful and practical, so that if, say, there was an occasion when one wanted two seconds of music, one could take *Atlas Eclipticalis* and play it for two seconds; it's unlikely because it takes too long to set the thing up. You could set up, however, one part of it very easily and quickly and do it for two seconds. Because I conceive that a long work with many parts can be expressed by any one of its parts or any number of its parts for any length of time. When you started this part of the conversation I found that I was thinking about the difference between prose and poetry. I was thinking that Webern particularly suggests poetry, and that this activity on my part suggests perhaps a big book that does not need to be read.

And also can bore you for long passages at a time, but still leave a mark.

Right, and you could read it, for instance, for any length of time. You could, in other words, have it around, pick it up, put it down, or you could settle down and read it for several hours. And you could, as in the case of *Finnegans Wake,* read it without understanding anything for a long time, and then suddenly you could understand something.—David Sylvester & Roger Smalley (1967).

Very little of my time is set aside for reading, but a great deal for writing. I don't read very much; for the last six or seven years I've been reading almost nothing but *Finnegans Wake.* That has obliged me to read a lot of books about *Finnegans Wake.* I could go on with that for many years.—John Roberts with Silvy Panet Raymond (1980).

Could you say a few words about your present concern with mesostics?

I take a name as a kind of discipline and the first line must have the first letter of the name and must not have the second letter of the name. That must appear in the second line. And so I am able to do that either by having syntactical ideas, as in the case of the mesostics on the name of Duchamp, or I can do it by chance operations, as in the case of the Merce Cunningham mesostics. There I applied the operations to the book on choreography by Cunningham and to thirty-two books from his library that had been useful to him in his work on the dance. So that those, even though they do not make any sense syntactically if you read them, the nonsense is the dance.

Why do you write these mesostics?

Questioning why we do what we do is very curious. I think we do what we do because we slept well and when we wake up we have energy and we try to think of what to do, and we find something to do and do it.

Is your present concern with mesostics a kind of splendid isolation?

No, it is my present concern with language. You see, language controls our thinking; and if we change our language, it is conceivable that our thinking would change. I noticed that all over the world language is changing. There was talk formerly of Esperanto, but it was too localized, because it used European languages only. But now, as people fly, we come to the ideas of Buckminster Fuller. As people move around the world, language begins to appear as something that separates people from people. Rather than a means of communication, it becomes a means of not-understanding. And so we see, for instance, images. In airplanes, instead of saying No Smoking, we frequently see a cigarette with an X over it, and that can be understood by everyone. And my mesostics became things that you can see and understand the way you understand "No Parking."

Do you make your experiments with nonsyntactical language because you feel somehow bound by syntactical language?

I think we need to attack that question of syntax. My friend Norman O. Brown pointed out to me that syntax is the arrangement of the army.

Yes, that reminds me of Nietzsche's saying that our need to have grammar is proof that we cannot live without God. If you are opposed to syntax, do you think that we do not need to have God.

Yes, and Duchamp too, when he was asked what he thought about God, said, "Let's not talk about that. That's man's stupidest idea."—Nikša Gligo (1972).

What about the mesostics? When did you start with this, and why do you put words in this very strange, but very structured literary form?

People are always asking me to do something, and I heard long ago that the Japanese people, when they wrote letters to one another, wrote poetry; and I found that if someone asked me to write something for them when they had a birthday, or some other reason, that if I used the name down the middle to make a mesostic, it entertained me more than if I just sat down and tried to think off of the top of my head something to say, because that discipline of writing the mesostics helped me get an idea.

And where did you start this?

I started it about fifteen years ago. Now I'm very good at it. I can do it quickly.

And you like more the mesostic than the acrostic?

I like the look of the margins being ragged on both sides. What I don't like about the acrostic is that the margin is straight up and down. I prefer to have the middle straight up and down.—Klaus Schöning (1982).

Your subsequent literary work has . . .

To do with *Finnegans Wake.* It's quite different from *Empty Words. Writing Through Finnegans Wake* and *Writing for the Second Time Through Finnegans Wake* have been mesostics on the name of James Joyce. That's a different discipline and doesn't involve chance operations, but involves something else entirely—painstaking examination.

Coupled with devices in selecting from Joyce's work to ensure that something other than the original Joyce emerges. What in past poetry have you been relating to?

When I was first aware of literature beyond high school, it was Pound and Eliot and Joyce and Stein and Cummings. And then I lost interest in literature in the thirties. I didn't become interested in the social concerns of Auden and Isherwood, and who were the others? I wanted a poetry that would continue from these five I just mentioned. It took a long time for that to come about.—Richard Kostelanetz (1979).

Your poetry in mesostics—the process of writing where the name of the person you're writing about is spelled in a vertical row within the text—led you to discover a means of translating any book into music. This happened while you were composing Roaratorio, an Irish Circus on Finnegans Wake. *How does it work?*

What I suggest people do is write *through* a book in order to reduce its length to a reasonable musical length. In the case of *Roaratorio* it's one hour, from *Finnegans Wake,* which is 626 pages to begin with, and becomes in my writing of mesostics on Joyce's name, something like 41 pages, and those 41 pages can be read comfortably in the space of an hour. The translation can also be identified by page and line, so that it's like a ruler going through the book.

I can go through the book and find out where I *hear* something, for instance: if the writer says someone laughed or a dog barked I can jot that down and I can identify that by page and line and I can then *insert* a barking dog or a crying child at the point that it belongs in relation to the ruler that I've already written. And if places are mentioned in the book, I can go to those places and make recordings and put them where they belong in relation to the ruler, and eventually I have a piece of music.—Paul Hersh (1982).

What are you working on now?

I'm writing now, through the *Cantos* of Ezra Pound, mesostics based upon Pound's name. And I'm just completing the fourth writing through *Finnegans Wake;* I've also started the fifth writing. It will be like *Mureau,* you know that text in which I use chance operations to locate different parts of Thoreau's *Journal.* This time through the *Wake* I will not go linearly, as I have been doing with the mesostics, but as in *Mureau,* I'll fly backwards and forwards.—Middlebury College (1981).

Can you tell us about Muoyce?

That's the first syllable of the word *mu*sic, and the name of *Joyce* without the *J.*

I some years ago wrote *Mureau,* which is music-Thoreau, and it was the subjecting of the journal of Thoreau to chance operations whereas this does the same to *Finnegans Wake;* and unlike my first four writings through *Finnegans Wake,* it is not made up of mesostics but is like *Mureau* a collage of typescript. Many of the words are brought together, as they are in the thunderclaps of *Finnegans Wake.*—Charles Amirkhanian (1983).

Instead of going from the beginning of the text to its end, I flew over *Finnegans Wake,* landing through chance operations here and then there, or on a letter, or a syllable, or a word, or a phrase.

Muoyce can begin anywhere in the book and move to any other point. It's perfectly aerial.—Klaus Schöning (1983).

And there's no punctuation. I think it is certainly the most difficult text to read [aloud] that I have ever encountered.—Charles Amirkhanian (1983).

When I first wrote the text, I had great trouble pronouncing it. I didn't know what the sound of it should be, or could be. I tried everything I could think of, and among the things I tried was whispering. When I whispered it, and voiced the italicized syllables, it clicked for me.—Klaus Schöning (1983).

It makes no sense [semantically]; but as I read it, and I'm sure as people hear it, ideas come into their heads; but the ideas are not so much coming by intention from me but simply as the result of the concatenation of phrases, words, syllables and letters.

So it's an evocation of sense.

I hope so, but not an intended sense. I think something automatically comes into it of *Finnegans Wake*—Joyce's concern with the church, and also with vulgarity.

How many times have you rewritten Finnegans Wake?

This is the fifth time, and the last time.

Why the last?

I'm not going to do it any more. That doesn't mean I'm through with the *Wake*, but I'm through writing through the *Wake;* but I enjoy reading it.—Charles Amirkhanian (1983).

Recently I wrote mesostics on the name of Ezra Pound all the way through the *Cantos*, which is over eight hundred pages; and I felt a little foolish doing it. I had never read the *Cantos* and there was a magazine editor who wanted me to do it, and so I thought I'd take this opportunity to get through the *Cantos*. Now that I've done so, I must say that I don't regard them as highly as I do the *Wake*. The reason is that there are about four or five ideas that keep reappearing in the *Cantos*, so that in the end the form resembles something done with stencils, where the color doesn't really change. There's not that kind of complexity, or attention to detail, as there is in Joyce. In the *Cantos* when something changes you can say, "Oh, there's *that* again."

In my book *Themes and Variations*, which was published this year, I wrote quite quickly and spontaneously about certain ideas whose subjects came about by chance operations. But then I used chance operations with regard to several such spontaneous writings, in order to get a final form, which I say in the introduction to the book, is not about ideas but hopefully is in a form which *produces* them.

Themes & Variations *is not only composed in mesostics but utilizes* renga, *a classical form of Japanese poetry in which several writers contribute one line each. How does* renga *affect the spontaneous production of ideas?*

If I have five texts and make a sixth text from the first line of any one of the five (as chance determines), and the second, again, from any one of the five, I then write a text which was not spontaneous but which was *written by different poems*, even though they were all written by me. It's as though they were different people or different times, so that something happens that was not in my mind, and which is not glued to my intentions.

Themes & Variations *is another step toward a text without syntax, something "polymorphic" in the Norman O. Brown sense and thus seems tied to the* Musicircus *or* Roaratorio.

Yes. This is what I enjoy most in art: some kind of activity which is not stuck to the creator's mind, but is free of it, so that it can be enjoyed in different ways by different people. I think fundamental to all these activities is the absence of intentions. You can, in the *Musicircus*, have an absence of intention through the *multiplication of intentions.*—Paul Hersh (1982).

What about when you were working with James Joyce, or works from the past—because you've isolated and changed, transformed older texts. We've been discussing whether that should be called a form of collaboration.

Well, if it's a collaboration, it's one-sided.

An involuntary collaboration.

I mean, poor Joyce, he has no way to fight back. The only thing that happens is that I'm obliged to give a percentage of my income to the Society of Authors, so that the Joyce side of the collaboration is now purely financial.

When you were working with Joyce, did you feel in contact? You're not doing a mustache on his Mona Lisa, you're not transgressing him. Or do you think it is transgression?

It has nothing to do with him. It's something else. He would have enjoyed it, and there are some Joyce scholars who think that Pound would have enjoyed my writing through the *Cantos.* Certainly there are more Joyce scholars who enjoy my writings through *Finnegans Wake* than Pound scholars who enjoy my writings through the *Cantos.*

And in a traditional paradise, you wouldn't have thought of presenting it to Pound or Joyce as a gift in your mind?

I would have, yes. I would have thought that. Not in my mind, but I would have actually sent it to them. I've always thought if I did work with somebody's work or have some kind of connection, I should let them know, if they were alive to know. For instance, one of my first such works was the setting of three short texts of Gertrude Stein, and I wanted very much to meet her then, and I remember thinking that anyone I wanted to meet might be in the neighborhood. So I actually looked through the telephone books of the Los Angeles area, thinking that Gertrude Stein might have a summer place or something, or a winter place. And I came up with some Gertrude Steins, but never with the real one.—David Shapiro (1985).

*Do you react to [*Finnegans Wake*] in a musical way or in a literary way?*

There's a strong connection between music and literature. The obvious connection produces songs and operas, and so forth; so that the arts which are so friendly are music, theater, literature, and dance—in other words, literature, when it is not read but comes into the theater or into the concert hall. I have recently written a number of texts in different languages which I don't know. And I also responded to a poem in Swedish, which I could not understand. Imagine the sound of the poem in Swedish and write it in English with a similar sound. It's very funny. I didn't think of doing that myself. I was asked to do it by Dick Higgins. He asked a number of people who did not know Swedish to translate the poem into English.

It made a very funny poem, but then one work that I like very much that I made this year is the French text, and the previous year I made a German text; and then when I was in Japan, I wrote a poem in Japanese. These I could not hear. All I could do was look. I could see Japanese, and so I wrote according to what I saw. And then I wrote a poem under the name of Octavio Paz in Spanish. So I'm getting to be multi-lingual, like a kind of hamburger.—Thomas Wulffen (1984).

What would Joyce think of your two writings through Finnegans Wake*?*

I don't know, but I suspect he would enjoy them.

Do you have a favorite masterpiece that hasn't been "deconstructed" or "declassified" yet?

What do you mean? Written through? At present I am in the process of writing through *whistlin is did* by the Australian poet Chris Mann, *The Agenbite of Outwit* by Marshall McLuhan, and the Bible.—Jay Murphy (1985).

We were wondering what you are working on now?

I'm writing a piece for orchestra "A Collection of Rocks", and I'm planning with the help of a mesostic-intelligent word processor, being programmed for me by Jim Rosenberg, to write through the Bible, the New King James Version. (It doesn't have as many "beholds" in it.) Left to myself I would have written all the mesostics on the name Jehovah, that is, for the Old Testament; for the New Testament, I will change to Jesus Christ. But at the suggestion of Klaus Reichert I am going to use not just this Christian name of Yahweh but the earlier Hebrew names as well. The first two mesostics on the name Jehovah go this way:

Jabal
hE was
tHe
Of
haVe
nAme
He

Just
walkEd
witH
gOd
filled withViolence
And
flesH

It's sort of Genesis in a nutshell. It's quite terrifying. That takes us through Genesis 6:12 in, so to speak, two steps. This is an example of a 100% mesostic. That is, between two capitalized letters of the name, neither letter appears. *Jabal* is the first word in Genesis that has neither J nor E after the J. *He* is the first word after *Jabal* that does not have a J or an E before the E nor an E nor an H after it. Of course it has nothing after the E except the *was* which I chose to include.—Kathleen Burch et al. (1984).

[My computer] is a great liberation. I have a program now, so that if I have a text in the memory, in any language, I start it going and it makes mesostics on any text I wish. And then after the mesostic is made—it gives only the spine, so to speak—then I can compare that with what's left over and make a poem, you see. I'm having a program made shortly so that I could every day, every hour or every minute make a new poem on the same subject, so that could kind of be as though poetry was put on the stove and was cooking, and you could taste it, and each time it would taste different.—Thomas Wulffen (1984).

At the moment, having, as I do, a computer, I'm able to work much more rapidly than formerly, so that I have a great deal of work that could be published. But I'm not publishing it as quickly as I could have formerly, because I think we're almost at a point of change. The change, I think, will go from a book-publication as we know it to some form of electronic publication. And electronic publication would not be something with paper and binding but would be something that you would simply have access to, as you do to the voice of a friend on the telephone; so that you would be able to dial, so to speak, a book and receive it on a screen or on some erasable material that you would have beside the computer. ☙My most recent book, *The First Meeting of the Satie Society*—it's over two hundred pages—can be accessed on the Art Com Electronic Network carried by the Whole Earth 'Lectronic Link—they did that in order to call it "WELL." For information, contact Art Com at 415-431-7524 for voice, or 415-332-6106 for modem [ENTER g acen AT THE OK: PROMPT]. It's free from the source, though you have to pay your phone bill, as we are getting rid of ownership and substituting use.❧—Birger Ollrogge (1985).

[Writing on a computer] does completely change your mind. When you write a text as I used to write with all the crossings out and everything, you have a picture of the past along with the present and you develop a maze. With the word processor you have only the present so that you're really in a new mental land. I think what it also shows is the disappearance of the middle-man. There is going to be a great directness between making something and its being enjoyed.—Deborah Campana (1985).

Technology essentially is a way of getting more done with less effort.

And it's a good thing rather than a bad thing. Oh, pick up any text published by the musicians union and you'll see that they don't like electronic music. But, electronic music is definitely here to stay. The publishers, my music publisher, my book publisher—they know that Xerox is a real threat to their continuing; however, they continue. What must be done eventually is elimination not only of the publication but of the need for photocopying, and connect it with the telephone so that anyone can have anything he wishes at any time. And erase it—so that your copy of Homer, I mean, can become a copy of Shakespeare, by just quick erasure and quick printing.—Sean Bronzell & Ann Suchomski (1983).

RADIO AND AUDIOTAPE

When did you first work creatively with radio?

When I went to Seattle and took the job as dance accompanist for the classes of Bonnie Bird, I was attracted there in the first place by the presence of a large collection of percussion instruments; but when I got there I discovered that there was a radio station in connection with the school, like a big outhouse. The same building is still there, though now it's used I think for pottery. But then it was radio, and we were able to make experiments combining percussion instruments and small sounds that required amplification in the studio. We were able to broadcast those to the theater which was just a few steps away, and we were able, of course, to make recordings and, besides making records, to use records as instruments.

How did you use records as instruments?

Well, the record makes a sound and the speed of the record changes the pitch of it, and the turntables that we had then one no longer sees; but each one had a clutch: you could move from one speed to another.

What did you do in the radio station that you couldn't do playing the records elsewhere live?

Well, the turntables were in the radio station, they were not movable, and they had speed controls.

What could you do with these speed controls?

Well, when you change the speed of the record, you change the frequency of the recorded sound. I used continuous sounds that were made for test purposes by the Victor Company, and they had both constant tones and tones that were constantly sliding in pitch through a whole range. Those records were used in the *Imaginary Landscape No. 1.*

Were the turntables played simultaneously?

No. That may have been the case somewhere in the piece, I forget; but they were played simultaneously with other instruments like cymbals, prepared piano, and so forth. Generally, the record player would play one record at a time and then I'd change it and play another record.

So you could go swiftly from one record to another.

Not swiftly, but you could go properly.

Was the sound modified at all after it went into the microphone?

No, no, I've never done much with sound modification.

Why not?

I found the sounds interesting as they were.—Richard Kostelanetz (1984).

The suitability of those (radio) sounds in combination with percussion was immediately evident to me. So, I made the first two "Imaginary Landscapes" always with some kind of technological thing in combination with percussion, and with prepared piano. Then, when I got to Chicago, I had a commission to do a piece for CBS and I worked with the sound effects engineer at the radio station in Chicago and he showed me the thunderous sound of the coil of wire in a contact microphone—which I loved. I used that in *Imaginary Landscape No. 3.* "Imaginary Landscapes" became the title that I used when I was using electric or electronic technology.—Thom Holmes (1981).

What was your next radio involvement—the Kenneth Patchen project?

Yes, I'd always admired the Columbia Workshop play programs, and you remember the story of the play that had to do with the end of the world and how the entire country thought it was true; so that not only I, but many other people, were interested in the Columbia Workshop plays. I appealed to Davidson Taylor here in New York to let me make the accompaniment to a Columbia Workshop play. I explained to him that my view of radio music was that it should follow from a consideration of the possible environmental sounds of the play itself; so that, if it was a play that took place in the country, it would be natural to have the sounds of birds and crickets and frogs and so forth. But, if it were a play that took place in the city, it would be natural to have the sounds of traffic. In other words, I wanted to elevate the sound effect to the level of musical instruments.

That appealed to him and so he asked me to suggest an author for the play. The first one I suggested was Henry Miller. I asked Henry Miller if he would write a play for me, and he said it would be better if I would first read his books. It was difficult at that time to read his books because they were considered pornographic, so he gave me a letter of special introduction to the New York Public Library when I was still in Chicago. I came to the New York library where he said his books actually existed, and I was able to read them. I didn't see the possibility of a radio play from those books and still felt that he should write something especially for the occasion. He didn't agree to do that. So Davidson Taylor said, well, who would be your next choice, and I said Kenneth Patchen. I had read and enjoyed *The Journal of Albion Moonlight* [1941].

I was now living in Chicago, and I'd made friends with the head of the sound effects department of CBS there. Since this was a CBS Workshop project that had a particular date and deadline, I asked him what sounds I could use; and he said there was no limit to what you could do. (Musicians frequently say this to you also; they say, write anything you like and we will do it.) So I proceeded. I used to go downtown into the Loop in Chicago and close my eyes and listen and I dreamed up through that listening all sorts of requests which I wrote down verbally and musically; and when I took them to the sound effects man, he then told me, if you please, that what I'd written was impossible.

Just as those solicitous musicians would tell you that the score you'd just given them was impossible.

Right, so I said, what's impossible about it? He said it would be so expensive. By this time the projected performance was only a few days away and my whole score, which was for an hour, yes, of music that I had written, was, he said, impossible. I had to write another hour in just a few days, and I used the instruments that I knew how to use—namely, the percussion instruments and records. The play that Kenneth Patchen had written was called *The City Wears a Slouch Hat.* I stayed up for about four days really without sleeping, just napping now and then; and I wrote. I was married then to Xenia Cage, and she would do the copying. We had the musicians on hand to play and so forth.

So they would play the new score as you were writing it down.

Essentially yes. I would write it, she would copy it, and they would play it.

Does that first score still exist?

No, I don't think so.

Can you reconstruct it? Could it be done, given technologies available now?

It might be able to be done, but I'm not going to do it.

How did you develop in the early fifties the notion of using radio as a musical instrument?

There was a tendency through the whole twentieth century, from the Futurists on, to use noises, anything that produced sound, as a musical instrument. It wasn't really a leap on my part; it was, rather, simply opening my ears to what was in the air.

Do you remember your thinking at that time?

Yes, my thinking was that I didn't like the radio and that I would be able to like it if I used it in my work. That's the same kind of thinking that we ascribe to the cave dwellers in their drawings of the frightening animals on the walls—that through making the pictures of them that they would come to terms with them. I did that later with the tape machine in Milan when I went to make *Fontana Mix.* I was alarmed over all the possibilities, so I simply sat down the first day I was there and drew a picture of the whole machine.

That dehexed it for you, so to speak.

Right. It's true.

Now why did you choose twelve *radios, rather than just one, for* Imaginary Landscape No. 4?

There're so many possible answers; I don't remember which one was in my head. One is the twelve tones of the octave, and the other is the twelve disciples, and so on. It seemed like a reasonable number.

It's said in the history books that when you saw them lined up, you said, "Ah, twelve golden throats." Now I assume that's ironic.

No. This particular radio I was using was advertised as a "Golden Throat."

But did you think of them as "golden throats?"

Yes, because, when I was walking along one of the streets in the fifties near Radio City and these radios were in the window, they were advertised as "Golden Throats," and I immediately decided to go to the president of the company, or the manager of the store, and ask for the loan of twelve of them. I did that, and he gave me the loan.

So, with your exclamation of "twelve golden throats," you basically gave him free advertising.

Exactly.

Didn't you have two operators for each radio?

Right. One controlled kilocycles and the other controlled the tone control and the volume.

And what instructions did you give the performers?

The parts were written in what we call proportional notation, where the notes are at the points in space that they should be in time. However, this is written in a space which changes with accelerandos and ritards; so that it's at the cross between conventional notation and proportional notation. *The Music of Changes* [1951] is at the same point, so it's written in 2/2 or 4/4. The space is observed, so that fractions of notes that are irrational can be placed in it by measuring them. Then I can go, for instance, from a note that's two fifths of a quarter to a note that's one third of a half, and so on, and measure each single fragment. In this case, because you're measuring, you need not add up to whole units; you can come out completely uneven.

Which is not so easy to do in straight musical notation.

No, but I was still using quarter notes and half notes, and half notes with fractions above them, very peculiar. Later, due to David Tudor's studying a form of mathematics, to take the trouble out of my notation and doing it successfully, I dropped all notion of meter and went directly into plain space equals time, which has enormously facilitated the writing of new music.

Were those twenty-four radio-performers musicians?

Yes, they were. They could all read notes, and there was a conductor who was beating 4/4 time.

Who was he?

I was doing it.

My recollection is that there was something special about what time of day this performance was.

The first performance had almost no sound in it. Two friends of mine at the time, Henry Cowell and Virgil Thomson, both attributed the absence of sound to the fact that it was late at night—it was nearly midnight. However, I knew that the piece was essentially quiet through the use of chance operations and that there was very little sound in it, even in broad daylight, so to speak.

Because the volume levels would always be . . .

. . . always very low.

What about your other works for radio at that time.

One is called *Radio Music* [1956] and what's the other one.

Speech *[1955] "for five radios and newsreader," it says in your catalogue.*

Speech, yes. Well they're slightly different, but the radio piece was written more or less to please the people who were disturbed over the *Imaginary Landscape No. 4* because it was so quiet. I forget what I did, but it can be played so as to be loud.—Richard Kostelanetz (1984).

I imagine that 50 percent of the automobiles on the highway have a radio going and are existing in a medium of music, though very third- and fourth-rate music. Now I do not believe that that kind of music does anything to enhance what is going on within those cars and automobiles; they'd do better just to listen to the whistling of the wind.

There's one station now on the radio [in New York] that reminds me of Satie, and that is WINS. Have you listened to it? It's a [continuous] news station; and the program, if you listen long enough as you are driving along the highway, more or less repeats itself in the same way that the *Vexations* of Satie would be repeated, because you come back to the weather at regular intervals and, in fact, to the same headline news.—Alan Gillmor & Roger Shattuck (1973).

When did you first encounter audiotape?

I must have first encountered it in Paris in the late forties, when I met Pierre Schaeffer who was the first to do any serious work from a musical point of view in relation to magnetic tape. He made every effort he could to get me interested in working along those lines, but I wasn't yet really ready. I was moving . . . Well, I was writing my *String Quartet* [1950], and I had written *Sonatas and Interludes* [1948]. I was gradually moving toward the shift from music as structure to music as process and to the use, as a result, of chance operations in composition. I might have been more cooperative with Schaeffer, but I wasn't. It didn't really dawn on me.

Because of notational problems?

No, my mind was being used in a different way; so that I wasn't as open as I might have been to the notion of music on magnetic tape then. That was '49.

In '52, when I worked with David Tudor and Earle Brown, we made several pieces—one by Earle, one by me, one by Christian Wolff, and one by Morton Feldman, with funding from Paul Williams. I made the *Williams Mix* [1953] then. All of that work was done with excitement over the possibilities of magnetic tape, and they were various. That's why I was anxious not to exploit them alone but with other people, because each mind would bring into the new possibilities a different slant; and that's certainly the case. Feldman was working with his early graph music, and it was just marvelous to come to a square on his graph paper with the number, say, 1,097 in it. That meant that we were to chop up a piece of recorded tape so that it formed 1,097 fragments and splice it back into the band, you know, at that point. I was very open at the time, and very interested in splicing tape and in making the music manually. I found various ways of changing sound not with dials but, rather, by physically cutting the tape.

Such as?

Well, the tape normally goes past the head horizontally, but if you cut it and splice it back diagonally . . .

You would have to cut it into pieces so small they would be no longer than tape is normally wide.

Yes, but you could get perfectly beautiful sounds by putting it at an angle to what it should have been.

That's terribly meticulous work.

Yes, and I was using chance operations, so that I was able to go from a vertical cut on the tape to one that was four inches long at an angle on quarter-inch tape.

It must have taken years.

Well, no, it took about a year with help to splice the *Williams Mix*, which was itself a little over four minutes of music.—Richard Kostelanetz (1984).

[All this effort] is a highly questionable process, in view of the electronic utilities we now have that produce with ease musics of much greater lengths and, if I may say so, greater variety. Well, maybe not greater variety—*Williams Mix* is actually very lively in its four minutes. It might be that the kinds of variation in *Williams Mix* that did result from splicing could happen with computer programming; I don't think they could happen with the manipulation of dials, but I do think they could happen with computer programming.—Bill Shoemaker (1984).

We [also] did the *Suite by Chance* of Christian Wolff, and we did the *Octet* of Earle Brown and we did the *Intersection* of Morton Feldman.

Do all these works still exist?

I believe they do.

All I know is your Williams Mix *from the 25th Anniversary Record.*

Earle's piece, the *Octet,* was made with the rubbish from the pieces by Feldman and Wolff and myself.

Using similar compositional operations?

Using his own composing means, but with regard to the sounds that were, so to speak, thrown away through the process of making other pieces.

You know that I regard the Williams Mix *as your most neglected masterpiece.*

Well, it's an interesting piece. One reason it could very well be neglected is that the score has nearly five hundred pages and, therefore, it has not been reproduced. The original is at Peters, I think. It would be too expensive to multiply it, so I don't think many people are aware of it. I have illustrated it in the notes to the Town Hall program.

The 25th anniversary album.

People have seen one page that is like a dressmaker's pattern—it literally shows where the tape shall be cut, and you lay the tape on the score itself.

On the scale of one to one?

One to one, yes.

So the tape is, in effect, the length of five hundred pages.

Yes, each page has twenty inches, two ten-inch systems, a little over a second in duration.

Which are, in the album illustration, reproduced on a single page, one atop the other. Your idea for this score is that it would be possible to reproduce the cuts with tapes other than what you used.

Yes. I labeled each entry in the score according to the categories which were A, B, C, D, E, and F and hoped with those categories to cover all possible environmental sounds. Then I took the various parameters of sound as little letters to follow those capital letters . . .

Of the categories.

So that you would know what kinds of transformations of those original environmental sounds had been made, whether the frequency had been changed or that the loudness had been changed and so forth; so if it was the same as it was originally, it was followed by a C. If it had been varied, it was followed by a V. So "ACCV" would be a sound, let us say, from the country that had remained as it was in two respects and had been changed in a third.

And this "ACCV" you would have gotten by chance operations.

Right. And then you could have a sound described as "AVVC" or "BCVC" or their combination "ACCCBCVC," and someone else then could follow that recipe, so to speak, with other sources than I had to make another mix. It really is very interesting, don't you think?

Fantastic, yes. As you say, the score is like a dressmaker's pattern. You just simply lay it out and duplicate its cuts on your tape.

One of the pages has a hole in it, which came from a burn from a cigarette. I was a great smoker in those days.

To me, two of the special qualities of the Williams Mix *are its unprecedented range of sounds and the rapidity of their articulation.*

Right. What was so fascinating about tape possibility was that a second, which we had always thought was a relatively short space of time, became fifteen inches. It became something quite long that could be cut up. Morty Feldman, as I told you, took a quarter of an inch and asked us to put 1,097 sounds in it, and we did it—we *actually* did it.

Within a quarter inch?

Which would be one sixtieth of a second, you see, we put 1,097 fragments.

Without mixing? You mean just little slivers of tape?

Little slivers of tape.

That's physically impossible.

No, no, we did it.

How?

By counting, and by hand.—Richard Kostelanetz (1984).

[Where else have you used audiotape?]

I have two pieces. They're called *Etcetera* and *Etcetera 2/4 Orchestras* (1986), and each piece is accompanied by a tape recording of the sounds in the environment where the music was written. In *Etcetera 1,* I lived in the country; in *Etcetera 2,* I lived in the city.

Did you collect those?

No, I didn't collect them; I just made a recording.

And they were just happening while you were recording.

While I was composing.

Have you used other natural phenomena in recorded pieces?

Well, not recorded pieces. I don't make recorded pieces. But in *Variations V* I used tapes of the drain, with the drops of water coming from them in the plumbing.

Did you adjust the plumbing in any way?

No. I just took it the way it was. And then those tapes were used in a situation where I couldn't control the sound coming out. It was controlled rather by the movement of a dance company, with respect to receivers. Some of the receivers were like antennas and some were like interruptions of photoelectric cells.—Tom Erikson (1987).

[When did you work again with radio?]

The next time I was conscious of radio was with the invitation from Frans van Rossum to make the *Sounday* in Amsterdam, and that was so extraordinary that I accepted it, extraordinary because it meant something like a twelve-hour broadcast with only an announcement at the beginning and one at the end and one in the middle. That was all. Otherwise, there was no interruption of the sound. So I put into the morning the pieces for Grete Sultan, the *Etudes Australes* for piano, surrounded by performances of *Branches,* the plant materials, cacti and all, and then I put into the afternoon the *Freeman Etudes* for violin.

Would these pieces be done simultaneously, or alternately?

No, the morning consisted of *Branches* mostly, and every now and then the *Branches* would stop and you'd hear a piano étude. The image I had in mind was that of going into one of those entertainment parks through those dark tunnels in a boat, and every now and then you'd see something lit up, some image.

And then in the afternoon the tunnel changed from being *Branches* to *Inlets,* the gurgling of the conch shells filled with water, and things that were heard changed from the piano études to the *Freeman Etudes* played by Paul Zukofsky, and then toward the end they changed to the voice of Demetrios Stratos singing the *Mesostics re and not re Merce Cunningham.*

How much of this was live, and how much was prerecorded?

It was all live. The whole thing was a performance which could be attended through the whole day by people in Amsterdam. It was after that performance that I met Klaus Schöning who had heard from Frans van Rossum that I had made a *Writing Through Finnegans Wake,* and he asked me if I would be willing to read it for his Hörspiel program in Cologne, and I said yes. Then when I returned to the United States, I received a letter from him asking me if, since I was willing to read it, would I be willing to write some music to go with it, and I again said yes, and out of that came *Roaratorio.*

What were your compositional ideas here?

Well, the text is mesostics on the name of James Joyce. It's not my first *Writing Through Finnegans Wake* but the second writing. It doesn't permit repetition of the same syllable for a given letter of the name. It was an attempt to shorten the first *Writing Through Finnegans Wake;* and it not only does not permit repetition of the syllable, but it doesn't permit the appearance of either letter between two letters of the name, so that . . .

So that if the A in one line is that axis of "jAmes," that syllable . . .

Can't represent the A of another James.

Or the S, between the A and S of "JAMES." Did I get it right?

No, between the J and the A you can't have another J or A, and the syllable that's used for the J can't again be used for the J; nor can the syllable used for the A appear again, and that ensures that the text will be shorter than the first one.

And by convenience one hour long.

I'm wondering, as I tell you all this, whether I'm telling you the truth. I think what happened with the second writing is just the following of *one* of those new rules which is the nonrepetition of the syllable. It's in the third writing that I followed the new rule which I call Mink's Law, because it was Louis Mink who suggested it.

That text, as you said, existed prior to your meeting Schöning, but the compositional idea for Roaratorio *came when he asked you to write some music for it.*

Then the question was what kind of music to write for the rest of that.—Richard Kostelanetz (1984).

It's called *Roaratorio, an Irish Circus on Finnegans Wake.* The work was done with John Fullemann, who's a sound consultant, using the facilities at IRCAM in Paris. We didn't use the computer, but we used all the advantages from 16-track machines, and so on. We ended with a piece that has sixty-four tracks. It's very, very thick. Very dense. In January there were some performances with some of the tracks taken out and put back in live with Irish musicians, and my voice reading my text which is called *Writing for the Second Time Through Finnegans Wake.* It was used as a ruler through the hour. By ruler I mean that it could be identified by page and line. And then there was a book published listing the places in *Finnegans Wake,* a very large number of places; and I reduced it to a reasonable number. I think I considered reasonable the number of pages in the *Wake* which is 626. And the book I think listed some four to five thousand places. So we recorded sounds from 626 of these places. And they're around the world, but most of them are in Ireland. So it gave me the opportunity to make a chance-determined trip through Ireland, which was very, very pleasant. That took a month. And then another month was given to the putting together of those sounds and others which came from other parts of the world and from the library of the West German Radio. The piece had been commissioned by that radio together with the Dutch-Catholic Radio and the South German Radio.

What kind of sounds did you choose from those places?

We would go to a place and then look for a sound that was distinctive, that is to say which wasn't a sound that would be found in other places. The sound which is predominant through the world is the sound of automobile traffic. And so we . . . Although the tapes include that, we had a tendency to look for other sound than that. We were very fond of birds and of streams, or dogs and chickens, babies and children. And then I also went through the *Wake* and listed all the words or phrases that suggested sounds. I called that—that's a long list—*Listing Through Finnegans Wake.* There was that work to be done, to record those sounds. And they were identified also by page and line, you see; so were the places.—Andrew Timar et al. (1981).

I had done a piece earlier, *Williams Mix,* in which I catalogued all sounds as A, B, C, D, E, and F; and we could do things to any sound that was satisfactory as *A.* I used the same kind of thinking with reference to this, because *Finnegans Wake* is so complicated and has so much in it.—Klaus Schöning (1984).

Then on top of that a circus was put of Irish traditional music and my reading of the text. And we put as many sounds as we could in the space of a month. And then we stopped arbitrarily because had we continued and recorded every sound, we would probably still be working. So the notion of being able to stop came to me from thinking of the Venus de Milo, who gets along so well without her arms; so that you could have a principle of thinking that something is complete at every stage providing equal attention is given to all of those parts. In this case the parts were two sixteen-track tapes and the work . . . and in relation to that listing and in relation to the places. So then we had, you might say we had A and B, the tapes, and then we had one and two, the work to be done, plus the Irish music, which didn't need much; it had been recorded in Ireland. And my reading took one day only. So we had a little over three weeks of work to be divided between A1, A2, B1, B2; and we kept them equal, giving equal number of days to each one of those things to be done.

And then the whole was structured using chance procedures?

We knew where the sounds were to go because of the book. But the other variables were determined by chance: how loud, whether they were short, medium or long. And instead of being precise about that, I was just rough. I would make a recipe through chance operations of how a sound should be, and then John Fullemann would . . . as the sound would go on he would do what he thought was short or what he thought was medium or what he thought was long.—Andrew Timar et al. (1981).

I think that remark of Valéry's that a work of art is never finished, it's just abandoned must be true of *Finnegans Wake.* And it was abandoned in our case, the *Roaratorio* on schedule. The people at IRCAM were very surprised. I'm sure the people who work there go and waste a few days at the beginning and then [expect], at the end, a few more [days] to be added on to the schedule. We set to work the moment we arrived, and we only worked ordinary days, you know, like eight hours or so. And then at the end they really asked me whether I wanted to stay longer. I said, no, we're finished. Because, you know, we planned to stop at the end of the month.—Andrew Timar et al. (1981).

I remember once, as we were making it, when you were then in Paris, you realized that we were covering up some sounds that you especially cherished with louder sounds; and the things that you had enjoyed were disappearing. I remember a walk back into the house where we were staying, and you were trying to persuade me to leave some of those nice sounds.

I remember; I loved them so much.

I said that I had work to do. I knew what it was, and I was going to finish it, willy-nilly; and that if you didn't like it when it was finished, you didn't have to take it.

You're right. This work, with you, was permanent learning for me.

One nice thing about it is that it always seems to be different. It's so complicated that you don't somehow hear the same thing twice.

You felt in the midst that I was a bit anxious about broadcasting these three thousand sounds. . . .

I said you must think not of the audience.

And if your station throws you out, we'll give you a job in America. I wrote it in my diary.

With all the work you've done now [with Americans], I'm sure you could get a job there like rolling off a log.—Klaus Schöning (1984).

[What was your next work for German radio?]

Each [scene in *Alphabet* (1982)] has its own characteristics in terms of the mesostics, in terms of the ideas, in terms of the characters. The dictionary was subjected to chance operations, and the encyclopedia, in order to find other characters and the stage properties. Then later, seeing that it would be nice to have music to go with it, or sounds, whatever you want to call it, I obtained those sounds also using the alphabet.

How did you get these sounds, which you called "rational" and "irrational"?

Rational sounds are sound effects. If, for instance, the scene includes opening a door, then the sound of opening a door will be a rational sound. Whereas in the same scene, if we don't have any mention of a parrot, a parrot would be an irrational sound. But it would also arise, if not only the letter P arose, but P having been obtained, you would then count the number of pages in the dictionary, and subject that to the chance operations, and then on two facing pages in the dictionary you would look for the sound. And if the parrot was there, you could use it, or whatever else you find—or a pump, a water pump. And now the irrational sounds can happen anywhere in a scene—therefore, they happen at a chance-determined point. Whereas the rational sounds can either happen where they belong, or they can happen at some other time than where they belong.

Sometimes illustrating and sometimes not-illustrating.

Or sometimes being. For instance, if in the scene, someone says, "The telephone rings," the telephone might ring when it is supposed to, in which case it's rational, or it could happen to ring earlier, in which case—when you hear the words "the telephone rings," you say, "Oh yes, I know the telephone rings." Or if it happens later, then the memory goes into operation. This is the Buddhist principle: everything is related. . . .

With everything?

Even irrational things are related to rational things, fortunately.

Your first idea was, you told me, "Please find a Chinese child who can speak German." Buckminster Fuller you had in, and we have George Brecht; and we have Teeny Duchamp, and you spoke the role of James Joyce.

I think there has been a great inclination in the aspects of theater to get rid of acting and to have the real McCoy. It began with Saroyan, I think. He thought instead of having an actor be a streetcar conductor, for instance, to have a streetcar conductor be a streetcar conductor. Or instead of having somebody represent Buckminster Fuller, to have Buckminster Fuller doing it.

But here we have a problem with the dead ones, the ghosts, who have to be represented by live people, unless—but this never occurred—to get some psychic person to go into a trance and speak voices. . . .

So you spoke the character of James Joyce.

That was because I like to read from *Finnegans Wake.*

So you spoke the real quotations of Joyce, and you spoke your inventions of what Joyce had perhaps said. And then—it's a nice idea, I think—you divided your friend Marcel Duchamp into two parts.

Divided him into two beings. Well, he did that himself. I don't know whether he would agree, but I ascribed his writings to his female alter ego, Rrose Selavy; and then, when he wasn't writing, but just saying something, I decided naturally that he was male.—Klaus Schöning (1982).

Just before beginning the production of HMCIEX *at WDR in Cologne, you'd been in Torino working with a thousand children. What was it like—a joyful coming together, like a children's music Olympiad perhaps.*

I think it turned out very well. There were a thousand children, from four years old to twelve. They sang the songs they learned in school. Some of them danced.

So the Olympic Games also bring together thousands of people peacefully fighting, we can say; and you agreed to make a composition for this event [the 1984 Olympics].

I had the idea of letting the countries be represented by their folk music. How many countries? There are 151 countries that have recognized Olympic committees. I don't know who does the recognizing. Some of them, of course, haven't accepted the invitation to come to Los Angeles, but that was a political decision, not an Olympic or athletic one. I decided for musical reasons to keep all 151 in the situation. I wanted the feeling of "Here Comes Everybody," and that's what the title is—the "H. C. E" of "Here Comes Everybody" alternating with the letters of the word "mix."

You always have a relationship with Finnegans Wake *and Joyce.*

I think the notion of a musical circus, which the children's work in Torino was, is just that—here comes everybody.

So you put in the folk music and the names of the countries, but in a very strange way.

I separated the names of all the countries into syllables, and I found that in the German pronunciation of them there were 520 syllables; but in the English pronunciation, there were 502. So by chance operations, I was able to locate one of either kind.

Let's turn to the music composition. We have 151 folk musics, on records and tapes from the WDR archive. How did you bring together all these musics?

I took the total length, in seconds, and submitted it to the *I Ching,* and I found that number of entrances of sounds I needed in that total length. Originally, the total length was to be fifty-five minutes. It has since been cut in half, because the work turned out to be so complicated that the amount of time I asked for, and which was available, was insufficient to do the splicing that became necessary. Through chance operations, the sounds came so close together the only way they could be realized was through splicing. It turned out, in the end, even when we cut the tape in half and superimposed the halves in a way to get the density that we might have had, there still was no time for the splicing.

But what we do have on the tape is the proper order of the sounds, and we have the proper dynamics, and we have the proper stereo locations, composed through chance operations. A further element of indeterminacy is that the splicing will not be according to a score but will be according to the circumstances of simply removing unnecessary silences from the unedited tapes, until we come to the proper lengths.

You told me that after you make this decision, you don't feel unhappy.

No, I feel liberated. There's something extraordinarily domineering about a score which one is trying to realize exactly. Long ago I moved to independence of parts, from a fixed score, a fixed relation. I look forward to hearing it. It will certainly be another example of nonintentional music, with the desire to free sounds from my notions of order, feeling and taste.—Klaus Schöning (1984).

Another thing that's equally shocking is the quality of television entertainment, which is being absorbed willy-nilly by so many people. That is what has kept me from supporting the so-called public broadcasting system, because they are as bad as the others, and I think their programs, for the most part, are very bad, and yet they're supposed to be so good, so elevated.—Geoffrey Barnard (1980).

I find the fund-raising as annoying (if not more annoying) than the commercials of the other stations—I end by not looking at it.

I think though, theoretically, if cables continue and multiply, that the television will become a kind of university; they'll have to have something to broadcast, and eventually they'll broadcast something interesting like the monkeys working with the dictionary or encyclopedia or the alphabet.—Jack Behrens (1981).

VISUAL ARTS

Most people don't realize how difficult it is to make modern art—because the mind is so much in control that it keeps people unpoetic and unimaginative. At the time that I met Mark Tobey there was a show involving watercolors in Portland, Oregon, and the public was indignant because it was still in the thirties and they didn't take modern art seriously then. They said that it should not be shown in the museums and that it was no good. So the people in charge of the museum put up blank paper on the opposite wall, divided the show into what the public could do and what the artists had done—and the public quickly learned that they didn't know how to criticize.—Robin White (1978).

So, in that [thirties] climate my involvement with painting (and I had done some painting) was toward abstract painting. I was impressed by the Bauhaus, for instance, and I was particularly impressed by Mondrian, or such a thing as Malevich's *White on White.* I was more or less of the opinion that representation in painting was not anything that could interest me. I was very much attracted by the fantasy of Klee, and even the late faces of Jawlensky. Curiously enough, with this love of abstract painting, I didn't so much enjoy Kandinsky as I did Klee and Jawlensky, so the story really isn't a clear line. Nevertheless, I didn't think of proper painting of the time as being anything but abstract. If I were going to paint, and I had meanwhile given up painting, it would be abstract painting, and it would tend toward geometric painting. That is the position that I held during the thirties, and I came to New York only to find the Surrealists in sway, with André Breton here, you see. So that the current involvement in painting at the time wasn't abstract at all, but was involved with symbols, and also their relations to the private aspect of an individual's life. Even though I enjoyed the friendship of an evening at parties and so forth of a number of those artists including Max Ernst, David Hare, etc., my heart didn't go out to Surrealism at all.

Even the idea of automatism?

Automatic art, in fact, has never interested me, because it is a way of falling back, resting on one's memories and feelings subconsciously, is it not? And I have done my utmost to free people from that.—Irving Sandler (1966).

Did Surrealism ever come to influence you in any way?

I never liked it.

For what reasons?

Because of its involvement with psychoanalysis.

What are your objections to psychoanalysis?

The same as Rilke's: "They might remove my devils, but they would certainly offend my angels." But my objection was also my own, it came from an analyst saying that he could fix me so that I'd write much more music and, as you have pointed out, I already write a sufficient quantity; so it's questionable whether I should do much more than I already do. It was such a fad. I think we are somewhat free of it now and I notice in society now a general willingness to criticize psychoanalysis. Surrealism is so closely connected with it—in my mind at least—that I didn't find it interesting. I found Dada much more interesting, in the same way I find the work of Rauschenberg and Johns interesting in the sense of Dada, and I find the recent Pop Art after them uninteresting in the sense of Surrealism, not a Surrealism of the individual but a Surrealism of the society.—John Roberts with Silvy Panet Raymond (1980).

Before we continue with the Surrealists, let me pick up something that happened to me when I was still on the West Coast, namely, the encounter with Morris Graves and Mark Tobey. And though I loved the work of Morris Graves, and still do, it was Tobey who had a great effect on my way of seeing, which is to say my involvement with painting, or my involvement with life even. I remember in particular a walk with Mark Tobey from the area of Seattle around the Cornish School downhill and through the town toward a Japanese restaurant—a walk that would not normally take more than forty-five minutes, but on this occasion it must have taken several hours, because he was constantly stopping and pointing out things to see, opening my eyes in other words—which, if I understand it at all, has been a function of twentieth-century art: to open our eyes; *not* to do as the Surrealists wish, that is to say, to make us less guilty perhaps, or something like that.

Or to certainly bring up unconscious matter.

Something like that. But this had to do with eyes, something that really I could use.

Just seeing what was there.

Just seeing what there was to see.

Now I don't remember the exact date of it, whether it was in the early or middle forties, but there was an exhibition at the Willard Gallery which included the first examples of white writing on the part of Mark Tobey. I liked one so much that I began buying it on the installment plan. I've since, unfortunately, sold it. It was a painting that had no representation in it at all, though his paintings including his white writing paintings frequently do have representational elements. This one had nothing. It was completely, so to speak, abstract. It had no symbolic references. It was a surface that had been utterly painted. But it had not been painted in a way that would suggest the geometrical abstraction that interested me, so it brought about a change. And also that walk to the Japanese restaurant brought about a change in my eyes, and in my relation to art, so that when I left the Willard Gallery exhibition, I was standing at a corner on Madison Avenue waiting for a bus and I happened to look at the pavement, and I noticed that the experience of looking at the pavement was the same as the experience of looking at the Tobey. Exactly the same. The aesthetic enjoyment was just as high. Now this didn't keep me from buying the Tobey, and painfully buying it. So, you have a change then in my view. Now this change, that was really the result of my involvement with Tobey, naturally opened my eyes to Abstract Expressionism, not to its intentions, but to its appearance.

In other words, I used Abstract Expressionism as though it were something I could use, not as something that had been given to me to understand, but as something that I could see in the way that I had been changed to see. What you have in the case of Tobey, and in the case of the pavement, and in the case of much Abstract Expressionism, is a surface that in no sense has a center of interest, so that it is truly distinguished from most art, Occidental and Oriental, that we know. The individual is able to look at first one part and then another, and insofar as he can, to experience the whole. But the whole is such a whole that it doesn't look as if the frame frames it. It looks as if that sort of thing could have continued beyond the frame. It is, in other words, if we were not speaking of painting, but speaking of music, a work that has no beginning, middle, or ending, nor any center of interest—we come back now to talk about art. So, this makes it clear that the experience of art is essentially not an objective experience, but rather a subjective experience. And it is available only to the people who are equipped to have it. I would agree that the world of that person has been changed, but I would say that it has been changed due to changes in his way of seeing. In other words, it has been changed, not from the Surrealist emphasis on the subconscious and the unknown area of the collective unconscious in dreams and all of that, and automatism, but it had been changed by things that are more daytime accessible, that is to say, by what we experience through our senses.

But there is a shift here from the intention of Abstract Expressionism to the way their works struck you. You were aware at the time of their intention.

Well, I was vaguely aware. I have become more aware as time has gone on. I never agreed with their intentions, if I know what they are, and I'm not really clear that I do know what they are.

I recall a few incidents that would lead me to believe that we always disagreed. For instance, it was clear to anyone in the late forties that the work of Bill de Kooning was of extreme interest. I recall a painting of his with which I had no difficulty whatsoever—a black and white one which was exhibited for a while at the very entrance of the Whitney Gallery when it was still on Eighth Street. In the black and white, which had no center of interest, etc., had been impressed some newsprint. You recall the painting?

Yes.

This painting was one of the most glorious paintings I have ever seen. Now, maybe Bill meant something else by it than the way in which I used the painting. But the painting, as far as I was concerned, was exhilarating and introductory to the very life that I was living, not to some insight on the part of Bill de Kooning, but life itself.

Did you get the same feeling with the work, say, of Ad Reinhardt or Barnett Newman?

Reinhardt—the work was so appealing that I tended to resist its appeal. To be perfectly frank, I think it's more recently that the work of Newman and Reinhardt have impressed me deeply. The present exhibition of *The Stations of the Cross* I think is superb, and I see now that it makes quite explicit what I would think are the intentions of Abstract Expressionism.

Or certainly part of them.

It would seem to be to me *truly* Abstract Expressionism.

The reason I raised their names at all was because Bill does *have this way of introducing material out of our experience in a way that they don't.*

He did for me in a way that I could understand in that black and white painting with the newsprint impressed.

Now things get mixed up, because I can use those *Stations of the Cross* by Newman perfectly well, although I think I could use them better had he included a fifteenth station, which would not leave us in the void, but which would bring us back to the image that comes at the end of the ten ox-herding pictures in the second version of Zen Buddhism, namely, the fat man returning to the village bearing gifts with a big smile on his face. Now this smile is largely missing from Abstract Expressionism. I remember hearing Harold Rosenberg say, after the exhibition of Pop and Op art a year and a half ago, "Where is all the suffering?" And I continually made it clear in my discussions of art that I prefer laughter to tears.

Now how did I come to that view? I came to it partly through recognition that if art was going to be of any use, it was going to be of use not with reference to itself, but with reference to the people who used it, and that they would use it not in relation to art itself, but in relation to their daily lives; that their daily lives would be better if they were concerned with enjoyment rather than misery—it seems evident. I came to it that way, and I came to it also through my personal need which had brought me to a study of Zen Buddhism.

We haven't mentioned one important figure in the whole setup, which is Jackson Pollock.

You were friendly with him?

Well, I more tried to avoid him. I did this because he was generally so drunk, and he was actually an unpleasant person for me to encounter. I remember seeing him on the same side of the street I was, and I would always cross over to the other side. Now and then I would be unable to avoid the encounter; we would meet, and he always complained that I didn't like his work enough. And I didn't. The first time I saw it was at Peggy Guggenheim's apartment uptown. She had a hallway downstairs and there was this enormous mural of his of . . . It seemed to me to be taken from the human body, and that immediately made my interest diminish. Then came along those things that you would think I would like, namely, the all-over dripped canvases. But I was familiar with Tobey, and Pollock's work looked easy in relation to Tobey's work which looked far more complex. It was easy to see that, from observing a large canvas of Jackson Pollock's, he had taken five cans or six cans of paint, had never troubled to vary the color of the paint dripping from the can, and had more or less mechanically—with gesture, however, which he was believing in—let this paint fall out. So the color couldn't interest me, because it was not changing. Whereas if you look at the Tobey, you see that each stroke has a slightly different white. And if you look at your daily life, you see that it hasn't been dripped from a can either.

But what about the pitch of intensity, the excitement?

Oh, none of those aspects interested me. They're precisely the things about Abstract Expressionism that *didn't* interest me. I wanted them to change my way of seeing, not my way of feeling. I'm perfectly happy about my feelings. In fact, I want to bring them, if anything, to some kind of tranquillity. I don't want to disturb my feelings. I don't want to spend my life being pushed around by a bunch of artists.

So actually de Kooning's late works of the forties probably were a bit more to your liking than the most aggressive expressionist in the fifties. . . .

I found the women very difficult to take. In fact, I didn't really like them. I can see that they're beautiful works of art, in fact great works of art, but if that's what art is, it doesn't interest me.—Irving Sandler (1966).

There is a paradox in modern art between the work of Albers on one hand and Pollock on the other. Rather than seeing these two things as opposites, I have tried to see them as the same thing, because you see these two tendencies everywhere in modern art—the one toward the symmetrical, and the other toward an overall surface without any center. They seem to be opposite, but I think the opposites are the same. I think the result of both is to engage the observer in his experience of each—namely, that when I look at the Albers and see it as symmetrical, I begin making a movement of my experience of looking which is not controlled by Albers but is original to me, because I'm not interested in symmetry. I can understand it immediately, so I begin traveling throughout the painting. And this is precisely what I do with Pollock; so my experience of the two, which appear to be different, is really very similar.—Lars Gunnar Bodin et al. (1965).

Do you think you need a lot of scholarship to see Duchamp's work?

I don't feel I need much scholarship to enjoy Duchamp as *I* enjoy him.

How do you enjoy him?

The way I do. Whether the way I enjoy him is the same way he intended, I have no way of knowing. I could have asked questions about that, but didn't.

Because you weren't interested?

No, no. I didn't want to disturb him with questions. Supposing he had not been disturbed by some question I had asked, and had answered it, I would then have had his answer rather than my experience. Furthermore, he left the door open by saying that observers complete works of art themselves. Nevertheless, there is still something hermetic or inscrutable about his work. It suggests scholarship, questions and answers from the source. I spoke to Teeny Duchamp once about this. I said, "You know, I understand very little about Marcel's work. Much of it remains mysterious to me." And she said, "It does to me too."—Moira & William Roth (1973).

Schoenberg himself was opposed to other people writing twelve-tone music. I asked him a question once about some twelve-tone problem, and he said, "That's none of your business." People can take the attitude, say to Oriental thought, that the goal is to sit cross-legged and to do deep breathing exercises and to follow the letter of the system of deep breathing. My attitude was not to do those things that Oriental people did but to find, if I could, the principle of Oriental thought. And the same thing with Schoenberg, the same thing with Duchamp. So I never asked Marcel any questions about his work. Maybe I learned this from Schoenberg, because when I asked Schoenberg something about his work, he said, "None of your business."

We think often in the West that we can ask someone who knows and he would give us the answer. But in Zen, if you ask the teacher the question and he gives you the answer, and if he asks you the same question and you give him back the answer, you get hit over the head. So it seemed to me it was improper to ask Duchamp questions. I already knew that Duchamp wasn't interested in music—almost not at all; so I knew in that situation, it would be absurd, for instance, to ask him, do you like what I did. Even to ask him "do you like" was out of the question.

So it happened I was walking on MacDougal Street in the Village, and he was on the same side that I was. That was the period when I didn't wish to bother him with my friendship, though I admired him. He may have asked me to come and see him, and I went to an apartment in the Village. I forgot who else was there. The one thing I remember from our conversation was that the talk turned to dope, and Marcel said that he didn't think that dope would ever be a serious social problem. And we said why not? He said people won't take any more dope than they now drink liqueurs.

Meaning by that alcohol?

No, crème de menthe, Cointreau, . . .

Later, it must have been in the early sixties, it just happened that one holiday season between Christmas and New Year's, when there are so many parties in New York, we happened to be invited to the same parties. Suddenly, I saw him every night, four nights in a row; and I noticed there was a beauty about his face that one associates, say, with coming death or, say, with a Velásquez painting. And I realized suddenly that I was foolish not to be with him, and that there was little time left. And so I said to Teeny [Mme. Duchamp], "Do you think Marcel would be willing to teach me to play chess?" Because I knew that that would be a way to be with him without asking him questions; or if I asked him questions, they would be ones it would be useful to know the answers to. And so she said, "Why don't you ask him yourself." So I went up to him and said, "Would you teach me chess?" And he said, "Do you know the moves; do you know how the pieces move?" And I said, "Yes, I know that"; and he said yes. And so we made an appointment, then, for me to go to his house; and after that, we were together as often as possible, at least once a week when they were in New York, or sometimes twice a week.—Alain Jouffroy & Robert Cordier (1973).

Do you think your idea of silence has anything in common with Duchamp?

Looking at the *Large Glass,* the thing that I like so much is that I can focus my attention wherever I wish. It helps me to blur the distinction between art and life and produces a kind of silence in the work itself. There is nothing in it that requires me to look in one place or another or, in fact, requires me to look at all. I can look through it to the world beyond. Well, this is, of course, the reverse in *Etant Donnés.* I can only see what Duchamp permits me to see. The *Large Glass* changes with the light and he was aware of this. So does a Mondrian. So does any painting. But *Etant Donnés* doesn't change because it is all prescribed. So he's telling us something that we perhaps haven't yet learned, when we speak as we do so glibly of the blurring of the distinction between art and life. Or perhaps he's bringing us back to Thoreau: yes and no are lies. Or keeping the distinction, he may be saying neither one is true. The only true answer is that which will let us have both of these.

Duchamp seems so much less physical in his art than you do.

A contradiction between Marcel and myself is that he spoke constantly against the retinal aspects of art, whereas I have insisted upon the physicality of sound and the activity of listening. You could say I was saying the opposite of what he was saying. And yet I felt so much in accord with everything he was doing that I developed the notion that the reverse is true of music as is true of the visual arts. In other words, what was needed in art when he came along was not being physical about seeing, and what was needed in music when I came along was the necessity of being physical about hearing. However, with *Etant Donnés,* we feel his work very physically, not abstractly, and in a way which can be deeply felt. Music is more complex, I think, than painting, and that's why chance operations in music are just naturally more complicated than they would be for painting. There are more questions to ask about a piece of music than there are about a painting.—Moira & William Roth (1973).

Of all the painters of the forties, Tobey would be the most central for you—the man whom you esteem the most.

And of his work the white writing which had no representational elements in it.

Now, the person who changed that for me, Bob Rauschenberg, made those black paintings which appealed not only to me, but to Franz Kline, who happened to be at Black Mountain the same summer [1948], and I would approach them [the Rauschenbergs] on several levels—either from the Tobey point of view or from the Mondrian point of view. Those black paintings could be approached exactly as I had approached Abstract Expressionism—namely, as a surface having no center of interest, which was not necessarily confined by the frame. Furthermore, the composition, if there was any, appeared to be Mondrianesque. Now that, at the time, made it possible for me to embrace it wholeheartedly, because of my previous involvement with geometrical abstraction and my devotion to Mondrian. Later when I wrote about Bob, it became the one problem that I had with his work: namely, why did he cling to geometrical abstraction? And particularly to those horizontals and verticals, you see.

One of the interesting things you said before was that you could use certain Abstract Expressionist works, or, say, the works of Tobey and de Kooning, because it reinforced certain tendencies in your own work, say, chance, for example?

No, I used it as I walked around the city.

I see. You didn't mean specifically in terms of your own work?

No, certainly not. That would happen, no doubt, and would happen in terms of reinforcing my notion that there needn't be a climax in a musical composition. Such influences—certainly. But the way to use visual work, it seems to me, is not by, certainly, a dialogue, that is to say transformed, but transformed as I just mentioned, but the immediate use would be to change my way of seeing. Wouldn't it?—Irving Sandler (1966).

I liked everything Bob [Rauschenberg] showed me, and he showed some earlier works. In fact, he gave me an early painting which had a Dada flavor, which was a collage of curious elements. Later he came into my house and painted over it, and I mention this in my article on him in which I say the door is open, and he comes in and paints, and what have we lost. . . . So I had to accept that because I was interested in his notion of impermanence. I had no argument against it. But then as Bob's work became more and more representational, my eyes were opened by him to representational things by way of seeing; he made it possible for me to see not just the pavement that Tobey had made it possible for me to see, in other words an all-over situation, but he made it possible for me to see a Coca-Cola bottle for heaven's sake.

Then there was a relation between that idea and the idea of using radios in your work.

Right. All of that goes together, then it brings back with great impact the work of Marcel Duchamp.—Irving Sandler (1966).

I think there's a slight difference between Rauschenberg and me. And we've become less friendly, although we're still friendly. We don't see each other as much as we did . . . I have the desire to just erase the difference between art and life, whereas Rauschenberg made that famous statement about working in the gap between the two. Which is a little Roman Catholic, from my point of view.

Meaning what?

Well, he makes a mystery out of being an artist.—Martin Duberman (1972).

I was not able to see Johns's work immediately. It was again through Rauschenberg that I was able to see Johns's work. And I continued, even though Rauschenberg had great enthusiasm for Johns's works, to have difficulty with it. In fact, the difficulties I had with Johns's work are among the difficulties I most cherish. They too have obliged me to change—not my eyes alone which needn't change. For instance, you can look at a Johns work without paying any attention to it, except with your eyes. And so enjoy it the same way you would enjoy Abstract Expressionism or Tobey or anything that was nonrepresentational. But if you accepted it as a flag or a target, for example, your mind has to change, and this has been why his work has been not weaker and weaker as time has gone on, but stronger and stronger. It has changed the nature of art criticism, and more potently so than the work of Bob Rauschenberg. And it has made re-emphatic, it seems to me, the work of Duchamp.

You're saying, then, that at one point Johns opened you up to that as well.

I don't take it as his opening me up to that; I take it as his changing my mind in terms of "Am I going to open myself up actually to include what it is he proposes, what it is he does. Am I going to change my mind, and my answer is yes." But then I qualify that answer with "yes, but with difficulties."—Irving Sandler (1966).

What questions come to mind when you think about Duchamp?

The things I think about him don't lead me to ask questions, but rather to experience his work or my life. At a Dada exhibition in Dusseldorf, I was impressed that though Schwitters and Picabia and the others had all become artists with the passing of time, Duchamp's works remained unacceptable as art. And, in fact, as you look from Duchamp to the light fixture (pointing in the room) the first thought you have is, "Well, that's a Duchamp." That's what I think, and that doesn't lead me to ask any questions. It leads me to the enjoyment of my life. If I were going to ask a question, it would be one I really didn't want to know the answer to. "What did you have in mind when you did such and such?" is not an interesting question, because then I have his mind rather than my own to deal with. I am continually amazed at the liveliness of his mind, at the connections he made that others hadn't, and so on, and at his interest in puns.

Would he pun when you talked to him?

He tried to every now and then. He liked it in conversation. He was very serious about being amused, and the atmosphere around him was always one of entertainment.

Would he talk to you about your work?

We really never talked about his work or my work.—Moira & William Roth (1973).

Another thing that Marcel used to talk about in those last years of his life, which recurred in his conversation—not with me but with other people, he would arrange it so that it came up. He'd say, "Why is it that artists are willing to let people look at their work from any distance?" And he, of course, was thinking of *Etant Donnés,* in which he obliges them to look through the peephole of the door. No one had thought, before he thought of it, of making a situation in which he would control the position of the observer, and for him to control, he who had been the one to remove control from art!—Terry Gross (1982).

One thing that was difficult for me to understand in Cadaqués was the attitude that Marcel had toward [Salvador] Dali. He admired Dali very much. Did you know that? The second year I went to Cadaqués Marcel asked me if I would like to visit Dali, and I said no. I was furious that all the postal cards in the local post office had photographs of Dali, and there were no cards of Duchamp. Poor Marcel. The next year, when I came back, he said, "I think you should visit Dali, whether you want to or not." I said okay. So he made an arrangement, and we all went over to see Dali and what's the lady's name.

Gala.

And the moment I entered the house, I just didn't feel at home. We sat in a large circle, and Marcel sat next to Dali; and I think it was outdoors in a kind of patio. And they served the pink champagne, and Dali talked all the time. Marcel never took his eyes off him. Marcel said almost nothing. Dali was perfectly happy talking as though he was the king, but the situation was the reverse, I thought.

Finally, Dali asked whether we wanted to see his painting. Marcel said, "Oh, yes." And we went into his studio, and here was this huge painting, oh, four times the size of that wall; and Marcel proceeded to admire it. And it was vulgar and miserable.

After Marcel died, I was back in Cadaqués, and I was invited to a house where Dali was. We sat next to one another at a luncheon. I was searching then to see if I could find in Dali something that might have attracted Marcel; and I happened to notice his eyes were very beautiful. I don't mean "beautiful" in the sense of being beautiful in themselves, but that they seemed honest, with some kind of transparency and even a certain simplicity; and that is the closest I've been able to get to an admiration of Dali.—Alain Jouffoy & Robert Cordier (1974).

At what point in your compositional career did you begin to treat musical scores as pictures too?

That arose as a by-product. The intention was to make a notation that would recognize that sounds did truly exist in a field; that our previous notation had not permitted our recognizing this fact or even acting on this fact; that we needed other notation in order to let sound be at any pitch, rather than at prescribed pitches. In order to do that, it had to become graphic; and in becoming graphic, it could accomplish this musical purpose.

When this Town Hall [twenty-fifth anniversary concert] came up, sponsored by Bob [Rauschenberg] and Jap [Johns], through their energy and everything, they wanted to ornament this occasion in such a way that it would be prominent in the society of '58 in New York. So they said we'll have an exhibition of your scores. I had not thought of them as art. That they thought of them as something to look at was, of course, gratifying.—Irving Sandler (1966).

And it was music that out of its own generosity brought me back to painting. It's not that I've given up music, but it's that in the late forties and early fifties it became clear that there's a physical correspondence between time and space. And music is not isolated from painting, because one second of sound is so many inches on tape. That means that the old metres of two, three and four are not longer necessary, and that space on a page is equivalent to time. Therefore, I began doing graphic notations, and those graphic notations led other people to invite me to make graphic works apart from music. And those led me in turn to make musical scores that were even more graphic, so that the whole thing is . . . I don't feel that I'm being unfaithful to music when I'm drawing.—Ev Grimes (1984).

How did your plexigrams come about?

They were commissioned by a lady in Cincinnati, Alice Weston, who has a certain interest in both music and painting. She has commissioned Gunther Schuller to do work, and it was through her and her husband that I was made composer in residence at the University of Cincinnati. Then she got the idea that though I had not done any lithographs, I could do some. She asked me to do some. Marcel had just died, and I had been asked by one of the magazines here to do something for Marcel. I had just before heard Jap [Johns] say, "I don't want to say anything about Marcel," because they had asked him to say something about Marcel in the magazine too. So I called them, both the Plexigrams and the lithographs, *Not Wanting to Say Anything About Marcel*, quoting Jap without saying so. What I did was to subject the dictionary to chance operations and to use the *I Ching* with respect to a dictionary that had images, and to make a transition from language alone to language with imagery and numbers, and then as I say in the preface to all that, I think Marcel would have enjoyed it. I found a remark of his after I had done the work, that he often enjoyed looking at signs that were weathered because, where letters were missing, it was fun to figure out what the words were before they had weathered. The reason, in my work, that they are weathered is because he had died. So every word is in a state of disintegration.

How did you like that business of actually putting it all together?

Well, I didn't do that work. It was done by Calvin Sumsion, I composed it. I wrote it. First we worked together, then I was able to tell him to do something, and then he would send back the work completed. Albers has used such methods—hasn't he with his own work?—or he gives it to some craftsman to do. Those things. Many artists now, when they don't know a particular craft, learn how to tell a craftsman what to do.

How did you like doing the lithographs and all that?

Oh, it's very exciting, and it made me understand why so many artists become alcoholics, because when you put a blank sheet of paper into the press and something actually happens to the paper when it comes out, it's so exciting that you just have to have a drink. Whereas with music, you can't drink, because the occasion of hearing the music is a public one, not a private one, and the drinking all takes place after the concert.—Paul Cummings (1974).

And I am making etchings. I've been doing a great deal of that in the last five years.

Etchings . . . not of scores?

No, graphic work, in a sense bringing to that graphic work ways of working that came from music. And now I notice this piece [*Thirty Pieces for Five Orchestras*] is responding to some of the ideas I got making etchings, to bring it back into music. That's how these metrical passages developed. I had templates which were . . . I took this size of paper, and I made a grid of 64 by 64 on it to work with the chance operations. And through chance operations I cut the piece of paper, the full size of it, into templates. Those templates, of squares and triangles and such, are so that the points of the shapes could become sounds. Or holes could be put in the shapes to produce sounds. And shapes when, through chance operations, were put on the sheets, sometimes projected off that way or this way. Well, if it came off this way [to the left], it would start one of these metrical situations going on the strong beat; and if it went off that way [to the right], it would start it off on the weak beats. And *where* it went off gave the pitch, because I had designed the paper to be completely sound. The reason these are so far apart is that the ledger lines of one instrument touch the ledger lines of the adjacent one. Then these will be the points inside or around the outside of the shapes and which of these possibilities you did was chance-determined, whether you were looking for the holes or the shapes themselves.

Do the etchings you're doing have anything to do with Thoreau's drawings?

Yes they do. I made one series which was called *17 Drawings of Thoreau.* I took, through chance, certain drawings of Thoreau and enlarged them through chance operations and so forth. But when I put them on the copper, everything was done so that the drawing would be clear. In other words, I was following the kind of advice that one would receive if one was moving toward high fidelity. Then, in a subsequent series, called *Changes and Disappearances,* I subjected all of those activities to chance operations. And the result is some of the drawings disappear, and some of them are only faintly visible, and so on. And then there is dry point, and I've learned to engrave. As that particular series continued, it moves from a kind of simplicity to quite a great complexity. Because I ask the question each time a plate reappears whether it's mobile or immobile; and if it's mobile, it receives a new image.—Andrew Timar et al. (1981).

Toward the end of the first day [in making a portfolio of seven prints called *Seven Day Diary*], *I Ching* chance operations were used with respect to two techniques—hard ground and drypoint—determining the tool to be used and the number of marks on a copperplate to be made with it. All marks were made without looking at the plate on which I was working. Lilah Toland kept count since I sometimes missed the plate.

What is the advantage of not knowing what you are doing?

It cheers up the knowing. Otherwise, knowing will be very self-conscious and frequently guilty.—John Ashbery (1978)

I was asked by a French editor who lives in Marseilles, André Dimanche. He makes a series of books; there will be fifteen. They're called Edition Ryoan-ji, which is the name of the garden in Kyoto that has the sand and fifteen stones in three groups. He asked me to make a cover for a book of my writing [*Le Livre des champignons,* 1983] that they are publishing in the series. The paper that he has is about this size [ca. 9 1/2" high, 18" wide]. I looked around the house for fifteen stones, and I simply drew around the stones at points determined by the *I Ching.* And I sent that result, which pleased me, to him, and it pleased him. That had fifteen drawings.

When I went to Crown Point Press, I took the stones with me. I began by drawing around the stones, as I had done for the drawing, but now on copper and drypoint. When we printed the result, it was absurd—absolutely uninteresting to look at. I worked for a week trying to find a way to print it that would give it a quality of being interesting, but it never became interesting. Then it occurred to me to have recourse to multiplicity, and so I multiplied fifteen by fifteen, which makes 225; and I drew around each one of the fifteen stones fifteen times, making three drypoints, which you see. When we printed them, they were immediately interesting. At least I think, and then people have told me they find them. . . . We say, when we like a work of art, that it is beautiful; but what we mean is that it's interesting, because the word "beauty" has no meaning other than we approve of it; the only reason we approve of it is that it keeps our attention. The reason they interest me is that I can look at them for a long, long time and I would never know the end of it; I see something I hadn't noticed before. This is also the case for me with the work of Mark Tobey, which I loved very much; so that these, in a sense, are my response to the work of Mark Tobey. In another sense, all of my work is a response to Mark Tobey.—Press conference, Cologne (1983).

Would you say something about the prints you will be doing at the Crown Point Press?

I began last January making prints by means of fire. I'm building a fire on the press and putting the dampened paper on the fire and then rolling it through and then later also branding it with an iron, Japanese iron teapot, like the one you saw this morning. Now I'm going to continue that in a more carefully controlled way and use chance operations with respect to the time the fire is allowed to burn the paper. Having found out the least amount of time necessary for a print, and the amount of time it takes to destroy the paper completely, and then to use chance operations, finding out through them, how many seconds the fire should continue.—Ellsworth Snyder (1985).

On the interplay between art and music:

I think that this is a realization in music that is different from what music was at the turn of the century. It was then that music so greatly influenced the visual arts as to be the excuse for the turn toward abstraction; you recall, cubism and so on. All the manifestos spoke of music as having already accomplished this that was now being done in painting. I think that much of what is being done since 1950 in music is a response to this question you spoke of in the visual arts which was the response to music, and that the dialogue continued because the physical circumstances are different to bring about changes. So that music's response now to the visual arts of the first half of the century produces a situation to which the visual arts must now reply, or may reply. I think it's already involved film, for instance, in the use of a plurality of screens rather than one. That *that* is like music without a fixed score.

You see this can proceed in many directions. Not just, dogmatically, one. It can proceed—there is one film I saw at Montreal['s Worlds Fair]; it was called *Labyrinth.* Now there was a case of several screens being used quite dramatically which I should say corresponded to a nineteenth century orchestration. So that one film related to another dramatically at special moments. And that if the films were not synchronized, fixed together, that the dramatic effect intended would not be gained.—Don Finegan et al. (1969).

Could you explain the function of silence in your music compared to the "white page" of Mallarmé?

I've always felt very close to Mallarmé; and the book that was published posthumously, *Le Livre,* also is very involved with chance operations, is it not? I often think of him, though I haven't studied Mallarmé closely. But one has the feeling of space in which a variety of things can be present.

But didn't you say, on the other side, at least concerning your music, that there is no such thing like silence?

Right. There always are sounds.

Well, just in comparison to Mallarmé's fear of the "white page?"

He had a fear of it?

In some way, yes, he had to write something on it at least—the fear of every author of having a white page in front of him.

Well, clearly, my silent piece doesn't express that fear but expresses the acceptance of whatever happens in that emptiness. And the same thing was expressed by that empty painting, that white painting of Bob Rauschenberg, which I mention in the note which precedes [the article on him in] *Silence.* It saw that the white paintings came first and my silent piece came afterwards. And Mallarmé preceded both.—Birger Ollrogge (1985).

I thought it would be interesting to speak about the nature of silence in three different arts, one of them film. By that means, perhaps, we might get a notion of what the nature of the film may be.

My normal reaction to film, my everyday reaction to it, is that I enjoy all of it. Many people enjoy poor films. I, with them, am overcome by the pleasure simply of looking at moving images.

On the nature of silence:

You know that I've written a piece called *4'33",* which has no sounds of my own making in it, and that Robert Rauschenberg has made paintings that have no images on them—they're simply canvases, white canvases, with no images at all on them—and Nam June Paik, the Korean composer, has made an hour-long film that has no images on it. Now, offhand, you might say that the three actions are the same. But they're quite different. The Rauschenberg paintings, in my opinion, as I've expressed it, become airports for particles of dust and shadows that are in the environment. My piece, *4'33",* becomes in performance the sounds of the environment.

Now, in the music, the sounds of the environment remain, so to speak, where they are, whereas in the case of the Rauschenberg painting the dust and the shadows, the changes in light and so forth, don't remain where they are but come to the painting. In the case of the Nam June Paik film, which has no images on it, the room is darkened, the film is projected, and what you see is the dust that has collected on the film. I think that's somewhat similar to the case of the Rauschenberg painting, though the focus is more intense. The nature of the environment is more on the film, different from the dust and shadows that are the environment falling on the painting, and thus less free.

These things bring me to my thought about silence: to me, the essential meaning of silence is the giving up of intention. As we might expect, few films follow silence in renouncing intention: when one looks at films (and I here lump together art films and Hollywood films) one sees that intention is almost never renounced. I think that the closest to the renunciation of intention—if we forget the Nam June Paik film which has no images on it whatsoever—would, in my experience, be through the films of Stan VanDerBeek, a renunciation of intention which is effected through the multiplication of images. In this multiplicity, intention becomes lost and becomes silent, as it were, in the eyes of the observer. Since he could not be looking at all five or six images at once but only at one particular one, the observer would have a certain freedom. However, even in this work of VanDerBeek, as in most dance, in fact, there seems to be an absolute unwillingness to stop activity, to renounce intention.—University of Cincinnati (1968).

On whether films must necessarily be "linear":

It isn't necessary. We see in the work of Stan VanDerBeek and others that it's perfectly reasonable to have things going on at the same time that aren't related, or as with the ONCE group in Ann Arbor, Michigan, during their sixteen mm Festival. There something else appeared. It appears in my experience more and more. They discovered with that film festival that the films could be poor, but that the combination of them was not poor. Now this is very much what Bucky Fuller says when he says "synergy," or what happens when we make an alloy of metals so that a strength comes from things that don't have that strength until they come together. So that the whole question of quality which has been of such concern to the university—or to the whole question of education, to teach the good rather than the bad—is put in question because the bad if it enters into an abundant enough situation is no longer bad. In fact, it's a little spicy.—Don Finegan et al. (1969).

Another way to get the absence of intention that I spoke of is through the multiplication of films, the multiplication of intentions. This was done by the Ann Arbor group when they had a festival of sixteen mm films. Now, though each of the films was full of intention, the sum result was an absence of intention. And that brings us to our daily experience.

Yet in one film I have seen in the [Cincinnati] festival—[Stan] Brakhage's *The Dead,* the one concerned with the tombs in the Parisian cemetery—I noticed that, at one point, there was something that looked like absence of activity—the point at which the camera moves behind the wall so that it couldn't see what it had been looking at.

It may be a good thing for film to introduce this lack of intention, this silence. Or, perhaps it may not: such limitation would confine film to the medium itself, to film. It may be because of this potential confinement in the nature of film that filmmakers have chosen to present images that travel so widely into the world.—University of Cincinnati (1967).

Any experimental musician in the twentieth century has had to rely on painters.

Why is that?

Because the notation of music was like Latin, and any divergent use of it was like Protestantism, and you couldn't expect the priests of the church to have any interest in what you were doing, because you were in a sense threatening the position of the whole Greek aspect of music, which is bound up in its notation, which is Greek to the layman. So, any lively musician—you just name them through the century—has had to go to poets and painters for friends.

But why have poets and painters been receptive in the first place?

Because they were the lively changers of art to begin with, and they did it by saying, "Well, look at music, music has done it already." Music was abstract before we were. All the early documents about abstraction, cubism, and everything, refer to music.—Irving Sandler (1966).

[*On the playing of his music as background during an exhibition of his visual art.*]

Don't play it all the time.

Why, could it be disturbing? I don't understand. If I hear two of your [music] pieces together, it is not disturbing to me.

At the Guggenheim Museum in New York, they always thought there was a close relation between music and art, and so they had music being played while we would look at the Kandinskys in their collection. I found it absolutely impossible.

What kind of music did they play?

The music that Kandinsky liked.

Cannot your lecture today be superimposed over your drawings?

I prefer the superimposition of things to be nonintentional, like the sound of traffic and church bells; that I can deal with. But when you play something which is from me, because you are looking at something from me, then you begin to make an intention.—Press conference, Cologne (1983).

DANCE

When I first saw modern dance, I saw Martha Graham, Doris Humphrey and Hanya Holm, and of those three I preferred Martha. I preferred *Celebration* and some of her solos. When her work became literary, as in *Letter to the World,* I grew disinterested in it. I begged Merce to leave her theater and to make his own. And I promised that I would help with music.—David Sears (1981).

How have all these things come together in your mind and work? You work in music, theater, writing, lecturing, dance . . .

Mushrooms . . .

That kind of range is very unusual today.

Don't you think again we would have to trace circumstances? When I was just beginning I wrote a piece for a clarinet solo. Since I knew it was difficult to play I called up the first clarinetist of the Los Angeles Philharmonic Orchestra. And when he looked at it, he said, "That's not the way to write music." He thought I should write like most writers, so he was not going to play it, and advised me not to do the sort of thing that I was committed to doing. Then I made another stab at getting this piece done, and it failed again. That time not because the clarinetist wasn't willing to play it but because he didn't have the time to devote to learning to overcome its difficulties, and didn't choose to overcome them. The circumstances again.

Then at just about that time I was called up by some modern dancers at UCLA, who actually wanted me to do something . . . and so I did it, and in that way I soon learned that if you were writing music that orchestras just weren't interested in—or string quartets, I made several attempts, I didn't give up immediately—that you could get things done very easily by modern dance groups. At the time I was interested in structure because I was fresh from working with Schoenberg. I thought that dealing with noises as I was I'd need another structure, so I found this time structure and immediately was able to give it to the dancers to work with. Time was a common denominator between dance and music, rather than being specific to music as harmony and tonality were. I freed the dancers from the necessity to interpret music on the level of feeling; they could make a dance in the same structure that a musician was using. They could do it independently of one another, bringing their results together as pure hypothetical meaning. And we were always delighted to see that what we brought together worked.—Michael Kirby & Richard Schechner (1965).

Most of my work with other people has been with dancers, and among dancers I've worked particularly with Merce [Cunningham]. The first thing I noticed in the thirties was that the modern dancers wanted to be first with respect to the music. They wanted the musician to be in a subservient position as far as the collaboration was concerned. They always finished the dance before inviting him to see it. This was opposite to the way a musician worked with ballet; there the music had to be finished before the ballet was begun. Neither way of working was to my liking, though I was willing to accept either. It would be better, I thought, if two people working together could work without either following the other. The best procedure, I thought, would be working independently, that is, in different places at about the same time and then later enjoying seeing/hearing the two works coming together, paying attention to them both as they happened rather than expecting something preconceived, or an approximation of it, to happen.—David Shapiro (1985).

I have never been satisfied with the Balanchine-Stravinsky collaborations which have been dependent on making ten ☙fingers❧ seem to be like two ☙feet❧, which is impossible. Therefore, in working with Merce, the first thing we did was to liberate the music from the necessity to go with the dance, and to free the dance from having to interpret the music. The way that was done was that I had established a rhythmic structure for music, since I didn't have access to a harmonic structure. And I made those rhythmic structures that are based on the square root, and then Merce would make a dance within that structure. I would make music within the same structure, and then the two could come together without in any way having forced each other in terms of details. Then the dance was independent, but in the same structure.

Then as my work continued, I gave up the need for structure by getting involved in process, and the dance was free to be in that process. The result is now two things that are not at all even structured the same way can go together.

In our collaboration, as it made itself evident in 1960 here in Europe, when Merce and Carolyn [Brown] performed with David Tudor and me, the response, particularly in Cologne, where there were many musicians who value my work, found that the dance was not as advanced as the music. Partly this was due to their unfamiliarity with dancing, and partly, I think, it's due to the nature of dancing, this two-legged business, which is dependent, for instance, on periodic rhythms—the mere action of walking or running is an old-fashioned notion which cannot in any way simulate the aperiodic rhythms of modern music.

In our present trip, take the response of, for instance, [Mauricio] Kagel in Cologne, who had seen the work of Carolyn and Merce together, and now sees the [entire dance] company. He was extremely impressed by the choreography and felt that something had changed, whereas all that changed were more people and the complexities that result from more people dancing together, to obscure the simpler aspects of dance and to introduce to the observer the more complex and seemingly more contemporary aspects.—Lars Gunnar Bodin et al. (1965).

I think it's well known by now, and less irritating than it used to be, that Merce and I introduced an independence of the music and the dance into our practices. People aren't annoyed by it anymore, because they've experienced it so many times it doesn't bother them.—David Sears (1981).

Schoenberg had impressed upon me the need in music for structure (the division of a whole into parts). He said this should be accomplished by means of harmony, tonality. I had no feeling for harmony. I was interested in noises. I had to find what would be the proper structure for noises, and when I found it—an empty time structure—I found a proper structure for collaboration between two arts such as dance and music. And that, of course, covers all sorts of things, singing, for instance, anything, in fact, that happens in time.

Could you explain?

It was already traditionally true in India, that the time-arts were not separate from one another, in fact they have a term—I'm not sure what it is—but there's a term that covers both dance and music, and time is of the essence there, because it is used by both arts.

Have you also ever worked with film, another time-art?

Not really in this sense. In my experience filmmakers are not interested in questions of structure.—David Shapiro (1985).

The mixing of music and "happenings"—isn't that an evolution?

As theater moves toward happenings, and toward the inclusion of the kinds of things, for instance, I include in music, in the piece that I described before as *o'oo"*, where anything we do is made apparent as music, when through happenings anything we do is made apparent as theater, then the discipline that dance is tends to disappear. This is precisely the situation in which Cunningham [now] finds himself—namely, he is devoted to the discipline of dancing. I think it is through the way in which he has handled that discipline and what he has done with it, in part and to other influences too, that the happening has come about; but this tendency is more, I think, toward the dance than away from it. And this is because he is one of those rare people who is, so to speak, born as a dancer. He didn't take on dancing, but rather was a dancer to begin with; so that it's difficult for him in view of the interest in happenings and the strong tendency in that direction, to do what an athlete or dancer must do—namely, to work every day in class. And this repetition of the exercises, which resemble print more than electronics, which resemble classical dancing more than happenings, is nevertheless physically necessary if he is to dance at all. I think this is his principal problem at the present moment. Were he to give up the daily class, all the dancing, as he has lived to do it, would become impossible, because the things that are done are athletic in character and are not possible unless you maintain a daily discipline in the same sense that one cannot high jump unless the body is physically disciplined. Now happenings do not require any discipline whatsoever. Now this is the position, somewhat heartrending, of Merce Cunningham, as I see it.

We have thought all along that if one writes something as a composer or writer that that work will live after we die, and so I've never considered that I've had to work day and night, because I have plenty of time. Furthermore, my work need not even be appreciated while I am alive, because it might be appreciated after I die. A dancer is not that way; a dancer is as impermanent as a flower that can only be seen while it is blooming.—Lars Gunnar Bodin et al. (1965).

I was brought up to worry. I am very good at worrying. I think if left to myself I wouldn't have much to worry about, but I manage to connect myself with many other people whose problems worry me. I'm very worried, for instance, about the Merce Cunningham Dance Company, because it seems to be almost impossible to make a physical situation which is reasonable and comfortable for so many people and to make it work economically.—Moira & William Roth (1973).

As Merce's work has developed, it satisfied me with respect to my love of theater. What is so amazing is that he is constantly making some discovery that alters. The work you see is different from what you experienced before.—David Sears (1981).

Are you going to do music for dance soon again?

Well, I've written this text which I'm beginning, and I'll go on with it, called *Empty Words;* and I think it will be very suitable for dance accompaniment. It doesn't make any ordinary sense, but I think we know now from our own experience (and we may as well cite Artaud again) that there isn't such a thing as a thing that doesn't make sense. So language that we thought had to make sense in a particular way can make sense in other ways. I can read you a little passage of this, which I think makes a great deal of sense, but what sense it makes we're not sure. You're not sure what it's saying, but you can get some kind of an idea.—Robert Cordier (1973).

Do you think of the music collaborating both with the set and the dancers?

The only thing I think about is that they are in theater and that theater involves primarily the two sense perceptions of seeing and hearing. I don't think that tasting, smelling, and touching, the other senses, are as much involved in theater as seeing and hearing. If you add tasting, smelling and touching to theater, you get ritual.

Seeing is very different from hearing. It's biologically different. It responds to physical laws differently. Kierkegaard noticed this in his praise of *Don Giovanni.* He loved Mozart's *Don Giovanni* more than any other work of any art because it was the freest from physical constraints. Whereas dancing, for instance, is an acceptance of physical constraints, a response to them and an enjoyment of them.

In terms of your collaborative work with Merce, your work remains indeterminate, while his . . . even though chance operations are used in the choreography . . .

It has to be fixed, because of the physical movements involved in dancing. There are no such dangers involved in a piece of music—nobody's going to get hurt—whereas dancers are going to get hurt if they bump into one another. And so they have to rehearse very carefully.

But in [Cunningham] Events, *though the sections from one dance collage with, into another, they still have rehearsed it.*

Oh yes. Otherwise if they used any energy at all, any great energy, it would be dangerous.

Could Merce dance an indeterminate solo? Or has he?

He was interested in indeterminacy in *Story* and *Field Dances* [in the 1960s]. These works are examples of it with the company. But the thing that led him away from that was his interest in high energy, because both those works had to be slow and careful.—David Shapiro (1985).

Four or five years ago, Cunningham would have said that the indeterminacy you can exercise in music is physically dangerous in dancing, because if two people moved with great strength, as they must to do certain things, and collide, you have something equivalent to a catastrophe which could make it impossible for either one of them to dance again. This is a problem with architecture—if the building is badly built, it will fall down. But then he has found ways to permit more freedom on the part of the dancers than formerly. In *Story,* for instance, the activity of the dancers is not as energetic as it is, say, in *Rune;* so should they bump into one another in *Story,* it might be inconvenient or ludicrous, but it wouldn't be physically dangerous.—Lars Gunnar Bodin et al. (1965).

Have you seen our *Dialogue* that Merce and I do together? Sometimes I move in that, from one part of the stage to the other. I just walk. I don't dance. But I do feel I'm aware that I'm on the stage with a dancer, so that because I move, that has to be thought of in relation to dancing. One couldn't avoid it. I don't alter it. I'm just aware that I'm moving where angels fear to tread.

What I try to get to, if I can, and I think I can get to it, is an enjoyment of all the moments. Not trying to single out a special moment. Special moments, of course, do come, admittedly; but I try to be open to every moment being special. In the theater and now when we're not in the theater, I want all the time to be special, rather than one moment, so that I would tend to not want to desire one thing more than another. My intention is not to have a desire. Or rather my desire is to pay attention to all of it. Insofar as I can. That's why I love the sound of this traffic, because I must say that there isn't a dull moment for me in this apartment. I listen to that sound all of the time, and Sixth Avenue is fantastic!—David Sears (1981).

I've noticed when I've seen dance that was not supported by the music, the dance immediately looks physically strong and rhythmic in its own right. Each movement looks like a rhythm in a way that it never does if it's going with the music. Now I simply can't enjoy that, two things happening in unison. It just drives me berserk.—David Shapiro (1985).

There is a dancer in the United States who in many respects is like Merce Cunningham, in the respect that night is like day, and that is Ann[a] Halprin; and her work is very much like the happenings, but it's very nocturnal, whereas Merce's work, except for the new dance called *Winterbranch* [1964], is not nocturnal at all but is, as it were, in full daylight. The thing that is similar between them is a complexity—many things going on at once, possibly in different rhythms, with different kinds of things happening simultaneously. Ann Halprin does not keep up the daily discipline that Merce does. When she has an idea for a dance, and wants to bring it about, she then searches for the discipline that will facilitate the things she wants to do, and wants her dancers to do; and so they make special exercises to enable them to do the particular dance that they want to do. That is her theory, and it results in a greatly different activity. There's a greater tendency toward lack of discipline in that whole way of working, whereas with Cunningham there's an equally great tendency toward discipline. And it is between these two things—that we will hopefully see as the same thing—that we are nowadays working.

What I'm hoping is that rather than seeing esthetics disappear between the different arts that we will understand these differences as coming from the physical nature of the arts themselves. And I think with Cunningham choreography that, even though many of the steps can be quickly related to ballet rather than Happenings, this can be enjoyed as dance; and the similarity between dance and happenings, or the common denominator, is theater. There is, nevertheless, a difference between dance and happenings—(a) having been born to do it; and (b) the question of discipline.

But these Happening events leave space for indeterminacy.

Yes. If you take a work of Ann Halprin's, which is quite complex and where the various people perform independently and yet with a very loose decision as to what will follow what, you will discover that most of the movement is not dangerous. Nor does it call for great physical exertion from anyone doing it. The result is the freedom is greater.

But observe the disciplines that are necessary for airplanes, particularly as they increase in speed—jet planes, therefore. You would think that, due to electronics, there would be a great deal of freedom; but you discover it is necessary to have a great deal of discipline. Otherwise, they would collide.

There are greater freedoms in the [dance] work of Yvonne Rainer than there are in Merce's work, and she has found ways to do that with her group, has she not?

In her group things, there's always been a complex structure, so that dancers usually know where they are going to be.

So you don't have much chance to fall into somebody. That approaches the dance, rather than happenings; but when she dances as a soloist, it gives the impression of great freedom, as though it might be different from time to time. In Merce's case, when he dances as a soloist, the movement tends to become more elaborate in details, wouldn't you say. I think that's because he has no wish to impose his understanding of details on another person. He's tried to find ways in which the people he's worked with would do what is natural to them. You might notice in his performances a great difference between [company dancers] Carolyn Brown and Viola Farber, and he doesn't give to Viola the kinds of movement that he gives to Carolyn, even though he asks them, in a piece like *Rune,* to do the same thing.—Lars Gunnar Bodin et al (1965).

[Where can modern dance go?]

The two things that music now is able to free itself from, as I see it, are pitches and rhythms, because those are the two aspects that were easily measured. It is difficult to measure tone quality or overtone structure, and also difficult to measure dynamics, but easy to measure tone and pitch; so as we give up those measurements, we're able to move into a field of activity.

Now in dance, if you give up things that correspond to rhythm and pitch—namely, movement on two legs—what do you have? It's almost as though you couldn't give it up. You could, as you suggested, have a film, or the movement as we do have now of abstract shapes on film, or transmitted on television; but that isn't the dance. And no matter how electronic our culture becomes, we will still have the question of two feet on the earth, and that very fact is going to produce dancers. There is nothing about scales and periodic rhythm in the art of music that makes them so eternally necessary. Rather, I would agree with Busoni, who says that music gains its true nature when it is free of all such physical necessities; and where we notate regular rhythms, as Busoni says, they come to life only with rubato, they come to life only with irregularity.

But in the very nature of the dance are such questions as balance, muscle control, left-right, left-right, etc.—Lars Gunnar Bodin et al. (1965).

SUCCESSORS

I often state, and believe to be true, that there is no piece of music written in the past thirty years that has not felt the influence in some measure of John Cage. I know of few composers who do not pay full respect to you regarding their own work. How do you react to this?

I try to be totally ignorant of that. That's the only way I know of to solve it. I don't think it's accurate, though. I think that when a person does something he does it originally, even if he's thinking of something he calls an influence. I really think that each person does his own work.

I guess the kind of influence I am referring to is that of, for example, [Witold] Lutoslawski, who, when I saw him a few years ago, claimed that his music was radically changed after he heard your Concert for Piano and Orchestra.

That's a very good example. He does say that he made certain changes in his work after hearing mine. What he did, of course, was original to him and exactly what I'm saying, so I don't feel any problem there at all and I enjoy his work when I hear it, and I enjoy it as *his* rather than as *mine.* I think that's what is good about my influence, if there is one, that there are more possibilities open to people than there were when I was young.

When I was young, you had either to follow Stravinsky or Schoenberg. There was no alternative. There was nothing else to do. You could perhaps have felt that you could follow Bartók, or you could have translated that Bartók into Cowell or Ives, but we didn't think that way then. We thought Schoenberg or Stravinsky, and the schools certainly felt that way. I think, for example, that folk music was thought of only in the way that Stravinsky thought of it. Now, of course, there are 1,001 things to do, and I think that that's partly a result of a kind of step that not only I took, but others took.

It would seem to be a more healthy situation now . . .

Well, it's certainly more suitable for a larger population, which is the case, too.—David Cope (1980).

How close a contact do you maintain with composers on the Continent?

Well, I see them when I'm there, and they see me when they're here.

Do you find ties between what you're doing presently and what they're doing?

Well, the Europeans are mostly involved in all sorts of things that I'm not involved in—control, center of interest, all such things. And I'm not involved in that and they tend to think, well, we can take these ideas of indeterminate things so far, and include it in a total picture which we will, of course, control. And I'm not even interested in whether they win and I lose.—Yale School of Architecture (1965).

When I first met Pierre Boulez in [Paris in the late forties], the smile, the energy, the brilliance of the eyes, all of it was electrifying to me; but in New York, I saw another side. Once, on our way back from Cape Cod, we ran out of gas. Pierre thought that was inelegant. I also remember a diner in Providence. Pierre was indignant over the service and the food, and I believe that he required us to leave. I was always frightened by his superior taste. He was always uncompromising. Things had to be exactly where they should be. I was still terribly poor. I wanted to make poverty elegant, but Pierre was not interested in that. What he wanted was an excellent richness. Everything had to be exactly right, aesthetically right. Once I dropped into my studio unannounced [where and when he was working] and he was wearing an elegant silk robe.

With Pierre, music has to do with ideas. His is a literary point of view. He even speaks of parentheses. All of it has nothing to do with sound. Pierre has the mind of an expert. With that kind of mind you can only deal with the past. You can't be an expert in the unknown. His work is understandable only in relation to the past.

After having repeatedly claimed that one could not do what I set out to do, Boulez discovered the Mallarmé *Livre.* It was a chance operation down to the last detail. With me the principle had to be rejected outright ☙by him❧; with Mallarmé it suddenly became acceptable to him. Now Boulez was promoting chance; only it had to be *his* kind of chance.—Joan Peyser (1976).

I think he [Karlheinz Stockhausen] was gifted. He had a number of children and they've all become musicians, haven't they? So there was some transmittable involvement with music. What is true of Stockhausen is that it seemed to us that the music was avant-garde, that it was making discoveries, but it wasn't doing that. It was actually very conservative. Nothing was being revealed; the old places of emphasis were being reaffirmed.—Morton Feldman (Bunita Marcus and Francesco Pellizzi) (1983).

Just this last November, I was in Metz and went to a lecture that Karlheinz gave, and I was astonished to see that his whole insistence on musicality as relationships and oppositions was very, very conventional, and not in any sense a discovery. He gave a detailed lecture in which he said that listening was actually listening to relationships. In my opinion, listening is listening to each sound. If you listen to the relationship, you lose those sounds.

Can you escape that? Isn't hearing simply recognizing the relationships of sounds?

In Karlheinz's case, you have to know that something is a close interval or a distant interval, and that one is the inversion of the other, and so forth; whereas, as I listen to these sounds around us, I hear them all without making any attempt at such relationships. We're quite different, so that when people think we're the same, they're quite mistaken.—David Stanton (1982).

You mention the relation of my activity to that of Merce Cunningham and David Tudor. And you ask if my activities would have been the same without those people. Certainly not. I have to work with other people and these two are two of the most mysterious and stimulating to me. I am not at all the kind of personality that either Cunningham or Tudor is. And it is for that reason that they fascinate me so much.

I think that the relationship is unique, after so many years, that the three of you were at the same time each following his own path, but you are something all together.

Yes, yes, it is quite marvelous. I often felt even that David Tudor is—good heavens, he must be at least twenty years younger than I am—always seemed to me to be older. I think he was born older but I was born very young and always was surprised that he was not a composer. And now I am very happy that he has become a composer, and the fact that he is a composer now has somewhat separated us, because we no longer perform together, except with Merce Cunningham; but then we come as two different people, where formerly we came, so to speak, as one person. I am delighted that this has happened, and I do not regret what could appear to be the loss of David Tudor. For instance, no one to my knowledge now plays the *Music of Changes* the way he did. However, the piece had a life while he played it.—Alcides Lanza (1971).

If you knew David Tudor, and worked with him as I did over a long period of time, you would say he's one of the great musical . . . I was going to say "minds." I would say that of Schoenberg. But David Tudor is not so much a musical mind as he is a musical . . . At that time, he was, as Busotti said, "a musical instrument." And when Busotti wrote a piece for him, he didn't say "for piano"; he said "for David Tudor," meaning him as an instrument. David still has that aspect in the society. I noticed him recently in California after a concert with the Cunningham Dance Company, and the young composers of the Bay Area flocking around him because of his technical knowledge and technical experience in the field of live electronics. And formerly, it was in the field of piano. And before that, it was in the field of the organ. But he was such an extraordinary musician that, if you were near him, and even now if you're near him, you don't need anything else. The world is immense through him, has no limits, has only inviting horizons.

Why do you suppose David never played any Ives?

I asked him why he didn't play Ives because that's the remarkable thing that is missing in his history. He said, "It's too difficult." And I don't know what that meant. That is why he's so fascinating. At first, I didn't know what he meant, because it was not too difficult from the point of view of his hands. He played the Boulez *Second Sonata,* which is more difficult. Either he told me or I then realized that he would have had to change his mind over into that of a transcendentalist, which he didn't wish to do. When he played the Boulez sonata, he read the poetry that Boulez was reading at the time—René Char. He learned the French language in order to read that poetry; he didn't know it until then. He became, insofar as he could, the composer. And he said it would be too difficult to do that in the case of Ives. Had he done it, we would have had performances of Ives that we haven't yet had.

This sounds very elitist, and I think I am actually an elitist. I always have been. I didn't study music with just anybody; I studied with Schoenberg. I didn't study Zen with just anybody; I studied with Suzuki. I've always gone, insofar as I could, to the president of the company.—William Duckworth (1985).

The other two people who have meant so much to me are not musicians but painters—Robert Rauschenberg and Jasper Johns.

Can you, so to say, project yourself with your imagination, and think if these people would have been the same by themselves not having had this relationship with John Cage.

No. We have to take a Buddhist attitude toward this business. We are all related and it was simply fortunate that we came together. My relationship with Jasper Johns is similar to my relationship with Cunningham and Tudor. That is to say, *I don't understand him.* My relation to Rauschenberg is quite different. I recognize Rauschenberg as myself, as if we were the same person. We do not even have to explain things to one another. I can have conversations with either Tudor or Cunningham, or Johns, in which I remain puzzled by what they say, even after many years. I never know what any one of those three is going to say, whereas I can predict, but still enjoy, what Rauschenberg could say, because he, like me, is interested in constant changing.—Alcides Lanza (1971).

My two closest friends among [visual] artists are [Robert] Rauschenberg and [Jasper] Johns. And I knew many of the other painters, but my kind of family attachment is to Rauschenberg and Johns. And then I always admired Duchamp so much that I couldn't speak straight, and about four or five years ago, I asked him to teach me chess, so I often was with him in his last years, and I love his work very much. Originally, I had liked abstract painting, and particularly Mondrian. And then it was Rauschenberg who opened my eyes to the possibility of something that wasn't abstract and then it's been so interesting because it was then Johns. I see Johns now more than any of the others. I like, let's see, of the ones since then, I think Claes Oldenburg.

Is there a connection?

Yes, I think so. One example with me is that my next project if I do do it—sometimes I have projects I don't do—is to make as realistically as possible a thunderstorm. To take an actual thunderstorm and to measure it and then to use the ten thunderclaps in *Finnegans Wake* and have them actually sung. To have components, electronic components, made so that what the singers sing is transformed to fill up the envelopes of the actual thunderclaps is the idea. And to have the strings pizzicato, which will make raindrops and the rain falling on different materials because the thunderclaps in *Finnegans Wake* are a history of civilization's technology. Well, that is, to my mind, a response to Jasper Johns' beer cans. Because it sets out to make something which is as much as possible this other thing.—Don Finegan et al. (1969).

La Monte Young is doing something quite different from what I am doing, and it strikes me as being very important. Through the few pieces of his I've heard, I've had, actually, utterly different experiences of listening than I've had with any other music. He is able either through the repetition of a single sound or through the continued performance of a single sound for a period like twenty minutes, to bring it about that after, say, five minutes, I discover that what I have all along been thinking was the same thing is not the same thing after all, but full of variety. I find his work remarkable almost in the same sense that the change in experience of seeing is when you look through a microscope. You see that there is something other than what you thought there was.

On the other hand, La Monte Young's music can be heard by Europeans as being European. For example, take the repetition of a tone cluster or a single sound at a seemingly constant amplitude over, say, a ten-minute period. The European listener is able to think, "Well, that is what we've always had, minus all the elements of variation." So they imagine, you see, that something is being done to them, namely, a simplification of what they're familiar with. My response is not that he is doing something to me, but that I am able to hear differently than I ever heard ☙because of what he has done❧.—Roger Reynolds (1961).

I was very impressed the other day when I heard Herbert Brun's *Infraaudibles,* which is also sound output from computer, a sound that was different from the sound of tape music or other forms of electronic music with which we are now familiar. It was an experience with which I was unfamiliar, not only with sound qualities and juxtapositions of them and the delicate changes within a sound with respect to its timbre, but also the pitch relations which were microtonal and which were not arranged, as I understand it, according to any scale. The pitches were chosen within fields set up by Brun, chosen by the machine according to random operations, ending up having microtonal pitch relations which are still extremely fresh and interesting to our ears. This will all lead to perceiving things with which we are unfamiliar, and, even if we don't perceive it in all of its details, we would have an experience which we have not yet had. I had this kind of feeling years ago with La Monte Young's music, for instance, and then again the other day with the sounds from Herbert Brun's piece. This would lead us to believe that this experience of being surprised by what it is that we experience will continue. The changes I'm speaking of are not slight ones but are almost as if it were another country, another continent, or another planet that had been discovered.—Larry Austin (1968).

Do you see any set of developments in the arts that you are especially interested in?

I don't know what you mean by set. I am not interested in organized art, e.g., the New Romanticism, New Wave, etc.—Jay Murphy (1985).

That interest in place in relation to music is a contemporary concern. For instance, I was in a hallway in the basement of Wesleyan University, Middletown, and there was a concert of students of Alvin Lucier there in which you could walk through a corridor and only at nodal points in the hallway did the sound become audible. In other words, you could pass through the sound physically, you could walk through it. It was electronics and the nature of the architecture—that close relation of sound and architecture also found in some pieces by Pauline Oliveros, just as that same concern for place arises in artists who deal with earthworks.—Bill Womack (1979).

In the forties I would pick up new books and see nothing interesting. It was in the fifties I became aware of Jackson Mac Low. I admit that his work was difficult for me at first, but Jackson faithfully sent me things as they appeared; he had been in my class at the New School.

In 1956.

And gradually I became devoted to his work and enthusiastic about it.

Jackson is a friend, whom I admire almost as much as you do, but it seems to me that Jackson, interesting as his methods are, missed the trick. He doesn't know that you have to cut it somewhere. That's why his pieces invariably go on too long. Even if you're involved with chance operations, the trick is that somewhere you must impose taste—you must decide that one procedure is not going to work any longer or that another device is a more inventive way of doing things.

That may occur in Jackson's work because, if he's using chance operations, he works with a rather limited reservoir of material, like a page from a particular book or something.

And then one not as interesting as Thoreau's Journal *or* Finnegans Wake.

And you immediately get the notion of repetition. Or if he's using the words that appear from a single person's name, as he often does, words naturally get repeated: repetition becomes the dominant characteristic of his work. I thought for a while that, since he was involved, as I am, with chance operations, I ought not to bother using chance operations with language; but then when I saw that I was interested in nonrepetition, it was as though I could enter the same field Jackson was in without stepping on his toes. And that's why I continued to do it.

Jackson's also very eclectic in his esthetics, as you know. He has expressionistic poems as well as those we've spoken about.

I first encountered this among artists, the people who painted oil paintings and who refresh themselves by painting watercolors. And I think that's what it is with Jackson. In order to refresh himself from the one, he does the other. I went to a reading the other night, and he read a more recent poem—in fact, he said it was a poem written that very day. It was another *Light Poem.* And it was more or less off the top of his head. It was that sort of thing. But, oh, Richard, his head has a lovely top, and the least thought that enters his head is a very good thought.

Really?

No, I think so, because it was really rather his least thoughts that were in the poem. And then there was another poet that evening whose considered thoughts were less entertaining than Jackson's offhand ones.

Are there any other writers that you . . .

And I think, in general, that we can say that the act of picking up a magazine or something to do with literature now is a less pat matter than it would have been in the thirties or even the fifties, because there's far more experimentation going on, so to speak, generally, than there was in those decades.

And "reading" has also become more problematic, in a fundamental sense.

And I've noticed too that an audience—for instance, the audience listening to Jackson read the other night at St. Mark's—was really attentive throughout and delighted with things that would have completely confused an audience of twenty years ago. Or at least twenty-eight years ago, twenty-five years ago.

You're calculating, I can tell, for the early fifties, which you regard as the extreme nadir of experiment in art in this country. Is 1953 your calculation?

No, 1952.—Richard Kostelanetz (1979).

Is it possible to say that the "Cagean" influence is also present in conceptual art?

I don't agree with that notion. I think that we are all together and that ideas are also equally available to us. For instance, two inventors invent the same thing at the same time. This must be that they didn't influence each other, but that they were influenced by the possibility of having that idea. So I think that what appears to be my influence is merely that I fell into a situation that other people are also falling into. And what is so nice about the situation is that it admits a great deal of variety. I would say that it admits more variety than if you fell into the twelve-tone system.

I have thought, for instance, that *4'33"*, which could be thought to be the source of my influence on conceptual art, was a very physical work, not conceptual. I thought of it as a quick way of hearing what there was to hear.—Alcides Lanza (1971).

[How else is the world of composition different now?]

Now young composers coming along tend not to think of entering that old structure of finding a publisher to publish their music—they'd rather distribute it themselves. They move about the world more or less as performers. The whole thing of the distribution of information in the form of correspondence is now worldwide. What does that bring about? It brings about a community of individuals who have no one ruling what they may not do. They are free in their musical actions from anything resembling economic or political structures. They are, so to speak, in an anarchic situation with a very few exceptions, and those exceptions are when, as with Nam June Paik and Charlotte Moorman, they step on prejudices which the society still maintains by means of its beliefs. Where else do they fail, in terms of the old structures? They fail when, through their actions to which they are dedicated, they are somehow not able to make a living and starve, or have to change their directions because of their desire for food and so forth. I think that all of these things go together in such a way that we don't have to solve just education or just art, but we have to change the entire society.—Robert Filliou (1969).

ESTHETICS

I said earlier that I was more interested in a mediocre thing that is being made now, which is avant-garde, than I am in the performance of a great masterpiece of the past.

The business of the great things from the past is a question of preservation and the use of things that have been preserved. I don't quarrel with that activity, and I know that it will continue. But there is another activity, one to which I am devoted, and it is the bringing of new things into being.

The difference between these two points of view is the difference between spring and summer.—Stanley Kauffmann (1966).

Oh, yes, I'm devoted to the principle of originality—not originality in the egoistic sense, but originality in the sense of doing something that it is necessary to do. Now, obviously, the things that it is necessary to do are not the things that have been done, but the ones that have not yet been done. This applies not only to other people's work, but seriously to my own work. That is to say, if I have done something, then I consider it my business not to do that, but to find what must be done next.—Roger Reynolds (1961).

Any ideas as to why people don't open their ears?

That's up to the psychologists. I can't understand why people are frightened of new ideas. I'm frightened of the old ones.

I think that the things that happen to us daily change our hearing and our whole experience. There have been known cases where the playing of new music took seventy-five rehearsals by trained musicians, and young students coming out of cornfields who had listened to the radio were able to play it with only two rehearsals.—Arnold Jay Smith (1977).

It's been suggested that the options that were so wide open twenty-five years ago just haven't been explored.

I think the musical world is in a very different situation than it was when I was young. When I was just beginning there were only two things you could do: one was to follow Schoenberg and the other was to follow Stravinsky. If you want to be a modern composer now, there are so many things to do, and people do them. Some of them don't even know who I am. And yet all that freedom exists. It comes about through a great change in technology and through a really changed world in which people who were formerly in cultures that were separate are now fully aware of each other. And it comes about through a greater number of people, so that there is, as Marshall McLuhan once said, a brushing of more information today than there was fifty years ago. It's a changed world. It's not a world in which we are obliged to follow a mainstream represented by X or Y.—Rob Tannenbaum (1985).

. . . we live in an age where everything is possible. Once we had the Mona Lisa, now we also have the Mona Lisa with a moustache.—Michael Zwerin (1983).

I think this question of music lagging behind the other arts is not necessarily always the case, that the arts can be seen as being in dialogue, and that at one point music may be in a position of not having spoken and not having replied to something that was said by another art earlier. And that would make it seem to be lagging. But when it does speak, it often adds something new to the dialogue, putting the other arts then in the lagging situation.—Alan Gillmor & Roger Shattuck (1973).

There was a movement in the '60s and early '70s toward making the process of composition audible within the music—in [Steve Reich's] Come Out, *[Alvin Lucier's]* I Am Sitting in a Room, *and so on. Has that ever held interest for you—to make the compositional process audible in your work?*

I think it was Steve Reich who said it was clear I was involved in process, but it was a process the audience didn't participate in because they couldn't understand it. I'm on the side of keeping things mysterious, and I have never enjoyed understanding things. If I understand something, I have no further use for it. So I try to make a music which I don't understand and which will be difficult for other people to understand, too.—Laura Fletcher & Thomas Moore (1983).

I like art to remain mysterious. I find that as long as a book or a painting or a piece of music is not understood by me that I can use it. I mean use it in order to employ my faculties. If I understand something I can put it on a shelf and leave it there. In the past I thought it had to do with the feeling in Europe of a tradition or the history, whereas we here in America have very little sense of history. We're so to speak tourists in our own country which really belongs to the Indians.—Birger Ollrogge (1985).

The attitude that I take is that everyday life is more interesting than forms of celebration, when we become aware of it. That *when* is when our intentions go down to zero. Then suddenly you notice that the world is magical.—Michael Kirby & Richard Schechner (1965).

The basic message of Silence *seems to be that everything is permitted.*

Everything is permitted if zero is taken as the basis. That's the part that isn't often understood. If you're nonintentional, then everything is permitted. If you're intentional, for instance if you want to murder someone, then it's not permitted. The same thing can be true musically. As I was saying before, I don't enjoy being pushed while I'm listening. I like music which lets me do my own listening.—Rob Tannenbaum (1985).

The concept of zero *is an important one to understanding both what you say and what you compose. It is, very honestly, a very difficult problem for me to imagine a zero to start with, no less to begin there in my composition. What techniques does one acquire to achieve this? Even more important, how do you renew that zero after a new discovery is made?*

It's a good question. It's exactly the problem that I face all the time, and it's very difficult, because we have a memory. There's no doubt of it. And we're not stupid. We would be stupid if we didn't have memory. And yet it's that memory that one has to become free of, at the same time that you have to take advantage of it. It's very paradoxical. Right now, I am refreshed and brought, so to speak, to zero, I think, through my work with Joyce.

I don't know how he actually worked. I know more than I used to know. Writers like Louis Mink and Adeline Glashine have helped. One of these mentions that you can't understand Joyce unless you have an unabridged dictionary and the eleventh edition of the *Encyclopaedia Britannica.* And if you have both you can then see doors open on passages in *Finnegans Wake* which are more or less lifted from one or the other. He used these reference texts in a way that facilitated and stimulated his work.

In my way, I do the same thing in my most recent work. The passage about water in the next to last chapter of *Ulysses,* which was Joyce's favorite chapter, was no doubt taken out of the encyclopedia just as I took some recent work relating to charcoal out of the encyclopedia. I added to it, of course—and I'm sure he did, too—but the skeleton was there for the having, so to speak. The dictionary is a gold mine and so is the encyclopedia. Joyce had that very great one, which I used to have as a child, but unfortunately no longer have. It was put in a garage in Southern California and mildewed; otherwise, I would try to get hold of it. Now it's very hard to find that edition.—David Cope (1980).

I dreamt once that I had composed a piece of music all notes of which were to be cooked and then eaten. On the way to the concert hall to perform this piece I stopped to rehearse and cooked the notes. Then around came a bunch of dogs and cats and ate them all up!—Jeff Goldberg (1976).

I have from time to time, either for myself or for others, made statements that are like manifestos. You know this is popular in the field of the arts—to say in a manifesto-style statement what distinguishes the contemporary or modern thing from what isn't. The first time I was asked to do it, I did it with regard to painting. I said that a painting was modern if it was not interrupted by the effect of its environment—so that if shadows or spots or so forth fell on a painting and spoilt it, then it was not a modern painting, but if they fell on it and, so to speak, were fluent with it, then it was a modern painting.

Then, of course, I have said the same thing about music. If the music can accept ambient sounds and not be interrupted thereby, it's a modern piece of music. If, as with a composition of Beethoven, a baby crying, or someone in the audience coughing, interrupts the music, then we know that it isn't modern. I think that the present way of deciding whether something is useful as art is to ask whether it is interrupted by the actions of others, or whether it is fluent with the actions of others. What I have been saying is an extension of these notions out of the field of the material of the arts into what you might call the material of society. If, for instance, you made a structure of society that would be interrupted by the actions of people who were not in it, then it would not be the proper structure.—C. H. Waddington (1972).

I had luncheon today with Marshall McLuhan, and when I'm with him I'm full of admiration for his ideas, because what he says I find illuminating and corroborative. Some things he says open my mind in ways that it hadn't been. But when he asks me a question, if he stops talking and asks me a question, I have great difficulty replying because I know that if I said anything that it would not be what he expected me to say, nor would he understand what I was going to say. I hadn't been able until today to know what the problem is. McLuhan is, as he has frequently said, a detective who observes patterns and points these out, and wishes through probing means and what not to make us aware of our environment; I think I've had somewhat the same intention. But it has not been patterns; it has been centers. McLuhan, evidently through being interested in patterns, is interested in relationships, and in pointing out these relationships. I have spent my life denying the importance of relationships, and introducing, in order to make it evident what I mean and what I believe, situations where I could not have foreseen a relationship.

Now this Happening at Black Mountain was such an occasion, and all of these people were given the possibility of performing, I admit, within compartments that I arrived at through chance operations. By compartments I mean periods of time during the total period when they were free to do whatever they wished, or to do nothing. Those mostly chose to do something. I had no knowledge of what they were going to do. I had a vague notion of where they were going to do it. I knew that M. C. Richards and Charles Olson would climb a ladder which was at a particular point.

I had less knowledge of what Merce and the dancers would do because they would move around. The thing had not been rehearsed. It had simply been planned. In fact, that very day before lunch it was planned, and it was performed before dinner. And we all simply got together and did these things at once.

And if we did bring about patterns, they were patterns which we had not measured—furthermore, which we didn't wish to emphasize. We simply wished to permit them to exist. I was straight from the classes of Suzuki. The doctrine which he was expressing was that every thing and every body, that is to say every nonsentient being and every sentient being, is the Buddha. These Buddhas are all, every single one of them, at the center of the Universe. And they are in interpenetration, and they are not obstructing one another. This doctrine, which I truly adhere to, is what has made me tick in the way that I ticked. And it has made the agreement and the disagreements, and it has made it possible for me to use some people's work in ways that they didn't intend it to be used. And then this doctrine of nonobstruction means that I don't wish to impose my feelings on other people. Therefore, the use of chance operations, indeterminacy, etc., the nonerection of patterns, of either ideas or feelings on my part, in order to leave those other centers free to be the centers.—Irving Sandler (1966).

We have the kind of attitude and use of art that has been handed down. Our experience now is being enriched not by losing the old because the new never takes the place of the old. We are discovering another use of art and of things that we have not considered art. What is happening in this century, whether you accept it or not, is that more and more there is no gap between art and life.—Stanley Kauffmann (1966).

I think the history of art is simply a history of getting rid of the ugly by entering into it, and using it. After all, the notion of something outside of us being ugly is not outside of us but inside of us. And that's why I keep reiterating that we're working with our minds. What we're trying to do is to get them open so that we don't see things as being ugly, or beautiful, but we see them just as they are.—Richard Kostelanetz et al. (1977).

Formerly, one was accustomed to thinking of art as something better organized than life that could be used as an escape from life. The changes that have taken place in this century, however, are such that art is not an escape from life, but rather an introduction to it.—Stanley Kauffmann (1966).

I was with de Kooning once in a restaurant and he said, "If I put a frame around these bread crumbs, that isn't art." And what I'm saying is that it is. He was saying that it wasn't because he connects art with his activity—he connects with himself as an artist whereas I would want art to slip out of us into the world in which we live.

I think that modern art has turned life into art, and now I think it's time for life (by life now I mean such things as government, the social rules and all those things) to turn the environment and everything into art. In other words, to take care of it, and to change it from being just a mess into being something which facilitates our living, instead of making us all miserable.—Robin White (1978).

Left to itself, art would have to be something very simple—it would be sufficient for it to be beautiful. But when it's useful it should spill out of just being beautiful and move over to other aspects of life so that when we're not with the art it has nevertheless influenced our actions or our responses to the environment.

But the environment is so crowded.

Well, that's one of the reasons we need some help with it. Not only is it crowded but it is sometimes what you might call constipated. We get ourselves into traffic situations either on highways or in supermarkets where, even if we're in a rush, it does us no good, because we have to go at a snail's pace if any pace at all. Not so long ago in New York I was brought to a complete halt because of two trucks, neither one of which would give in to the other. At such points if we have paid attention to modern paintings and to modern music, we can shift our attention to the things that surround us—things to hear, things to see.—Robin White (1978).

Music is about changing the mind—not to understand, but to be aware. The understanding mind is what you get when you go to school, which is boring and of no use whatsoever. The experiencing mind is what we need because it stands us in good stead whether things are going smoothly or not; it finds tranquility in the least tranquil situation.—Michael John White (1978).

A mind that is interested in changing, though, such as the mind of Ives, is interested precisely in the things that are at extremes. I'm certainly like that. Unless we go to extremes, we won't get anywhere.—Cole Gagne & Tracy Caras (1980).

I don't trust my imagination. I know what my imagination is, and what I'm interested in *is* what I *don't* know. The logical mind is offended when anything comes in that isn't within the range of its imagination, whereas the accepting mind is delighted.—Roy M. Close (1975).

Why is it necessary to compose?

We spoke about that earlier but not thinking in these terms of why is it necessary? I'll give you an answer, if you want one, I often give. When the sixth patriarch of Zen Buddhism was being chosen, the fifth one arranged a poetry contest, and each one had to tell his understanding of enlightenment. The oldest monk in the monastery said, "The mind is like a mirror. It collects dust and the problem is to remove the dust." There was a young fellow in the kitchen, Hui-neng, who couldn't read and couldn't write, but had this poem read to him and said, "That isn't very interesting." And they said, "Well, how do you know?" And he said, "Oh, I could write a much better poem, but I can't write." And so they asked him to say it, and he did; and they wrote it, and it was: "Where is the mirror and where is the dust?" He became the sixth patriarch. Now, several centuries later in Japan, there was a monk who was always taking baths. So a young student said to him, "If there isn't any dust, why are you always taking baths?" And the old one replied, "Just a dip, no why."—Yale School of Architecture (1965).

[Does your music reflect your emotional life?]

My feelings belong, as it were, to me, and I should not impose them on others. Besides, the ancient Indians listed only nine basic emotions ❧the four white ones: the heroic, the erotic, the mirthful, the wondrous; tranquility in the center; the four black ones: fear, anger, disgust, sorrow☙. If the first composer in history had expressed all nine, what would be left for the rest of us to do?—Joseph H. Mazo (1983).

Then how does emotion fit into your work

It doesn't fit into my work. It exists in each person, in his own way; but I'm not involved with that.

But you're still feeling emotions.

I have emotions, but I don't try to put them into my work.—Thomas Erikson (1987).

Do you associate them with excess?

You could associate them with all kinds of things—with jealousy, hatred, fear, anger, sorrow. All the good ones can be turned into bad. Most murders come from people who love one another. Love, in fact, is said to make people blind. "I was blindly in love." You could get run over. Emotions have long been known to be dangerous. You must free yourself of your likes and dislikes.

But my likes give me pleasure.

If you give up that kind of pleasure, your pleasure will be more universal.

You mean constant?

I mean both constant and more spacious.—Lisa Low (1985).

Say Abstract Expressionism really is the expressionism of the artist's feelings through his gesture and art; then isn't he doing it rather poorly?

How could he do better?

He is not forcing you to pay attention at any particular point on the canvas, is he?

No, but on the other hand, you're constantly aware of his process.

Yes, well there I'm all in agreement. All of those things I agree with. You say he's trying to put something across.

Yes.

He's not doing it.

Well, it's this that he wants to put across to a large degree—his own image, of course, which Harold Rosenberg calls identity.

Yes, I began to be disgusted with such ideas.—Irving Sandler (1966).

Since your ego and your likes and dislikes have been taken out of your compositions, do you still view them as your compositions, in the sense that you created them?

Instead of representing my control, they represent questions that I've asked and the answers that have been given by means of chance operations. I've merely changed my responsibility from making choices to asking questions. It's not easy to ask questions.

Is that one of the aspects that makes it experimental music, still?

Yes, and experiments on my part, rather than someone else's.

And the asking of the questions actually is a process of invention.

That's what I trust.

Cartridge Music *is a good example. There's a sense in which you could say that* Cartridge Music *will always sound like* Cartridge Music. *That piece will always give the impression of being the same piece even though from event to event very different things will happen, because of the primary invention of the medium within which the sounds operate, the cartridges themselves. To that extent you could say that any John Cage piece will always sound like both itself and a John Cage piece. Do you think that's true?*

Partly.

To what extent isn't it true?

Well, I always enjoy remembering the circumstance in Beverly Hills when I was having a drink with a friend of mine whose name I've forgotten, and she had a recording that was being played while we were talking and drinking in another room, and it struck me as being a very interesting piece. I asked her what it was, and she said, "You can't be serious!" It was a piece of mine. Which I didn't recognize.

Did you find out what the piece was?

It was actually *Cartridge Music.* When David Tudor and I recorded it for Mainstream, Earle Brown's record company, he asked us whether we wanted to hear the final mix, and both of us said that we didn't want to hear it, and so that was probably the first time I had heard it.—Tom Darter (1982).

[What prompts you to compose?]

My composition arises out of asking questions. I am reminded of a story early on about a class with Schoenberg. He had us go to the blackboard to solve a particular problem in counterpoint (though it was a class in harmony). He said, "When you have a solution, turn around and let me see it." I did that. He then said: "Now another solution, please." I gave another and another until finally, having made seven or eight, I reflected a moment and then said with some certainty: "There aren't any more solutions." He said: "OK. What is the principle underlying all of the solutions?" I couldn't answer his question; but I had always worshipped the man, and at that point I did even more. He ascended, so to speak. I spent the rest of my life, until recently, hearing him ask that question over and over. And then it occurred to me through the direction that my work has taken, which is renunciation of choices and the substitution of asking questions, that the principle underlying all of the solutions that I had given him was the question that he had asked, because they certainly didn't come from any other point. He would have accepted that answer, I think. The answers have the question in common. Therefore the question underlies the answers.—David Cope (1980).

The need to change my music was evident to me earlier in my life. I had been taught, as most people are, that music is in effect the expression of an individual's ego—"self-expression" is what I had been taught. But then, when I saw that everyone was expressing himself differently and using a different way of composing, I deduced that we were in a Tower of Babel situation because no one was understanding anybody else; for instance, I wrote a sad piece and people hearing it laughed. It was clearly pointless to continue in that way, so I determined to stop writing music until I found a better reason than "self-expression" for doing it.

The reason that I finally found was in Oriental traditions; however, a friend of mine found it expressed by an English composer as late I think as the seventeenth century. It was this: "The purpose of music is to sober and quiet the mind thus making us susceptible to divine influences." I then determined to find out what was a "quiet mind" and what were "divine influences."—Maureen Furman (1979).

You intend to express something with your work, don't you?

It's not that I intend to express one particular thing, but to make something that can be used by the person who finds it expressive. But that expression grows up, so to speak, in the observer.—Birger Ollrogge (1985).

So I want to give up the traditional view that art is a means of self-expression for the view that art is a means of self-alteration, and what it alters is *mind*, and mind is in the world and is a social fact. . . . We will change *beautifully* if we *accept* uncertainties of change; and this should affect any planning. This is a *value.*—C. H. Waddington (1972).

On January 28, 1949, you spoke at the Artists School, and your topic was Indian sand painting.

No, it was just sand painting.

Sand painting—not Indian?

No, sand painting. I took, of course, Indian sand painting as the reason for the title, and I spoke of it. But I was promoting the notion of impermanent art, and I was extending it certainly away from Indian sand painting to our own work as we are now making it.

Did you allude to Pollock at all in that? He too once wrote about Indian sand painting; it was an influence on him.

I can see how it could have been; but his work had a permanence, so that he was concerned really only with the fact of gesture, and perhaps of painting on a surface which was on the floor.

And your primary point was . . .

I was not thinking of gestures; I was thinking of impermanence and something that, no sooner had it been used, was so to speak discarded. I was fighting at that point the notion of art itself as something that we preserve. That was my intention in that speech.—Irving Sandler (1966).

What is an experimental act, and how does it relate to so-called experimental music?

Experimental music can have many definitions, but I use the word *experimental* to mean making an action the outcome of which is not foreseen.—Roger Reynolds (1961).

I think that even when two pieces are diametrically different from each other—as are the *Freeman Etudes* for violin solo, which is written out in detail and in which there are no indeterminate aspects at all, and, on the other hand, the silent piece, *4′33″*, from the early '50s, where the performer has nothing to do and the audience has nothing to do but listen, no matter what the sounds are—that the common denominator between those two pieces is central to my work: namely, to find ways of writing music where the sounds are free of my intentions.—Bill Shoemaker (1984).

I frequently say that I don't have any purposes, and that I'm dealing with sounds, but that's obviously not the case. On the other hand it is. That is to say, I believe that by eliminating purpose, what I call *awareness* increases. Therefore my purpose is to remove purpose.

It's very simple to show, and we've already talked about it. If I have a particular purpose, and then a series of actions comes about, and all I get is an approximation of my purpose, then nothing but a sort of compromise or disappointment can take place. And perhaps that still takes place when my purpose is to remove purpose, namely, I see that I haven't really done it. But at least I'm going along in that general direction.—Roger Reynolds (1961).

I can distinguish three different ways of composing music nowadays. The first is well known—that of writing music, as I do. It continues. A new way has developed through electronic music and the construction of new instruments of making music by performing it rather than writing it. And a third way has developed in recording studios, which is similar to the way artists work in their studios to make paintings. Music can be built up layer by layer on recording tape, not to give a performance or to write music, but to appear on a record. This last, begun in popular music, will continue in serious music. Together with these changes we have the changes that affect the rest of our lives—the great multiplicity of musics, the interpenetration of cultures formerly separate, Orient and Occident, the coming into general usage of many new technologies, and the vastly increased number of people living, who affect one another.—Ilhan Mimaroglu (1985).

I understand the word "structure" as the division of the whole into parts. And I would apply the usefulness of the idea of structure to a work of art that sets out to be an object, namely, to have a beginning, middle, and end. And if one is making a work, which I do often, that is not an object, but a process, then that concern doesn't enter in and the question of whether it is better or not better, is not to the point. I think, perhaps, if you were not involved with process, as I often am, but were involved with object, that the question of what would be a better object than another object is very hard to decide. Perhaps one would say that an object that had never been seen before was more interesting than one with which one was familiar. One might. Certainly, I early felt the desire to get free of any kind of musical structure that had three parts the first and last of which were the same.—Richard Kostelanetz et al. (1977).

Let me add something that I think might illuminate this. What is the primary concern of the dramatist and the actor? It is content, in any way that you interpret content. But Marshall McLuhan in his work on mass media begins by saying that content is of no importance. He says "the medium is the message." And he says you can come to this conclusion and this awareness only if you divorce yourself from thoughts of content. This is very similar to my statement about divorcing oneself from thoughts of intention, they go very well together. What does McLuhan see as activity for an artist? It's perfectly beautiful, and every time we see it now we enjoy it: he says all we have to do is brush information against information, and it doesn't matter what. By that brushing we will be made aware of the world which itself is doing that.—Michael Kirby & Richard Schechner (1965).

Did your study of Zen reaffirm certain ideas you had had [about harmony] early in life—Zen was not so much a revelation to you as it was something that you were compatible with all along?

Don't you think that's how it is with us in anything? Sometimes compatibility hides itself. Probably, we are ultimately compatible with everything, but we make it impossible for things to reach us, or they just don't cross our paths, or some such thing. There are problems inside and outside that keep us from going in certain directions. But the directions we do go in are, don't you think, more often than not, ones that we're actually prepared to go in.

I've lately been thinking again about *Silence,* which is the title of my first book of my own writings. When I was twelve years old I wrote that oration that won a high school oratorical contest in Southern California. It was called "Other People Think," and it was about our relation to the Latin American countries. What I proposed was silence on the part of the United States, in order that we could hear what other people think, and that they don't think the way we do, particularly about us. But could you say then that, as a twelve year old, that I was prepared to devote my life to silence, and to chance operations? It's hard to say. We could say that in a sense we're prepared, but then in another sense not.—Cole Gagne & Tracy Caras (1975).

When I first made the transition from a continuity that I was directing, as it were, to one which I wasn't directing, I still had a certain knowledge of the possibilities. And so, seeing that there were some that would be pleasing, I did, at first, wish that they would come up, rather than the ones I didn't know were pleasing; I discovered that they altered my awareness. That is to say, I saw that things I didn't think would be pleasing were in fact pleasing, and so my views gradually changed from particular ideas as to what would be pleasing, toward no ideas as to what would be pleasing. Therefore, when you ask, do I "have difficulty in implementing" my philosophical positions, I don't try to have any of those things.

In other words, I try, rather, to keep my curiosity and my awareness with regard to what's happening open, and I try to arrange my composing means so that I won't have any knowledge of what might happen. And that, by the way, is what you might call the technical difference between indeterminacy and chance operations. In the case of chance operations, one knows more or less the elements of the universe with which one is dealing, whereas in indeterminacy, I like to think (and perhaps I fool myself and pull the wool over my eyes) that I'm outside the circle of a known universe, and dealing with things that I literally don't know anything about.—Roger Reynolds (1961).

I would say that the highest discipline is the discipline of chance operations, because chance operations have absolutely nothing to do with one's likes or dislikes. The person is being disciplined, not the work.—Roy M. Close (1975).

When I first began to work on "chance operations," I had the musical values of the twentieth century. That is, two tones should (in the twentieth century) be seconds and sevenths, the octaves being dull and old-fashioned. But when I wrote *The Music of Changes,* derived by chance operations from the *I Ching,* I had ideas in my head as to what would happen in working out this process (which took about nine months). They didn't happen!—things happened that were not stylish to happen, such as *fifths* and *octaves.* But I accepted them, admitting I was "not in charge" but was "ready to be changed" by what I was doing.—C. H. Waddington (1972).

You use the I Ching *to make choices in composition. Is this use of it separate from the book's guiding or spiritual purposes?*

Yes. It's not entirely separate from it, but I don't make use of the wisdom aspects in the writing of music or in the writing of texts. I use it simply as a kind of computer, as a facility. If I have some question that requires a wise answer, then of course I use it that way. On occasion I do. But if I want to know which sound of one hundred sounds I'm to use, then I use it just as a computer.

Is this considered an improper use of the book?

By some people, I think, who are superstitious about it. The mechanism by means of which the *I Ching* works is, I think, the same as that by means of which the DNA—or one of those things in the chemistry of our body—works. It's a dealing with the number sixty-four, with a binary situation with all of its variations in six lines. I think it's a rather basic life mechanism. I prefer it to other chance operations. I began using it nearly thirty years ago, and I haven't stopped. Some people think that I'm enslaved by it, but I feel that I am liberated by it.—Cole Gagne & Tracy Caras (1980).

I always admired [Duchamp's] work, and once I got involved with chance operations, I realized he had been involved with them, not only in art but also in music, fifty years before I was. When I pointed this out to him, Marcel said, "I suppose I was fifty years ahead of my time."

Was there any difference between his idea of chance and yours?

Oh yes. I hear from people who have studied his work that he often carefully chose the simplest method. In the case of the *Musical Erratum,* he simply put the notes in a hat and then pulled them out. I wouldn't be satisfied with that kind of chance operation in my work, though I am delighted with it in Marcel's. There are too many things that could happen that don't interest me, such as pieces of paper sticking together and the act of shaking the hat. It simply doesn't appeal to me. I was born in a different month than Marcel. I enjoy details and like things to be more complicated.

Duchamp wasn't uncomplicated though?

He was less complicated than someone else doing the same thing would have been. I think the difference between our attitudes toward chance probably came from the fact that he was involved with ideas through seeing, and I was involved through hearing. I try to become aware of more and more aspects of a situation in order to subject them all individually to chance operations. So I would be able to set a process going which was not related to anything I had experienced before.—Moira & William Roth (1973).

When I was conducting a contemporary music ensemble, and we did some of your pieces, that was one of the hardest things to get across to the students. We were doing Theater Piece *where each player creates his or her own specific performance instructions, and some of the players said, "Given that this is going to appear random to the audience, can't we do anything?" What would be your answer to that?*

Well, if they do just anything, then they do what they remember or what they like, and it becomes evident that that's the case, and the performance and the piece is not the discovery that it could have been had they made a disciplined use of chance operations.

So if they do that discipline, it becomes a discovery for them.

And for the audience, which can immediately tell whether someone's doing something in a disciplined way or in an improvised way. Most of the performances of *Theater Piece* are not good because people don't understand the need for discipline.—Tom Darter (1982).

Some composers recently have admitted a degree of chance to their compositions but have retained generally traditional methods by and large. You have noted that this practice reveals a "carelessness with regard to the outcome." Would you elaborate on that comment?

If one is making an object and then proceeds in an indeterminate fashion to let happen what will, outside of one's control, then one is simply being careless about the making of that object.

You don't think, then, that it is valid for a composer to wish that a certain aspect or section of his work will have a changing face while the general language and substance remains controlled.

I think I know what you're referring to and it's a very popular field of activity among composers at the present time. That is to say, to have certain aspects of a composition controlled, if I understand you, and others uncontrolled. Well, what is maintained here is the concept of *pairs of opposites:* having black and white, as it were, and then composing with the play of these opposites. One can then engage in all of the games that academic composition has led us to know how to play. One can balance this with that, produce climaxes, and so on. I'm afraid all I can say is that it doesn't interest me.

It doesn't seem to me to radically change the situation from the familiar convention. It simply takes these new ways of working and consolidates them with the old knowledges, so that one remains at home with one's familiar ideas of the drama—of the play of the opposites. So, one wouldn't have to change one's mind. Whereas, I think we are in a more urgent situation, where it is absolutely essential for us to change our minds fundamentally. And in this sense, I could be likened to a fundamentalist Protestant preacher.

Stockhausen has recently employed a system of composition that involves the selection of one technique at a time from a number of different ways of working, and an attempt to let any one of them move into play. This gives the impression of a rich reservoir of contemporary techniques, so that in a repertoire of, say, seven or eight compositional techniques, indeterminacy would play the part of one, and you could call on it, as it were, when you had some use for it. But, that doesn't require a change of mind from what one previously had, and so nothing fundamentally different is taking place.

I think one could see it very clearly in terms of painting. You could have certain parts of a canvas controlled and others quite chaotic, and so you would be able to play, as it were, in the same way in which you had played before. What we need is a use of our Art that alters our lives—is useful in our lives. We are familiar with those plays of balance, so they couldn't possibly do anything more to us, no matter how novel they were, than they already have done. "New wine in old bottles."—Roger Reynolds (1961).

Another idea in *Cartridge Music* is not just transforming sound, but that of performers getting in each other's way in order to bring about nonintention in a group of people, so, if one person is playing a cartridge with an object inserted in it, another one is turning the volume down independently. I've never liked the idea of one person in control.

On Stockhausen's control of his music . . .

His interest is in the result rather than the process. When I visited the fine potter in Japan—one of the living treasures of Japan—he sat down at the wheel and said, "I'm not interested in the pot; I'm interested in making it. . . ."—Thom Holmes (1981).

What I would like to find is an improvisation that is not descriptive of the performer, but is descriptive of what happens, and which is characterized by an absence of intention. It is at the point of spontaneity that the performer is most apt to have recourse to his memory. He is not apt to make a discovery spontaneously. I want to find ways of discovering something you don't know at the time that you improvise—that is to say, the same time you're doing something that's not written down, or decided upon ahead of time. The first way is to play an instrument over which you have no control, or less control than usual. The next way is to divide empty time into rooms, you could say. In those rooms try to make clear the fact those rooms are different by putting different sounds in each room. If, for instance, I made this sound in a two-minute period—say, we now begin a two-minute period [taps rock on table after a pause of several seconds], I don't need to make the sound again in that two-minute period. I could have made the sound then or at any other time. Instead of making it once I could make it several times, but if I made it several times, it is at that point that I could move toward my taste and memory.

Repetition is necessarily a function of memory?

It has a great deal with do with it, don't you think? You have to remember to keep a regular beat. You have to know where the beat is. You have to remember where it was. To become free of that is what interests me. There is a beautiful statement, in my opinion, by Marcel Duchamp: "To reach the impossibility of transferring from one like object to another the memory imprint." And he expressed that as a goal. That means, from his visual point of view, to look at a Coca-Cola bottle without the feeling that you've ever seen one before, as though you're looking at it for the very first time. That's what I'd like to find with sounds—to play them and hear them as if you've never heard them before.—Bill Shoemaker (1984).

You know Schoenberg said that everything is repetition—even variation. On the other hand, we can say that repetition doesn't exist, that two leaves of the same plant are not repetitions of each other, but are unique. Or two bricks on the building across the street are different. And when we examine them closely, we see that they are indeed different in some respect, if only in the respect of how they receive light, because they are at different points in space. In other words, repetition really has to do with how we think. And we can't think either that things are being repeated, or that they are not being repeated. If we think that things are being repeated, it is generally because we don't pay attention to all of the details. But if we pay attention as though we were looking through a microscope to all the details, we see that there is no such thing as repetition.

How was it performing, for example, the 840 repeated da capos *of Erik Satie's* Vexations*? What grew out of that, although it has repetition?*

It does [have repetition, as you say]; but as [the performance] continued, we heard that it does not—that each time it was played, it was different.

Can it thus be heard as an indeterminate piece?

As we heard that piece over and over again, our attention became very sharp, very clear; so that every slightest deviation from what it had been became clear. It was like a sharpening of the faculty of listening.

How many hours did it take?

Eighteen hours and forty minutes.—Birger Ollrogge (1985).

After the first performance of Vexations *in New York you noted that "something had been set in motion that went far beyond what any of us had anticipated." What exactly did you mean by that statement?*

If you know a piece of music, as we did, and you're going to do it 840 times, and you know that you've planned to do that, and you're committed to do it, there's a tendency to think that you have had the experience before it has taken place. And I think that this idea is basic, is it not, to what is called conceptual art?

Right, except it doesn't even have to take place.

Right. I have often been connected with conceptual art because of my interest in such things as playing Satie's *Vexations.* But I feel very differently. I think that the experience over the eighteen hours and forty minutes of those repetitions was very different from the thought of them, or the realization that they were going to happen. For them to actually happen, to actually live through it, was a different thing. What happened was that we were very tired, naturally, after that length of time and I drove back to the country and I slept I think for, not eighteen hours and forty minutes, but I slept for, say, ten hours and fifteen minutes. I slept an unusually long period of time; and when I woke up, I felt different than I had ever felt before. And, furthermore, the environment that I looked out upon looked unfamiliar even though I had been living there. In other words, I had changed and the world had changed, and that's what I meant by that statement. It wasn't an experience that I alone had, but other people who had been in it wrote to me or called me up and said that they had had the same experience.—Alan Gillmor & Roger Shattuck (1973).

Chance operations are a discipline, and improvisation is rarely a discipline. Though at the present time it's one of my concerns, how to make improvisation a discipline. But then I mean doing something beyond the control of the ego. Improvisation is generally playing what you know, and what you like, and what you feel; but those feelings and likes are what Zen would like us to become free of.—Stanley Kauffmann (1966).

The difference is that improvisation frequently depends not on the work you have to do [that is, the composition you're playing] but depends more on your taste and memory, and your likes and dislikes. It doesn't lead you into a new experience, but into something with which you're already familiar, whereas if you have work to do that is suggested but not determined by a notation, if it's indeterminate, this simply means that you are to supply the determination of certain things that the composer has not determined. Who is going to think of the *Art of the Fugue* of Bach, which leaves out dynamics altogether, who is going to think of that as improvisation?—Tom Darter (1982).

Have you developed any satisfactory methods using improvisation to play what you don't already know?

Finding, as with the conch shells in *Inlets,* an instrument over which I have no control, or less control than usual. Another example is if you use as a percussion instrument a music stand which has a faulty relation between the part that holds the music and the three legs that support the stand. If I hold the three legs in my hand—the stand is upside down—and move the top part on the wooden floor, then because of the faulty relationship, I won't always get a frictional sound. But, sometimes, I will. It's a little like driving a bumper car in the fun house, where you have less control than usual over which direction the vehicle takes. That interests me. But, say you have control, then it is a matter of how to occupy your intentions in such a way that you move into areas with which you're unfamiliar, rather than areas based on memory and taste. One of the ways I've found I call "structural improvisation." Given a period of time, I will divide it. Say we have eight minutes. We'll divide it into sections of either one, two, three, or four minutes long, or three parts—four minutes, three minutes, one minute, in any order—or whatever. Then, if I have ten sounds, I can find out through the use of chance operations which of those ten sounds go in the first section, which go in the second section, and which go in the third. Then I improvise using the number of sounds that have been determined for the first section, the number of sounds for the second and the number of sounds for the third, and I will have an improvisation which is characterized by a change of sound at those different times, no matter what I play.—Bill Shoemaker (1984).

Why is it so rare to find independence in music performance?

In the West, people who improvise have thought it's more human not to have their own ideas and be doing their own work, but rather to be influenced and to respond to what someone else does. And that has characterized jazz improvisation; so that if one of them got loud, they'd all get loud. The opposite is true of improvisation traditionally in India, where the intention of one musician will be to confuse the other. It was Henry Cowell who first introduced me to this idea that Indian improvisation was in the nature of a contest. He also gave me the idea that a concert should be a situation not of togetherness but of contest, that would bring each person up, so to speak, to his highest point of energy, and to increase the use of the faculties, instead of becoming slouchy and careless.

Are young people active in popular musics eager to have contact with you and know what you think of their kind of music?

Very rarely. Mostly when that question is put, it is hoped that I will say that I like it, but I don't have much experience of it. The last direct experience I had of it was in Chicago in '67, '68, or '69, when I was invited by a group of black musicians to come and play with them. And they also asked me to criticize what they were doing. I said, "Well, play," and they did.

And I said to them that one of the troubles was that when they got loud, they all got loud. And they said, "How could we change that?" They were willing to change. I said that perhaps if they didn't sit together, those of them who could move through space should get away from one another. Some of them couldn't carry their instruments—the double bass was too big, and, of course, the piano—so that when one of them got loud, the others wouldn't be impelled to be so loud. That day, when we practiced together, and I played with them too, they did very well, and they enjoyed what happened—a kind of independence of a plurality of jazz spirits, and an extension of that idea of freedom of the soloists to all members of the group.

Popular music must be very boring and monotonous to you to listen to.

I have spent my life with music; and even though I like to have an open mind, I still have a closed mind in many respects. And what I try to close myself to is things that I'm too utterly familiar with. It's very hard for me to listen to music nowadays with a regular beat; so that I have a hard time to begin with, with most popular music. On the other hand, some of it gets free of it. Rock seems to me to get free of it, because it calls so much attention to loudness that you forget the beat.—Frans Boenders (1980).

When I listen to jazz, I don't find it as interesting as people tell me it is.—Rick Chatenever (1982).

How do you consider new popular music—punk, New Wave?

What is the New Wave? I don't really know what it is. If you could point it out to me, I might have some reaction.

It's very simple, three-, four-chord stuff, aggressive, fast.

There's a good deal of dancing on the part of the performers?

Usually jumping up and down.

I've seen something like that. It was entertaining to see but not very engaging.

But they use very dissonant sounds; I wonder how you felt about that?

I have no objection to dissonance.

I know you have no objections, but I wanted to know whether you felt any pleasure that things were coming round to your way of thinking.

But this isn't, is it? Isn't it a regular beat?

Not all the time.

I think it's part of show business.

Aren't you?

No.

In a marginal way?

No, I'm much more part of music as a means of changing the mind. Perhaps if you want to say that, I wouldn't myself.

Opening up the mind.

A means of converting the mind, turning it around, so that it moves away from itself out to the rest of the world, or as Ramakrishna said, "as a means of rapid transportation."

So your music in itself is not that important.

The use of it is what is important.

The use rather than the result.

That's what Wittgenstein said about anything. He said the meaning of something was its use.—John Robert with Silvy Panet Raymond (1980).

Would the same be true for the popular music that we hear everywhere in public places. Would that kind of music be better, or more interesting, or more appealing, if it were to be played in a more independent way?

The only way I have thought of improving popular music, so that I, for instance, could enjoy it would be to have lots of it, lots of different kinds of it, in the same room. Then the situation would at least give me something to do.

To give you a choice?

Not a choice, but how to resolve the complexity.

Well, I've developed that a good deal in my work—the notion of a musicircus, of many different things going on at once. You can have soft things going on at the same time as loud things, and all you have to do to hear the soft things is go closer.—Frans Boenders (1980).

Do you think there is a place in your music for nonmusical performers—people without musical training—to perform your compositions musically?

Some of my compositions can be done that way.

Do you think that would help escape the idea of an improviser performing what he already knows, what he's familiar with, what he's already played? Someone who isn't familiar with anything along those lines might create something on the spur of the moment, not more original, but perhaps fresher.

No, I don't think so. Because when people don't know anything about music and improvise it, as for instance Kurt Schwitters did, you get something that is elementary from a musical point of view because it begins again from a kindergarten level. Schwitters was fascinated by things like sequences and repetitions, but beginning at another level, another pitch level—and those ideas are no longer necessary. And yet from the point of view of a person who has no musical experience, they're fascinating. That's what happens with a good deal of electronic music now. Because the people who use electronics for the most part skip the business of studying music and so, frequently, like Pierre Schaeffer in France, they do things that are not really interesting musically. Because they don't have any musical experience. I don't mean that one has to study music to do interesting electronic music. But what I do mean is that one shouldn't become fascinated by elementary musical devices simply because one hasn't had any musical experiences.—Art Lange (1977).

Can one have so much music that one no longer needs it?

Well, I already have that situation, but it doesn't do me any good because I have a great deal of music. You know, I go, through circumstances, to a number of concerts, but I certainly don't search them out. I go only through circumstances and I don't keep any records, I don't have any radio or any TV. So that I don't have any reliance on needing to have music because I have always sounds around me. Nevertheless, I'm a musician and I make music and I am able to listen to other people's music.

Will it suffice one to read the manuscript of a piece of music?

That's not my point. My point is the reverse. It has been thought in the past that music was something that existed in a person's mind and feelings and that he wrote it down and that he had heard it before it was audible. My point has been that we don't hear anything until it is audible. At least I don't. And if I did hear something before it was audible, I would have had to take solfège, which would have trained me to accept certain pitches and not others. I would then have found the environmental sounds off tune, lacking tonality. Therefore I pay no attention to solfège. I don't have perfect pitch; I simply keep my ears open, my mind empty but alert. Period. And the result is that I can hear things that are off tune, on tune—I suppose it makes a difference, but not one that I approach in terms of value. I try to approach each sound as *itself.* Now I find I can do that better with sounds that *aren't* music than sounds that *are* music; but I try to make my own music, and I notice that more and more people are making music that is, *like* the environment.

Is this a kind of ultimate abstractness?

No, I would say rather an ultimate reality, wouldn't you?

We had an argument after playing two tapes made by a composer here named Wolf Rosenberg, and he was defended by Herbert Brun, who's done some beautiful work here with computer music. Herbert Brun was insisting that anything we do is artificial, and I disagreed and said that I knew perfectly well that in my experience they are not artificial. Now what would make sounds artificial would be that one wasn't really interested in them or paying attention to them, and that what was of concern to one was the relationship to the sound. This notion of relationship actually makes the sound unimportant. You could have a musical idea and express it, let us say, in lights or something. Or some other relationship maybe applies. I have become interested not in relationships—though I see that things interpenetrate—but I think they interpenetrate more richly, more abundantly, when I don't establish any relationship. So one of the first things I've done, which it seems to me is what nature has done, too, is not to make a fixed score. When I have three sounds, I don't think that one must come first, and then the next, and then the other, but that they can go together in any way, and that's exactly what happens to the birds and the automobiles and so on. At any rate that freedom from a fixed relation introduces me to the sounds of my environment.—Don Finegan et al. (1969).

The interview before this one was conducted by two ladies from Montreal, and they had gotten the notion of interviewing not just me but some other people—they may very well interview you. But they started out from Murray Schafer and his book on tuning the world, and the ideas of sound and environment, and so on. And their last question to me was, "What would be the ideal environment acoustically?" And I said, "You must look at your question and see what it is you're saying; it just doesn't make sense." I said, "The environment is there, and the ideal is in your head." And the two were quite astonished. Fortunately, we had talked a good deal before so that they understood what I was saying.—Morton Feldman (Bunita Marcus and Francesco Pellizzi) (1983).

I made a decision in the early fifties to accept the sounds that are in the world. Before that I had actually been naïve enough to think there was such a thing as silence. But I went into an anechoic chamber in Cambridge, at Harvard University, and in this room I heard two sounds. I thought there was something wrong with the room, and I told the engineer that there were two sounds. He said describe them, and I did. "Well," he said, "the high one was your nervous system in operation and the low one was your blood circulating." So that means that there is music, or there is sound, whether I intend it or not.—Maureen Furman (1979).

I then realized that I was, so to speak, a walking concert and that I didn't really intend to be that. I saw myself at a crossroads of either going as most people do, in the direction of their intentions or in the dirction of freeing the music from my intentions.—Ellsworth Snyder (1985).

What silence is is the change of my mind. It's an acceptance of the sounds that exist rather than a desire to choose and impose one's own music. That has been at the center of my work ever since then. I try when I make a new piece of music to make it in such a way that it doesn't essentially disturb the silence which already exists.

You spoke of the difference between accepting the sounds that exist and imposing one's own music. Could you explain that?

Daisetz Suzuki put that relationship between the two this way: he drew this shape on the board:

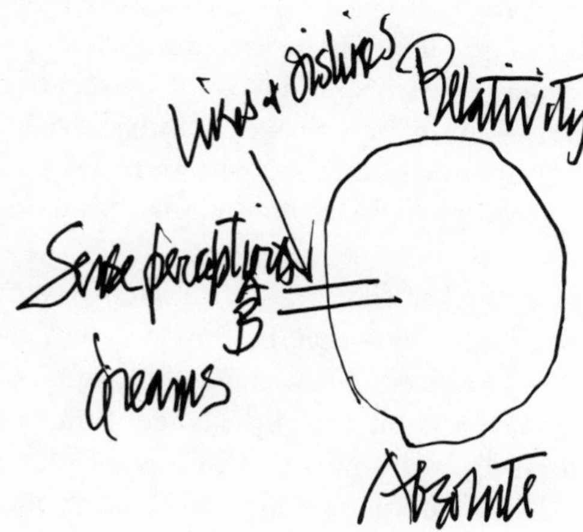

He said, "This is the structure of the Mind, and this (B-A) is the ego. The ego can cut itself off from this big Mind, which passes through it, or it can open itself up." He said, "Zen would like the ego to open up to the Mind which is outside it. If you take the way of cross-legged meditation, when you go *in* through discipline, then you get free of the ego." But I decided to go *out.* That's why I decided to use the chance operations. I used them to free myself from my ego.

I have faith that if I do this honestly, it will bring me full circle.—Maureen Furman (1979).

I just was in San Francisco and then I went to Santa Cruz to see my friend Norman O. Brown, who has written those beautiful books, *Life Against Death* and *Love's Body,* and we had very interesting conversations.

And that thing that Jesus said in the New Testament came up, about considering the lilies, which is a kind of silence; but now we know, through science, that the lilies are extremely busy. We could say that Jesus was not thinking scientifically, or not thinking microscopically, or electronically; but then we could agree with him, because the work of the lilies is not to do something other than themselves. In other words, it is not production of something else; it is rather reproduction of themselves. And that perhaps is the proper work for us all, and that, I think, could bring us back to silence, because silence also is not silent—it is full of activity.—Alcides Lanza (1971).

I remember being with an older composer who was concerned about my use of the word "nature" in connection with my explanation of musical ideas. He said he'd always thought of nature as something that should be gardened, controlled, so that the aspects of it that were uncomfortable could be removed so that one could escape being bitten.—Jeff Goldberg (1976).

Progress may be the idea of *dominating* nature. But in the arts, it may be *listening* to nature. In the forties, I conceived the idea of a piece *with no sounds in it,* but I thought it would be incomprehensible in the European context. Five years later, I was inspired to do it by seeing the paintings of Robert Rauschenberg—one of which was a canvas with no paint on it. Charles Ives wrote a romantic essay about sitting in a rocking chair, on the front porch looking out toward the mountains, "listening to your own symphony."

I once went to a Quaker meeting—with silence—and found myself thinking of what I should *say*—that is, how to dominate the meeting (Faustian!)—and then I realized that was not the point—not to dominate, but to listen. And to listen to silence. By silence, I mean the multiplicity of activity that constantly surrounds us. We call it "silence" because it is free of *our* activity. It does not correspond to ideas of order or expressive feeling—they lead to order and expression, but when they do, it "deafens" us to the sounds themselves.—C. H. Waddington (1972).

I think of my effort as a way of showing that it is possible to write music in different ways, but never with reliance on harmony or tonality. When I visited Joseph Schillinger, he had up near the ceiling of his apartment the octave marked as it would be if it followed Helmholz's book, or if it followed the vibrations of the string—that is to say, if it was true to nature. Then he had marked in different colors, with the natural in black, the others—those divisions of the octave that had been most accepted in the course of history. Not a single one of them coincided with natural harmonies. Every one of them was a convention. We are moving in directions away from theory in this century. We are beginning to listen even to thunder and birds and electronics and other noises.—Arnold Jay Smith (1977).

I have always sought out loud sounds, when I can find them, and I have asked people to make them louder . . . and most people run away from those situations. They put their fingers in their ears or protect themselves, something like that. I didn't find it necessary. The loudest one I think I heard was in a research center for architecture near London. They had a reverberation chamber, and I was able to hear very low sounds very, very loud. And I kept indicating I wanted it louder; finally, it was as though I was being massaged by the sound. It was quite a marvelous experience. Because the Japanese aesthetician, when I talked to him about hearing with the ears, you know, he said, "Remember that one can also hear with his feet."

What distinction I could draw between music and sound is: if I rent a car and when I put on the brakes they squeak and the whole car shakes, then the squeak is indicative of some malfunctioning of the car, and so stops me from using my aesthetic faculties. But otherwise I would include the very same sound if it didn't have all those other danger signals connected with it. After we like loud things, then, of course, we can get interested in very soft things.—Don Finegan et al. (1969).

I wanted to be quiet in a nonquiet situation. So I discovered first through reading the gospel of Sri Ramakrishna, and through the study of the philosophy of Zen Buddhism—and also an important book for me was *The Perennial Philosophy* by Aldous Huxley, which is an anthology of remarks of people in different periods of history and from different cultures—that they are all saying the same thing, namely, a quiet mind is a mind that is free of its likes and dislikes. You can become narrow-minded, literally, by only liking certain things, and disliking others. But you can become open-minded, literally, by giving up your likes and dislikes and becoming interested in things. I think Buddhists would say, "As they are in and of themselves," whether they are seen as aspects of nirvana, or whether they are seen as aspects of *samsara,* daily life. Now this may seem to be far away from music, but I don't think it is. Here where I live you see no musical instruments. But it seems to me that we are surrounded by sound. What I'm hearing are the sounds of traffic.

In general, the proliferation of noise and musics . . .

Well, the proliferation of music is more difficult for me than the proliferation of traffic sounds. The thing that makes Muzak tolerable is its very narrow dynamic range. It has such a narrow dynamic range that you can hear many other things at the same time as you hear Muzak. And if you pay attention carefully enough, I think you can put up with the Muzak—if you pay attention, I mean, to the things that are not Muzak.—Ev Grimes (1984).

There's another aspect of noise, or of ambient sound, that is not so easy to enjoy but which, glory be, I'm beginning to enjoy; and that is the sounds that don't change—for instance, the hum of a refrigerator, or a humidifier. You know as well as I do that, over and over again in our twentieth-century environment, we come into situations where some sound is immobilized. And what is it doing? It's stationary; it's not only remaining the same sound, but it's remaining in the same place. So what does that make us experience—I keep saying "experience" instead of "think."

But what does it make us experience? It makes us experience something to do with space, to do with sculpture, to do with architecture. What these constant sounds are is points in space. If I can have in a room five feedbacks or hums or drones, I can now enjoy that situation with great pleasure. It gave me an experience for which I'm actually starved, because I avoided sculpture all of the time I was younger. I had at one time a mobile that Calder gave me, and it took up too much room; and so I hung it from the roof, and it seemed to me to spoil the view, so I gave it to a friend. And I had another sculpture by another artist, David Hare, and I always felt I had to feed it. I felt so conscious of it I didn't feel alone in the room; I felt this sculpture is there. So I got rid of it. And now that I'm on my last legs, I need sculpture; and I'm getting it first of all through plants. And the plants have introduced me to stones, and it may be those stones that are introducing me to fixed sounds like burglar alarms, which I'm actually beginning to enjoy.—Joel Eric Suben (1984).

From a musical point of view, and I'm sure from the visual point of view, one thing makes everyday life far more fascinating and special than, say, concert life. That is the variety of sound with respect to all the other things, including space. When we make electronic music, we have to flood the hall with sounds from a few loudspeakers. But in our everyday life sounds are popping up, just as visual things and moving things are popping up, everywhere around us. I would like to imitate that—to present fantastic architectural and technological problems. That's how the theater will be. We have in America two or three loudspeakers in a theater, in Europe they have them up in the teens, and I think in the hundreds in Russia, so that sounds can move or appear to come from any point in space, generally around the hall. I would also like it to appear, as I think it will with transistor means, in the center of the space. And then there's mobility too. When a fly buzzes past me now I have, from an artistic point of view, a frightful problem. But it's quite reasonable to imagine that we will have a loudspeaker that will be able to fly through space.—Michael Kirby & Richard Schechner (1965).

Sounds should be honored rather than enslaved. I've come to think that because of my study of Buddhism, which teaches that every creature, whether sentient (such as animals) or nonsentient (such as stones and air), is the Buddha. Each being is at the center of the universe, and creation is a multiplicity of centers.—Joseph H. Mazo (1983).

In Buddhism there is the term *Yatha butham,* which means "just as it is"—and this is what appeals to me, though I see every now and then that some people are interested in symbols. But what they mean by symbols seems to be different from what I thought they meant. There's a very fine fellow I'm working with on *HPSCHD,* and his name is Calvin Sumsion—he's in the design department, and he used the word "symbol" enthusiastically the other day; it dawned on me that what he meant was a representation of visual things, rather than abstraction, and that all he meant by "symbols" was that. He didn't mean, for instance, that a dove means "peace." He meant that a picture of the dove was a symbol of the dove. And that's very different from what I would have meant, so I'm getting more interested in symbols.—Don Finegan et al. (1969).

[What music do you find worth listening to?]

I think the term "worth listening to" depends on who's listening. I think it would be right to say that no matter what, if it is sounds, one would listen to it. I haven't yet heard sounds that I didn't enjoy, except when they become too musical. I have trouble, I think, when music attempts to control me. I have trouble, for instance, with the "Hallelujah Chorus." But if the sound is unintentional, then I have no problem.—Rob Tannenbaum (1985).

[But can't music so strong—music so "moving," as we say—be justified on religious or political grounds?]

This use of music though, which bows to the audience, and does so confessedly, I think is the opposite of what seems to me to be a true revolutionary attitude, because it takes the status quo and comforts it. It doesn't do what I've said music ought to do: to make people stronger, and to change them.

I know a lot of people are very responsive to that kind of [programmatic political] music.

I have difficulty with it because it's so pushy. It has precisely in it what government has in it: the desire to control; and it leaves no freedom for me. It pushes me toward its conclusion, and I'd rather be a sheep, which I'm not, than be pushed along by a piece of music. I'm just as angry, or refusing to go along, with the "Hallelujah Chorus" as I am with the Attica one [a composition by Frederic Rzewski]. The moment I hear that kind of music I go in the opposite direction. And they use the technique of repetition, and of sequence, incessantly. And I can do without that.—Geoffrey Barnard (1980).

How do you listen to music?

I listen to the sounds, and I like the sounds not to be enslaved so that when a whole scale passage goes by where they all have the same color, I think, "Oh, those poor things—lined up like kids in a school with the same uniform on." Now and then something happens that seems to make the sound have its own life. I listen to that . . . and that's why I so much enjoy the sounds of my environment, whatever they happen to be, because the rhythm and everything about them has a beautiful freedom. When I am composing I keep that fact of everyday ambient noise as a kind of model.—Geneviere Marcus (1970).

A great many people would be baffled by the suggestion that they should respond neither emotionally nor intellectually to music. What else is there?

They should listen. Why should they imagine that sounds are not interesting in themselves? I'm always amazed when people say, "Do you mean it's just sounds?" How they can imagine that it's anything but sounds is what's so mysterious.

They're convinced that it's a vehicle for pushing the ideas of one person out of his head into somebody else's head, along with—in a good German situation—his feelings, in a marriage that's called the marriage of Form and Content. That situation is, from my point of view, absolutely alarming.

I had just heard *The Messiah* with Mrs. Henry Allen Moe, and she said, "Don't you love the 'Hallelujah Chorus' " and I said, "No, I can't stand it." So she said, "Don't you like to be moved?" and I said, "I don't mind being moved, but I don't like to be pushed."

What do you think the harmful effects of that marriage are for an audience?

What it does is bolster up the ego. It is in the ego, as in a home, that those feelings and ideas take place. The moment you focus on them, you focus on the ego, and you separate it from the rest of Creation. So then a very interesting sound might occur, but the ego wouldn't even hear it because it didn't fit its notion of likes and dislikes, its ideas and feelings. It becomes not only insensitive, but, if you persist in annoying it, it will then put cotton in its ears. So if it isn't sufficiently insensitive to the outside, it will cut itself off from possible experience.

Is it possible to listen to The Messiah *in such a way that the sounds can be taken simply as themselves?*

I think so. But you'd have to listen to a lot of other music at the same time, in some kind of *Apartment House* situation. Then it might be very entertaining. You can get rid of intention by multiplying intention. That's what's at the basis of my work with *Musicircus,* which is in *Apartment House.*—Cole Gagne & Tracy Caras (1980).

How do you like your listeners to come to a concert? Do you like them to know certain things, or have certain attitudes?

They should be ready for a new experience, and the best way to be ready for a new experience is to be attentive and empty. By empty is meant open—in other words, the like and dislike of the ego doors should be down. And there should be a flow so that the experience of listening can come in.

I think that there is a distinct difference between . . . I think that the most pointed way to put this distinction is by using the word "understanding" as opposed to "experience." Many people think that if they are able to understand something that they will be able to experience it, but I don't think that that is true. I don't think that understanding something leads to experience. I think, in fact, that it leads only to a certain use of the critical faculties. Because . . . say you understand how to boil an egg. How will that help you in cooking zucchini? I'm not sure. One could make the point more dramatically by saying, "How will that help you to ride horseback?" But that probably goes too far. I think that we must be prepared for experience not by understanding anything, but rather by becoming open-minded.

You talked about understanding as opposed to experiencing. Would you like to see people experiencing more music?

I think that that's very important. I think in the first experience involving music, as opposed to understanding music, the first thing is to learn to listen. And I suppose that most would think that that's so simple to do that there's no problem. And actually there is no problem, but it's a question of whether or not one does it. Some people, for instance, develop ideas about what are good sounds and what are bad sounds. And they don't want to hear the bad ones. I had a composer friend who was that way. The result was that he couldn't stand the sounds of traffic, which I love. He had to put cotton in his ears to keep them out. Many people in our society now go around the streets and in buses and so forth playing radios with earphones on and they don't hear the world around them. They hear only the music that they've chosen to hear, or whatever it is they've chosen to hear. I can't understand why they cut themselves off from that rich experience which is free. I think this is the beginning of music, and I think that the end of music may very well be in those record collections.

The nature of listening is the experience of hearing something and then realizing that you're no longer hearing it and that you're hearing something else. This is part and parcel of hearing. When you look at a painting, you don't have the impression that the painting is disappearing. But as you listen to sounds, you have the impression that they're gone, and that others have taken their place. And you're brought right by paying attention to events in time. All you need to see is you're brought into direct contact with ephemerality.—Ev Grimes (1984).

You've commented that most audiences go to a concert with the feeling that something is being done to *them, instead of going with the attitude that they have to take an active role. Could you be more specific about what you think they should be doing?*

The two things that they shouldn't be doing are the things that they generally think they should be doing: one is responding emotionally, and the other is responding in terms of relationships of sounds. I don't think either one should be done.

A great deal of the education has taught them to do just what I've said they shouldn't do. So then the average person goes on to say—or at least is quoted as saying—that he doesn't know anything about music (as the educated suggest that he should do), but that he knows what he likes. So he searches to see whether he likes something or not. Then the first time he's rubbed the wrong way, he says, "I don't like it." That can be because something is too loud, or too dissonant, or too this, or too that.—Cole Gagne & Tracy Caras (1980).

So it's exclusively the reader or the listener of your music who is doing something with your works?

Yes, the response, I think, finishes it. I think we've been moving from ownership to use.—Birger Ollrogge (1985).

In some of your potentially thicker compositions, people often complain that they can't pick out anything because so much is going on. Is that a failure of their ears, or an attempt to lay an expectation on what they are hearing?

I think so. I myself enjoy a complex situation in which I can place my attention one place or another. I then am drawn inevitably to the nature of my experience as coming from my own center rather than from some other center. I think each person should listen in his own way, and if there are too many things for him to listen to, and if in that complex he then listens to whatever, he will have his own experience, and there will be a strength and validity in that which is much greater than, say, listening to one thing and not knowing at the end what it was that you heard or whether you were listening properly.—Tom Darter (1982).

Does it sadden you when a piece you've written provokes a violent response?

It happened to me recently in Colorado. I was giving a performance which many people in the audience found not at all beautiful but very boring, and after twenty minutes they began a kind of concerted attempt to bring the performance to a halt. I must confess that I would have been happier if that hadn't taken place, but I think that our experiences ought not just sadden us or make us happy. I think that if my work were not disgruntling to some people, I'd be even more disturbed.—Jeff Goldberg (1976).

To live well you have to hear what there is to hear, rather than what you think there's going to be to heard. When I go to a concert, I want to hear music that I've not heard before. I don't generally go to a concert now to hear anything with which I'm familiar, or which I know that I'll like. I go in order to hear something that I've never heard before. In fact that's the same intention that I have when I write a piece of music which I've never heard before—to make a kind of discovery if I can.—Tom Darter (1982).

How do you respond to critics who say that your pieces are too long?

Well, they're thinking of art as entertainment, and that isn't what art is about. I would say, to put it as simply as I can, that art changes our minds. After all, boredom is not perpetrated upon you; it's you who create the boredom. So my music isn't boring. The person who said it is has just found a way to be bored.—Jeff Goldberg (1976).

[Why do you object to the recording of music?]

I don't like recordings because they turn music into an object, and music is actually a process that's never twice the same. If you turn it into an object, then you have the kind of musical experience that resulted, for example, in the amusing remark of a child . . . I was present when Stravinsky conducted one of his early pieces for orchestra, one of the ballets; and after it was finished, the child turned to his father—they were sitting in front of me—and he said, "That isn't the way it goes." I told that story to someone else recently, and he knew of a child who turned to his father and said, "Why don't they turn the record over? And play the other side?"

So actually records are creating a whole new set of expectations in listeners.

Right, right, so that the record listeners are not really prepared for listening to live music. I have a very dear friend, the important violinist Paul Zukofsky, for whom I'm writing the *Freeman Etudes.* He has his own recording company because he believes that records are more faithful to music than live performances. He believes that in the course of a live performance both the performer and audience are in an unpredictable, uncontrollable situation, and that things happen that could be corrected, so he moves, actually, toward an idea which is the ideal of the music as it was written, and he veers away from music as it happens in the course of circumstances that involve performance. I don't agree with him.—Tom Darter (1982).

All [hi-fi records do] is move toward a faithful reproduction of something that's already happened. I think if you're going to have all that equipment you should be able to distort the sound too. Hi-fi is only one point on a circle, and most people stick with that one point, but it's more intelligent to start going around the circle.

I don't collect records, including my own, and I don't get a great deal out of popular music now that the more or less revolutionary aspect of rock is more or less quiescent. I can see that a musician could decide that, in this society, recordings would be the way to make it if your music is going to reach the people. On the other hand, I know that I don't like to listen to records as much as I like to listen to silence. . . .—Jeff Goldberg (1974).

Do you think that, as the years go by, more people will compose with the methods you've brought forth?

No, I think we're going in a multiplicity of directions. If I performed any function at all, it's one that would have been performed in any case: to take us out of the notion of the mainstream of music, and into a situation that could be likened to a delta or field or ocean, that there are just countless possibilities.

And you think that would have happened anyway, without your music?

I think so. I think that our ideas that seem to be novel are merely ideas that one or another of us is about to have. At the time that I was using the Magic Square, Wyschnegradsky on the other side of the Atlantic was also using it, and I had no connection with him. At the time that Edison invented the electric light, someone else did it too but didn't get to the post office soon enough!—Cole Gagne & Tracy Caras (1980).

Some people say that we are now in the time of postmodernism, and that we've had a lot of . . .

That we've had enough modern music?

They think that the idea of avant-garde is finished. How do you see this?

I think that people always hoped that it would be finished, but that the trouble is that it never will be finished. The reason that it won't be finished is because the avant-garde is synonymous with invention, discovery and change; and these are essential qualities so that they will always be here to irritate people.—Thomas Wulffen (1984).

You said in a lecture: "The past must be reinvented, the future must be revised. Doing both makes what the present is. Discovery never stops." Is the avant-garde dead?

People ask what the avant-garde is and whether it's finished. It isn't. There will always be one. The avant-garde is flexibility of mind. And it follows like day the night from not falling prey to government and education. Without the avant-garde nothing would get invented.—Stephen Montague (1982).

PEDAGOGY

The moment something is in danger of being lost, like the art of formal gardening, or the kind of music that was played at that time, people rush to its assistance specifically with the purpose of saving it. We have societies for the ancient music of our cultures and others. There are people out there who live for nothing else. If some form of ancient art hasn't been preserved, those people will say, "Oh, that gives me something to do." The moment there would be any sign of music disappearing, the number of musicians would increase alarmingly. From the point of view of making a living, music is absolutely useless. The only way Americans make a living in music is by teaching.—Arnold Jay Smith (1977).

What consequences do you think this new situation in music will have for music education?

Conventional music education is something that can only infuriate anyone who is at all interested in living. No matter what aspect of it you think of, you get angry almost immediately. The idea that a small child should be put in front of a piano and be made to read notation which is the equivalent of Greek or Latin is ridiculous. Unless the child loves music inordinately, he will soon learn to hate it positively. The first thing that happens is that his eyes are engaged and his ears are shut. So that playing music in terms of music education has absolutely nothing to do with ears or the enjoyment of sound. It has only to do with reading, and reading something equivalent to Greek or Latin because the notation is no longer useful for the music of the twentieth century. It's only useful for previous centuries. So for our young children to have the good fortune to be brought into the twentieth century, and to be immediately educated as though they were in a previous century, is some form of social insanity.—Lars Gunnar Bodin et al (1965).

I remember when I was in grammar school the people used to put the needle down on the record for just a few seconds and then pick it up and we all had to tell who had written it, and then when [the composer] died and so forth—things were getting confused because you couldn't tell whether the sounds were men, or the men were sounds (we spoke in fact of those sounds—if we got a star for it, we said Beethoven or Mozart or Haydn instead of saying what the sounds . . . instead of listening to the sounds really). Then, after studying music, if you're lucky you can come back to the direct hearing of sounds—hopefully.—Jack Behrens (1981).

In the field of music you mentioned it seemed impossible to get rid of harmony and, yet, once it was done, the whole field of music was changed. What would be the equivalent in the field of education?

Well, one would have to look at the educational system and try to see what its nature is, so to speak, essentially, when it does not have any of the structures which have been placed over it by means of social agreement or conventions. One of the first things that you would get rid of in education that has nothing to do, obviously, with education, is all the business of bureaucracy, which would include forms and the filling out of forms, certificates of degrees, prizes, anything that would indicate the manner in which the thing should be accomplished. Education should become a field in which it was uncertain either that anyone would become educated, or uncertain that they were not educated before they entered the experience of becoming educated. Buckminster Fuller, whom I visited recently, said that when a child is born he is, so to speak, completely educated. He has in his body all that is meant, ultimately, by the word "education." He doesn't need anything else than to be born.—Robert Filliou (1970).

We have made our government and our educational system such that . . . we have made people bad. We've forced them to be bad. The whole thing of competition in schools, where it begins, and how it stands in society, the competition enforces dishonesty. Mao Tse-tung says that we must firmly believe that the great masses of humanity are good. I'm perfectly willing to agree with that, provided we don't educate them to be bad.

The same [grammar school] teacher, who thought she was teaching me music appreciation, also told me that I had no voice. I had wanted to join the glee club, and when she tested my voice she said, "You don't have a voice." It wasn't until I was thirty-five years old that I sang. Our whole education has been to stop singing and to inspire cheating. If you don't know what the music is and who the composer is, you can peek over your neighbor's shoulder. You learn very quickly, and if you cheat sufficiently, you'll be rewarded with a silver star, and you might even get into the regional contests.

My early relation to the educational system was when I recognized that it wasn't doing what I needed. I simply dropped out of school. I left. Thoreau, too, stopped teaching. He went to Harvard University to learn to teach, and he came back to Concord and they required that he dress in a particular way to teach. They were more strict then than now. They also required that he punish students who didn't do what they were supposed to do. He refused to do either of those things, and so he stopped teaching.—Ellsworth Snyder (1975).

The entire social structure must change, just as the structures in the arts have changed. We believe, I think, since this has been accomplished in the arts in this century, that it is an indication, at least in the minds of the artists, that there is a need for it to happen in the other fields of society, particularly in terms of political and economic structures and all the things that go beside, like educational structures.

I think, first of all, we need a situation in which nothing is being transmitted: no one is learning anything that was known before. They must be learning things that were, until this situation arose, so to speak, unknown or unknowable—that was due to the fact of the person coming together with other people or, so to speak, coming together with himself that this new knowledge which had not been known before could become known.

Now I don't think we need do anything else other than make an empty canvas upon which this education can be painted. We don't need anything more than an empty space of time in which this music could be performed, if education were music. And when we have now an empty canvas or an empty space of time, we know in the areas of art that we don't need to do anything to those in order to have the esthetic experience—they already are that. So, we could say of the educational experience that we do not have to consciously learn anything in order to learn something.

This story occurs over and over again in the annals of Zen Buddhism—the student who comes to the teacher and begs him for instruction. The teacher says nothing—he's just sweeping up leaves. The student goes off into another part of the forest and builds his own house; and when he is finally educated, what does he do? He doesn't thank himself; he goes back to the teacher who said nothing and thanks him. It's this spirit of not teaching that has been completely lost in our educational system.

More service with less input of human labor?

It will happen in all sorts of ways. One way is this: speaking of education, changes in education and how they will come about—people will notice more and more, as they already do, that within five years after you get a Ph.D. from a given American university in a particular field, all the things that you learned in the course of your education are no longer of any use to you. This is due to the fact that changes are happening more rapidly than they happened earlier, that the techniques involved, the information useful, etc., are not the ones which you were taught. So, one will become skeptical about what the function of education is, and ultimately, what one will have to do is to give each individual, from childhood, a variety of experiences in which his mind is put to use, not as a memorizer of a transmitted body of information, but rather as a person who is in dialogue: A, with himself and B, with others as though they were him too.—Robert Filliou (1970).

You should know Buckminster Fuller's book, *Education Automation*, in which he suggests a space that is without partitions, in which a variety of activities is going on and the attention of the student could be at one place or another—rather than being forced to focus on a single thing that often isn't even of his choice. I think this is a good principle which can be stated in many ways. One is: where you see a boundary, remove it (or partition, to remove it). And if you *must* have them, then have them movable; and where you have—as Fuller says—a choice between fixity and flexibility, choose flexibility. This is a very good rule.—Don Finegan et al. (1969).

Now, there is near Chicago at the present moment a school without partitions. There are a large number of classes where, in the study of one subject you would at least be hearing, since there are no partitions, not only the information in your subject, but the information in the adjacent subject. Now it is conceivable that there would occur at this point, even if you didn't change your seat, what McLuhan refers to as the brushing of information against information. Now, when you see this that is being transmitted to you as being nothing but information and when you see a different kind of information on the other side of the table, and when in your mind these two things come together, very often a third thing, or even a larger number of things occur in your mind. Your mind invents or creates, so to speak, from this brushing; and it is there that we need to be if we are going to be learning something that we did not yet know—where the learning process now takes place outside of us, obliging us to imitate it, the new knowledge only comes into existence in our heads.—Robert Filliou (1970).

There's a very curious thing about the United States that hasn't yet been mentioned that makes it different from the rest of the world. It is that we have these schools with the young people in them, and these schools continue, for the most part, up through the universities. Let's say that many, many people get a college education.

Now, as long as they are being educated, they have had access to art, theater, etc. They use it, take it seriously, and they believe in it.

Then, when they graduate from that school situation, they discover that they are in a society that has absolutely no serious use for art. Anything but art is important.

Now the proof of this is that if then you do go against society, as it were, and insist upon being an artist, and do some lively work, where is your audience? Your audience is back in the school from which you graduated. You can't sustain yourself as a performing artist in this country without performing year after year on tours that don't take you to the adult audiences, but rather take you to the school audiences.

Neither in Japan nor in Europe would the universities dream of having you perform for them because they're busy studying.

Furthermore, they have a long tradition, not in the schools, but among the adults, of taking art seriously. We have a tradition of thinking that art is a good thing [for adults] to forget.—Stanley Kauffmann (1966).

We're certainly going to have controls of one kind or another, but if we could put them, get them placed some place, where we wouldn't notice them, that would be the goal of society, don't you think? I don't notice for instance all the control they put into making the telephone. And I don't notice the whole history of plumbing and everything when I turn on the faucet, but it is there. What I don't want is to get involved in it politically. The value judgment thing is the political idea. Like all the value judgment that runs through the university teaching, it's political.

Since you place so much emphasis on youth, what do you think about their present incubators, the universities?

As they exist now, they are places where people go in order to get degrees in order to get jobs in order to enter this prison we've talked about. The university itself is modeled on the idea of the prison, so you get used to the idea of prison already while you're being educated. . . . "If you don't do as we say you'll do, we'll fail you." You know all about that. But, in that university, more and more things are changing, and freedom is creeping in. You hear such expressions as "the free university," or you hear of students taking advantage of the university without being enrolled, and of deciding themselves when to leave. Or you hear of the university permitting people to choose their own studies and not bother with the curriculum or degrees, and more and more teachers are willing to teach without giving grades, etc., so that this change is entering into that very situation which was bolstering up the old, so that we have this overlap situation that we're living in and that's why we're frequently confused by what's happening around us. Sometimes it's happening for old reasons which are dying, and sometimes it's happening for new reasons which are coming into being.—Geneviere Marcus (1970).

The great trouble with the universities is that they limit hours, schedule classes, arranging things so that you run from one thing to the other like an idiot. The very first thing you should think of doing in a university is not to schedule things, because that isn't the way people live. The only time you should do that in your living is when you have to make a train or an airplane or something; then you have to get there on time. But the rest of the time you don't have to do that.—Don Finegan et al. (1969).

From a positive, new society point of view, the university is gradually becoming like life. It is beginning to include in it all the things that are in life, so ultimately when there is nothing to do in the way of work, but, say, one hour's work per year, then we could just spend our entire life in the university. But then we would have to make it into a nonpolice situation which we would enjoy being in, because we would never graduate. It would be in other words a place in a community abundantly implemented so that anything you thought of doing or studying could be done, and if you needed help to learn to use such and such a tool for something, there would be someone around who would be willing to help you. That would be a university. That could be life, and we have all kinds of signs like that, like community centers and so forth, where people can go freely and use materials and make things and do things—or the public library where people can go and read anything they want.

What about human relationships? The family structure may be disintegrating.

The reason it's disintegrating is because we have separated all the generations. We put our children away from us with baby-sitters. When they get older, we send them off to school. When they graduate, we send them off to the army. When they get out of that, if they're still alive, we give them jobs that nearly kill them. And then, when they lose their minds slightly, we send them off to insane asylums, and when they break our rules, we send them to prison; and when they get old enough, we send them to senior communities. We haven't a moment in our society now when we don't manage to get rid of us.—Geneviere Marcus (1970).

I want to add one more thing. More and more recently, to the benefit of the entire world, the ideas of Buckminster Fuller are being brought to our attention. He envisages a society that, by using its intelligence and the resources of the world, will bring about a global village in which each one of us to fulfill his responsibility to society will not have to do more than one hour's work per year.

Then he makes curves, showing that the need for people in certain activities is going down remarkably. For instance, one of my second cousins in Buffalo who works for Union Carbide told me that they just introduced a computer that makes it possible to fire 955 out of 1,000 people.

Now, at the same time that those people don't have that work to do, notice what is happening to our universities all over the country. They are having to expand. More and more people are going into the universities. More and more unemployment is occurring in our adult situation.—Stanley Kauffmann (1966).

The ideas about the university that have struck me as most interesting are those of Ivan Illich and Buckminster Fuller. Illich speaks of "deschooling society," and Fuller speaks of changing both the university and society so that no one ever graduates. In both cases, the idea is to keep the process of learning and the interest in learning going—not stopping it and not institutionalizing it.

On the "compartmentalization" of academic departments:

There's a very interesting book by Edgar Anderson, who's an economic botanist. It's called *Plants, Man, and Life,* I think, and in it he shows . . . Well, as we know, our ways of growing plants are to grow only one plant; the result is that each plant is separate from the others. But when one mixes the plants up, and it looks almost as though it were not agriculture but was wild, then everything regenerates everything else and it becomes a healthy situation for the plant. I would say in life, too. The only kinds of ideas that really interest me in any of the arts are ideas that also work in our lives, or with plants—where, after all, our problem is that we're individuals, that we're members of society, and that society inhabits an environment—and that's Nature. And these things have to work together. This business of organization which is so inherent in education has many, many dangers—and it has also many usefulnesses, as we know. For instance, if someone telephoned a number, dialed a number and got just *anybody* each time, and the person *changed* each time, the telephone system would be of little use to us. It's there that we need some kind of order. And if I turned on the water, and not water but dust came out, or wine, or something else—there might be times when it would be pleasant, but other times it would be useless. We need to place organization where it is useful, and we need to place disorganization or unpredictability of interpenetrations elsewhere. And more and more, whether we place it or not, this is happening because of communications. You know what I mean.—Don Finegan et al. (1969).

You want to know the basic thing I am interested in? The basic thing, I would say, is to do nothing. The second thing would be to do, so to speak, what enters one's head. It should not be fixed in advance what that would be.

I think, as far as our lives and behavior are concerned, that we are on the search for clues as to how to proceed and how to behave in this very complicated historical moment of the old structures remaining and new structures becoming either evident or desired. You see it everywhere. And then, we determine our actions by those clues, once we're convinced of their usefulness and validity, and try to apply them. The first one I've given you seems so little and so difficult, because it's so basic—that idea that we're being educated without being educated. Well, let's see if we could add something. If we add something, it should be added in the spirit of that basic nothing and not be antagonistic to it. Because, if we got rid of this new basis, we would have gotten into what you spoke of—namely, a new structure that might be as bad as the old one eventually. So we must somehow keep free of replacing, filling up, that emptiness with a new structure. So we're already close to a new principle that we can recognize, coming from many different directions. For instance, a man named Avner Hovna wrote an article in one of the UNESCO publications on the effect on society of automation—the sum of which, as far as I recall, is that we must substitute flexibility values for continuity values. Now, we know immediately when we think now of education that our educational structure, as we know it, is characterized by continuity values—it has always resisted even the most recent aspect of the continuity: namely, the avant-garde. But we don't want that continuity value—we have no use for it. We need flexibility value. So, our education must be characterized by anything that leads toward change in flexibility. Therefore, coming back to the architecture of the school—a big, empty space in which the students are not obliged to sit on one chair, but are free to move from chair to chair.

And also from time to time, I suppose.

From time to time.

One of the big problems now is that we have schedules, hours. . . .

This must be refused. Anything that represents a continuity from one day to the next should be changed to something that represents flexibility from one day to the next. Anything resembling an interruption, a distraction, should be welcomed. Why? Because we will realize that by these interruptions and distractions and flexibilities we enrich the brushing of information against information, etc.—Robert Filliou (1970).

There is a tendency because of the structure of universities to think that if you enter a building marked "Music" and go all the way through it, you'll come out a musician. This isn't true. Morton Feldman said it is a question of who is teaching. The matter of people meeting people is very important. Finally, the meeting has to be with yourself. The university doesn't encourage meeting with yourself because it's constantly offering the opportunity to do something other than meet yourself.

I don't think that the arts can be taught. I think that the process of teaching should be a meeting between the teachers and the students and in that exchange it is not certain who is going to learn. It's very possible that the teacher will learn more than the student—at least this is how Schoenberg's book *Harmonielehre* begins. He says, "I learned this book from my students." I'm reluctant to teach because I think that it would take too much time. I realize that teaching has a function in society, but I choose to fulfill that function not individually, but by means of continuing my work writing both words and music and giving in that way an example.—*Works and Days* (1969).

In traditional Asian art, structures of precise form are very important. Can the kind of opening of mind that chance operations aims for take place in traditional forms? Do they differ in their arising from your own work?

Where there is a dependence on precise art forms and esthetic principles, something like education (learning) is going on. I have been for many years now more involved in postgraduate experience. In fact, I discourage teaching. I want to go on studying.—Bill Womack (1979).

In Fuller's never-ending university he suggests that we take down the walls between the various rooms so that when you go, say, to study music, you might hear a little bit from the next class over (because there wouldn't be any wall between you) which might be on some other subject such as electrical engineering; I'm sure the mind is such that connections would be made and they might be very refreshing.

Once when I was at Wesleyan University I didn't have to teach but I did now and then give a class. When I was asked to teach musical composition, I introduced the students to the work of Marcel Duchamp; and since that wasn't about music but was about things that you could see rather than hear, what they read had different effects—it was received in an original way by each of the students—so that when the students brought compositions resulting from that information they were all different, whereas if the teaching had been more musical they would all have done more similar things. The fact that they were different was refreshing because it made it clear to the students that they weren't in a state of competition with one another but were in a state of discovering something that they were unfamiliar with.—Jack Behrens (1981).

Can [students] experience things without having to value them is a blunt way of saying it, and I think they can. And I think they'll be able to experience them more openly in a greater variety of ways if the notion of valuing them is removed. In education, at least when I went to school—you may be more liberated now—you weren't allowed to value Shakespeare, for instance, in your own way. You had to value it in the jury's way or the teacher's way. And this is unfortunate. It has the effect for many people of removing any interest in Shakespeare. Because Shakespeare simply then becomes the subject of an examination, and not of an experience. He becomes a path to a degree or something like that, which isn't Shakespeare at all. So I'd say get rid of examinations. I think that if things are going to be criticized and looked at, they should be looked at not by a jury but by all the people; and that one very good practice that's developing now is not to hand in the papers to the teacher—one wants to lose the distinction of teacher and student and to simply develop the notion of a society which has young people, older people, inexperienced people, experienced people, all willing to help one another. They have now much to give to one another. The teachers can learn much from the students. Just as the students can on occasion learn something from the teachers. But mutual learning will take place better if the distinction is obscured. It can only be obscured if the students give their work to themselves as well as to the teacher. And then have surveys taken of what people's reactions were today, if you wanted to know them, rather than making judgments. More and more one would get busy if the university permitted people to be busy not doing particular things, but doing many things. Then there will be less and less time for foolishness like evaluating and talking about something that is already done.

The example of this that I sometimes give are the anarchists in the Ohio farming community in the last century who were so busy working that they didn't bother with any meetings to talk. They didn't have anything to talk about because everything was being done. The example is from a beautiful book called *Men Against the State*, and it's a survey of American philosophical anarchism in the nineteenth century. With the conclusion—among the things that are concluded—of the fact that anarchism at the time the book was written was more or less defunct politically ☙socially❧, but was still visible in the manifestos of ☙individual❧ artists in which the spirit, the anarchist spirit, is still alive. But you feel it in Thoreau's essay on "Civil Disobedience" where he says the best government will be that which is no government at all. The best university will be that which is no university at all. And [Buckminster] Fuller says we want a university from which we never graduate. There is no question of graduating because the whole society has turned into a university—and what university is that? It's a place where one is allowed to do research on one hand, invention, creation, etc., and/or all these things to affect one another and so make society lively. And if it were a good university who would want to graduate from it?—Don Finegan et al. (1969).

[What about Black Mountain College, which seemed more "successful" at educating artists?]

The Black Mountain community seemed really marvelous and certainly marvelous in relation to any other school in the country. And since then the question that's so frequently asked is, "What school now comes the closest to what Black Mountain was?" And many schools have tried to do that, but I don't think have succeeded. The closest, for me, to an experience comparable to Black Mountain was the summer workshop at

Emma Lake in Saskatchewan from the University of Saskatchewan, and which I have written a text about, "Emma Lake," in *A Year from Monday.* In each case, the number of people was comparable, around a hundred people. And it may be that one of the great problems for other schools that would like to be like Black Mountain is that their numbers are different. When you have several thousand, you simply don't have the possibilities that you have when you have one hundred.—Mary Emma Harris (1974).

In the case of Black Mountain College, the arts were very compatible with the university because that's what was there. There was almost nothing else there [in 1952–53], though I think there was a class in mathematics or physics. Mostly, it was the arts. What was very enlightening about Black Mountain was that you didn't have to come to an end of it; you didn't graduate from it. You were just as much in it when you left as when you were there. That comes as close to anything in the American experience to Fuller's notion that we should have a university from which we don't graduate. If one did wish to graduate one could. But the Black Mountain faculty didn't graduate him or examine him. They imported people from more structured places to give those examinations and to give grades.

I was invited to Black Mountain to teach music composition, and I didn't have any students [in 1952]; nobody wanted to study with me. This didn't keep me from staying there, and it also didn't keep the students from talking with me. I think what actually happened at Black Mountain was that many things were taught without there being any assigned times for that exchange to take place. It really took place when people were together, and they were together primarily when they were hungry. The food wasn't particularly good, but everyone ate in the same place and looked out at the view across the lake. There were mountains in the distance and there was an island in the lake. The librarian said the tree on the island was in the wrong place.—*Works and Days* (1979).

[One student at Black Mountain] was averse to studying with anyone, since he would prefer to have taught. He was very bright. What was interesting about him, and the reason why I asked whether he's still alive, is that he told me that he had very little time to live and that he was going to die in six months. Well, of course, he didn't. I said, "That makes no difference whether you're going to die in six months or six years or sixty years. I'm also going to die, and death isn't part of our concern. Our concern is what we are going to do while we're alive." And so I refused to commiserate with him over the fact that he was going to die. I had a very good friend, Hazel Dreiss, a bookbinder in San Francisco, who had been told by doctors that she was going to die in six months, and she had lived—and as far as I know, she still lives—longer than anyone else. And

I bet you a nickel that Jay Watt is still living. He also got involved, after he left Black Mountain, in a rather killing relation to drinking and perhaps even to dopes and things; I don't know.—Mary Emma Harris (1974).

[How does one tell] teachers from students without a program?

I think one would have a file, available night and day—twenty-four-hour access—of ideas given both by the faculty and by the student body in the university situation. You might think of other files; I think especially of one. Things to do. Things that need to be done. As though the world were a house—which it is—that we're all living in and it's in a bad way—and it really is. I think it really needs "cleaning up," you know; fixing up, so it works. And there are all kinds of other things to do. And if people jotted these down and then cross-referenced them—where a given thing to do crops up in several different fields so that you could happen upon it in this file, not just in one place, but in all the places that it really had reference to—that thought would become enormously stimulating to the whole community. And there could be things to do that went all the way from being practical to being impractical, which would involve—if they were accomplished—invention, etc.

You see, there are some obvious things that teachers have to learn from the students. And curiously enough they're what the teachers used to be teaching the students: reading, writing, and arithmetic. Very few of the teachers any longer know how to do any of these three things in terms of the computer. Whereas many of the students do, because it's their baby, so to speak. Whereas it came after *we* were grown up, so we don't know anything about it; in fact, we're a little bit frightened by it. We need help—and whose help? Very possibly the help of the students to do our programming. Maybe. Now what can we really give them? And when we ask ourselves that question we really wonder. Mostly, they don't need anything from us and would like us to have something to do. Let us say for us to be students, too, which is what I think the subtitle of Fuller's book is—"Returning the Teacher to His Studies."

Don't they need us just merely as a disguise or an excuse for being in a certain place?

Well, that's the attitude that life consists of games, and that was necessary when there were boundaries. In fact you can't play a game unless you *do* have boundaries and *do* have signs that this place is not this other place. That this university is not downtown. This university is not a TV set. Except on occasion when the program is "educational." But it will be better if we stop playing that game. If, for instance, the religious spirit instead of taking place just because there are a bunch of priests around takes place as it did with Thoreau, walking naked, as he did, in a stream in the middle of Concord—did you know that? That was one of the things he did in Concord that made his "religious" neighbors a little upset.

But how far do you take this idea? Only into the arts? How does it fit in with social responsibility, as in training the doctor, training the engineer . . . ?

But then we have our heads to use, and we should use them. I gave the illustration of the telephone and the water faucet and there will be areas that require another attitude than the one I'm suggesting, but certainly all this will have to do with mind, and changing it—which is, say: philosophy, religion, mythology, arts, and then psychology; I suppose sociology, the enjoying of nature through the sciences. But then science is at that point of the naming of things. Taxonomy in botany is something like the telephone, organization has to take place; otherwise, the telephone is of no use to us. If we give names to all the various mushrooms, then we ought to find some way of knowing which mushroom is which, and this is the thing people are working on now with the computer. The previous taxonomies have been hopelessly inefficient at being useful, so we're trying to get useful ones. And where that kind of practicality is of the essence—and is otherwise foolishness—there we need organized ways of doing things. But in all the rest of human activity I think that the E. E. Cummings title might be an inspiration—two plus two *Is Five.* It's at that point where all the rationality is precisely a nuisance and it is of no service to us and ought to be put down under, as Norman O. Brown says, as though in a sewer, where we don't have to even think about it.—Don Finegan et al. (1969).

And the first thing I announced was that everyone in the class would get an A because I am opposed to the grading in schools. Well, when this news got around the campus the size of the class increased to 120 people who all wanted to have A's. Gradually, it settled down to about 80 people who came to the class all the time. But even those who just came and registered got an A. My first talk to them explained my point of view. And that included the fact that we didn't know what we were studying. That this was a class in we didn't know what. And in order to make that clear that we would subject the entire University Library to chance operations, to the *I Ching,* and each person in the class would read, say, five books or parts of five books, if the books were too long, and the *I Ching* could tell them which part to read. And in that way we would all have, I thought and they agreed, something to talk about, something to give one another. Whereas if we did as other classes do and all read the same book and knew what we were doing, then we could only be in the position of competing with one another to see which one understood the most. Whereas in this other class we all became generous to one another, and the conversations were unpredictable.—Hans G. Helms (1972).

I think the various conventional forms that afflict the university at the present time should be bypassed, or steps should be taken to remove them. For instance, I was once talking with Varèse on the subject of harmony, which now takes a year to be taught in a university. We both agreed that anything useful about harmony could be taught in one half hour.

I would suggest that instead of there being *required* studies, they should simply be made available, in an environment which is conducive to people becoming interested. The interest in such general questions should arise in the student, rather than being forced upon him. The reason I dropped out of college was because I was absolutely horrified by being in a class which had, say, two hundred members, and an assignment being given to have all two hundred people read the same book. I thought that if everyone read the same book, it was a waste of people. It was sufficient for one person to read the book and then somehow through that person, if the book had anything in it, everyone could get it, by talking with the person who had read the book. But to look at those desks with everybody reading the same book, that struck me with horror, so I marched away and went into the stacks of the library. I read books as irrelevant to the subject as I could find; and when the questions were given for the examination, I got an *A*. I thought there was something wrong with that system, so I dropped out of college.

I think this notion of a curriculum and practices such as having people read the same standard text are based on the conviction that at the basis of learning is language, which is understood by each person; and that people would not be able to communicate unless they had the same information. Now in the arts at the present time, this is not what obtains. Today, all through the world which uses modern art, what we have are *intermedia*. It is extremely common practice that many things go on at once. In a theatrical or musical or any such situation, the center of interest is nowhere to be observed; it is interesting all over.

This means that the basic notion of an agreed-upon language is being given up. The characteristic of one of our events, that includes music, and action, and film, and slides, and so forth, and which is present in what we call serious art, and in rock and roll performances with films and stroboscopic lights, with dark light and all these things—the characteristic thing is that after two people have experienced it they would be able to converse and exchange their experiences, which have been *different.* I don't think syntax or language in a conventional sense took place; it is something far more all-pervasive which took place. Two people in such a situation, with the activity surrounding the audience, might have their backs to one another and literally see different complicated things, though they were present at the same event. And that is our life experience. Why are these arts the way they are? They are not that way in order to simply break the laws of art; they are, rather, that way in order to introduce us to the life we are living, so that we can, as you say, participate in it.

Now, the situation we have here right now, the discussion in this room, is an excellent one for education; and it also occurs, doesn't it, at the graduate level. Ought it not to sweep down through and penetrate the whole university? That is to say, people coming together and exchanging their information; and then, through the *brushing* of their information together, one with the other, stimulating further perhaps unwritten information—people acting together synergistically, rather than each one as in a factory doing exactly the same thing as the others.—C. H. Waddington (1972).

I have no formal contact with the students at all, and I stay quite a bit away from the University [of Illinois] and don't even present myself. It was controversial whether to invite me there in the first place, and the faculty in the music school was divided, as you can imagine; some thought that if I came it would be a disaster, and others thought it would be very good. And I think in the end I disappointed everyone. Although I'm not pushing myself forward, some students make their way over here, and one of them, I recall, last year even expressed a kind of gratitude to me for not teaching. He said, "I hear you're going to teach next year," and there were some people who said, "Why should he be here if he's not doing anything in the way of teaching?" And I said, "Well, I don't think I'll do it." Then he said, "I think that it's very good not to." They know that I'm here and if they wish to see me, they can; and if they don't need to, they don't have to. And I put up a sign saying, "Anyone who wants to see me, may." Which they didn't read. People read less and less of those notices, you know.

Except one day I got a note from a student saying he would like to meet me any time that I wished—you know, that I was free. So I replied and said that he could call and that I was free most any time, and he hasn't called. Peculiar, isn't it?—Don Finegan et al. (1969).

John, you said you had spent a year, or more than a year, studying Oriental thought and philosophy. This is not just reading one book about it. You went quite deeply into it. Now, possibly because of where it comes in most people's lifetime, the university conventionally is a place where people tend to want to go fairly deeply into something or another. They should be able to select what they go deeply into, and it might be a mixture of Oriental philosophy and bacterial genetics, or some other eccentric combination of disparate subjects; but it seems to me, there is an advantage in going deeply into something.

I think that society, in one way or another, should recognize the value of doing this, but to have a large number of people going deeply into the same thing, not of their own will, but because it was considered good for them, is not going to accomplish that goal. When you said that a poet and artists and so forth should be in university communities, I think the advantage from that would be that by their activities the students would see that these people were *devoted* to what they were doing. I think that we study, we teach, throughout our lives, whether we hold classes or not; and we do it by this effective means of example.—C. H. Waddington (1972).

I don't teach. I give lectures, or I . . . I asked David Tudor years ago how I should behave in these university situations. And he said, "Think of yourself as a hit-and-run driver." Well, David Tudor is an altogether marvelous person, but he also has a very shocking mind, and that was a shocking statement. But it's also very perceptive. I can, I think, teach well, but I don't teach because it requires too much time from my point of view. For instance, I do not think that a teacher should teach something to the student. I think the teacher should discover what it is that the student knows—and that's not easy to find out—and then, of course, encourage the student to be courageous with respect to his knowledge, courageous and practical and so forth—in other words, to bring his knowledge to fruition. Don't you think?—Ev Grimes (1984).

Would you say anything to young people about discipline and training?

No, I don't think we could say anything that will actually help because if someone says something and then someone else does what they are told to do, it doesn't work out right. It has to be original. It has to come from all the calls that come to that individual, whether from inside or from outside. Don't you think?

In painting, for instance, there are people whose work is representational to begin with and it becomes abstract later in their lives, and vice versa. I think what we have done with our lives is not something to be imitated. Each person's life is original. It could go from A to B, or it could go backwards from B to A, or it might go to a completely other letter, or to a series of different letters or in circles. I think the important thing is—I don't know if you would agree, but I think you might, though maybe you won't—that it must begin by a conscious decision to give yourself up, to devote yourself. Whatever direction, whatever path, it comes through the decision to devote yourself, to pay attention to all the things outside of yourself, to give yourself up.—Rose Slivka (1978).

People complained who knew Thoreau; he was a controversial figure and he was adverse to schools, you know—he was a teacher for a little bit, but he left the educational system quickly. His neighbors complained that he did nothing, and even Emerson complains that all he was worth was as captain of the Huckleberry Party, but history has proved otherwise. Three instances: India—through Gandhi, through Thoreau—changed a whole political structure; the Danes—through the essay on "Civil Disobedience"—successfully fooled Hitler's occupation; and Martin Luther King. There you see: all that's needed is re-examination, really, of our value system with regard to what people do. Poets down through the ages, and saints and so forth, have *advised* inactivity. And we haven't listened—at least the universities haven't listened. Yet they're willing to teach the poetry. It's a very strange situation.—Don Finegan et al. (1969).

We want to see the world as a university from which we never graduate. This trend is already showing. In the mid-West, and I am sure in many other places, they have what they call a mid-Western complex of universities, and a student can take advantage of the services of any of those places and still be effectively in his own university or his Alma Mater. In other words, I think the notion of Alma Mater ought to give way to just "world."—C. H. Waddington (1972).

SOCIAL PHILOSOPHY

Every being is the Buddha just as, for the anarchist, every being is a ruler. Now, my music liberates because I give people the chance to change their minds in the way I've changed mine. I don't want to police them.—Michael John White (1982).

We need first of all a music in which not only are sounds just sounds but in which people are just people, not subject, that is, to laws established by any one of them, even if he is "the composer" or "the conductor."

The situation relates to individuals differently, because attention isn't focused in one direction. Freedom of movement is basic to both this art and this society. With all those parts and no conductor, you can see that even this populous a society can function without a conductor.—Michael Nyman (1973).

When I think of a good future it certainly has music in it but it doesn't have one kind of music. It has all kinds. And it goes beyond anything that I can imagine or describe. I would like any kind of music because people have different needs. And some music, for instance, which would not be useful to me at all might be very useful to someone else. I have little need for jazz, I can get along perfectly well without any jazz at all; and yet I notice that many, many people have a great need for it. Who am I to say that their need is pointless?—Hans G. Helms (1972).

If you want to make music in this society, the only alternative is to make it yourself, or to train a group of people to do what you have in mind to do. That's what's taking place particularly with electronic composers. They have become, so to speak, troubadours. I remember David Tudor saying in his inimitable manner, "I want to have an instrument that only I know how to play." And now he's got it through his electronic circuitry; and when he plays, it's extremely mysterious and extremely marvelous.—Joel Eric Suben (1984).

Have you, or anyone else, ever used your music for political or social ends?

I am interested in social ends, but not in political ends, because politics deals with power, and society deals with numbers of individuals; and I'm interested in both single individuals and large numbers or medium numbers or any kinds or numbers of individuals. In other words, I'm interested in society, not for purposes of power, but for purposes of cooperation and enjoyment.—*Source* (1969).

The American painters, the people that you've worked with, like Rauschenberg and Jasper Johns—have they had a great influence on you as a musician?

In the first place, I don't agree with the notion of influence. In the second place, if we're going to have any influences, they're apt to be more lively if they come from outside the field we're working in.

The final thing that I think influences my action more than anything is social concerns, so I try not to write a piece unless it is useful as an instance of society. I don't mean to say that I think I've solved anything socially in the music, but I've tried to give instances of improvements in society. In this particular piece at the opera [*Etcetera*], I made a paradox. I experience it, but I'm not sure that I believe it. What it is is a situation in which one can either be governed, or one cannot be governed. In the last paragraph of the essay on "Civil Disobedience," Thoreau says that a government is like a tree; and when people ripen, they are like fruit that drop away from the tree. So this piece, *Etcetera* [1973], is that tree with the fruit, some of it on the tree and some of it dropping off.—Robert Cordier (1973).

I agree that technology opens up new possibilities to us but I think that finally what we are dealing with is what we were always dealing with, namely, mind. What technology seems to me to open us to in the way of landscape is precisely that—something which cannot be measured the ways things formerly were measured. So that, to make this very specific, instead of being given a beat in music or a scale as we were given centuries ago, we now have the whole field of sound, and it behooves us, even if we use scales and even if we make melodies and even if we proceed metrically, to think as though we were not doing that, but were in the larger field where there is no beat and where there is no measurement.—Richard Kostelanetz et al. (1977).

I have a feeling that at present the world has lost a sense of unity at almost all scales, from the individual through these intermediate neighborhood groupings right up to the world scale. The question is, do you need to re-create the sense of unity?

I don't find the notion of unity . . .

I should not have said "unity"; I should have said "wholeness."

Well, how was it that you should have said wholeness and you did say unity? I have been thinking about this question of unity and multiplicity, and for myself I prefer multiplicity. It seems to me to conform more with our circumstances than unity does.

Unity was a mistake; come on to wholeness.

But the mistake is very revealing. Wholeness—the only objection I can see to wholeness is that it suggests that there are boundaries to the whole, and then wholeness is like unity. I would rather have "open-ness," not unity or wholeness but open-ness—and open-ness particularly to things with which I am unfamiliar. I think that in society the stranger has always had a great integrating effect.—C. H. Waddington (1972).

Do you feel that the state of the world is essentially complex or simple?

Complex.

Can it be simplified?

I don't think it can be simplified unless someone sets out to control it, and I wouldn't want to live in that kind of world. Would you?—David Stanton (1982).

If one compares, for instance, the music of Bach and Mozart, you can take a small section of Bach and all the voices in the music will be observing the same kind of movement. That is to say, if the movement is chromatic all of the voices will be moving so; or if the unit or the module is rhythmically the sixteenth note, then if you add up all the voices you get a steady movement of the sixteenth note. That brings about a state of "wholeness" or "unity," which is a great contrast to Mozart. In Mozart, taking just a small section of the music, you are very apt to see not one scale, but I would myself see three. You would see one of the large steps made by arpeggiation of the chords; you know—thirds and fourths; then you would see diatonic scales, making use of the combination of whole steps and half steps; and you would also see chromatic passages, all within a small area sequence. They would generally be going together so that you have differences working together, in Mozart's case, to produce what you might call a harmonious wholeness.

But with new changes in music—those that we have had recently—we no longer see the coming together of disparate things as requiring harmony. In fact, if harmony is required or imposed by the composer, it acts in our ears now to obscure the differences of the individual sounds. For instance, in Indian music, to hold improvisation together and to make it meaningful to the society, there were several devices—there was the drone, so that one could measure the different pitches with respect to this constant drone; and you could measure the time with respect to the unstated but understood drum beats. We are now capable, as musicians, of hearing *any* sounds in *any* combination. The first musician to announce this possibility, by the way, was Debussy, already over fifty years ago.

I believe in *dis*organization; but I don't see that in terms of nonparticipation or isolation, but rather precisely as a complete participation. Those rules of order must have been put there in order, as we say, to hold things together. Now, when they are taken away—if we take them away and don't have them—we discover that things get along perfectly well.—C. H. Waddington (1972).

The important thing is to see the world as a single place, as Buckminster Fuller does, and to see our problems as global and to, as quickly as possible, free the world from the quarrels of nations and make it a single place that starts out with intelligence to solve its problems.—Monique Fong & Françoise Marie (1982).

I believe that everything communicates, that I communicate just as well by saying nothing as by saying something.

It's very rare.

It's also very Christian. Jesus, for instance, pointing to the lilies of the field, said, "Look, they don't do anything." It doesn't work. No one can say that nature, or those flowers, are inexpressive. They're very expressive, and they're not saying a word.

No, I think our teaching, and our ideas, particularly about music, have become controlled mostly by German ideas and you still see it. The other day, I picked up the lectures Stravinsky gave at Harvard University—they're called *Poetics [of Music]*—and I looked at the end, because it is generally at the end of a book that they say finally what it was all about. He said that the thing that interested him was unity in the situation of variety, and he wanted to find the single thing that brought together all the differences. And he recognized this as an ideal which he believed. We all believed it until we began to examine it. When we examine it, we see it is a purely German idea, it's a fascist idea really, which wants to find not the blackness in the black and the whiteness in the white, but wants to find the whiteness in the blacks too, and wants everything to be white.—Regina Vater (1976).

What are you thinking about now?

A year and a half ago I was invited to the University of Hawaii, which has an East-West Center. They have a festival of music there which brings two people from the Orient representing music and art and two people from the Occident. I was there for a month, and while I was there a man from our State Department gave a talk at the university. I didn't hear the talk, but I read about it in the newspaper the next day. The headlines were: WE ARE LIVING IN A GLOBAL VILLAGE, WHETHER WE LIKE IT OR NOT. And then to prove it he said there were fifty-five global services then in operation that could not observe political boundaries because of the techniques involved. Unfortunately, I was slow-witted. I just let that come in. I didn't let it go out the other ear, though, it just stayed in my head; but I didn't do anything. Then this September on the way to Ann Arbor I was in Kennedy Airport having a cup of coffee, and there was a group of Japanese people and one American standing near me. Since I'd been in Japan twice, I feel friendly to all Japanese. So I began chatting with them, and after I told them what I did, I asked them what they did. They were all telephone men and the

American was from Los Angeles and the Bell Telephone Company. So I thought I'd mention these global services, and I did, and the American calmly said, "It's now sixty-one." Again, I was slow-witted and I didn't say, "Where do I get the list?" But in the meantime I had thought about the island of Oahu where I had been living that month. It's divided by a mountain range and it's crenelated at the top and that crenelation was for the purpose, formerly, of protecting oneself while sending poisoned arrows down the other side. Now that mountain range is tunneled and the utilities are in use for both sides, that is to say, electricity, telephones, etc. I deduce from this whole business that we are in a period of history when all the things we are presently complaining about are part of the dying structure of politics and economics, and that coming into being, without our being informed, is an utterly different global village social situation. And this is what is interesting me now. And this is what art, it seems to me, has been involved in too. And in this connection the two minds who are articulate and write books and so forth that seem to be pertinent are: Buckminster Fuller and Marshall McLuhan.

I said in my talk that what we want now is quantity; we get quality automatically. It seems to me to have been the effect of modern art in this century to change our way of seeing such that wherever we look we may look esthetically. This is what is happening in the field of music, now, and when it finally gets around to all of our ears, we will discover that our ears are open to the ambient sound, no matter where we are, and that we will be able to enjoy it esthetically. This applies also to theater. In other words, wherever you are you will be able to look, listen, etc. to the experience around you esthetically. Now, since this is true and since these changes that I just now spoke of socially and technologically and so forth are taking place, what we would like is to live longer. And furthermore we may very well. Maybe not I, because I'm already disintegrating, but those who aren't so much so. You already know (don't you) or sense that life is going to be extended far beyond what we now think reasonable.

You used the word "play" several times, speaking against it.

Yes, I don't like it. I mean I don't like the idea that that is what art is. The reason I don't is because my. . . . I read part of that book called *Homo Ludens* [by Johan Huizinga], do you know it? It discusses man as the playing one and the whole business of setting up rules whereby a game may be played, furthermore setting up a place in which to play in all kinds of ways producing separation from the rest of the world. All of that annoys me. And then invention, you see, which I'm so involved in, is bad because it changes the rules. And that's what I mean when I refer to spoilsport because an inventor simply ruins the game. But I don't think we're playing games. I like to play games, but I don't think of art as being that. I think that we should treat politics and economics, as they are now dying, as games, and I think we should treat this new thing coming into being as inviting celebration. Now I don't think that it is *we* who are celebrating. I think that it is *it* that's celebrating. I prefer that notion to the notion of games.—Yale School of Architecture (1965).

How do you feel about having power?

I think we should go over our language and remove all words having to do with power. There are a number of composers who are interested in music becoming more political. They say that our social situation boils down to who has power and who doesn't. If that were so, I'd want to be one of those who were powerless. I was that way as a child, never attracted to the bullies. I was always rather pleased with that Christian statement that if you are hit on one cheek the proper action is to turn the other.

I don't like the words "greatest" or "strength." People are simply different from one another. The last time I had my ⟨astrological⟩ chart done I went because I was getting self-conscious in an irritating way due to the fact that I'm well known. People are constantly asking me questions or I'm constantly having to say something. I was feeling this so much that I was reluctant to take engagements at universities, or to talk or do anything. The woman who did my chart ⟨Julie Winter⟩ said I had better adapt myself to the circumstances because I was going to be even better known than I am now. So I've had to adjust my mind to the business of enjoying it. But when you steer yourself in that direction you can be bumped into, because you're steering in the fog. That's what the Zen monk meant when he said, "Now that I'm enlightened I'm just as miserable as ever." Now that I've decided to enjoy being well known I can hate it just as much as ever.—Jeff Goldberg (1976).

Sometimes people ask me what is the goal of technology. I say we really need a technology that will be so excellent that when we have it we won't even know it's there. And I see this recurring in all fields now; the proper goal, I don't like the word "goal," but let's use it, the proper goal of each activity is its obviation. Wouldn't this be a lovely goal, now, for politics, for economics?—David Sylvester & Roger Smalley (1967).

I'm very sad, and this is a source of confusion for me, I'm very sad to see throughout our society now a struggle for power. Instead of this struggle for separatist ⟨devisive⟩ power, we should recognize as Mao did in China that there was a serious problem that required an intelligent solution. Well, he said that it involved power but the expression of power that I think was the most effective in China on Mao's part was the long retreat which is remarkably like something that Martin Luther King might have proposed or Gandhi.

Do you think that a nonviolent revolution in the U.S. could be successful?

I think so. When I say I think so you have to realize it's wishful thinking.

There is very often in my recent work a sense of theater, that is to say, an inclusion of what will be seen, not only of what will be heard, and often the performances include things that seem pointless or humorous to audiences because, as with the sounds, the theater is chance-determined and often in ways that are not determined by me but are a result of the performers' actions, so that people who expect to hear something in my music are often put off by that inclusion of the theatrical, just as people who go to one of my lectures expecting to hear something about music, hearing something about Mao or mushrooms, think that they somehow made a mistake in coming to the lecture. But all of this arises from my conviction which I've had now for twenty-five years, I suppose, since my serious involvement with Oriental thought, when I asked myself why do we write music, I came to the conclusion initially that it was in order to produce a revolution in the mind, and that now I would say it would be or hopefully would be, and yet I've just been skeptical about that, it could further revolution in the society.—Hans G. Helms (1972).

It would be good if we could make our changes nonviolently. That's how changes in art take place. The reason why we know we could have nonviolent social change is because we know we have nonviolent art change. We mustn't believe that you can only change by killing because you can also change by creating.—Regina Vater (1976).

We are, if I may say so, a corrupt society. I'm very impressed by an article I read recently in *The New York Review of Books* by Mary McCarthy. She has been a critic of Vietnam and is still a critic of Vietnam because Vietnam continues even though President Nixon tells us that it has stopped. McCarthy sees Watergate as a continuation of Vietnam; she sees it as a silly and pathetic attempt on our part to atone for our true crime, which is Vietnam. But Vietnam is not, I would say, our only crime. We have also ruined our environment. We've done everything in order to be selfish. We should listen now to Mao Tse-tung who points out that the earth in which capitalism grows is just pure selfishness. What was Nixon's excuse for continuing in Vietnam and now in Cambodia? It was to come out of that whole thing as he says with some kind of face or self-respect. It all turns back on the self, and here I would like, if you permit me, to criticize the entire tradition of Christianity. I think the Golden Rule, which is often thought of as the center, really, of Christianity, is a mistake: "Do unto others as *you* would be done by." I think that it is a mistaken thought. We should do unto others as *they* would be done by.—Alan Gillmor (1976).

Mao Tse-tung has the notion of gradually raising up the popular acceptations, so that you would go from the primary level to the other one up to the tertiary, if you followed the Mao Tse-tung idea. My notion is that we should act as though everyone has graduated from school, and live in a world, and jump into it, and so make it. In other words, the Buddha, when he was asked how enlightenment came, whether it came gradually or suddenly: Mao Tse-tung says gradually; the Buddha said gradually and then in the very next paragraph ❧in the Lankavatara Sutra☙ he says suddenly, and gave instances from nature. And it's true that things happen gradually, as the germination of seeds in nature, but it's also true that things happen suddenly through earthquakes or through lightning and such things. And I'm for the latter.—Geoffrey Barnard (1980).

Have you read the writings of Mao? Well, in one of them he says, "We must be absolutely convinced of the goodness of human nature." And there is a tendency in the West to be convinced of the badness of human nature.

Are you convinced of the goodness or of the badness of human nature?

It is essential that we be convinced of the goodness of human nature, and we must act as though people are good. We have no reason to think that they are bad.

What do you mean saying that we do not have reason to think that they are bad? What about Hitler, the Second World War . . . ?

Well, of course, the whole involvement with power, with profit, and so forth have made it so that we have taught people to be bad. But by nature they are good. Do you see? So we must simply change our educational system. In the United States, everything is done to make people as bad as possible. And the way you do that is the following: If you have forty children, you give them all the same book to read. You could have them read forty different books, and that would be beautiful; but instead you give them one book to read, and they must all read the same one. Then they must pass an examination to see which one did the best. That immediately reduces human nature, because the one who does badly begins to think of copying what the one who did well did—in other words, stealing. Then the one who begins to think of winning the second time, and so we produce a society that is not bad by nature but that has been taught to be bad. I think that it is astonishing, with all that education, how good people are.

I noticed in New York, where the traffic is so bad and the air is so bad, everything, and the food, and the coffee, everything, and the streets are falling to pieces, you get into a taxi and very frequently the poor taxi driver is just beside himself with irritation. And one day I got into one and the driver began talking a blue streak, accusing absolutely everyone of being wrong. You know he was full of irritation about everything, and I simply remained quiet. I did not answer his questions, I did not enter into a conversation, and very shortly the driver began changing his ideas and simply through my being silent he began, before I got out of the car, saying rather nice things about the world around him.

So that is the type of education you would use instead?

It was the one proposed by Thoreau, it was the one proposed by Gandhi, it was the one proposed by Martin Luther King. It was the one practiced by the Danes in opposition to Hitler. It was what is called passive resistance.—Nikša Gligo (1972).

I'm afraid that my optimism is "personal." On the other hand—that is to say, on the hand of society—these wars, in the Middle East, Falkland Islands, Iran-Iraq, are like an unnecessary disease, in which society is an individual that is attacking itself. Say the destruction is very great—with atomic weapons and so forth—I think there would still be life; that life may or may not be the life of human beings, but there would still be life. I'm also convinced that life takes place on other planets.—Paul Hersh (1982).

How do you feel about the safety of the world for future generations, given the extraordinary stockpiling of nuclear weapons, and the rapid and seemingly uncontrollable arms buildup throughout the world, and the rampant international spread of nuclear technology?

Perhaps a holocaust is necessary to bring us to our senses, hopefully not too complete a one.

How do you feel your attitudes on these issues are expressed in your work as an artist? Whether or not they are, what do you think is the desirable relation between such admittedly social and political considerations and art?

Art as I see it has to do with changing the mind, turning it away from the confines of ego (art in my opinion is not self-expression) and getting it to flow outward through sense perceptions full circle (the relative, the absolute) and inward through the dreams (Suzuki: the structure of the mind and the philosophy of Zen Buddhism). I agree with the late Marshall McLuhan that through electronics we have extended the central nervous system. The world being a mind can change its mind. The present internationalism is schizophrenia. If art were more socially effective than it is it could be the pleasing alternative to holocaust. It could persuade people (all of them) to change their minds.—Jonathan Brent (1981).

My notion of how to proceed in a society to bring change is not to protest the thing that is evil, but rather to let it die its own death. And I think we can state that the power structure is dying because it cannot make any inspiring statements about what it is doing. I think that protests about these things, contrary to what has been said, will give it the kind of life that a fire is given when you fan it, and that it would be best to ignore it, put your attention elsewhere, take actions of another kind of positive nature, rather than to continue to give life to the negative by negating it.

The summer before last, I organized a group in New York of all sorts of people who were at one time engaged in protest. I asked them to discuss, once a week through the summer, what one could do to change society other than to protest it. There were some twelve to twenty people at each meeting, so there were many minds, many sets of experiences—and the only solutions we could all agree upon were the projects and works of Buckminster Fuller.

This is something which is coexistent with the evil. The technology is developing in spite of, or at least coexistent with, the power and profit structures.—C. H. Waddington (1972).

Does it mean that you are apolitical?

Well, I think of myself as an anarchist. And Mao himself, when he was younger, was very much involved with anarchist thought. But through the exigencies of the political situation, he made a solution to the Chinese problem that found him involved in a political change.

But your acting might seem anarchy to me, although you are absolutely convinced that it is a perfectly set order. Let us take an example: when you and David Tudor perform both your musics together, as you sometimes do, your actions might seem anarchic to the listener, although there must be a sort of nonanarchic corresponding attitude toward David Tudor as your co-performer, in spite of the fact that your two pieces are conceived as completely independent.

It is a very simple example of anarchy because two of us were working together, but independently. I was not telling David Tudor what to do, nor was he telling me what to do, and anything that either of us did worked with everything the other did.

Does it mean that your anarchy supposes the communication without preagreement or without the fixed codes of perception?

Right! When we have the facility to do and to work without constraint, or when we have the things that we need to use, I think we have all that we need. We do not need to have the laws that tell us not to do this but to do something else. Thoreau said that the only reason to have the laws and governments is in order to keep two Irishmen from fighting in the street. I would rather have a few murders here and there than our war in Vietnam. And they could be murders of passion, rather than the cold useless murders we now have. We have what you might call "mass media murders."

I think that there must be found a kind of common denominator between those who, like Mao, rely on power and those, like Fuller, who have faith in the goodness of material, of material having. You see, Fuller like Mao believes in the goodness of human nature, and he thinks that what makes people bad is the fact that they do not have what they need. If they had what they needed, they would be less selfish than they are when they do not have what they need.

I have noticed too with our mushroom society in New York that when the weather is dry and there are few mushrooms, the people are very secretive and selfish and they do not let anyone know that they have found something, they hunt very quickly. But when the weather is very wet and there are lots of mushrooms, they become extremely unselfish and generous and even give mushrooms away.

I noticed too with myself that as I have what I need, I look at our large stores in New York and I do not see anything that I want.—Nikša Gligo (1972).

I want the police *not* to control traffic of private cars, but to maintain a fleet of communal cars that we can use when we wish, and leave when we are through.

I agree with McLuhan's idea that electronics has extended the central nervous system, and that this network is now becoming a world mind; and that the new psychoanalysis is to deal with the malfunctions of this *world mind*. . . .

I am wondering about the necessity of expressing a thought, since this thought is usually already in the world mind. When I express what is a new idea to me, I often find later that someone else has already said it.

We need to move from a fixed view to a larger view, which pictures man belonging to a family, city, nation, and world; then in a religious view, belonging to everything.—C. H. Waddington (1972).

My concern toward the irrational, and my belief that it is important to us in our lives, is akin to the use of the koan in Zen Buddhism. That is to say, we are so accustomed and so safe in the use of our observation of relationships and our rational faculties that in Buddhism it was long known that we needed to leap out of that, and the discipline by which they made that leap take place was by asking a question that could not be answered rationally. Now they discovered that when the mind was able to change so that it was able to live not just in the rational world but wholly, and in a world including irrationality, that then one is, as they said, enlightened. Now in connection with the thought of Marshall McLuhan we know that we live in a period of the extension of the mind outside of us, in the sense that the wheel was an extension of the power that we have in our legs to move, so we now with our electronics have extended our central nervous system not only around the globe but out into space. This then gives us the responsibility to see enlightenment, not in terms of individual attainment, but in terms of social attainment, so that at that point we must say that the world as we now see it is intolerable. Do you follow? Now on the individual level, now as ever and forever more, it will be possible to see each day as excellent, *Nichi nichi kore ko nichi,* but in social terms, in terms of the extension of our minds outside of us, which is our present situation, we must see the necessity for the training and discipline of all creation such that life in this intolerable situation will work. Now I needn't, need I, point out intolerable things going on nowadays. They're too evident. We know them without even mentioning them. Our heads are full of them. You must make the world so that those things don't take place. This divisiveness of intention and purpose and competition in the world between the nations. The wars, the dog eat dog, the piggishness, is utterly intolerable. And we must see—I don't know how to say it in Japanese, I must learn—that it would be "each day is a miserable day" as long as, for instance, one person is hungry, one person is unjustifiably killed, etc., etc.

But how does art help?

I may be wrong, but I think art's work is done. I could be right in terms of my own work, with respect to it. I must be wrong certainly with regard to other people's work, with respect to it, but as far as I'm concerned twentieth-century art has done a very, very good job. What job? To open people's eyes, to open people's ears. What better thing could have been done? We must turn our attention now I think to other things, and those things are social.

So you must logically give up composing.

No, no, let's not be logical. We're living in this rational-irrational situation. I can perfectly well do something illogical. I can do something unnecessary. I can fulfill invitations. I can invite myself to do something frivolous. I can be grand at one moment and idiotic the next. There's no reason why I shouldn't. I might even from time to time need a little entertainment!—David Sylvester & Roger Smalley (1967).

I think that there are two most important things to steer us in what is obviously a changing and complex situation. One, which I've already mentioned, is to choose flexibility when one can, as opposed to "fixity"; that's extremely relevant with regard to anything you can think of—it's like a basic principle. Another basic principle, I think, is to choose abundance, rather than scarcity. Be wasteful, rather than pinchpenny. Get as much as you can out of all that there is to be had. Have it even if you don't use it, or even if you use it badly as a gadget.

On working with what one has:

That's all right; one can, but one must also be aware of why one doesn't have the other—and that the reason is simply an economic one. We have a very funny society now; we have—I don't know what the exact figures are, but we're all aware that the nature of the situation is this: in this century more new ideas have come into existence, more awarenesses, and technological developments than in all of history put together, and we expect in the next ten years to have more ideas than we've already had in this century. In other words, we're in the situation Fuller grasped, and we're at the critical point—and as we start going up, *it* will go up very quickly and easily. That the society should have functioned as long as it has, divisively, one part of it against another part and doing its finest efforts in time of war rather than in time of life, is a curious thing—in that this element of competition should have been idealized as necessary for what one calls "motivation," "impetus," and so on, and has been imbedded in our educational system and in much of everything else. So we know that we *have* these machines, we know that we have these ideas, but we also know that we don't have access to them for economic reasons—and those economic reasons are part of that competitive business. And yet all it was to begin with was the human race on earth, and somehow it must be brought to that again, making use of the things it has been able to think of, rather than dividing the usefulness of those things within society so that you have a division of haves and have-nots. What we need is to have a whole world of haves. Now one way to move or to checkmate—or to fool's-mate—the economic structures that now exist is to break down the boundaries between *your* university and other universities increasingly—to throw a stone, so to speak, into the economic structure as into a lake and to let its effects spread out—so that your usefulness is put together with the usefulness of other like institutions. So that if one of you had such-and-such a machine, another of us might make the effect of throwing this stone so great that there wouldn't be anything that you didn't have access to.

I would include the sciences, too, and I think there are scientists here, scientists at the University of Illinois, for instance, inviting teachers from other departments to teach subjects that they don't know. The plan is to bring about a fructifying in a situation that has been stultified. And it can break across boundaries—but we've said this already. Every boundary you see, I think, you should try to see if it can be removed. Is it something that is really necessary in the sense that the telephone is or that the water faucet is, or is it something that simply satisfies a bureaucracy? I mean, was it a necessary boundary or wasn't it? And if it wasn't necessary, then I think you can expect that the good it did in the past when it was separating things can be kept when it isn't separating things. I had a curious experience yesterday. I had an appointment and I wasn't clear as to where the Coordinated Science building was, so I dropped first into the one that has that name on it, which is an old building. And looking for the room number I practically went through the whole building—because no one in the building knew where the room numbers were, and they were poorly organized. but in the course of that I saw all kinds of things that I wouldn't see in a music school, or at home, or in a supermarket—all kinds of machinery, and things that were strange—almost like going to a foreign country; and then I finally got into the new building that the room is actually in, and it, too, has many different kinds of things in it that aren't ever connected with music—or painting or sculpture—which could be refreshing.—Don Finegan et al. (1969).

We won't have just one way of living that everyone has to follow. We should have a variety of ways and then we should have a possibility of other ways than we thought of so that everyone lives as he needs to live, rather than as other people think he should live. He should live as he needs to.

And are you enough of an optimist to think it's possible?

Yes, because I think the larger number of evils that would come from that freedom are currently the result of the division of the world into those who have and those who don't have and the resulting. . . . If everyone had what he needed to live, many of the evils that currently take place would not, because the people wouldn't be struggling to get something illegally that they needed, they could have it. The first problem, in other words, of the global village is to give absolutely everyone what he needs to live, regardless. So that, at the present time, would mean water and electricity and food and shelter and so on. They need food—and there is, of course, a variety of foods. Some people need one kind of food, and other people need another kind of food.

One of our business advisers in Brazil, in recent years, advised the people there to stop growing black beans and to substitute soybeans because they would make more money with soybeans; but Brazilians are devoted to black beans and rice—that's the basic food and diet. They took the advice of the American people, got rid of the black beans, and put in soybeans. For a while, they made a lot of money, but then the prices slumped. Now, they have to import black beans from other countries at enormously high prices. It's a mistake. I don't want any meat, but there are, I suppose, people who want meat.

But at what level does it stop? Do junkies get their heroin? In their minds they think they need it.

I can see that it is a very serious question. I wouldn't question the fact that heroin is the wrong thing to have. I know that [for some] people maybe heroin takes the place of food for them. I know that cocaine did in Peru; it took the place of food and clothing. They could starve without feeling hunger, and they did not feel the cold by taking cocaine. Perhaps the cocaine should be available, and the heroin, without any restrictions; but it should be made clear how dependent one becomes on it. If you wanted to live that way, what it would be like. It shouldn't be made financially difficult to have, because they kill and do all sorts of things for that.—Monique Fong & Françoise Marie (1982).

There are so many things now, and one's more and more aware of things to do. This, of course, is a problem, I think, that should be solved by each individual, don't you? What is it he is willing to devote his time to? It's as simple as that. Then Margaret Mead suggests that since we live longer now we might change, and there's no reason—against this is flexibility as opposed to fixity—no reason to think that it's virtuous to remain one thing throughout one's life; that the dedication could take some other form, as moving from music to botany—or maybe finding a connection between the two. That we used to live long enough to devote ourselves to one thing, but now we live longer so we could be devoted to many, or—giving up this notion of "mainstream" in history, and seeing that we're going in many directions—we ourselves could explore. And I think then a reasonable thing to do—if one also gave up competition—would be to do those things that no one else was doing, and being informed, of course, at the same time about what *was* being done; improving our communications so that we would know what was going on, and then do something that was not being done. I asked Fuller, for instance, once when I became extremely interested in his notion of a house that was unattached to the earth for its utilities—I said, "Are you working on that?" He said, "I don't need to," and I said, "Well, what do you mean by that?" And he said: "Well, they're doing it in the space program." In the space program. From his point of view, one of the major values of the exploration in space is that it is necessary to produce a contained house for long trips whereby one can live comfortably without attachment to the earth. That would mean that we can live in wilderness, or on tops of mountains, or in the Arctic regions, or on the oceans—so that the whole perspective with regard to the problems of overpopulation disappears. Because even in Japan the mountains are relatively uninhabited. Then, in a paper I had from Fuller just recently, he indicated—as I indicate in the field of music—that the *goal*—going toward the rainbow, so to speak—is not to have any. That is to say, an architecture which doesn't appear to be an architecture will be a marvelous place to live; and a music which isn't music, and yet satisfies one's musical inclinations, is what I have now: namely, the ambient sounds. I find the sounds around me more to my enjoyment than any music I know of; and I have that all the time, and it's constantly changing. And that can be had—it's harder for us to envision it in the case of shelter, but apparently Bucky Fuller envisions it; I've seen it—in his terms. That is to say, two transparent geodesic domes, one within the other, with plants placed between the two; so that you would be living, so to speak, in a garden and have both—as though you were "sheltered" and as though you were not.—Nikša Gligo (1972).

What do you perceive to be the major political/social/economic issues of today, nationally and internationally?

I refer you to R. Buckminster Fuller's recent book, *Critical Path.* We look forward to the cessation of nationalism and internationalism, the use of intelligence rather than power for bringing about an equation between human needs and world resources such that the present division of mankind into "haves" and "have-nots" will no longer obtain. The law instead of protecting the rich from the poor should change so that poverty is agreeable, as it was for Thoreau.—Jonathan Brent (1981).

But what then about the usage of mass media? If you plead for the multiplicity of message, which comes out from your music, isn't it in contradiction with the one-dimensional orientation of mass media message? Did you happen perhaps to use some of the mass media in the way of your compositional technique, so that they go on with the idea of the multiplicity of centers?

No. You know that I come from the United States and the mass media in the United States are largely concerned with the commercials. We have very little access to it, except sometimes to our educational TV; and there I made recently a thirty-minute TV program that was interesting, but that was seen by very little mass. In general, there is very little opportunity to do something with the mass media, except in terms of advertising.

But if you have free hands to do what you want, and if the mass media are not so conditioned, what would you do then?

I do not know much how to answer "if" questions. If I were doing it, then I think I might have an idea; but until I am in a position to do it, I really do not know what I would do. But you see, I think that the mass media are different than they might be in a good future. In the same way that the publication of music is different now than it would be in a good society. By a good society I mean a situation in which there would be no traffic jams. In the field of music now we have, I think, not more publishers than we had, let us say, in the nineteenth century. But we have an enormously larger population. And we have far more people writing music now than in the nineteenth century, so that for many who write music now there is no opportunity for music either to be heard, or to be published, or to be used in any way. If we use our technology in a way that any person could reach any other person in terms of performance and in terms of publication, let us say, communication, I think it would be better than the way we now use our technology. I think particularly of a telephonic arrangement which includes the ability to transmit printed and graphic material. This technological capability already exists in the United States, but it is used only by the industry, government, and our army. We could expect that it could eventually be available to civilians, so that simply by dialing one would be able to have a book or a piece of music immediately in hand and substitute it at any moment for something else. One would then use the telephone numbers as library numbers. In other words, I look forward in mass media to a greater multiplicity and variety of communication means.

The only advantage in America is that the audience, since it is largely students, is an audience of people who are not yet involved in making their own living, so that they are not integrated into the capitalistic society yet.

During the last few years we witnessed the sudden reacceptance of your music in a new, fresh way, with new positive impulses.

But I do not think that it is my music. I think it is the aggregate of the ideas.

I think your music, your way of living, everything included in it.

I think that . . . Well, I do not know what I think. I wish all the people well, and I hope as I have already said for practical anarchy.

[*Is it coming?*]

I think there is a strong and growing revolutionary spirit in the United States. I think too, as population increases, we can expect a majority of people to become younger, that is to say, the average age will go down rather than up, and then when it gets truly into the student level, since those students are not yet members of the self-interest society, that they could change things. You see, when the Russian Revolution took place, it took place on the basis of the worker and the Chinese revolution took place on the basis of the peasant. The question is where will the American revolution take place. It ought to take place with the largest number of people; hopefully it will be the students.

So you agree with the student movement of '68?

Yes, but so far the students have not taken technology sufficiently seriously. I think that is the only difficulty. I was asked by the Revolutionary Student Congress at Cornell University to take part in what amounted to a festival of lectures, and I found that if I wanted to telephone the Central

Office of the Committee, I could not reach anyone because they did not have a sufficient number of telephones. And the whole organization was poor.—Nikša Gligo (1972).

I noticed an interesting correspondence between the Bauhaus in Germany and Mao. In English there is a book of Moholy-Nagy's called *The New Vision,* and this book was very influential for my thinking. Near the beginning of Moholy's book there is a circle which describes the individual, an individual human being, and shows that the individual is totally capable, that is to say, each person is able to do all the things that any human being can do. But through circumstances and so forth we often become specialists rather than whole people. Well, one of the things that Mao has insisted upon for the Chinese is that if there is an army that everyone is in it, if there is agriculture to do everyone should do it, if the land is to be changed so that it will not be flooded periodically, everyone in the community goes to work to bring about this change, even those who are old, even those who are young, so that the experience of the family has been extended through Mao's influence, so that in a sense the nation itself is a family. And I find this very beautiful.—Hans G. Helms (1972).

Were you active in the sixties in anything?

No. My activity is anti-institutional. I work best as an individual, not as one sheep in a herd of sheep. I've made lots of statements of a social nature. They're all rather anarchistic. I was recently asked to sign a petition against atomic energy. But I wrote back saying I wouldn't sign it. I wasn't interested in critical or negative action. I'm not interested in objecting to things that are wrong. I'm interested in doing something that seems to be useful to do. I don't think critical action is sufficient.

Do you vote?

I wouldn't dream of it. I'm looking forward to the time when no one votes. Because then we wouldn't have to have a president. We don't need a president. We can get along perfectly well without the government. What we need is a little intelligence which we don't have at all.

It requires so much responsibility on the part of the people though.

But the kind of responsibility that is given the government now is of no use to anyone. All the nations do is make trouble for each other.—Robin White (1978).

I think we must distinguish very clearly nowadays between government and utility. I do not think we should think of utilities as forms of government, because they're obviously necessary; otherwise, the great population of the earth is not going to be able to exist. Utilities are made in such a way that they reach all the various peoples, and what we need is a situation in which the world is not divided, as it is so dramatically in South America, between those who have and those who do not have; it must be a world for people who have, all of them have, and that can only come about through the utilities, whereas the governments discriminate between those who *should* have and those who *shouldn't* have. Therefore, we do not need government; what we need is utilities.

The utilities include shelter, food, clothing, air (because now we are ruining the air), water, energy, and you can go on; but that is the basis, and the direction. I will not say that someone should love someone else; we must each be left to discover the beauty of love. But we must not be forced, as the religions ask us, to love one another, because it doesn't do any good if you love someone when you also keep them hungry.—Alcides Lanza (1971).

Technological achievements should not *determine* what we do, but they should be *utilities, channels,* through which we express whatever we want to.

There are public utilities in the body—nerves, blood vessels . . .

Would you say the body is nothing but utilities?

The publishing of music is oppressed by "middlemen" who are *not* open channels but are determining what gets published.

The biological model of society is really not an organism but an ecosystem. There are no "middlemen" in an ecosystem, but each component is interacting directly with other components.

The telephone system is not a "system of systems," but a *utility.* We need to make our utilities functional throughout the world. We should want our organizations to *allow things to happen* (and *more* things than otherwise, without organization), but they should not determine *what* happens.

When I dial, I want to *get what I expect to get;* but in my music, I want *space for surprise.* I want us not to be inhabitants, but tourists, meeting new experiences; drawn to them. My attention was attracted to the "x-quantities"—to the things outside of formal teaching, to the innovative things.—C. H. Waddington (1972).

It's becoming more evident that politics consists of games. And that the partners change, and so on. And that the people we used to like—for instance, when I was young we liked the Chinese very much, and my uncle, who couldn't have been more conservative, thought the Japanese were terrible, and he was rather pleased when the Japanese seemed to more people to be terrible. And the Chinese, good. But now it's changed the other way; fortunately the poor man is dead, so he doesn't have to be confused—as I'm sure he would have been, because he was opposed to Communism to begin with; but then to have to be opposed to the Chinese for that reason. . . . I think much in our society becomes endurable if it's realized that it's a game; and not more serious than that, even though many are evil games with evil consequences. But I think we must change to a society which sees that we are facing problems which require solutions, and that, as we ought to know by now, they include our minds. The problems range all the way from enjoying life—I say that in relation to our minds—to relating the world's resources to the world's people so that everyone has what he needs to live—we can call that making the World Mind work.—Don Finegan et al. (1969).

Do you think that artists should do something about it?

I think the real changes that will take place in society will take place primarily through our renunciation of government and our concern with the earth as a problem in relation to the living of human beings. I think that modern art and modern music have served to draw the attention of the individuals to the enjoyment of the world around them. I think that more recently music more than painting, because of the social nature of music (since music requires a group of performers, generally speaking). . . . I think that the ways in which we now perform music already suggest that change from government to utilities. And when you can see that work in art, then you can have more courage that it will work in the world *outside* of art.—Alcides Lanza (1971).

If anyone examines his circumstances he will see that the government enters into them very little. This is again something that Thoreau said in the essay on the duty of "Civil Disobedience," that the only time he had direct contact with the government was when the tax collector came. That was why he chose not to pay his taxes, in order to make it evident to the government that he was not in agreement with it. We, of course, have more contact with the government than he did, and it largely comes through our driving automobiles. We live in continual terror of the policeman, whether we're driving or whether we're parking.

We contact the government more, but we contact it actually very little. If you just made a kind of sketch for yourself, conscientiously, over a period of a week, and you said whether or not you were doing your work or whether or not you were being imposed upon in some way by the government, your work, of course, wouldn't bring you into contact with the government; but the government would stop you when you were going too fast or when you parked in the wrong place, and you would find that it would happen very little.

We need certain things to be facilitated, and our government is now acting to make even the utilities almost impossible. They've made the water so we can't drink it, throughout the country, and now they're making the transportation, at least in New York City, exorbitantly expensive. The other day I got on an empty bus, and paid fifty cents; and to the poor people who get on the bus, fifty cents is a lot of money.—Ellsworth Snyder (1975).

How would you describe your politics?

I'm an anarchist.

Like Thoreau?

I don't know what the adjective is—pure and simple [anarchist], or philosophical, or what; but I don't like government! And I don't like institutions! And I don't have any confidence in even good institutions. I won't even support something like the Wilderness Society, and I love mushrooms, the forests, and all that. But I *hate* what those institutions are doing to them. Do you know what they do? They buy up a big piece of what you might call wilderness, or wasteland, land that no industry or metropolis has thought suitable for a city or a factory. Then they make rules that you can't pick anything. You have to approach the whole thing as a museum: in the name of saving the wilderness, but with no good reason or purpose.

Do you pay taxes or do you follow Thoreau's example?

I keep on paying my taxes, which Thoreau wouldn't have done, but I do it in order to be free of the things the government could do to me in revenge. I want to be able to continue my work, so in that situation I do what the government requires, but no more. Thoreau didn't pay taxes, because he could continue his work, in which no one was interested while he was alive, in or out of jail. My situation is the reverse. Many, many people are interested in what I am doing, so I must continue and keep moving.—Stephen Montague (1982).

If one were to say something to the "establishment," what would one say at this juncture?

Well, I would say that intelligence is lacking in our leadership, whether it be the leadership of the government itself or the leadership of our various institutions, that we should put on our thinking caps. Second, I think we lack conscience. So much of my thinking is dependent on one hand on Fuller, where intelligence is so pertinent, and on the other hand on Thoreau, where conscience is so important. When we see that a situation is evil, we should do our best not to give it our devotion.

No one seems to know, for instance, now in New York, how to solve the economic problem of the city. President Ford complains about the way we run the city of New York, that we spend too much money, and the situation is what they call nicely "in default," whereas actually it's bankruptcy. The funny thing about President Ford's remark is that the United States is bankrupt, and other nations, too, are bankrupt. They have a habit of being bankrupt. They solve this by having confidence in one another.

And what we are pretending now is that we could get along without having confidence in one another municipally. What we need to do, of course, is what Bucky has said for a long time, and that is to stop living separated from the next ones, so that instead of living in New York City as distinguished from Philadelphia or other cities, to live in this megalopolis that actually goes over the whole earth, and the wildernesses where there aren't great populations are like Central Park. The world is one place, and we must come to see it as such.—Ellsworth Snyder (1975).

Money is not money anymore. It's credit. Credit is confidence. A bank will extend credit to you if it has confidence in you. All it needs to do is extend confidence to everyone.

Yes, but we'll still have to pay the bills.

More and more the paying of bills is nothing but numbers. All the government will eventually have to do is decide to give basic economic security to everyone. It's already set up the computer way of handling it. We use credit now much more than we use money. All we have to do is extend it and not require people to pay bills at the end of the month. I think this is inevitable; otherwise we will continue the present division between haves and have-nots and the consequent wars, imprisonment, and everything else that is no longer tolerable.

We already know we can get all the work done if each of us does one hour's work a year. But in order to keep our universities and our economic structure going, we have to fool ourselves and act as though we didn't have the means to get rid of work, and we keep up that old equation of work equals money equals virtue. What we need is a situation where we don't do any work except work we need to do. Now, you see, we're doing work that we don't want to do simply in order to get money in order to have our uncles and aunts think we're good children. I think one of the things will be, as McLuhan says, that we will realize that work is obsolete and we will make a society in which we mean what we do and are totally involved in what we do rather than only involved in order to make a living.—Geneviere Marcus (1970).

The situation is frightful, absolutely frightful. On top of which you then wonder: What can I do? Shall I remain in America, shall I leave the country? But when you leave or have even the thought of leaving, you realize that you are being faithless to the best in America: Buckminster Fuller, for instance, who insists that we live in the world. There is no way to throw yourself out of America. In fact, wherever there is Coca-Cola, and there's Coca-Cola perhaps everywhere except in the Peoples' Republic of China, you have America.

Now, people will tell you that there are good things being done in

America, and they will point to the educational system or to the hospitals or to the insane asylums or to the National Wildlife Preserves. Well, now just take one of them which would seem to be the most innocent, the National Wildlife Refuges. What has happened is there is a confession that nature has been ignored by our search for money and industry and progress and so forth. So that in order to have any of it left we must put a fence around it. Then, if you notice when you go to those places, with very few exceptions you are not allowed to treat nature as man traditionally treated it. You can have no relation to it except that of audience. In my last text I refer to the National Wildlife Refuges in the United States as the museumization of nature.—Hans G. Helms (1972).

We are living in an étude period of history, in which, if we don't learn how to do what we have to do, we may very well destroy ourselves. What we have to do appears to many to be the impossible, but what we have to do is to approach the Earth as a single place not divided into nations in which all the people living here have what they need. So we need first of all an equation between world resources and the people living on the Earth; and second we need a way of looking at humanity that isn't as schizophrenic as the present nationalistic way of looking. We now have our futures in the hands of politicians who have only their own prestige at heart, so that we have a foolish war like the Falklands war because of the hopelessness of the political situation in both England and America. I mean, no one really likes Mrs. Thatcher, and no one likes that junta arrangement in the Argentine. Both of them welcomed the war in order to increase their public prestige, and that has nothing to do with the resolution of the problem between humanity and natural resources. What we have now is humanity divided into the rich and the poor.

We have to see the earth as Buckminster Fuller does, that the Earth is one Earth, and that the thing we need isn't politics but intelligence, and we need the proper functioning of the utilities, and that for the whole Earth rather than for just chosen parts of it. I think, for instance, that the Jewish notion of a chosen people is an entirely wrong idea; that the whole, all of the people who are alive, are chosen.

People often object to my work as not being political, and I'm not interested in power politics. I'm interested in the use of intelligence and the solution of impossible problems. And that's what these *Etudes [Australes]* are all about, and that's what our lives are all about right now. But I'm not interested in the difference between communism and capitalism or between Democrats and Republicans. I think they are all impossible. And I think the thing that's wrong about capitalist countries is that there's a marriage between industry and government, and that the government, like the Reagan government right now, is on the side of industry more than it is on the side of the consumers. Reagan doesn't care whether you can buy the products or not. What he cares about is whether or not they're going to be manufactured. He doesn't like communism because it doesn't leave free enterprise open. Part of my being well known is that I'm often asked what I think about the world situation, and when Reagan recently went into Germany, I was asked by *Die Welt,* a large German newspaper, what I thought of Reagan and his domestic policies and his international policies, and whether I would vote for him, but I wouldn't vote for *anyone* for president. I don't think we need a president. What we need is a solution of our present problems, which are global, not national. The fact that we have different nations makes every nation want to have the atom bomb and destroy all the others, and that will destroy all of us. We don't *need* nations. What we need is a recognition of the fact that we live on one Earth and we live together. And that we have mutual—that we have the same problems, all of us. We don't *need* any poor people. We need everyone to have what he needs to live.—Tom Darter (1982).

We thought it might be interesting to ask you about your concerns or ideas about technology today.

You know that I follow the ideas of Buckminster Fuller. The increasing number of people and the constantly changing relation between human needs and world resources make it possible for more people to live on the earth comfortably. Of course, we can imagine it now. But we haven't yet done it, because we still have a society divided between those who have what they need, and those who don't have what they need. Simply as a project for the future, technology is essential.

You think that technology is perhaps also dangerous?

It's dangerous if it's in the hands of people who don't have the intention to solve the problems unselfishly of humanity in relation to the world.

Where do you think we're headed now?

I think that each day we are headed toward a better situation than any given one we hear in the news. We feel when you get tired that it's a little foolish to be optimistic, but I have the feeling that optimism is the natural state of the human *attitude.* And that it's only fatigue that makes one pessimistic, even if the situation is very difficult.

Do you think that inclination is strong enough to be successful?

We have yet to see. We live in a fantastic time, where we're all aware that a mistake, even something unintended on the part of the person who did it, might bring about the destruction, the wholesale destruction, of the planet.

I think it would be very good if we could pull ourselves up, so to speak, out of the present situation and come into another one that involved intelligence rather than political bickering.

I think it's clear that as long as we have *nations* we have jealousy and fear too, so that the threats to global well-being will remain until we stop that inefficient work between nations. Optimism can stem now from the fact that in the nineteenth century, I think both Italy and Germany are two instances, nations were simply a collection of principalities. So that it could be, still—with a play of intelligence—that the global problems would be addressed. And there are many of us who feel this way.

How would you see this happening? What would be a way of that happening now?

There would have to be some intelligence. *Or* some threat that would draw the whole thing together. Don't you think that instead of being threatened from outside we could become so foolish, interiorly, through giving up our leadership to movie stars, or something worse, that we could then opt for an intelligent solving of real problems rather than the creation of imaginary ones? The imaginary ones being simply contests between *leaderships.* The governments are no longer representative of the people. They're just games being played by the leaders. If you fly around globally, and happen to talk with someone from any country—China, Russia, it doesn't matter what country, but take the ones we think might be enemies—you'll find that they're not enemies, that they're just like *us* and that you feel that almost immediately.

Where or how are we to gain intelligence?

Here's another thing to support optimism, which might answer that question. Industry is already supranational. Coca-Cola sees no boundaries to its commerce. So, we should study the ways of industry, in order to behave, ourselves, globally, as industry behaves. They do it out of greed. We should do it out of the desire to make the *house* we live in, which is the whole place, in good working order. It's now a kind of mess. The games that have been and are still being played have made it very, well, dirty. The environment hasn't been treated properly. It isn't ruined yet, but when you have a *lake* that can be set on fire, something is wrong.

Many people would tend to say, well, man makes nature. It doesn't matter. We can restructure the whole world. So we don't have trees anymore—we'll have nice concrete.

This is one of the reasons I so love Oriental thought: that nature is part of its thinking, rather than something to be tossed aside, in that fashion. I have trouble when there seems to be only the thought of man and society. Whereas, it's so different from those Chinese pictures of the landscape, when you look for a man and finally you see him down in the corner.

What bothers a lot of people is the fear that they might lose something.

They should ask themselves whether they *use* those things that they fear to lose. Very often they don't even use those things. People speak, for instance, of the Bible but don't read it. And Shakespeare and so on. Don't read it, and don't go to see any of it. And yet feel it's something they *own.* It's a mistake. I think there should be more general access to all of culture, that culture should become more and more electronic, that there should be general access, as there is with the telephone book.

And it would remove, again, that thing of ownership, and emphasize—what is more important than ownership, I think—*use.* This was a principle in Thoreau's life. He objected to people owning the land who didn't use it. And he pointed out in his journal that he used other people's property, where they didn't use it. He knew how to get across someone's land, and the owner had to be *led* by him through his own land. It seems so strange that the land should be owned by people who aren't there. There's an unwritten law among mushroom lovers, and in Germany I think it holds: that whoever *sees* a mushroom owns it, no matter what land it's on.

I think a great deal has to change. And I think we have a tendency to think that change is impossible, but we have examples of change in the past. Don't you agree?

Yes. It just seems that change might be resisted to the point, for instance, with the possibility of nuclear war, that we're going to wait until we're pushed *to do something, and that push will be too big and there will be nothing left.*

I understand. Fuller has said that invention is more thoroughgoing in the case of military endeavors, that once the war is fought those accomplishments of inventions are given over to the peaceful—the conduct of peace. What we have to do is change that. So we don't, as you say, kill ourselves before we get to use it.—Sean Bronzell and Ann Suchomski (1983).

What we need is a society based on the final possibility: finally we are able to have unemployment. Most people will tell you that this idea of loving unemployment is foolishness, because they are afraid that all those people who have nothing to do will go out and murder one another. This is simply like the bankruptcy of the city, the bankruptcy of the whole society; we don't have confidence in one another. Think of yourself and imagine whether you would murder other people if you had nothing else to do. You know perfectly well that you wouldn't. Why should we think so badly of other people?

This means that as people are "brought up," it would have to be a concern that they understand that there is something for them to do that is not employment. We've made it look as if you are either employed or you are in mischief, and the kind of work we're talking about we have been allowed to call only "artish."

But we should also not be afraid of *not* working. Now I'm speaking of not writing music, not painting, and I believe Robert Louis Stevenson and many others wrote about the virtues of idleness. Thoreau himself never took a job. His father ran a pencil factory. Thoreau invented the pencil [as we know it]; he was the first one to put a piece of lead down the middle of a piece of wood. Before him, people dug a groove down a piece of wood and dug a groove in another piece of wood, put lead in one of the grooves and then pasted the other one on top. He was the first one to drill a hole in a piece of wood and put lead in it. But he refused to make a fortune on it. People said, "You'll make your fortune on that." He said, "What do you mean?" They said, "Oh, make more." He said, "No, one is enough."—Ellsworth Snyder (1975).

Is this attachment to work necessary, we must ask ourselves? When McLuhan approaches this problem in his books, he speaks of our future activity, and many other people now do too, of being one not of work but leisure. What's the difference between work and leisure? He seems to think that the difference is whether or not we are completely involved. If it is work, we will be doing it not because we want to, but because we are obliged to, in order to make money. If it is leisure, we will do wholly what we do, we will be completely involved, without having the feeling that we have been forced to to this by someone else. If what I do can be done by computer, then I need to find something else to do. I am not interested in the result of my activity. I am interested in being alive.—Lars Gunnar Bodin et al. (1965).

Have you seen this book out called *Megatrends?* It's just out. I read it in a glancing-at-it way in Houston the other day. We're moving, the author says, from an industrial society to an information society, which is to say, from manual labor to unemployment. And our high degrees of unemployment that we now hear of—all the way from 9 percent unemployed to as high as 40 percent in Puerto Rico. I think in Detroit it's now 14 percent. If we change from seeing that as a threat to seeing that as an advance toward our proper goal, the whole thing could turn from negative to positive.

What would you do with the argument that nothing will get done that way?

Well, there are now factories in Japan where robots are making robots.

And this information is in that book. The tendency is definitely toward a society based on unemployment. Our educational system now is based upon preparing people for employment; yet even when I was young, it was known that university graduates were frequently unemployed. And in the first great depression there were university graduates going around sustaining themselves by going through people's garbage. We already know that's wrong.

But, what is basically wrong is that one should be educated in order to get a job. We now know that there isn't enough work, really, to go around. That we *have*, through invention, which is a good thing, now reduced the necessity for work. So that you really have to put your mind to it to figure out what to do. You have to *create*, not foolish jobs, but a use of your time that is interesting to you, that you can devote yourself to. You almost know, I'm sure, that most jobs you would get are not things you would devote yourself to, or want to.

If we could see that we don't have to be employed then how we are going to spend our time is the question. There's a company in Italy called the Olivetti Company that has been very enlightened in all of its history. And it always trains its employees in the use of their leisure time. So that when they would retire, they would already know things to do that they enjoyed. So they could continue. And now they are retired at the age of forty-five. And that was just a recognition on the part of the company of the state of affairs which is brought about by technology.—Sean Bronzell and Ann Suchomski (1983).

What we want is the peace which passes understanding, and which goes into daily experience. Some Christians thought it passed understanding and went off into heaven, which is just too spooky for words; but that's not the case with this peace. It's down-to-earth peace, don't you see?—Michael John White (1982).

The other day, when I was talking with the art students, I was asked if there was some way to sum up John Cage, and what he's about—what he has spent his life doing.

You know my answer to the Midwestern journalist, wasn't it, who wrote me asking me to summarize myself—in a nutshell, he said. So I said, "Get out of whatever cage you're in."—Ellsworth Snyder (1985).

CODA

Jacqueline Bossard a posé à John Cage le questionnaire de Marcel Proust:

Quel est pour vous le comble de la misère?

I prefer laughing to weeping; even so I'm against the current political economic structures (power and profit).

Où aimeriez-vous vivre?

Where I am.

Votre idéal de bonheur terrestre?

The general presence of intelligence among human beings, and the nonobstruction of nature (ecology).

Pour quelles fautes avez-vous le plus d'indulgence?

My love of music.

Vos héros de romans préférés?

It's been a long time since I've read any novels. I'm reading now the *Journal* of Thoreau.

Votre personnage historique préféré?

The Buddha.

Vos héroïnes dans le vie réelle?

The women I meet.

Vos héroïnes dans la fiction?

See above.

Votre peintre favori?

I try not to develop "favorites" and "preferences." In that way I find I remain curious and attentive to what I happen to encounter.

Votre musicien préféré?

See above.

Votre qualité préférée chez l'homme?

See above.

Votre qualité préférée chez la femme?

See above.

Votre vertu préférée?

See above.

Votre occupation préférée?

See above.

Qui auriez-vous aimé être?

I consider myself fortunate to be alive.

Le trait principal de votre caractère?

A happy disposition.

Ce que vous appréciez le plus chez des amis?
See above.
Votre principal défaut?
See above.
Votre rêve de bonheur?
See above.
Quel serait votre plus grand malheur?
See above.
Ce que vous voudriez être?
See above.
Le couleur que vous préférez?
See above.
La fleur que vous aimez?
See above.
L'oiseau que vous préférez?
See above.
Vos auteurs favoris en prose?
See above.
Vos poètes préférés?
See above.
Vos noms favoris?
See above.
Les caractères historiques que vous méprisez le plus?
See above.
Le fait militaire que vous admirez le plus?
I don't like structures that require the military.
Le don de la nature que vous voudriez avoir?
I accept what I have.
Ce que vous détestez par dessus tout?
See above.
Comment aimeriez-vous mourir?
That's a mystery the solution of which interests me very much.
État présent de votre esprit?
See above.
Votre devise?
?

ACKNOWLEDGMENTS

The following acknowledgments represent an extension of the copyright page:

Artforum (February 1965), by permission of the publisher.

"The Changing Audience for the Changing Arts/Panel," *The Arts: Planning for Change* (American Council for the Arts, 1966), by permission of the publisher.

PERSPECTA 11: The Yale Architectural Journal (1967), by permission of the publisher.

Cinema Now (University of Cincinnati, 1968), by permission of Michael Porte and Hector Currie.

Response to questionnaire, *Source* 6 (1969), by permission of Larry Austin.

New England Conservatory discussion (1976), by permission of the New England Conservatory of Music.

Middlebury College Magazine (Winter 1981), by permission.

Press conference, Cologne (1983), by permission of Bill Ritchie and Kathan Brown.

John Ashbery, "Cheering Up Our Knowing," *New York* (April 10, 1978), by permission of the author.

Larry Austin, interview in *Source: Music of the Avant Garde* 2, no. 2 (1968), by permission of the author.

Jack Behrens, interview in manuscript (1981), by permission of the author.

Mark Bloch, interview in manuscript (1987), by permission of the author.

Lars Gunnar Bodin/Bengt Emil Johnson/Deborah Hay, reprinted by permission of L. G. Bodin and Deborah Hay.

Frans Boenders, from an audiotape, by permission of the author.

Jacqueline Bossard, *Musique de tous les temps,* supplement au # 52, décembre 1970, by permission of Ornella Volta.

Jonathan Brent, *Tri-Quarterly* 52, a publication of Northwestern University (Evanston, IL), by permission of the publisher.

Sean Bronzell and Ann Suchomski, interview in *Catch* (Knox College), by permission of the faculty advisor.

Anthony Brown, interview in **asterisk,* by permission of the interviewer.

Kathleen Burch et al., interview in *The guests go in to supper* (Oakland, CA: Burning Books, 1986), by permission of the publisher.

Deborah Campana, by permission of the interviewer.

Rick Chatenever, "Cage's 'Found Sound,'" *Santa Cruz Sentinel* (August 20, 1982), by permission of the publisher.

Roy Close, reprinted from the *Minneapolis Star* (April 18, 1975), by permission of the interviewer.

Robert Commanday, reprinted from *San Francisco Chronicle/This World* (November 10, 1968), by permission of the interviewer.

David Cope, interivew in *The Composer* X & XI, by permission of the interviewer.

Robert Cordier, by permission of the interviewer.

Paul Cummings, interview in manuscript, by permission of the interviewer.

Tom Darter, "John Cage," reprinted from *Keyboard* (September 1982), by permission of GPI Publications, 20085 Stevens Creek, Cupertino, CA 95014. Copyright © 1982 by GPI Publications.

Gwen Deely, previously unpublished interview, by permission of R. Gwen Deely.

Martin Duberman, from *Black Mountain* (1972), by permission of Martin Bauml Duberman.

William Duckworth, interview in manuscript, by permission of the interviewer. Copyright © 1987 by William Duckworth.

Morton Feldman (B. Marcus and F. Pellizzi), conversation in *RES, Journal of Anthropology and Aesthetics* 6 (Autumn 1983), by permission of the publisher.

Robert Filliou, from *Teaching and Learning as Performing Arts* (König, 1970), by permission of the publisher.

Don Finegan et al., "Choosing Abundance," *North American Review* (Fall 1969 & Winter 1970), by permission of the publisher. Copyright © 1969, 1970 by the University of Northern Iowa.

Laura Fletcher and Thomas Moore, interview in *Sonus* 3 (1983), by permission of the publisher. Copyright © 1982 by *Sonus.*

Monique Fong and Françoise Marie, unpublished interview, by permission of Monique Fong (Wust).

Maureen Furman, "Zen Composition," *East West Journal* (May 1979), by permission of the publisher. Copyright © 1979 by *East West Journal.*

Cole Gagne and Tracy Caras. "Interview with John Cage," *New York Arts Journal* 1, no. 1 (1975); copyright c 1975 by Cole Gagne and Tracy Caras. Interview in *Soundpieces* (Scarecrow, 1982); copyright c 1982 by Cole Gagne and Tracy Caras. Both reprinted by permission of the interviewers.

Anne Gibson, interview for radio series "J. S. Bach: A Celebration of Genius" (CBC, 1985), by permission of the producer.

Alan Gillmor, interview in manuscript, by permission of the interviewer.

Alan Gillmor, and Roger Shattuck, interview in manuscript, by permission of the interviewers.

Nikša Gligo, original English transcript, by permission of the interviewer.

Jeff Goldberg, "John Cage Interview," *Soho Weekly News* (September 12, 1974), by permission.

———. "John Cage Interviewed," *Transatlantic Review* 55/56 (May 1976), by permission.

Ev Grimes, by permission of the interviewer. Copyright © 1985 by Ev Grimes.

Terry Gross, "Fresh Air," WHYY-FM (September 10, 1982), by permission of the interviewer.

Mary Emma Harris, interview in manuscript, by permission of the interviewer. Copyright © 1987 by Mary Emma Harris.

Hans G. Helms, by permission of the interviewer.

Paul Hersh, *Santa Cruz Express* (August 19, 1982), by permission of the publisher.

Paul Hertelendy, *San Jose Mercury News* (August 19, 1982), by permission of the interviewer.

Dick Higgins, interview in manuscript, by permission of Richard C. Higgins.

Thom Holmes, "The Cage Interview." *Recordings* 3, no. 3 (1981), by permission of the publisher.

Ray Johnson, unpublished letter (1987), by permission of the author.

Michael Kirby and Richard Schechner, "An Interview," *Tulane Drama Review* 10, no. 2 (Winter 1965), by permission of the publisher, MIT Press.

John Kobler, "Everything We Do Is Music," *The Saturday Evening Post* (October 19, 1968), by permission of the author.

Richard Kostelanetz, interviews with John Cage, by permission of the author. Copyright © 1981, 1987 by Richard Kostelanetz.

Richard Kostelanetz et al., symposium in Marilyn Belford and Jerry Herman, eds., *Time and Space Concepts in Art* (Pleiades Gallery, 1980), by permission of Joellen Bard.

Art Lange, "Interview with John Cage 10/4/77," *Brilliant Corners* 8 (Winter 1978), by permission of the interviewer.

Alcides Lanza, " . . . We Need a Good Deal of Silence. . . ," *Revista de Letras* 3, no. 2 (September 1971), by permission of the interviewer.

Lisa Low, *Boston Review* (July 1985), by permission of Lisa Elaine Low.

Geneviere Marcus, *Coast FM& Fine Arts* (March 1970) and a personal letter (1986), by permission of the author.

Joseph H. Mazo, by permission of the author.

Ilhan Mimaroglu, from the sound track of "The Question," a film in progress, by permission of the interviewer.

Stephen Montague, "Significant Silences of a Musical Anarchist," *Classical Music* (Rhinegold Press/London, May 22, 1982), by permission of the author.

———, interview in manuscript (1982), by permission of the author.

Jay Murphy, "Interview: John Cage," *Red Bass* 8/9 (1985), by permission of the interviewer.

Arlynn Nellhaus, *Denver Post* (July 5, 1968), by permission of the publisher.

Max Nyffeler, *Dissonanz* 6 (September 1970), by permission of the interviewer.

Birger Ollrogge, interview in manuscript (1985), by permission of the interviewer.

Tim Page, "A Conversation with John Cage," *Boulevard* 3 (Fall 1986), by permission of the interviewer.

Joan Peyser, from *Boulez: Composer, Conductor, Enigma* (Schirmer Books, 1976), by permission of the author. Copyright © 1976 by Katomo Ltd.

Susan Reimer, The *Post* (Ohio University, April 10, 1973), by permission of the author and the publisher.

Roger Reynolds, "Interview," *Generation* (1961), by permission of the author.

Moira and William Roth, "John Cage on Marcel Duchamp," *Art in America* (November-December 1973), by permission of the publisher and the authors.

Irving Sandler, previously unpublished interview (1966), by permission of the author. Copyright © 1987 by Irving Sandler.

Klaus Schöning, previously unpublished interviews, by permission of the author.

David Sears, *Dance News* (March 1981), by permission of the author.

David Shapiro, "A Collaboration in Art," *Res, Journal of Anthropology and Aesthetics* 10 (Autumn 1985), by permission of the author.

Bill Shoemaker, "The Age of Cage," *down beat* (December 1984), by permission of *down beat* magazine.

Rose Slivka, from *Craft Horizons* (December 1978 & February 1979), by permission of Rose C. S. Slivka.

Arnold Jay Smith et al., symposium in *down beat* (October 20, 1977), by permission of *down beat* magazine.

Stuart Smith, "Interview with John Cage," *Percussive Notes* 21, no. 3 (March 1983), by permission of the publisher. Copyright MCMLXXIII by Percussive Arts Society.

Ellsworth Snyder, two previously unpublished interviews (1975 for Wisconsin Public Radio; 1985), by permission of the interviewer.

David Stanton, *Southern California Magazine* (1982), by permission of the interviewer.

David Sterritt, "Composer John Cage, Master of Notes—and Sounds," *Christian Science Monitor* (May 4, 1982), by permission of the publisher. Copyright © 1982 by The Christian Science Publishing Society. All rights reserved.

Joel Eric Suben, interview on audiotape (1983), by permission of the interviewer.

Harry Sumrall, *San Jose Mercury News* (May 2, 1986), by permission of the author.

David Sylvester and Roger Smalley, "John Cage Talks," BBC (1967), by permission of the BBC and Roger Smalley.

Rob Tannenbaum, "A Meeting of Sound Minds," *Musician*, by permission of *Musician* magazine and the author's agent, March Tenth, Inc.

Andrew Timar et al., "A Conversation with John Cage," excerpted from *Musicworks* 17 (Fall 1981), by permission of the publisher (1087 Queen St. West, Toronto, Ontario M6R 2N1).

Calvin Tomkins, *The Bride and the Bachelors* (expanded ed., Viking, 1968), by permission of the author.

Regina Vater, interview in manuscript (1976), by permission of the interviewer.

C. H. Waddington, *Biology and the History of the Future* (Edinburgh University Press, 1972), by permission of the publisher.

Anne Waldman, *Talking Poetics from Naropa Institute* (Shambhala, 1978), by permission of Anne Waldman, editor.

Michael John White, "King of the Avant-Garde," *Sunday Observer* (September 26, 1982), by permission of The Observer Magazine, London.

Robin White, interview at Crown Point Press, Oakland, CA, *View* 1, no. 1 (1978), by permission of Point Publishers.

Thomas Wufflin, "An Interview with John Cage," *New York Berlin* 1, no. 1 (1985), by permission of the publisher.

Walter Zimmerman, "Desert Plants: John Cage," *Inselmusik* (Beginner Press, 1981), by permission of the author.

Michael Zwerin, from *International Herald Tribune* (1982) and *Close Enough for Jazz* (Quartet Books, 1983), by permission of the author.

Everything else by John Cage, with his permission. Copyright © 1987 by John Cage.

Every effort has been made to verify the spelling of all proper names and to trace the ownership of all copyrighted material, in addition to making full acknowledgment of the latter's use. If any error or omission has occurred, it will be corrected in subsequent editions, providing that appropriate notification is submitted in writing to the author.

BIBLIOGRAPHY

Alcatraz, Jose Antonio. "John Cage: El Sonido como centro del universo." *Excelsior* (February 29, 1976).

———. Interview with John Cage. *Excelsior/Plural* 56 (May 1976).

Amirkhanian, Charles. Interview on audiotape, 1983.

Anon. "Sound Stuff." *Newsweek,* January 11, 1954.

———. "It's electronic ballet—or 48 hours of bad plumbing." *Daily Mail,* November 22, 1966.

———. "Quiet composer voices loud ideas." *Scottsdale* (AZ.) *Daily Progress,* April 4, 1975.

———. "Arts." *Reporter* (Buffalo), October 19, 1978.

Ashbery, John. "Cheering Up Our Knowing." *New York,* April 10, 1978.

Austin, Larry. "*HPSCHD.*" *Source* 2, no. 2 (1968).

Bakewell, Joan. "Music and Mushrooms—John Cage Talks About His Recipes." *The Listener* 87 (June 15, 1972).

Barnard, Geoffrey. *Conversation Without Feldman.* Darlinghurst, N.S.W. (Australia): Black Ram Books, 1980.

Bither, David. "A Grand Old Radical." *Horizon* 23, no. 12 (December 1980).

Bloch, Mark. Interview in manuscript, 1987.

Bodin, Lars Gunnar, and Bengt Emil Johnson. "Bandintervju med Cage." *Ord och Bild* 74 (1965). (Original English tape, with Deborah Hay as a third interviewer, supplied by Bodin.)

Boenders, Frans. "Gesprek met John Cage. De cultuur als delta." In *Sprekend gedacht* (Bussum, 1980).

Bossard, Jacqueline. "Posé à John Cage le questionnaire de Marcel Proust." *Musique de tous les Temps* (December 1970).

Bosseur, Jean-Yves. "John Cage: "Il faut forger un nouveau mode de communication orale." *La Quinzaine littéraire,* December 15, 1973.

Brent, Jonathan. "Letters." *Tri-Quarterly* 52 (Fall 1981).

Bronzell, Sean, and Ann Suchomski, "Inter-view with John Cage." In *Catch.* Galesburg, IL: Knox College, 1983. Reprinted in *The guests go in to supper,* edited by Melody Sumner. Oakland, CA: Burning Books, 1986.

Brown, Anthony. Interview in **asterisk: A Journal of New Music* 1, no. 1 (1975).

Burch, Kathleen, Michael Sumner, and Melody Sumner. "Interview with John Cage." In *The guests go in to supper,* edited by Melody Sumner. Oakland, CA: Burning Books, 1986.

Cage, John. "John Cage in Los Angeles." In *Artforum* (February 1965), reprinted in *Looking Critically,* edited by Amy Baker Sandback. Ann Arbor, MI: UMI Research, 1984.

———. "Questions." *Perspecta* 11 (Yale School of Architecture, 1967).

———. Response to questionnaire. *Source 6* 3, no. 2 (July 1969).

———. "Art in the Culture." (A symposium with Richard Foreman and Richard Kostelanetz) *Performing Arts Journal* 10–11 (1979). German translation in *Theater heute* (January 1980).

———. In *Biology and the History of the Future,* edited by C. H. Waddington. Edinburgh: Edinburgh University Press, 1972.

———. Press conference, Cologne (1983), videotaped by Bill Ritchie.

Cage, John, and Merce Cunningham. "Questions Answered and Unanswered." *Middlebury* (Winter 1981).

Cage, John et al. *Cinema Now* (Cincinnati: University of Cincinnati, 1968).

———. "The University and the Arts: Are They Compatible?" *Works and Days* 1, no. 1 (Spring 1969).

———. "10 Questions: 270 Answers." *The Composer* X-XI (1980).

Campana, Deborah. Interview in manuscript, 1985.

Chatenever, Rick. "Cage's 'Found Sound.' " *Santa Cruz Sentinel,* August 20, 1982.

Close, Roy M. "Music creator Cage finds his ideas in nature." *Minneapolis Star,* April 18, 1975.

Commanday, Robert. "Composing with the Camera." *San Francisco Chronicle/This World,* November 10, 1968.

Cope, David. "An Interview with John Cage." *Composer Magazine* 10–11 (1980).

Cordier, Robert. "Etcetera pour un Jour ou Deux." *Had* (Paris, 1973). (Original English tape supplied by the interviewer.)

Cummings, Paul. "Interview: John Cage [May 2, 1974]" (in manuscript at the Archives of American Art).
Daney, S., and J. P. Fargier. Interview with John Cage in *Cahiers du cinéma* 334–35 (April 1982).
Darter, Tom. "John Cage." *Keyboard* (September 1982).
Deely, Gwen, with Jim Theobald. "Oral Defense of Thesis, Hunter Electronic Music Studio, December 20, 1976" (in manuscript).
Duberman, Martin. *Black Mountain: An Exploration in Community.* New York: Dutton, 1972.
Duckworth, William. "Anything I Say Will Be Misunderstood [1985]." *Bucknell Review: John Cage at 75* 33, no. 2 (1988).
Erikson, Tom. Interview in manuscript, 1987.
Feldman, Morton, and John Cage. "A Radio Conversation." *Circuit* (Spring-Summer 1967).
Feldman, Morton (Bunita Marcus and Francesco Pellizzi). "John Cage." *Res* 6 (Autumn 1983).
Filliou, Robert. "John Cage." In *Teaching and Learning as Performing Arts/Lehren und Lernen als Aufführungskünste* (New York-Köln: Verlag Gebr. Koenig, 1970).
Finegan, Don et al. "Choosing Abundance/Things to Do." *North American Review* 6, nos. 3 & 4 (Fall and Winter 1969).
Fletcher, Laura, and Thomas Moore. "An Interview [with John Cage]." *Sonus: A Journal of Investigations into Global Musical Possibilities* 3, no. 2 (1983).
Fong, Monique, and Françoise Marie. Interview in manuscript, 1982.
Freedman, Guy. "An Hour & 4′33″ with John Cage." *Music Journal* (December 1976).
Furman, Maureen. "Zen Composition: An Interview with John Cage." *East West Journal* (May 1979).
Gagne, Cole, and Tracy Caras. "An Interview with John Cage [1975]." *New York Arts Journal* 1, no. 1 (May 1976).
———. "John Cage [1980]." *Soundpieces: Interviews with American Composers.* Metuchen, NJ: Scarecrow, 1982.
Gena, Peter. "After Antiquity: John Cage in Conversation." In *A John Cage Reader,* edited by Peter Gena et al. New York: C. F. Peters Corp., 1982.
Gibson, Anne. "CBC Interview re Bach," November 1985 (in manuscript).
Gillmor, Alan. "Interview with John Cage [1973]." *Contact* 14 (Autumn 1976). In Swedish, "Intervju med John Cage." *Nutida Musik* 21, no. 1 (1977/780).
Gillmor, Alan, and Roger Shattuck. "Erik Satie: A Conversation [1973]." *Contact* 25 (Autumn 1982).
Gligo, Nikša. "Ich traf John Cage in Bremen." *Melos, Zeitschrift fur Neue Music* 1 (January-February 1973). (English transcript provided by the author.)
Goldberg, Jeff. "John Cage Interview." *Soho Weekly News,* September 12, 1974.
———. "John Cage Interviewed." *Transatlantic Review* 55/56 (May 1976).
Green, Blake. "John Cage: Old Guard of Music's Avant-Garde." *San Francisco Chronicle,* 1985.
Gregson, David. "John Cage makes his music at random." *San Diego Union,* April 29, 1986.
Grimes, Ev. "John Cage, Born 1912" (in manuscript), 1984.
Hahn, Otto. "Merce Cunningham." *L'Express,* 11 June, 1964.
Harris, Mary Emma. Interview 1974 (in transcript).
Helms, Hans G. "Gedanken Eines Progressiven Musikers uber die Beschädigte Gesellschaft." *Protokolle* 30 (März 1974). Reprinted in *Musik-Konzepte Sonderband: John Cage,* edited by Heinz-Klaus Metzger and Rainer Riehn. München: Text + Kritik, 1978.
Hersh, Paul. "John Cage." *Santa Cruz Express,* August 19, 1982.
Hertelendy, Paul. "John Cage Sprouting at UC." *San Jose Mercury News,* January 24, 1980.
———. "John Cage Rolls Dice at Cabrillo Music Festival." *San Jose Mercury News,* August 19, 1982.
Higgins, Dick. "John Cage Interview [November 1976]" (in manuscript).
Holmes, Thom. "The Cage Interview." *Recordings* 3, no. 3 (1981).
Jouffroy, Alain, and Robert Cordier. "Entendre John Cage, entendre Duchamp." *Opus international* 49 (March 1974). (Original English tape supplied by Robert Cordier.)
Kauffmann, Stanley, moderator. "The Changing Audience for the Changing Arts/Panel." In *The Arts: Planning for Change.* New York: Associated Councils of the Arts, 1966.
Kirby, Michael, and Richard Schechner. "An Interview." *Tulane Drama Review* 10, no. 2 (Winter 1965).
Kobler, John. "Everything We Do Is Music" *The Saturday Evening Post,* October 19, 1968.
Kostelanetz, Richard. "John Cage in Conversation, Mostly About Writing." *New York Arts Journal* 19 (1980). Reprinted as "John Cage (1979)," in Richard Kostelanetz, *The Old Poetries and the New.* Ann Arbor: University of Michigan Press, 1981.
———. "John Cage." *The Theatre of Mixed Means.* New York: The Dial Press, 1968; London: Pitman, 1970; New York: RK Editions, 1980.

Kostelanetz, Richard, and John Cage. "A Conversation About Radio in Twelve Parts" [1984]. *Bucknell Review: John Cage at 75* 33, no. 2 (1988). Preprinted, abridged, in *Musical Quarterly* 72, no. 2 (1986).

Kostelanetz, Richard et al. Symposium on "Time and Space Concepts in Music and Visual Art," (1977). In *Time and Space Concepts in Art,* edited by Marilyn Belford and Jerry Herman. New York: Pleiades Gallery, 1979.

Lange, Art. "Interview with John Cage 10/4/77." *Brilliant Corners* 8 (Winter 1978).

Lanza, Alcides. " . . . We Need a Good Deal of Silence . . ." *Revista de Letras* 3, no. 2 (September 1971).

Lebel, Jean-Jacques. "John Cage entouré de nus, vite." *La Quinzaine littéraire* (December 15, 1966).

Littler, William. "Roaratorio an Irish circus of words blended with sound." *Toronto Star,* January 1982.

Low, Lisa. "Free Associaton." *Boston Review* (July 1985).

Marcus, Geneviere. "John Cage: Dean of the Musical Avant-Garde." *Coast FM& Fine Arts* 11, no. 3 (March 1970).

Mazo, Joseph H. "John Cage Quietly Speaks His Piece." *Bergen Sunday Record,* March 13, 1983.

Mimaroglu, Ilhan. "Interview with John Cage." *Discotea* (November 1965).

———. Interview, 1985 (in the sound track of a film in progress).

Montague, Stephen. "Significant Silences of a Musical Anarchist." *Classical Music* (May 22, 1982).

———. Interview (in manuscript), 1982.

Morera, Daniela. "John Cage: i suoni della vita." *L'Uomo vogue* (Marzo 1976).

Murphy, Jay. "Interview: John Cage." *Red Bass,* nos. 8–9 (1985).

Nellhaus, Arlynn. " 'New' Music a Wirey Maze." *Denver Post,* July 5, 1968.

Nestyev, Israil. "Antimuzyka pod Glogom 'anarkhil.' " *Sovetskaya Muzyka* 37 (September 1973).

Nieminen, Risto. "John Cage marraskuussa 1982. Taide on itsensa zyollistamista." *Synkooppi* 13 (June 1983).

Nocera, Gigliola. "Alla Ricerca del silenzio perduto." *Scena* 2, no. 2 (April 1978).

Nyffeler, Max. "Interview mit John Cage." *Dissonanz* (Zurich) 6 (September 1970).

Ollrogge, Birger. Interview December 28, 1985 (in manuscript).

Page, Tim. "A Conversation with John Cage." *Boulevard* 1, no. 3 (Fall 1986).

Patterson, Suzy. "Original Approach to Ballet." *Journal Herald* (Dayton), December 31, 1966.

Peyser, Joan. *Boulez: Composer, Conductor, Enigma.* New York: Schirmer Books, 1976.

Rasmussen, Karl Aage. "En samtale med John Cage—maj 1984." *Dansk Musiktidsskrift* 49 (1984–85).

Reimer, Susan. "Music & dance: directing traffic." The *Post* (Ohio University) April 10, 1973.

Reynolds, Roger. "Interview." *Generation* (January 1962). Reprinted in *John Cage.* New York: Henmar Press, 1962; and *Contemporary Composers on Contemporary Music,* edited by Elliott Schwartz and Barney Childs. New York: Holt, 1967.

Roberts, John, with Silvy Panet Raymond. "Some Empty Words with Mr. Cage and Mr. Cunningham." *The Performance Magazine* 7 (1980).

Rolland, Alain. "Entretien avec John Cage." *Tel Quel* 90 (Winter 1981).

Roth, Moira, and William Roth. "John Cage on Marcel Duchamp." *Art in America* (November-December 1973).

Sandler, Irving. "Recorded Interview with John Cage (May 6, 1966)" (in manuscript).

Sarraute, Claude. "Cage et Cunningham à l'Opéra." *Le Monde,* Novembre 2, 1973.

Schonberger, Elmer. " 'Ik componeer arme muziek voor arme mensen.' De toevalsmanipulaties van John Cage." *Vrij Nederland,* June 3, 1978.

Schöning, Klaus. "Silence Sometimes Can Be Very Loud." In *Hörspielmacher.* Königstein/Taunus, Athenäum, 1983.

———. "Gesprach uber *James Joyce, Marcel Duchamp, Erik Satie: Ein Alphabet.*" *Neuland* 6 (1984–85).

———. "Gesprach zu *Muoyce.*" In a broadcast transcript from Westdeutscher Rundfunk, June 12, 1984.

———. "Gesprach zu *HMCIEX.*" In a broadcast transcript from Westdeutscher Rundfunk, July 10, 1984.

Sears, David. "Talking with John Cage: The Other Side." *Dance News* (March 1981).

Shapiro, David. "On Collaboration in Art." *Res* 10 (Autumn 1985).

Shoemaker, Bill. "The Age of Cage." *down beat* (December 1984).

Slivka, Rose. "Lifecraft." *Craft Horizons* (December 1978 & January 1979).

Smalley, Roger, and David Sylvester. "John Cage Talks" (BBC, 1967). Reprinted in concert programme, Royal Albert Hall, May 22, 1972.

Smith, Arnold Jay. "Reaching for the Cosmos: A Composers' Colloquium." *down beat* (October 20, 1977).
Smith, Stuart. "Interview with John Cage." *Percussive Notes* 21, no. 3 (March 1983).
Snyder, Ellsworth. "A Conversation with John Cage [1975]" (broadcast over Wisconsin Public Radio).
———. "John Cage Interview, North Carolina School of the Arts [1985]" (in manuscript).
Stanton, David. "John Cage: A Composer of Personal Vision." *Daily Trojan—Southern California Magazine* 61 (April 19, 1985).
Sterritt, David. "Composer John Cage, Master of Notes—and Sounds." *Christian Science Monitor,* May 4, 1982.
Sumrall, Harry. "Cage in Ferment." *San Jose Mercury News,* May 2, 1986.
Sykes, Jill. "Breaking out of art's cage." *Sydney Morning Herald,* March 19, 1976.
Tannenbaum, Rob. "A Meeting of Sound Minds: John Cage + Brian Eno." *Musician* 83 (September 1985).
Tarting, C., and André Jaume. "Entretiens avec John Cage." *Jazz Magazine* 282 (January 1981).
Tierstein, Alice. "Dance and Music: Interviews at the Keyboard." *Dance Scope* 8, no. 2 (Spring/Summer 1974).
Timar, Andrew et al. "A Conversation with John Cage." *Musicworks* 17 (Fall 1981).
Tomkins, Calvin. *The Bride and the Bachelors* [1965]. Expanded edition. New York: Viking, 1968.
———. *Off the Wall.* Garden City: Doubleday, 1980.
Varèse, Edgard, and Alexei Haieff. "Possibilities: Questioned by 8 Composers." *Possibilities* 1 (Winter 1947–48).
Vater, Regina. Interview on audiotape, 1976.
Vignal, P. du. "Le repas viet–namien de M. Cage." *Art Press* 1 (December 1972-January 1983).
Waldman, Anne, and Marilyn Webb, eds. "Empty Words, IV [1974]." *Talking Poets from the Naropa Institute,* vol. 1. Boulder: Shambhala, 1978.
White, Michael John. "King of the Avant-Garde." *Observer (London),* September 26, 1982.
White, Robin. "John Cage." *View* 1, no. 1 (April 1978).
Womack, Bill. "The Music of Contingency: An Interview." *Zero* 3 (1979).
Wulffen, Thomas. "An Interview with John Cage." *New York Berlin* 1, no. 1 (1984). German translation in *Zitty* (March 1985).
Zimmerman, Walter. "Desert Plants: John Cage." *Inselmusik.* Köln: Beginner Press, 1981.
Zwerin, Michael. "Silence, Please, for John Cage." *International Herald Tribune,* September 24, 1982.
———. *Close Enough for Jazz.* London: Quartet Books, 1983.

SOME OF THE INTERVIEWERS

CHARLES AMIRKHANIAN has been music director of KPFA in Berkeley, CA, since 1969. At the age of five in 1950, he remembers, he got his first John Cage record from his father.

JOHN ASHBERY is a distinguished American poet and art critic.

LARRY AUSTIN, a composer, directs the Center for Experimental Music and Intermedia at North Texas State University, Denton, and, as he writes, "has worked musically with John Cage on many occasions since the mid-sixties in California, Florida, New York, and Texas."

JACK BEHRENS teaches music at the University of Western Ontario in London, Canada.

MARK BLOCH is a multimedia artist living in New York.

LARS GUNNAR BODIN & BENGT EMIL JOHNSON are Swedish composers and cultural executives. DEBORAH HAY, in 1965 a dancer in the Merce Cunningham Company, has lived in Austin, TX, since 1976.

FRANS BOENDERS is a Belgian-Dutch broadcaster, critic, essayist and poet. A senior producer at Belgian Broadcasting, he has made many cultural radio programs and documentary films.

SEAN BRONZELL & ANN SUCHOMSKI, once students at Knox College, Galesburg, IL, now live in Chicago.

ANTHONY BROWN, formerly an editor of **asterisk* in Ann Arbor, now lives in Yipsilanti, MI.

KATHLEEN BURCH, MELODY SUMNER & MICHAEL SUMNER are the editors and publishers of Burning Books in Oakland, CA.

DEBORAH CAMPANA completed a doctoral dissertation, "Form and Structure in the Music of John Cage," at Northwestern University in Evanston, IL, where she lives.

RICK CHATENEVER is a staff writer/reviewer, as well as associate entertainment editor, of the *Santa Cruz Sentinel.*

ROY CLOSE has been music critic of the St. Paul (MN) *Pioneer Press and Dispatch* since 1981; previous to that, he worked for the *Minneapolis Star.*

ROBERT COMMANDAY is a staff writer for the *San Francisco Chronicle.*

DAVID COPE is a composer teaching at the University of California at Santa Cruz. Formerly the editor of *The Composer,* a periodical, he also authored *New Directions in Music* (1971).

ROBERT CORDIER is a bilingual theater director who has worked in both France and America.

PAUL CUMMINGS has written and edited many books about American art.

TOM DARTER has been the editor of *Keyboard.*

GWEN DEELY wrote her M.A. thesis on "The Making of a Composer: John Cage's Early Years in New York City (1942–49)"; she has recently been working in computer programming in New York City.

MARTIN DUBERMAN authored *Black Mountain* (1972), among other books of American cultural history.

WILLIAM DUCKWORTH (1943—) is a composer presently teaching at Bucknell University. His M.A. thesis was devoted to Cage's music.

THOMAS ERIKSON, a resident of San Francisco, writes that he is "a free-lance photographer primarily interactive with people in the art of music."

MORTON FELDMAN (1926–87) a composer, taught for years in the Department of Music at the State University of New York at Buffalo.

ROBERT FILLIOU (1926–87) was a French artist working in several media, including language.

DON FINEGAN, RALPH HASKELL & RALPH KOPPEL all taught visual art at the University of Northern Iowa.

LAURA FLETCHER & THOMAS MOORE were graduate students at the University of Maryland, College Park.

MONIQUE FONG is a U.N. interpreter who has translated Cage into French; FRANÇOISE MARIE is her daughter.

COLE GAGNE & TRACY CARAS are respectively a music critic and an attorney living in New York City. Together they produced *Soundpieces: Interviews with American Composers* (1982).

ANNE GIBSON is an executive producer in the music department at the Canadian Broadcasting Corporation.

ALAN GILLMOR is a musicologist presently teaching at Carleton University in Ottawa.

NIKŠA GLIGO is a music writer living in Zagreb.

JEFF GOLDBERG, born in Philadelphia in 1948, edited *Contact,* a poetry magazine in his home city, and then worked in New York City journalism as an editor and interviewer.

EV GRIMES, residing in Grand Isle, VT, co-produced the John Cage seventieth birthday celebration for National Public Radio's "The Sunday Show."

TERRY GROSS hosts the interview magazine "Fresh Air" for Philadelphia's public radio station WHYY-FM.

MARY EMMA HARRIS recently completed a book and curated an exhibition, both about the arts program at Black Mountain College.

HANS G. HELMS (1932—) authored *Fa:m' Ahniesgwow* (1958), among other German books. Recently a resident of New York City, he has returned to Köln.

PAUL HERTELENDY has written widely on music and dance. He also holds a doctorate in engineering.

DICK HIGGINS (1938—) is an artist/writer living in New York who has known Cage since attending his New School classes in the late fifties.

THOM HOLMES is a music writer and book producer living in Cherry Hills, NJ.

RAY JOHNSON is a visual-verbal artist who has known John Cage for over thirty years. *Correspondence* (1976) was a book and exhibition of his letters.

MICHAEL KIRBY & RICHARD SCHECHNER are professors in the graduate performance studies program at New York University and, separately, the authors of many books about theater.

JOHN KOBLER, once a staff writer at *The Saturday Evening Post,* recently finished a book about Igor Stravinsky.

ART LANGE is a poet and music critic, who edited *Brilliant Corners: A Magazine of the Arts* from 1975 to 1979, and is currently editor of *down beat.*

ALCIDES LANZA, born in Argentina in 1929, presently teaches at McGill University in Montreal.

LISA LOW is a professor of English literature at Cornell College, Mt. Vernon, IA.

GENEVIERE G. MARCUS is co-president of Equal Relationships Institute in Pacific Palisades, CA.

JOSEPH H. MAZO, dance critic for *Women's Wear Daily,* has published *Dance Is a Contact Sport* and *Prime Movers: The Makers of Modern Dance in America.*

ILHAN MIMAROGLU is a Turkish-born composer who also works in New York as a record producer.

STEPHEN MONTAGUE (1943—) is an American composer/pianist living in London. His compositional interests include music for traditional ensembles, as well as electroacoustic music, music theater, mixed media, dance and video.

JAY MURPHY is a free-lance critic and journalist living in Tallahassee, FL, where he edits the activist arts publication *Red Bass.*

MAX NYFFELER, a pianist and journalist, lives in Köln and Zurich, where he works as an editor for Pro Helvetia.

BIRGER OLLROGGE lives in West Berlin. Among the books he has translated into German are Daniel Charles' and John Cage's *For the Birds.*

TIM PAGE, music critic for New York *Newsday,* also hosts a music program on WNYC-FM.

FRANCESCO PELLIZZI is an anthropologist who edits the periodical *Res.*

JOAN PEYSER (1931—), the author of *Boulez* (1976), recently published a biography of Leonard Bernstein.

SUSAN REIMER is now a sportswriter for the *Baltimore Sun.*

ROGER REYNOLDS (1934—), a composer, teaches at the University of California at San Diego. He authored *Mind Models* (1975).

MOIRA ROTH, an art historian and critic, also teaches at the University of California at San Diego. She authored *The Amazing Decade: Women and Performance Art in America 1970–1980* (1983).

IRVING SANDLER is a professor of art history at SUNY-Purchase and the author of *The Triumph of Abstract Expressionism* (1970) and *The New York School* (1976).

KLAUS SCHÖNING is staff producer for Hörspiel (audio art) at Westdeutscher Rundfunk in Köln and the editor of several books of and about audio art.

DAVID SEARS is a dance critic presently living in Brooklyn.

DAVID SHAPIRO (1947—) is a poet and art critic teaching at several universities in the New York City area.

ROGER SHATTUCK (1923—) is Commonwealth Professor of French at the University of Virginia and the author of several books, mostly about French literature.

ROSE SLIVKA was for many years the editor of *Craft Horizons.*

ROGER SMALLEY (1943—), a British composer and pianist, is currently Senior Lecturer in the music department of the University of Western Australia.

STUART SMITH (1948—) is a composer, poet, essayist and editor teaching in Baltimore. A percussionist, he was editor-in-chief of *Percussive Notes Research Journal* from 1982 to 1984.

ELLSWORTH SNYDER is a pianist residing in Madison, WI, best known for his performances of twentieth-century and avant-garde works. He also deserves credit for writing the first doctoral dissertation on John Cage.

DAVID STANTON has published in *The Piano Quarterly,* the *Los Angeles Times, Chamber Music America* and the *Croton Review.*

DAVID STERRITT is film critic of the *Christian Science Monitor,* where he also writes regularly on music, theater and dance.

JOEL ERIC SUBEN, a composer and conductor, is music director of both the Peninsula Symphony (VA) and the Brooklyn Heights Music Festival (NY). He also teaches at the College of William and Mary (VA).

HARRY SUMRALL, at present a music writer for the *San Jose Mercury News,* has written about popular culture, as well as music, for several publications.

ROB TANNENBAUM contributes to *The Musician,* among other magazines.

CALVIN TOMKINS (1926—) is a staff writer for *The New Yorker* and the author of several books about modern art.

REGINA VATER, an artist born in Brazil, is presently living in Austin, TX.

C. H. WADDINGTON was a noted biologist interested in other things as well.

ANNE WALDMAN is a poet and editor living in Boulder, CO.

ROBIN WHITE worked as an editor at *Artforum* in New York and at Crown Point Press in Oakland, CA; she is presently executive director of the Media Alliance in New York.

THOMAS WULFFIN is a cultural journalist living in West Berlin.

WALTER ZIMMERMAN is a composer and editor living in West Germany.

MICHAEL ZWERIN has written regularly for the *International Herald Tribune* and other magazines. *Close Enough for Jazz* (1983) is a kind of autobiography.

RICHARD KOSTELANETZ (1940—) has written and edited many books of and about contemporary art and literature. As a media artist, he has worked in audiotape, videotape, holography and film.

ABOUT THE AUTHOR

Richard Kostelanetz (1940–   ) has written and edited scores of books of and about contemporary art and literature. As a media artist who has received many grants and residencies, he has worked in audiotape, videotape, holography and film. He lives in New York City.